HCI Challenges and Privacy Preservation in Big Data Security

Daphne Lopez
VIT University, India

M.A. Saleem Durai
VIT University, India

A volume in the Advances in Human
and Social Aspects of Technology
(AHSAT) Book Series

Published in the United States of America by
IGI Global
Information Science Reference (an imprint of IGI Global)
701 E. Chocolate Avenue
Hershey PA, USA 17033
Tel: 717-533-8845
Fax: 717-533-8661
E-mail: cust@igi-global.com
Web site: http://www.igi-global.com

Library of Congress Cataloging-in-Publication Data

Names: Lopez, Daphne, 1967- editor. | Durai, M. A. Saleem, 1974- editor.
Title: HCI challenges and privacy preservation in big data security / Daphne
    Lopez and M.A. Saleem Durai, editors.
Other titles: Human computer interaction challenges and privacy preservation
    in big data security
Description: Hershey, PA : Information Science Reference, [2018] | Includes
    bibliographical references and index.
Identifiers: LCCN 2017012033| ISBN 9781522528630 (hardcover) | ISBN
    9781522528647 (ebook)
Subjects: LCSH: Big data--Security measures. | Personal records--Access
    control. | Privacy, Right of. | Human-computer interaction--Security
    measures.
Classification: LCC QA76.9.A25 H3956 2018 | DDC 005.8--dc23 LC record available at https://
lccn.loc.gov/2017012033

This book is published in the IGI Global book series Advances in Human and Social Aspects of Technology (AHSAT) (ISSN: 2328-1316; eISSN: 2328-1324)

British Cataloguing in Publication Data
A Cataloguing in Publication record for this book is available from the British Library.

All work contributed to this book is new, previously-unpublished material.
The views expressed in this book are those of the authors, but not necessarily of the publisher.

For electronic access to this publication, please contact: eresources@igi-global.com.

Advances in Human and Social Aspects of Technology (AHSAT) Book Series

ISSN:2328-1316
EISSN:2328-1324

Editor-in-Chief: Ashish Dwivedi, The University of Hull, UK

MISSION

In recent years, the societal impact of technology has been noted as we become increasingly more connected and are presented with more digital tools and devices. With the popularity of digital devices such as cell phones and tablets, it is crucial to consider the implications of our digital dependence and the presence of technology in our everyday lives.

The **Advances in Human and Social Aspects of Technology (AHSAT) Book Series** seeks to explore the ways in which society and human beings have been affected by technology and how the technological revolution has changed the way we conduct our lives as well as our behavior. The AHSAT book series aims to publish the most cutting-edge research on human behavior and interaction with technology and the ways in which the digital age is changing society.

COVERAGE

- Cultural Influence of ICTs
- Cyber Bullying
- Technology and Social Change
- Technoself
- Information ethics
- Computer-mediated communication
- Digital Identity
- ICTs and social change
- End-User Computing
- Cyber Behavior

IGI Global is currently accepting manuscripts for publication within this series. To submit a proposal for a volume in this series, please contact our Acquisition Editors at Acquisitions@igi-global.com or visit: http://www.igi-global.com/publish/.

Titles in this Series

For a list of additional titles in this series, please visit:
https://www.igi-global.com/book-series/advances-human-social-aspects-technology/37145

Optimizing Human-Computer Interaction With Emerging Technologies
Francisco Cipolla-Ficarra (Latin Association of Human-Computer Interaction, Spain & International Association of Interactive Communication, Italy)
Information Science Reference • ©2018 • 471pp • H/C (ISBN: 9781522526162) • US $345.00

Designing for Human-Machine Symbiosis Using the URANOS Model Emerging Research ...
Benjamin Hadorn (University of Fribourg, Switzerland)
Information Science Reference • ©2017 • 170pp • H/C (ISBN: 9781522518884) • US $125.00

Research Paradigms and Contemporary Perspectives on Human-Technology Interaction
Anabela Mesquita (School of Accounting and Administration of Porto, Polytechnic Institute of Porto, Portugal & Algorithm Research Centre, Minho University, Portugal)
Information Science Reference • ©2017 • 366pp • H/C (ISBN: 9781522518686) • US $195.00

Solutions for High-Touch Communications in a High-Tech World
Michael A. Brown Sr. (Florida International University, USA)
Information Science Reference • ©2017 • 217pp • H/C (ISBN: 9781522518976) • US $185.00

Design Solutions for User-Centric Information Systems
Saqib Saeed (Imam Abdulrahman Bin Faisal University, Saudi Arabia) Yasser A. Bamarouf (Imam Abdulrahman Bin Faisal University, Saudi Arabia) T. Ramayah (University Sains Malaysia, Malaysia) and Sardar Zafar Iqbal (Imam Abdulrahman Bin Faisal University, Saudi Arabia)
Information Science Reference • ©2017 • 422pp • H/C (ISBN: 9781522519447) • US $215.00

Identity, Sexuality, and Relationships among Emerging Adults in the Digital Age
Michelle F. Wright (Masaryk University, Czech Republic)
Information Science Reference • ©2017 • 343pp • H/C (ISBN: 9781522518563) • US $185.00

For an enitre list of titles in this series, please visit:
https://www.igi-global.com/book-series/advances-human-social-aspects-technology/37145

701 East Chocolate Avenue, Hershey, PA 17033, USA
Tel: 717-533-8845 x100 • Fax: 717-533-8661
E-Mail: cust@igi-global.com • www.igi-global.com

Editorial Advisory Board

Table of Contents

Detailed Table of Contents

Chapter 1

Gunasekaran Manogaran, VIT University, India
Chandu Thota, Albert Einstein Lab, India
Daphne Lopez, VIT University, India

Big Data has been playing a vital role in almost all environments such as healthcare, education, business organizations and scientific research. Big data analytics requires advanced tools and techniques to store, process and analyze the huge volume of data. Big data consists of huge unstructured data that require advance real-time analysis. Thus, nowadays many of the researchers are interested in developing advance technologies and algorithms to solve the issues when dealing with big data. Big Data has gained much attention from many private organizations, public sector and research institutes. This chapter provides an overview of the state-of-the-art algorithms for processing big data, as well as the characteristics, applications, opportunities and challenges of big data systems. This chapter also presents the challenges and issues in human computer interaction with big data analytics.

Chapter 2

P. Geethanjali, VIT University, India

Most of the assistive devices are of user contact based control like body-powered prosthetic hand, joystick control of wheelchair, sip-and-puff, etc. and have a limited number of control movements. The performance of these assistive devices improves using bio-signals/gesture based control embedded in the processor. Gesture based control is widely used in wheelchair navigation control, communication with external world for neuromuscular impaired subjects. On the other hand, bio-signals are used widely in prosthetic devices, wheelchair control, orthotic devices, etc. with pattern recognition based control strategy. The choice and number of features used in pattern recognition for accurate control of assistive device is crucial. Further, these features performance also varies with the classifier. The appropriate selection of combination of pattern recognition will enhance the accuracy. This chapter focuses on bio-inspired techniques in selection of features and classification for the pattern recognition based assistive device control.

Data privacy plays a noteworthy part in today's digital world where information is gathered at exceptional rates from different sources. Privacy preserving data publishing refers to the process of publishing personal data without questioning the privacy of individuals in any manner. A variety of approaches have been devised to forfend consumer privacy by applying traditional anonymization mechanisms. But these mechanisms are not well suited for Big Data, as the data which is generated nowadays is not just structured in manner. The data which is generated at very high velocities from various sources includes unstructured and semi-structured information, and thus becomes very difficult to process using traditional mechanisms. This chapter focuses on the various challenges with Big Data, PPDM and PPDP techniques for Big Data and how well it can be scaled for processing both historical and real-time data together using Lambda architecture. A distributed framework for privacy preservation in Big Data by combining Natural language processing techniques is also proposed in this chapter.

Information security is a prime goal for every individual and organization. The travelling from client to cloud server can be prone to security issues. The big data storages are available through cloud computing system to facilitate mobile client. The information security can be provided to mobile client and cloud technology with the help of integrated parallel and distributed encryption and decryption mechanism. The traditional technologies include the plaintext stored across cloud and can be prone to security issues. The solution provided by applying the encrypted data upload and encrypted search. The clouds can work in collaboration; therefore, the encryption can also be done in collaboration. Some part of encryption handle by client and other part handled by cloud system. This chapter presents the security scenario of different security algorithms and the concept of mobile and cloud computing. This chapter precisely defines the security features of existing cloud and big data system and provides the new framework that helps to improve the data security over cloud computing and big data security system.

Big data is information management system through the integration of various traditional data techniques. Big data usually contains high volume of personal and authenticated information which makes privacy as a major concern. To provide security and effective processing of collected data various techniques are evolved. Machine Learning (ML) is considered as one of the data technology which handles one of the central and hidden parts of collected data. Same like ML algorithm Deep Learning (DL) algorithm learn program automatically from the data it is considered to enhance the performance and security of the collected massive data. This paper reviewed security issues in big data and evaluated the performance of ML and DL in a critical environment. At first, this paper reviewed about the ML and DL algorithm. Next, the study focuses towards issues and challenges of ML and their remedies. Following, the study continues to investigate DL concepts in big data. At last, the study figures out methods adopted in recent research trends and conclude with a future scope.

Advances in recent hardware technology have permitted to document transactions and other pieces of information of everyday life at an express pace. In addition of speed up and storage capacity, real-life perceptions tend to transform over time.

However, there are so much prospective and highly functional values unseen in the vast volume of data. For this kind of applications conventional data mining is not suitable, so they should be tuned and changed or designed with new algorithms. Big data computing is inflowing to the category of most hopeful technologies that shows the way to new ways of thinking and decision making. This epoch of big data helps users to take benefit out of all available data to gain more precise systematic results or determine latent information, and then make best possible decisions. Depiction from a broad set of workloads, the author establishes a set of classifying measures based on the storage architecture, processing types, processing techniques and the tools and technologies used.

Chapter 7
M. A. Saleem Durai, VIT University, India
Anbarasi M., VIT University, India
Jaiti Handa, VIT University, India

As the volume of data is increasing with time the primary issue is how to store and process such data and get useful information out of it. Analysis of classification algorithms and MapReduce programming model has led to the conclusion that the distributed file system and parallel computing attributes of MapReduce are good for designing classifier model. The major reason for it is parallel processing of data in which data is divided and processed in parallel and the output from each is reduced further for a single output. In this paper, we are going to study how to use MapReduce model to build classifier model. We are using cancer dataset to predict if a person has cancer or not by using Naive Bayes and KNN classification algorithms. We have compared them on the basis on computational time and the factors like sensitivity, specificity, and accuracy. In the end, we would be able to compare these two algorithms and tell which one works better on MapReduce programming model

Chapter 8
Balajee Jeyakumar, VIT University, India
M.A. Saleem Durai, VIT University, India
Daphne Lopez, VIT University, India

Deep learning is now more popular research domain in machine learning and pattern recognition in the world. It is widely success in the far-reaching area of applications such as Speech recognition, Computer vision, Natural language processing and Reinforcement learning. With the absolute amount of data accessible nowadays, big data brings chances and transformative possible for several sectors, on the other hand, it also performs on the unpredicted defies to connecting data and information. The size of the data is getting larger, and deep learning is imminent to play a vital role in big data predictive analytics solutions. In this paper, we make available a brief outline of deep learning and focus recent research efforts and the challenges in the fields of science, medical and water resource system.

Foreword

Human Computer Interaction has spectacularly changed computing. The aim is to develop acceptable standards in aspects as display resolution, use of color, and navigation around an application. HCI focuses on discovering methods and techniques that support people in usability and user experience. Desktop applications, internet browsers, handheld computers, and computer kiosks make use of the prevalent graphical user interfaces (GUI). Voice user interfaces (VUI) are used for speech recognition and synthesizing systems, and the emerging multi-modal Gestalt User Interfaces (GUI) allow humans to engage with embodied character agents in a way that cannot be achieved with other interface paradigms. Instead of designing regular interfaces, the different research branches have had different focus on the concepts of multimodality rather than unimodality, intelligent adaptive interfaces rather than command/action based ones, and finally active rather than passive interfaces.

Big data can be defined as large amount of data that cannot be processed using traditional database systems. Data from various sensors, hospitals and social networking sites are a rich source of information for big data. This rampant growth of data leads to various challenges in today's digital world where data publishing plays a major role in every aspect of health and economics. The type of big data ranges from unstructured text to highly structured data. This huge amount of data with diverse dimensionality raises two fundamental challenges in big data domain: storage and processing of raw data. Big data integration can be used to build ecosystems that integrate structured, semi-structured and unstructured information from the published data. But, the major concern is with the privacy constraints in data publishing. Privacy can be defined as the right of individuals to determine how and to what extend information about them is communicated to others. As such, there is a strong demand to investigate information privacy and security challenges in Big Data.

This book collects high-quality research papers and industrial practice articles in the areas of HCI Challenges for Big Data Security and Privacy. It includes research and development results of lasting significance in the theory, design, implementation, analysis of human-computer interaction. Additionally, the book will explore the impact of Privacy Preserving big data in healthcare, industry, government and public sectors.

Gunasekaran Manogaran
Vellore Institute of Technology University, India

Gunasekaran Manogaran *is currently pursuing PhD in the Vellore Institute of Technology University. He received his Bachelor of Engineering and Master of Technology from Anna University and Vellore Institute of Technology University respectively. He has worked as a Research Assistant for a project on spatial data mining funded by Indian Council of Medical Research, Government of India. His current research interests include data mining, big data analytics and soft computing. He is the author/co-author of papers in conferences, book chapters and journals. He got an award for young investigator from India and Southeast Asia by Bill and Melinda Gates Foundation. He is a member of International Society for Infectious Diseases and Machine Intelligence Research labs.*

Preface

Human-computer interaction (HCI) provides services and features to interact between people and computers (Dix, 2009). User interface developed with the help of various software's and algorithms. Nowadays, there is a need of efficient interactive computing systems with advance HCI for human use. In order to develop an efficient human computer interaction model, the HCI designers should reduce the barrier between the human's cognitive models (Rogers, 2007). Human-computer interaction models are most often used in cognitive engineering.

The possible ways to interact the computer and human is listed below:

- Desktop appliance
- Internet browsers
- Handheld computers
- Computer kiosks

The Association for Computing Machinery (ACM) defines human-computer interaction as "a regulation concerned with the plan, assessment and completion of interactive computing systems for human exploit and with the study of most important phenomena adjoining them". Human–computer interaction focuses on developing various interactive models, cognitive systems and API from behind acquaintance on both the appliance and the human side (Khan et al., 2014).

Computer graphics, programming languages, operating systems and advance environments are available in machine side to develop the interactive models. Communication assumption, graphic and manufacturing design disciplines, cognitive psychology, linguistics, social sciences, social psychology, and human factors are used to develop the human computer interaction model in machine side.

Human computer interaction models are also called as human machine interaction (HMI), computer human interaction (CHI) or man machine interaction (MMI) models.

Features and applications of human computer interaction models include:

- Algorithms and techniques for designing a new computer interfaces.
- Developing programming languages and library functions to implement the interface.
- Evaluating the developed and implemented human computer interfaces with respect to their usability and desired goals.
- Studying the implications and importance of human computer interfaces.
- Identifying the conceptual frameworks and environments to implement the human computer interface models such as identifying the values of inspire computational design and computer interface.

ORGANIZATION OF THE BOOK

The book is organized into eight chapters. A brief description of each of the chapters follows:

Chapter 1 provides an overview of the state-of-the-art algorithms for processing big data, as well as the characteristics, applications, opportunities and challenges of big data systems. The author also presents the challenges and issues in human computer interaction with big data analytics.

Chapter 2 focuses on bio-inspired techniques in selection of features and classification for the pattern recognition based assistive device control. This chapter also reviews gesture based control in wheelchair navigation control, bio-signals in prosthetic devices, wheelchair control, and orthotic devices.

Chapter 3 reviews the various challenges with Big Data, PPDM and PPDP techniques for Big Data and how well it can be scaled for processing both historical and real-time data together using Lambda architecture. A distributed framework for privacy preservation in Big Data by combining Natural language processing techniques is also proposed in this chapter.

Chapter 4 presents several recent cryptographic approaches that make such processing possible for varying classes of analytics. In addition, this chapter also reviews the security and performance characteristics of each of these schemes and summarizes how they can be used to protect big data analytics.

Chapter 5 reviews the security issues in big data and evaluated the performance of ML and DL in a critical environment. At first, this chapter reviewed about the ML and DL algorithm. Next, the study focuses towards issues and challenges of ML and their remedies. Following, the study continues to investigate DL concepts in big data. At last, the study figures out methods adopted in recent research trends and conclude with a future scope.

Chapter 6 analyses and compares recent approaches for classifying measures based on the big data storage architecture, processing types, processing techniques and the tools and technologies.

Chapter 7 presents details about how to use MapReduce model to build classifier model. The authors argue that it is possible to maintain Internet security and hence facilitate e-businesses, if adequate importance is placed on technical security measures. The authors present a study on cancer dataset to predict if a person has cancer or not by using Naive Bayes and KNN classification algorithms.

Chapter 8 presents an outline of deep learning and focus recent research efforts and the challenges in the fields of science, medical and water resource system.

Daphne Lopez
VIT University, India

M. A. Saleem Durai
VIT University, India

REFERENCES

Dix, A. (2009). Human-computer interaction. In L. Liu & M.T. Özsu (Eds.), Encyclopedia of database systems (pp. 1327–1331). Springer.

Laurel, B., & Mountford, S. J. (1990). *The art of human-computer interface design.* Addison-Wesley Longman Publishing Co., Inc.

Robertson, I. T. (1985). Human information-processing strategies and style. *Behaviour & Information Technology*, *4*(1), 19–29. doi:10.1080/01449298508901784

Rogers, Y., Sharp, H., Preece, J., & Tepper, M. (2007). Interaction design: Beyond human-computer interaction. *networker, The Craft of Network Computing*, *11*(4), 34.

Wang, L., & Sajeev, A. S. M. (2007, January). Roller interface for mobile device applications. In *Proceedings of the eight Australasian conference on User interface* (Vol. 64, pp. 7-13). Australian Computer Society, Inc.

Acknowledgment

I would like to express my gratitude to the many people who saw me through this book; to all those who provided support, talked things over, read, wrote, offered comments, allowed me to quote their remarks and assisted in the editing, proofreading and design.

Chapter 1
Human–Computer Interaction With Big Data Analytics

Gunasekaran Manogaran
VIT University, India

Chandu Thota
Albert Einstein Lab, India

Daphne Lopez
VIT University, India

ABSTRACT

Big Data has been playing a vital role in almost all environments such as healthcare, education, business organizations and scientific research. Big data analytics requires advanced tools and techniques to store, process and analyze the huge volume of data. Big data consists of huge unstructured data that require advance real-time analysis. Thus, nowadays many of the researchers are interested in developing advance technologies and algorithms to solve the issues when dealing with big data. Big Data has gained much attention from many private organizations, public sector and research institutes. This chapter provides an overview of the state-of-the-art algorithms for processing big data, as well as the characteristics, applications, opportunities and challenges of big data systems. This chapter also presents the challenges and issues in human computer interaction with big data analytics.

DOI: 10.4018/978-1-5225-2863-0.ch001

1. INTRODUCTION

1.1 Background and History of Big Data

Data generation speed and amount of data has increased over the past 20 years in different fields. A report published in 2011 from International Data Corporation (IDC) states that, the overall generated and stored data size in the globe was 1.8ZB ($\approx 1021B$), which enlarged by almost 9 times within 5 years (Lopez et al., 2014). Due to the enormous growth of world data, the name of big data is essentially used to express massive datasets. In general, big data analytics is requires advance tools and techniques to store, process and analyze the huge volume of data. Big data consists of huge unstructured data that require advance real-time analysis (Lopez and Gunasekaran, 2015). Thus, nowadays many of the researchers are interested in developing advance technologies and algorithms to solve the issues when dealing with big data. In order to discover new opportunities and hidden values from big data, Yahoo developed the Hadoop based tools and technologies to store and process the big data. Nowadays, private organizations are also interested in the high prospective of big data, and numerous government agencies declared vital ideas to speed up the big data research and applications. Two leading scientific journals such as nature and science are also opened special issues to solve and discuss the challenges and impacts of big data. In recent years, big data plays a vital role in Internet companies such as Google, Facebook and Twitter. For example, Google handles nearly 100 Petabyte (PB) and Facebook produces log data of over 10 Petabyte per month. A popular Chinese company, Baidu, analyzes data of 10 Petabyte (PB), and Taobao, a subsidiary of Alibaba, produces data of 10 Terabyte (TB) for online trading per day. Sources of big data and the corresponding mining techniques are depicted in Table 1. State of-the-art tools and technologies to handle big data are depicted in Table 2.

1.2 Big Data and Its Market Value

Nowadays, Big Data has been playing a vital role in almost all environments such as healthcare, education, business organizations and scientific research. There is a strong relationship in Big Data and IoE (Internet of Everything). In general, IoE applications are used to capture or observe some specific values to find the hidden values and take better decisions. When the device is connected to the Internet, it always senses the specific metric and stores those metrics into a connected data stores. This would increase the size of the data stored in a data store. Hence, high end devices and scalable storage systems are needed to store such huge size of data. The amount of data to be stored and processed becomes an important problem in real life. Relational data base management system (RDBMS) is generally used to store the traditional data but day by day the volume, velocity and variety of sensor data is growing towards the Exabyte. This requires advanced tools and techniques to store, process and display such large amount of sensor data to the end users. Hence, Big Data tools are often used to process such huge amounts of data. This would increase the economy and market of the Big Data analytics. The report "Big Data Market by Component (Software and Services) states that "The Big Data market is expected to grow from USD 28.65 Billion in 2016 to USD 66.79 Billion by 2021 at a high Compound Annual Growth Rate (CAGR) of 18.45%". For the purpose of the report, 2015 has been considered as the base year and 2016 as the estimated year for performing market estimation and forecasting. 10V's of big data is shown in Figure 1. Various big data analytical algorithms are shown in Figure 4.

1.3 Big Data in Healthcare

In recent decades, big data analytics also impact more in healthcare (Lopez and Sekaran, 2016). Nowadays, health care systems are rapidly adopting clinical data, which will rapidly enlarge the size of the health records that are accessible, electronically (Shan et al., 2012). Concurrently, fast progress and development has achieved in modern healthcare management system (Hayes et al., 2014). A recent study expounds, six

Figure 1. 10V's of big data

use cases of big data to decrease the cost of patients, triage, readmissions, adverse events, and treatment optimization for diseases affecting multiple organ systems (Feldman et al., 2013). In yet another study, big data use cases in healthcare have been divided into number of categories such as clinical decision support (with a sub category of clinical information), administration and delivery, consumer behavior, and support services (Lopez and Manogaran, 2017). Jee et al. described that how to reform the healthcare system based on big data analytics to choose appropriate treatment path, improvement of healthcare systems, and so on (Parthasarathy et al., 2011; Fageeri et al., 2014; Manogaran et al., 2016). The above use cases have utilized the following big data in health care implementation. 1. Patient- centered framework produced based on the big data framework to approximate the amount of healthcare (cost), patient impact (outcomes), and dropping readmission rates (Tang et al., 2010). 2. Virtual physiological human analysis framework combined with big data analytics to create robust and valuable solutions in silico medicine (Sharma et al., 2015).

1.4 Cloud Computing With Big Data Analytics

Cloud computing has revolutionized the way software services and computing are delivered to the clients on demand. Cloud providers offered the components of cloud computing that includes Software as a Service (SaaS), Platform as a Service (PaaS) and Infrastructure as a Service (IaaS). Normally, cloud providers are named as cloud service providers or CSPs. Amazon Simple Storage Service (Amazon S3) is the first cloud service offered to the end users by Amazon in 2006. There after large number of cloud providers are developing variety of cloud services such as Apple, IBM, Joyent, Microsoft, Rackspace, Google, Cisco, Citrix, Salesforce. com and Verizon/Terremark. Users are using cloud computing through networked client devices such as desktop computers, smart phones, laptops, tablets and any Ethernet enabled device such as Home Automation Gadgets. More number of cloud applications allows end users to access cloud without any definite applications and software. Web user interfaces such as HTML5 and Ajax can achieve a similar or even better look and feel to native applications.

1.5 Big Data Applications

Big Data has gained much attention from many private organizations, public sector and research institutes. It is observed that, in recent decades, big data has been playing a major role in all fields (Varatharajan et al., 2017b). In this section explains how the real-time applications of big data are likely to grow in the future and how they will essentially shape our day-to-day environment. The push towards collecting and

Figure 2. Big data challenges

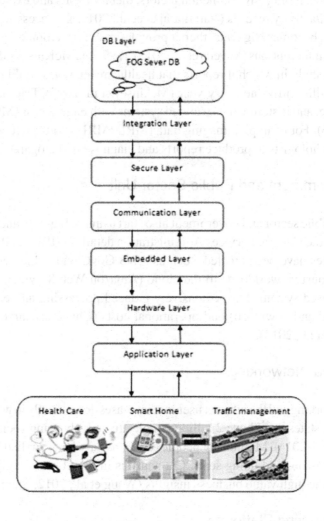

analyzing large amounts of data in diverse application domains has motivated us to use variety of applications such as Health and human welfare, Nature and natural processes, Government and the public sector, commerce, business and economic systems, social networking and the internet, and computational and experimental processes (Kambatla et al., 2014). Big Data Challenges are shown in Figure 2.

1.5.1 Hospitals and Healthcare Institutes

In general, Clinical data are classified as following types such as electronic medical records (EMRs), pharmaceutical data, imaging data, data on personal practices and preferences (including environmental factors, dietary habits and exercise patterns), and financial/activity records (Varatharajan et al., 2017a). Successfully combining all these data becomes Big Data, then it provides major development in well-being, delivery and interventions (Vayena et al., 2015). Recently, McKinsey Global Institute conducted a study in which it reports that healthcare analytics could produce more than $300 billion in value every year (Mckinsey.com, 2015). Data is collected at point-of-care, and is stored in distributed systems with huge access (Manogaran and Lopez, 2016). For example, imaging data (MRI, fMRI) is often accessed overseas by skilled radiologists to produce reports and diagnoses (Manogaran et al., 2017a).

1.5.2 Government and Public Sector Unit

Recently, Public sector and government also start using of big-data analytics to store and process the General Services Administration details (WIRED, 2016). Business cloud services have been created, such as AWS GovCloud, which entirely aim to transfer exhaustive workloads to the cloud (Amazon Web Services, 2016). Thus, Big Data based systems have extensively reduced processing and execution time (both upload and download) and operational costs (Chandrasekaran and Kapoor, 2011; Kim et al., 2014).

1.5.3 Social Networking

Social networking and the internet users are increases dramatically in worldwide. The latest report states that above 2 billion people are actively using social media each month (Kemp, 2014). Monitoring people emotions have been applied in many areas to solve big issues and doing sentiment analysis in social networking data is help to increase the high value business insights (Wang et al., 2012; Shah et al., 2015).

1.5.4 Computing Platforms

Nowadays computing platforms most often uses big data to get high value insight. For example, Astro-physical simulations, quantum-mechanical modeling (Pandey et al., 2015), Geospatial modeling (Mhlanga et al., 2015) are use Big Data computational platforms and Big Data tools to model the huge size of real time streaming datasets to bring in qualitative and quantitative changes in the near future (Reed et al., 2015).

1.5.5 Nature and Natural Processes

Big data also use to save nature and natural processes as copious data being collected linking to our environmental footprint and its noticeable impact. Natural related data is normally collected from satellite imagery, sensors and radars to monitor the extreme weather events, deforestation and urban encroachment. Thus, big data analytics has major impact in, including sustainable development (Gijzen et al., 2013), land and water resources management (Wang et al., 2013), environmental impact assessment (Howe et al., 2008), natural resource management (Hampton et al., 2013) and global warming and climate change (Jang et al., 2015; Manogaran and Lopez, 2017a).

1.6 Solving Big Data Storage Challenges With Private Cloud

Private clouds are used to store and share data for one organization and do not share physical resources to others (Manogaran and Lopez, 2017b). Resources of the private cloud can be provided externally or in-house. Private clouds is always use virtualized on-premises computing resources and storage to present a devoted cloud that a industry owns and operates. In general, due to regulatory or security limits Organizations requiring direct cloud environment control. An organization must maintain and handle infrastructure costs and technical or architectural issues that arise. As a result, organizations normally don't deploy Big Data on private clouds. A classic fundamental prerequisite of private cloud deployments are security regulations and requirements that require a strict partition of an organization's data storage and processing from malicious or accidental contact through shared resources.

In addition, private cloud setups are demanding because financial merits of scale are typically not possible within most projects and organizations despite the consumption of industry standards. The return of investment contrast to public cloud offerings is hardly ever acquired and the operational cost and risk of failure is also important. Nevertheless, users maintain private visualized isolated storage and processing methodologies. Security concerns, which attract a few to accept private clouds or custom deployments, are for the huge majority of users and projects unrelated (Manogaran et al., 2017a). Visualization is always used to access other customers' data tremendously tricky. Real time issues about public cloud computing are more ordinary similar to data lock-in and irregular performance of individual instances (Manogaran et al., 2017b). The data lock-in is a typical soft assess and works by assembly data inflow to the cloud provider open or extremely economical. The replication of data out to local systems or other providers is often more costly. This is not an impossible problem and in practice promotes to consume extra services from a cloud provider as an alternative of transferring data in and out for various processes or services. Typically, this is not reasonable anyway due to complexities and network speed around processing with many platforms (Manogaran et al., 2017c).

1.7 Solving Big Data Storage Challenges With Public Cloud

Public clouds that are offered by third-party providers is used to share and process physical resources and storage. As public cloud providers maintain numerous users, the processing platform is far more scalable and more than that of private cloud. To lower operating costs, unused resources are unconstrained once the processing job is ended. Public cloud provides a "utility" computing model, and is supreme for on-demand Big Data applications. Public clouds share physical resources for data storage, transfers and analyzing. It is approximately certain that in the cloud, data will be unencrypted. In addition, if public cloud uses a PaaS-based application or SaaS, unencrypted data will also approximately stored in the multitenancy platform (Manogaran et al., 2017d).

Recently, many organizations especially small and midmarket businesses promoters are use cloud based software applications from an external service provider to store their transactional data. If the organization maintains deep historical data in that cloud service, it might already have collected in Big Data levels. Value added analytics services such as marketing optimization, churn analysis, or off-site backup and archiving of customer data is provided by extending the cloud service provider functions; it might make intelligence to influence that rather than store it all in-house. Dedicated Hadoop cluster for huge size extract-transform-load (ETL) process on unstructured data sources is used to provide access to the public cloud applications such as multichannel marketing, geospatial analytics, social media analytics, elastic data-science sandboxing and query-able archiving. Public cloud providing might be the only possible alternative if the user need to process the data that include petabyte-scale, streaming, multi-structured and Big Data.

1.8 Solving Big Data Storage Challenges With Hybrid Cloud

Hybrid clouds combine public and private cloud, enabling services to drift between the two clouds using orchestration. In hybrid cloud, cloud bursting is known as the private cloud can use public cloud resources when additional compute is necessary. Private cloud manages basic workloads, whereas public cloud resources temporarily contain spikes in demand. This feature is used when the user processing Big Data in cloud. Nevertheless, organizations hardly ever use hybrid clouds for Big Data analytics since public cloud is effortless and takes benefit of any long-term cost allowances from the public cloud provider.

As hybrid cloud architecture combines public and private cloud deployments, there is a need to achieve the following features such as elasticity and security, provide cheaper base load and burst capabilities. Some business organizations experience small periods of enormously high loads. For example, as a result of online shopping offer and advertising events like sponsoring an admired television occasion. In general, these events can have massive economic impact to organizations if they are provided very worst service. In order to overcome this issue, hybrid cloud presents the opportunity to serve the base load with in-house services and lease for a short period. This needs a big deal of operational ability in the organization to effortlessly scale between the public and private cloud. Familiar tools and technologies for hybrid or private cloud deployments are already available such as Eucalyptus for Amazon Web Services. On the long-term extra expenditure of the hybrid cloud approach often is not reasonable since cloud providers present most important discounts for multi-year commitments. This would cause shifting base load services to the public cloud attractive since it is accompanied by an easier deployment policy.

1.9 Internet of Things

The Internet of Things (IoT) is a connection of physical objects such as devices, vehicles, buildings and other items-embedded with electronics, software, sensors, and network connectivity that enables these objects to collect and exchange data. 'Thing' refers to a device which connected to the internet and transfer the device information to other devices. An interesting trend contributing to the growth of IoT is the shift from consumer-based IPv4 Internet of tablets and laptops, that is, Information Technology (IT), to an Operational Technology (OT)-based IPv6 Internet of Machine-to-Machine interactions. This includes sensors, smart objects and clustered systems (for example, Smart Grid) (rank-watch, 2016). The IPv6 Internet is one of the most important connectivity of the IoT, as it is not possible to add billions of devices to the IPv4 Internet. Layered Architecture of IoT is shown in Figure 3.

2. INTRODUCTION TO HCI

Human-computer interaction (HCI) provides services and features to interact between people and computers (Dix, 2009). Various Fields in HCI is shown in Figure 5.

2.1 Human Computer Interaction Models

Human computer interaction models are developed based on various development models such as:

- Unimodal HCI system
- Multimodal HCI system

Figure 3. Layered architecture of IoT

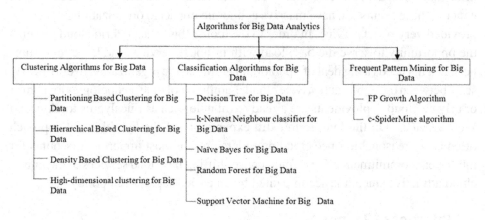

Table 1. Source of big data and the corresponding mining techniques

S.No	Sources of Big Data	Type of Data	Data Mining Technique/ Methodology	Reference
1.	Healthcare	Electronic Health Record (EHR)	Natural Language Processing (NLP)	(Byrd et al., 2014; Manogaran and Lopez, 2017e)
		Medical Imaging Data	Content based Image Retrieval System	(Müller et al., 2004)
		Genetic Data	Penalized Logistic Regression	(Wu et al., 2009)
2.	Social Networking	Text Data	Sentiment Analysis	(Feldman, 2013)
		Graph Data	Community Detection	(Parthasarathy et al., 2011)
			Social Influence Analysis	(Tang & Liu, 2010)
			Collaborative Filtering	(Sharma & Sethi, 2015)
3.	CCTV Surveillance	Video	Labor based Surveillance Systems	(Shan et al., 2012)
4.	Sensor Data	Unstructured Data	Contextual Anomaly Detection	(Hayes et al., 2014)
5.	Machine Generated Data	Log File	Frequent Pattern Mining	(Fageeri et al., 2014)

Figure 4. Various big data analytical algorithms

2.1.1 Unimodality HCI System

Unimodality based human computer interaction models are relies on numeral and variety of its inputs and outputs (Robertson, 1985). This type of human computer interaction interfaces based on only one modality is called unimodal. Unimodality based human computer interaction models are further divided based on the nature of different modalities such as:

- Audio-Based Interaction Models
- Sensor-Based Interaction Models
- Visual-Based Interaction Models

Drawbacks of Unimodal human computer interaction models are mentioned below:

Table 2. State of-the-art tools and technologies to handle big data

S. No	Task	Tool	Description
1	Data Storage and Management	Hadoop	Hadoop implements a master–slave architecture that consists of a namenode and datanode. The namenode controls the access of all datanodes. The main responsibility of datanodes is to manage the storage of data on the nodes that are running. Hadoop splits the huge file into a number of blocks and these blocks are stored in the datanodes of the system.
		Cloudera	Cloudera has provides an integrated platform for big data named as Enterprise Data Hub. Cloudera offers a service to store, process, and analyze all their data, allowing them to enlarge the significance of existing investments while providing primary ways to obtain value from their data.
		MongoDB	MongoDB is a type of document-oriented database and freely available online. MongoDB does not follows traditional rows and columns format. Instead, it uses built in architecture of collections and documents. In general, documents in the MongoDB contain sets of key-value pairs.
		Talend	Talend is an open source software that offers number of services includes data quality management, data integration and data storage. Talend consists of Master Data Management (MDM) function, which combines applications, streaming data, and function integration with fixed data quality.
2	Data Cleaning	OpenRefine	OpenRefine is also called as GoogleRefine used to clean the messy data. OpenRefine freely available online to investigate large amount of data sets quickly and merely even if the data is not in structured format. OpenRefine wiki and Github are provided to solve the user issues.
		DataCleaner	DataCleaner is used to transforms the messy semi-structured data sets into clean readable data sets that many of the visualization organizations can read. In addition, DataCleaner also provides data management and data warehousing services for end users. Though, DataCleaner is not open source, the company provides a trial version for a specific period.
3	Data Mining	RapidMiner	RapidMiner is used to provide an integrated environment for text mining, machine learning, data mining predictive analytics and business analytics. RapidMiner offers APIs to integrate our own specialized algorithms. It is used for various data mining operations including data collection, data visualization, data validation and optimization.
		IBM SPSS Modeler	IBM SPSS Modeler is developed for performing data mining operations includes analyzing data and developing analytic assets. The term *analytic asset* represents the variety of features that solve a business issue. The analytic asset performs the following operations: combines data from three historical data sources, C5.0 decision tree algorithm is used to build the model and results are displayed as tables.
		Oracle Data Miner	Oracle data mining provides various services include make predictions, discover business insights and influence their Oracle data. Oracle data mining also provides user to discover most excellent customers, behavior of the customer, and build company profiles. The Oracle Data Miner GUI allows business analysts, data analysts and data scientists to work with data inside a database using a rather elegant drag and drop solution.
		Teradata	Teradata is used to consolidate data from variety of sources and make the data available for analysis. It also provides end-to-end services and solutions in big data and analytics, data warehousing and marketing services. Teradata also provides various services including business consulting, implementation and training and development.
4	Data Analysis	Qubole	Qubole is used to improve the speed and scalability of big data analytics operations against data stored on Google, Amazon Web Service or Microsoft Azure clouds. Qubole also supports Hive, Spark and Presto to process the data in different data centers.
		BigML	BigML is used to simplify the difficulties in traditional machine learning libraries. BigML provides a powerful Machine Learning service with simple graphical user interface to import data and find predictions out of it. It allows users to use their models for data processing and predictive analytics.

Figure 5. Various fields in HCI

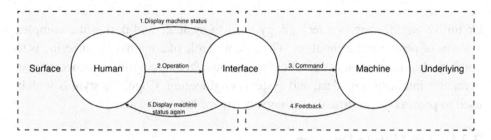

- Interfaces and API developed in Unimodal human computer interaction models are not like nature
- Unimodal human computer interaction models are developed for very small average of users
- Unimodal human computer interaction models not applicable to a different group of users
- Disabled, untrained and illiterate people are not possible to use the unimodal human computer interaction models
- Universal interface is not provided in the unimodal human computer interaction models

2.1.2 Multimodal HCI System

Multimodal human computer interaction models use a variety of independent channel signals with multiple modalities to develop the interaction model between a user and a machine. More than one modes of input is used in the multimodal interface to develop the API and Interface for human-computer interaction model.

Advantages of Multimodal human computer interaction models are mentioned below:

- Interfaces and API developed in Multimodal human computer interaction models are visualized naturally and easy to use
- Multimodal human computer interaction models are used to a different group of users
- Illiterate and disabled people can use the multimodal human computer interaction models without any additional knowledge and study
- Example multimodal human computer interaction model is "Put That There" demonstration system

2.2 Cognitive Engineering

Cognitive engineering is a technology used to evaluate and design the complex systems of people and technology. The essential role of cognitive engineering is to combine the information and practice from human factors, cognitive science, human computer interaction models, and systems engineering. Cognitive style is widely used to process the information of personality for any individual.

2.3 HCI in Mobile Devices

Nowadays, many mobile devices are produced with small size. Hence, there is a need to develop an efficient human interaction model. In order to overcome this issue, touch screen display system is introduced with good touch input or a miniature keyboard. Text input method is also considered as an additional interaction model for communication between human and machine. In addition, BlackBerry has introduced miniature thumb keyboards to enhance the existing human computer interaction methods. Moreover, smart touch keyboards (STK) is inbuilt with the current generation of smart mobile phones.

2.4 Operating Systems for Mobile Devices

Nowadays, various types of operating systems have developed to run the mobile phones. Microsoft Windows Mobile uses Windows operating system originally developed by Microsoft Corporation. The version of Windows operating is system is updated regularly. It is observed that Microsoft has released Windows Mobile 6.1 version on April 1, 2008 with an extension of Windows Mobile 6 platform. The enhanced Windows mobile operating system solves various issues with the exiting Windows operating systems. The essential role of Windows Mobile 6.1 version makes it easier to stay linked and supervise our life from just about everywhere. The following devices use the Windows operating systems it include Pocket PCs, Transportable Media Centers, Smart phones, and onboard computers for convinced automobiles.

2.5 Challenges of HCI in Mobile Devices

Nowadays, the process of human computer interaction is increasing more and more complex. In order to catch up with the transitory and prompt transformation, various advance operating system, programming languages and more reliable human computer interaction models are required. In order to develop the market, the mobile and electronic development industries must solve the interface issues arise in the newly developed mobile phones and computers (Wang et al., 2007).

HCI challenges in mobile phone are classified into two types as follows:

- Hardware Challenges
- Software Challenges

2.5.1 Hardware Challenges

Mobile phone users require the mobile phones with very small size and small weight. Hence, there is a need to develop efficient mobile phones with less size and good human computer interaction model. Hence, it is difficult to develop an efficient human computer interaction model for small size of mobile devices.

2.5.2 Software Challenges

There is a need to develop an efficient algorithm as well as programming models to interact the device without need of any additional requirement. In order to overcome this issue, various advanced software's are used to enhance the existing development platform.

3. HCI WITH BIG DATA

Data visualization methods are used to visualize the results in understandable format. Human computer interaction models are widely used to develop the data visualization methods that efficiently visualize the big data. In general, x- and y- axes of graphs are widely applied to visualize any type of data. The users must identify when to use which types of visualization for visualizing big data with the help of human computer interaction models. The important issue with human computer interaction models is to identify the solutions when the data overloaded. It is important to use filtering methods to build meaningful knowledge from the raw data.

3.1 Data Visualization and Human Perception

Data visualization is an efficient method since it makes the stability between insight and cognition. Data visualization is also used in decoding the important information in a way that human eyes can distinguish and our brains can recognize. The main goal of the data visualization method is to interpret conceptual information into image representations that can be effortlessly, professionally, precisely, and significantly decoded.

3.2 HCI Architecture

HCI systems architecture is classified as follows:

- User inputs and machine outputs in the system
- Variety of inputs and outputs in terms of modality
- Interaction between the inputs and outputs

Various HCI Systems Interfaces are listed below:

- Command Line Interface System
- Menu Driven Interface System
- Graphical User Interface System
- Natural Language Interface System

3.3 Human Interaction With Machines and Computers

3.3.1 Audio Based HCI

The audio based HCI systems are worked based on the data collected by diverse audio signals. The data collected from audio signals can be high reliable and cooperative. The following components are widely used to collect the audio signals such as Microphone, speech recognition instruments and natural language processing methods.

The classification of Audio based Human computer interaction models are listed below:

- Speech Recognition
- Auditory Sentiment Analysis
- Speaker Recognition
- Human Made Noise Detection
- Sign Detections
- Musical Communication

3.3.2 Visual Based HCI

Visual based human computer interaction models are use cameras to observe the machine vision. Various visual signals are identified from the cameras and transferred to the machine with the help of interaction models and interfaces.

The classification of Visual based Human computer interaction models are listed below:

- Facial Appearance Investigation
- Body association tracking
- Motion recognition
- Look recognition

3.3.3 Sensor Based HCI

Visual based human computer interaction models are use various sensors to observe the input from the human. The collected information from the sensor is transferred to the machine with the help of human computer interaction models and interfaces/API.

The classification of Sensor based Human computer interaction models are listed below:

- Motion Tracking Sensors
- Motion Tracking Digitizers
- Pen Based Interaction
- Haptic Sensors
- Force Sensors
- Mouse, Keyboard, Joysticks

CONCLUSION

Big data analytics requires advanced tools and techniques to store, process and analyze the huge volume of data. Big data consists of huge unstructured data that require advance real-time analysis. Thus, nowadays many of the researchers are interested in developing advance technologies and algorithms to solve the issues when dealing with big data. This chapter provides an overview of the state-of-the-art algorithms for processing big data, as well as the characteristics, applications, opportunities and challenges of big data systems. This chapter also presents the challenges and issues in human computer interaction with big data analytics.

REFERENCES

Byrd, R. J., Steinhubl, S. R., Sun, J., Ebadollahi, S., & Stewart, W. F. (2014). Automatic identification of heart failure diagnostic criteria, using text analysis of clinical notes from electronic health records. *International Journal of Medical Informatics*, *83*(12), 983–992. doi:10.1016/j.ijmedinf.2012.12.005 PMID:23317809

Dix, A. (2009). *Human-Computer Interaction. In L. Liu & M.T. Özsu (Eds.), Encyclopedia of Database Systems (pp.* 1327–1331). Springer.

Fageeri, S. O., & Ahmad, R. (2014). An efficient log file analysis algorithm using binary-based data structure. *Procedia: Social and Behavioral Sciences*, *129*, 518–526. doi:10.1016/j.sbspro.2014.03.709

Feldman, R. (2013). Techniques and applications for sentiment analysis. *Communications of the ACM*, *56*(4), 82–89. doi:10.1145/2436256.2436274

Hayes, M. A., & Capretz, M. A. (2014, June). Contextual anomaly detection in big sensor data. In *Proceedings of the 2014 IEEE International Congress on Big Data* (pp. 64-71). IEEE. doi:10.1109/BigData.Congress.2014.19

Lopez, D., & Gunasekaran, M. (2015). Assessment of Vaccination Strategies Using Fuzzy Multi-criteria Decision Making. In *Proceedings of the Fifth International Conference on Fuzzy and Neuro Computing (FANCCO-2015)* (pp. 195-208). Springer.

Lopez, D., Gunasekaran, M., Murugan, B. S., Kaur, H., & Abbas, K. M. (2014). Spatial Big Data analytics of influenza epidemic in Vellore, India. In Big Data (Big Data), 2014 IEEE International Conference on (pp. 19-24). IEEE.

Lopez, D., & Manogaran, G. (2016). Big Data Architecture for Climate Change and Disease Dynamics, Eds. Geetam S. Tomar et al. The Human Element of Big Data: Issues, Analytics, and Performance, CRC Press, USA.

Lopez, D., & Manogaran, G. (2017). Modelling the H1N1 influenza using mathematical and neural network approaches. *Biomedical Research*.

Lopez, D., & Sekaran, G. (2016). Climate change and disease dynamics-A Big Data perspective. *International Journal of Infectious Diseases*, *45*, 23–24.

Manogaran, G., & Lopez, D. (2016). Health Data Analytics using Scalable Logistic Regression with Stochastic Gradient Descent. *International Journal of Advanced Intelligence Paradigms*, *9*, 1–15.

Manogaran, G., & Lopez, D. (2017a). Spatial cumulative sum algorithm with big data analytics for climate change detection. *Computers & Electrical Engineering*.

Manogaran, G., & Lopez, D. (2017b). Disease surveillance system for big climate data processing and dengue transmission. [IJACI]. *International Journal of Ambient Computing and Intelligence, 8*(2), 88–105.

Manogaran, G., & Lopez, D. (2017e). A Gaussian process based big data processing framework in cluster computing environment. *Cluster Computing,* 1–16.

Manogaran, G., Lopez, D., Thota, C., Abbas, K. M., Pyne, S., & Sundarasekar, R. (2017d). big data analytics in healthcare Internet of Things. In Innovative Healthcare Systems for the 21st Century (pp. 263-284). Springer International Publishing.

Manogaran, G., Thota, C., & Kumar, M. V. (2016). MetaCloudDataStorage Architecture for Big Data Security in Cloud Computing. *Procedia Computer Science, 87,* 128–133.

Manogaran, G., Thota, C., Lopez, D., & Sundarasekar, R. (2017c). Big data security intelligence for healthcare industry 4.0. In *Cybersecurity for Industry 4.0* (pp. 103–126). Springer International Publishing.

Manogaran, G., Thota, C., Lopez, D., Vijayakumar, V., Abbas, K. M., & Sundarsekar, R. (2017a). Big data knowledge system in healthcare. In *Internet of Things and Big Data Technologies for Next Generation Healthcare* (pp. 133–157). Springer International Publishing.

Müller, H., Michoux, N., Bandon, D., & Geissbuhler, A. (2004). A review of content-based image retrieval systems in medical applications—clinical benefits and future directions. *International Journal of Medical Informatics, 73*(1), 1–23. doi:10.1016/j.ijmedinf.2003.11.024 PMID:15036075

Parthasarathy, S., Ruan, Y., & Satuluri, V. (2011). Community discovery in socialnetworks: Applications, methods and emerging trends. In C. C. Aggarwal (Ed.), *Social network data analytics* (pp. 79–113). United States: Springer. doi:10.1007/978-1-4419-8462-3_4

Robertson, I. T. (1985). Human information-processing strategies and style. *Behaviour & Information Technology, 4*(1), 19–29. doi:10.1080/01449298508901784

Rogers, Y., Sharp, H., Preece, J., & Tepper, M. (2007). Interaction design: Beyond human-computer interaction. *netWorker. The Craft of Network Computing, 11*(4), 34.

Shan, C., Porikli, F., Xiang, T., & Gong, S. (Eds.). (2012). Video Analytics for Business Intelligence. In C. Shan, F. Porikli, T. Xiang et al. (Eds.), Video analytics for business intelligence (Vol. 1, pp. 309–354). Berlin: Springer.

Sharma, S., & Sethi, M. (2015). Implementing Collaborative Filtering on Large Scale Data using Hadoop and Mahout, *International Research Journal of Engineering and Technology*, 2(4).

Tang, L., & Liu, H. (2010). Community detection and mining in social media. *Synthesis Lectures on Data Mining and Knowledge Discovery*, 2(1), 1–137. doi:10.2200/S00298ED1V01Y201009DMK003

Varatharajan, R., Manogaran, G., Priyan, M. K., Balaş, V. E., & Barna, C. (2017b). Visual analysis of geospatial habitat suitability model based on inverse distance weighting with paired comparison analysis. *Multimedia Tools and Applications*, 1–21.

Varatharajan, R., Manogaran, G., Priyan, M. K., & Sundarasekar, R. (2017a). Wearable sensor devices for early detection of Alzheimer disease using dynamic time warping algorithm. *Cluster Computing*, 1–10.

Wang, L., & Sajeev, A. S. M. (2007, January). Roller interface for mobile device applications. In *Proceedings of the eight Australasian conference on User interface-(Vol. 64,* pp. 7-13). Australian Computer Society, Inc.

Wu, T. T., Chen, Y. F., Hastie, T., Sobel, E., & Lange, K. (2009). Genome-wide association analysis by lasso penalized logistic regression. *Bioinformatics (Oxford, England)*, 25(6), 714–721. doi:10.1093/bioinformatics/btp041 PMID:19176549

Wu, X., Zhu, X., Wu, G. Q., & Ding, W. (2014). Data mining with big data. *IEEE Transactions on Knowledge and Data Engineering*, 26(1), 97–107. doi:10.1109/TKDE.2013.109

ADDITIONAL READING

Curran, R. J., & Haskin, R. L. (2010). *U.S. Patent No. 7,840,995*. Washington, DC: U.S. Patent and Trademark Office.

Demchenko, Y., Zhao, Z., Grosso, P., Wibisono, A., & De Laat, C. (2012, December). Addressing big data challenges for scientific data infrastructure. In *Proceedings of the 2012 IEEE 4th International Conference on Cloud Computing Technology and Science (CloudCom)* (pp. 614-617). IEEE. doi:10.1109/CloudCom.2012.6427494

Fernández, A., del Río, S., López, V., Bawakid, A., del Jesus, M. J., Benítez, J. M., & Herrera, F. (2014). Big Data with Cloud Computing: An insight on the computing environment, MapReduce, and programming frameworks. *Wiley Interdisciplinary Reviews: Data Mining and Knowledge Discovery*, 4(5), 380–409.

Gade, S., Pathan, A., Tomar, S., &Razdan, S. (2016). Big data on cloud using Hadoop. *Imperial Journal of Interdisciplinary Research, 2*(7).

Gai, K., Qiu, M., Zhao, H., & Xiong, J. (2016, June). Privacy-aware adaptive data encryption strategy of big data in cloud computing. In *Proceedings of the 2016 IEEE 3rd International Conference on Cyber Security and Cloud Computing (CSCloud)* (pp. 273-278). IEEE. doi:10.1109/CSCloud.2016.52

Gijzen, H. (2013). Development: Big Data for a sustainable future. *Nature, 502*(7469), 38–38. doi:10.1038/502038d PMID:24091969

Hashizume, K., Rosado, D. G., Fernández-Medina, E., & Fernandez, E. B. (2013). An analysis of security issues for cloud computing. *Journal of Internet Services and Applications, 4*(1), 1–13. doi:10.1186/1869-0238-4-5

Hongbing, C., Chunming, R., Kai, H., Weihong, W., & Yanyan, L. (2015). Secure big data storage and sharing scheme for cloud tenants. *Communications, China, 12*(6), 106–115. doi:10.1109/CC.2015.7122469

Inukollu, V. N., Arsi, S., & Ravuri, S. R. (2014). Security issues associated with big data in cloud computing. *International Journal of Network Security & Its Applications, 6*(3), 45–56. doi:10.5121/ijnsa.2014.6304

Kambatla, K., Kollias, G., Kumar, V., & Grama, A. (2014). Trends in big data analytics. *Journal of Parallel and Distributed Computing, 74*(7), 2561–2573. doi:10.1016/j.jpdc.2014.01.003

Katal, A., Wazid, M., & Goudar, R. H. (2013, August). Big data: issues, challenges, tools and good practices. In *Proceedings of the 2013 Sixth International Conference on Contemporary Computing (IC3)* (pp. 404-409). IEEE. doi:10.1109/IC3.2013.6612229

Kim, G. H., Trimi, S., & Chung, J. H. (2014). Big-data applications in the government sector. *Communications of the ACM, 57*(3), 78–85. doi:10.1145/2500873

Kune, R., Konugurthi, P. K., Agarwal, A., Chillarige, R. R., & Buyya, R. (2016). XHAMI–extended HDFS and MapReduce interface for big data image processing applications in cloud computing environments. *Software, Practice & Experience*.

Lynch, C. (2008). Big Data: How do your data grow? *Nature, 455*(7209), 28–29. doi:10.1038/455028a PMID:18769419

Marchal, S., Jiang, X., State, R., & Engel, T. (2014). A big data architecture for large scale security monitoring. In *Proceedings of the 2014 IEEE International Congress on Big Data (BigData Congress)*, (pp. 56-63). IEEE. doi:10.1109/BigData. Congress.2014.18

Pandey, A., & Ramesh, V. (2015). Quantum computing for big data analysis. *History (Historical Association (Great Britain)), 14*(43), 98–104.

Ranjan, R., Georgakopoulos, D., & Wang, L. (2016). A note on software tools and technologies for delivering smart media-optimized big data applications in the cloud. *Computing, 98*(1-2), 1–5. doi:10.1007/s00607-015-0471-8

Reed, D. A., & Dongarra, J. (2015). Exascale computing and big data. *Communications of the ACM, 58*(7), 56–68. doi:10.1145/2699414

Sabahi, F. (2011). Virtualization-level security in cloud computing. In *Proceedings of the 2011 IEEE 3rd International Conference on Communication Software and Networks (ICCSN)*, Xi'an, China (pp. 250-254). IEEE. doi:10.1109/ICCSN.2011.6014716

Sharma, G., Arora, N., & Rai, A. (2016). Use and impact of big data in cloud computing. *Global Journal for Research Analysis, 4*(12).

Shmueli, E., Vaisenberg, R., Elovici, Y., & Glezer, C. (2010). Database encryption: An overview of contemporary challenges and design considerations. *SIGMOD Record, 38*(3), 29–34. doi:10.1145/1815933.1815940

Subashini, S., & Kavitha, V. (2011). A metadata based storage model for securing data in cloud environment. In CyberC (pp. 429-434).

Vayena, E., Salathé, M., Madoff, L. C., & Brownstein, J. S. (2015). Ethical challenges of big data in public health. *PLoS Computational Biology, 11*(2), e1003904. doi:10.1371/journal.pcbi.1003904 PMID:25664461

Wang, W., Chen, L., Thirunarayan, K., & Sheth, A. P. (2012). Harnessing twitter "big data" for automatic emotion identification. In *Proceedings of the 2012 International Conference on Privacy, Security, Risk and Trust (PASSAT), and 2012 International Conference on Social Computing (SocialCom)*, Amsterdam, Netherland (pp. 587-592). IEEE.

Wang, X., & Sun, Z. (2013). The design of water resources and hydropower cloud GIS platform based on big data. In *Geo-Informatics in Resource Management and Sustainable Ecosystem* (pp. 313–322). Springer Berlin Heidelberg. doi:10.1007/978-3-642-41908-9_32

Wu, X., Zhu, X., Wu, G. Q., & Ding, W. (2014). Data mining with big data. *IEEE Transactions on Knowledge and Data Engineering, 26*(1), 97–107. doi:10.1109/TKDE.2013.109

Chapter 2
Bio-Inspired Techniques in Human-Computer Interface for Control of Assistive Devices:
Bio-Inspired Techniques in Assistive Devices

P. Geethanjali
VIT University, India

ABSTRACT

Most of the assistive devices are of user contact based control like body-powered prosthetic hand, joystick control of wheelchair, sip-and-puff, etc. and have a limited number of control movements. The performance of these assistive devices improves using bio-signals/gesture based control embedded in the processor. Gesture based control is widely used in wheelchair navigation control, communication with external world for neuromuscular impaired subjects. On the other hand, bio-signals are used widely in prosthetic devices, wheelchair control, orthotic devices, etc. with pattern recognition based control strategy. The choice and number of features used in pattern recognition for accurate control of assistive device is crucial. Further, these features performance also varies with the classifier. The appropriate selection of combination of pattern recognition will enhance the accuracy. This chapter focuses on bio-inspired techniques in selection of features and classification for the pattern recognition based assistive device control.

DOI: 10.4018/978-1-5225-2863-0.ch002

INTRODUCTION

Pattern recognition is a method of identifying the input information into particular category/class from various classes. Various researches have been carried out in improving control of intelligent assistive devices in the various stages of pattern recognition techniques, namely data preprocessing, feature extraction, feature selection/reduction, classification along with the development of control strategy of electric motor. In pattern recognition, the data usually considered as the raw measurements or raw values taken from the subjects to be classified. A simple block diagram of pattern recognition based control of assistive devices is shown in Figure 1.

The term feature in pattern recognition, refer to the result of the transformations applied to the raw data in order to transform them into another domain or space using time domain/ frequency domain/ time-frequency domain technique. Although, many features can be extracted from raw data for decoding intention and not all of them possesses discriminant capabilities. Some of the extracted features could cause confusion and degrade the classifier. Further, smaller the dimension of the feature vector, lesser the computation time and memory requirements. Therefore, choice of features or reduction of features is essential. Feature dimension reduction provides a method to decide whether it is necessary to include more features that would significantly contribute to the performance of the classifier. It is not a trivial to select the best set of features or the best transformation. The features must be selected or transformed based on the given problem. For the feature selection, some neural networks, population based bio-inspired techniques can be used. The features selection process involves choice of subset of extracted features in feature space by starting with all/without features or subset consisting of random features from the feature space. Feature selection process in the context of assistive devices will be reviewed later in this chapter. The Fourier transform and time-frequency transom yield coefficients of larger dimension and few of its coefficients carry the useful information to obtain the good classification performance. In literature, researchers applied feature reduction using linear or nonlinear projection of features to transform high dimensional feature space to lower dimensional feature space. A very popular method of feature reduction is principal component analysis (PCA) in which the features are projected to lower dimensional space to visualize the underlying class

Figure 1. Block diagram of pattern recognition based control of assistive device

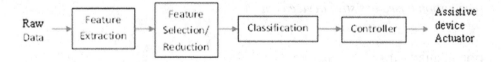

by linear projection. There are other many feature reduction approaches like linear discriminant analysis (LDA), fuzzy discriminant analysis (FDA), self-organizing feature map (SOFM), kernel-based FDA, etc. are discussed in literatures.

BACKGROUND

The feature selection aims to cut the dimensionality by eliminating irrelevant and redundant features, thus considering a subset of features that characterize the best discrimination of patterns. Since, it is difficult to find the discriminant features and selection algorithm using population based technique, use evaluation function to find the features of good discriminating capability. Feature selection would ease the problem of over fitting and reduces the classifier computation time. The existing feature selection techniques in the literature are divided as filters and wrappers according to their dependency on the classification algorithms. Typically, feature selection techniques could be useful in supervised or unsupervised learning algorithms. The filter approach is independent of classification algorithm and uses statistical properties to identify the relevant features. Due to this capability, filter approach is computationally preferred than the wrapper approach. However, it has disadvantage of local optimal solution due to its single iteration. The wrapper approach is based on a classification algorithm need more computation time, but more accurate than the filter approach. The hybrid approach combines the advantages of the filter and wrapper.

Feature selection based on a search strategy is necessary to explore the feature space. However, an exhaustive search from the feature space is computationally difficult, starting from an empty/full feature set for the entire/no feature set with all possible combinations to decide the relevance features. This exhaustive search takes $2n$ possible combination and computationally very expensive. Therefore, heuristic or population based search techniques have been employed.

Various search algorithms that differ in their optimality and computational cost have been utilized by the researchers to search the solution space. Bio-inspired computation algorithms have been successfully applied to the feature selection approach using wrapper approach. The bio-inspired computation algorithm has been an active research area in various disciplines such as image processing, signal processing, electrical drives, power system, data mining, rehabilitation engineering, load forecasting, curve fitting, etc. due to their capability maximize or minimize the objective function. These computation algorithms are stochastic techniques and found to be computationally efficient than the deterministic approaches. The various bio-inspired computational techniques are population-based search techniques include Evolutionary Programming (EP), Evolutionary Strategy, (ES) Genetic Algorithm

(GA), Particle Swarm Optimization (PSO), etc. to find the optimal solution. The bio-inspired technique, neural network (NN) is useful in identification of the category from the input feature. These bio-inspired algorithm find potential application, not only in feature selection, feature classification and also in the development of control of assistive devices.

The bio-inspired computation in rehabilitation engineering is useful at two different control levels, i.e. feature selection, classification for high level and identification of parameters of the drive, development of controller for the drive at a low level to do the desired movement control in assistive devices.

This chapter aims to cover various bio-inspired computation approaches in the context of dimensionality reduction, classification, parameter identification, controller in rehabilitation engineering are discussed in detail. Most literatures, demonstrates the application of EEG signals, EMG signals, EOG signals, speech signals, etc. and not much definite study describes the various bio-inspiring computation involved in the development of assistive devices in various stages in real-time. This chapter covers the applications of bio-inspired algorithm in various perspectives. This chapter describes various bio-inspired techniques and algorithm widely considered in assistive device control. Subsequently, the application of the approaches in assistive devices is discussed.

BIO-INSPIRED TECHNIQUES

The biologically inspired (or bio-inspired) paradigms have ability to solve complex problems to simple problems with little or without the knowledge of the system. Bio-inspired algorithms conceive a natural phenomenon through adaptation possesses the speed, robust capabilities for solving computationally complex optimization, controller and decision-making problems in a number of fields. The neural computing had been formulated in late 1960's and the concept of evolutionary computation had been proposed in early 1970's. Most applications of neural network (NN) have been in control engineering and decision making application. The evolutionary computation techniques have been in optimization of drive parameter and feature selection to the classifier. The techniques are briefly discussed in the following subsection

Artificial Neural Network (ANN)

Researchers are inspired by the human brain and its capability of solving control problems, decision making problems, etc. The human brain, consists of densely interconnected neurons and forming the synapses between the interconnection. Each neuron is composed of cell body a processing element, input units called dendrites and an output is transferred via axon. The information is transferred from one neuron to another neuron, when the electric potential due to release of ions from the synaptic junction, reaches a threshold called an action potential. The network receives input data from the sensory system and process the input to perform a complex task.

An artificial neural network also consists of a computing element which receives input signals. Each input has an associated weight to express the strength or importance of the signals which are analogous to synapse in biological brain. The weights are adapted through the learning process. The computing element transforms the weighted sum of input using the transfer function/activation function to a specific output. An artificial representation of a neuron with three inputs $[P_1, P_2, P_3]$ and an output is shown in Figure 2. The inputs are connected with weights $[W_1, W_2, W_3]$.

The output of the neuron is given as $f(P_1W_1 + P_2W_2 + P_3W_3)$. The weights are calculated using supervised learning rule or unsupervised learning rule. In supervised learning, weights are calculated during the training phase using input and output pattern, whereas in unsupervised learning, the prior output is unknown for the training input. During training the neural network maps the input to output to perform optimization, clustering. Supervised training is suitable for solving complex pattern recognition problems.

There are many activation functions to transform the input to the output. The widely-used activations function is unipolar binary, bipolar binary, logarithmic sigmoidal activation function, tan sigmoidal activation, linear function. The activation functions are functions of weighted sum of input X, the mathematical model of the widely used activation function is given below in equations (1)-(5).

$$\text{Unipolar binary} = \begin{cases} 1; & X > 0 \\ 0; & X < 0 \end{cases} \tag{1}$$

Figure 2. Structure of three input neuron

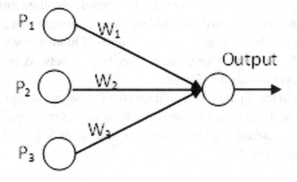

$$\text{Bipolar binary} = \begin{cases} 1; & X > 0 \\ -1; & X < 0 \end{cases} \tag{2}$$

$$\text{Logarthmic Sigmod} = \frac{1}{1 + e^{-x}} \tag{3}$$

$$\text{Tan Sigmod} = \frac{1 - e^{-x}}{1 + e^{-x}} \tag{4}$$

$$\text{Linear } y = x \tag{5}$$

In literature, different types of ANN architecture are available such as the single layer perceptron, multilayer perceptron, Hopfield network, Hamming network, Kohenen's self-organizing maps, and so on. Each type of ANN exhibits different properties due to the connection between neurons, i.e. architecture, activation function, and learning algorithm to adjust the weights. The number of input and output neurons depends upon the application to be solved. The architecture of ANN, learning algorithm for adjusting weights is chosen depending upon the nature of the problem. From all these types of ANNs, in this chapter a widely used multilayer perceptron and self-organizing feature map are discussed in this chapter

Multilayer Perceptron (MLP)

A single layer perceptron network has a layer of neurons with connected weights and suitable to solve only linearly separable problems. The multiayer perceptron (MLP) is a feedforward, neural network to overcome the limitation of the single layer perceptron network, consists of hidden layer between input and output layer of neurons. The number of hidden layers and units of hidden layers varies with the complexity of the problem. A structure of three layered network with input, hidden and an output layer is shown in Figure 3.

The neurons in the input layers and does not process and accept inputs, neurons in hidden layer perform computation and output layer for accepting the signal of output. There are different learning algorithms and the widely-used approach is the back-propagation algorithm.

Figure 3. Multilayer feedforward neural network

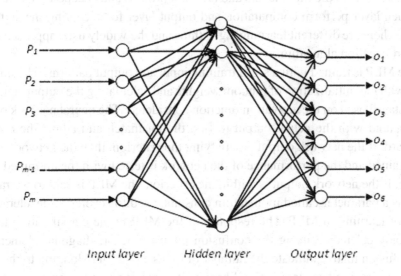

Input layer   Hidden layer   Output layer

The MLP is trained with a set of training input and output patterns. The training starts with the initialization of random weights and calculating the output signal for every stage based on the activation function considered. The neural network output is compared with the actual output to find the mismatch and adjust the error in backward. If the network output is satisfying the criterion, then the network is said to be trained and the performance of the network is tested with the untrained input pattern. If the network output is within the criterion, the MLP is said to be trained. There is a parameter called momentum constant, used to accelerate/decelerate the speed of learning in MLP. The response of the MLP in the classification task is commonly calculated using the confusion matrix. The off-diagonal elements of the confusion matrix indicate the number of times a pattern belonging to the class i, was misclassified as class j. The diagonal of confusion matrix corresponds to an accuracy of classification. Since each class pattern may be confused with another class pattern. Therefore, the sum on each row and column may be different from 100%. The generalization capability of the neural network, is checked using cross-validation process.

The objective of cross-validation is to determine the weights that maximize the accuracy of prediction. The K fold cross validation is carried out by dividing the training pattern U into K equal parts, i.e., $Ui = i = 1, 2, \ldots\ldots$ In the ith fold of the cross validation, the set U_i is used for testing and the remaining $K-1$ sets are used for training the NN. After all K folds of cross validation, over the K folds, the weights of highest predication accuracy is chosen.

The neurons in the input layers and does not process and accept inputs, neurons in hidden layer perform computation and output layer for accepting the signal of output. There are different learning algorithms and the widely used approach is the back-propagation algorithm.

The MLP is trained with a set of training input and output patterns. The training starts with the initialization of random weights and calculating the output signal for every stage based on the activation function considered. The neural network output is compared with the actual output to find the mismatch and adjust the error in backward. If the network output is satisfying the criterion, then the network is said to be trained and the performance of the network is tested with the untrained input pattern. If the network output is within the criterion, the MLP is said to be trained. There is a parameter called momentum constant, used to accelerate/decelerate the speed of learning in MLP. The response of the MLP in the classification task is commonly calculated using the confusion matrix. The off-diagonal elements of the confusion matrix indicate the number of times a pattern belonging to the class i, was misclassified as class j. The diagonal of confusion matrix corresponds to an accuracy of classification. Since each class pattern may be confused with another class pattern. Therefore, the sum on each row and column may be different from 100%. The generalization capability of the neural network is checked using cross-validation process.

Kohonen Self-Organizing Maps (KSOM)

A Kohonen self-organizing map (KSOM), (Kohonen, 1995) is an unsupervised neural network used for clustering input patterns. In addition to clustering, the network reduces the size input vector by mapping into lower dimension map. This network is commonly known as self-organizing map (SOM), find application in signal processing, image processing, decision making, etc. The SOM is a feedforward network consists of input layer and D dimensional computational/output layer.

The dimension D could be one or two. The neurons in computational layer are defined with topological neigbours based on neigbouring function. The neighboring neurons are defined based on Gaussian function or distance based function varying in number from dozen to thousands. Every neuron in computational layers is connected to input neuron with weights. The structure of 1-D, SOM is shown in Figure 4.

The unsupervised training for clustering starts with input data without class labels for good representation of the training data set as possible. The unsupervised network weight is updated based on competitive learning. During training, the network weights are initialized from the initial random weight values and distance between input vector and weight vectors are calculated. The winner as well as neighbouring neurons weights is updated during the training. The training continues until the

Figure 4. 1-D SOM Structure

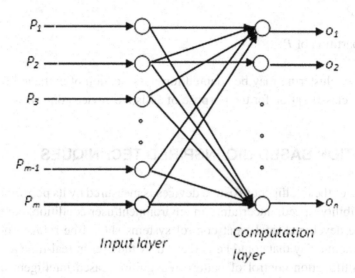

Input layer   Computation layer

clustering of training vector stabilizes by repeated exposing of input. However, SOM is not widely used for clustering of input in control of assistive device.

SOM is preferred to reduce the dimension of feature vectors. The number of feature weight elements is equal to the input feature vector in the feature space. In case of feature selection, SOM is trained similar to clustering. The weight vector with large value of weight preserves the information and those features are considered for further processing. Therefore, dimension of the feature is reduced from original dimension to lower dimension without losing much information.

Fuzzy Clustering

The fuzzy approach for transition of fuzzy sets consisting of classes of objects is gradual and not binary 0 or 1. This is the convenient form for representation of uncertain data. The information is represented using linguistic variables like slight, small, large etc. The degree of transition depends on level of uncertainty.

The objective function for clustering in P with sum of square error is given below.

$$J = \sum_{j}\sum_{k} v_{jk} \left\| p_k - c_i \right\|^2 \qquad (6)$$

where

$C = (c_1, c_2, c_3, \dots, c_i)$ denotes center of cluster for weighting exponent of membership

V is the c-partition of P

The fuzzy clustering may be adapted for classification of extracted features in the stage of classification for the purpose of assistive device control.

POPULATION BASED BIO-INSPIRED TECHNIQUES

The success of the intelligent assistive devices is measured by its performance, like safety, flexibility, speed, uncertainty in environment/user condition, etc. and cost. Further, the developed intelligent control systems should be robust and operate devices without delay that could be perceived by the user in real-time application.

The multifunction control of pattern recognition based intelligent devices is limited due to copious data from a number of sensors and or due to extraction of features using frequency and time-frequency techniques. A copious amount of data and or features leads to increased computation cost and time-delay in operating the assistive devices. Among several factors, the performance of classification is characterized by the features which represent the particular category/class of patterns and hence, the performance of the assistive device at an intelligent/high level control in case of pattern recognition based systems. This in turn necessitates the application of dimension reduction techniques, namely feature selection and feature reduction in pattern recognition techniques to reduce the input data to the classifier. The dimension reduction techniques may improve the classification task by eliminating the redundant and irrelevant spurious data leading to reduced time and computational burden. The estimation of motor parameters is vital in developing the controller for assistive devices. The poor estimation of parameters of motors may leads to poor design of controller and leads to instability.

In order to alleviate the problem of computation burden and parameter identification in case of assistive devices, population based bio-inspired search techniques are proposed in the literature developed from nature motivation. The advantage of these techniques over other techniques is that knowledge of the system or problem is not required and can be solved to reach the global optimum solution. Typically, the nature inspired algorithms may be based on biological behaviour of organisms (e.g. bat, firefly, swarm etc.) or based on physics/chemistry such as gravitation, central force, river formation, etc. These algorithms are studied to improve the performance of the system or solve the problem under study. Although there are plenty of nature inspired algorithms have been developed such as evolutionary algorithms (EA), particle swarm optimization (PSO), ant colony optimization (ACO), Bats algorithm, gravitational search algorithm, etc. In this chapter, starting with evolutionary algorithms and other widely used optimization techniques in feature selection process and motor parameter estimation has been discussed.

The evolutionary algorithms are inspired from biological process based on mutation, fitness, social interaction and reproduction. Search techniques based on components of evolutionary framework include genetic algorithm (GA), evolutionary strategy (ES), evolutionary programming (EP) and genetic programming (GP) (Back, 1996). These algorithms differ in technical representation for example representation of candidate solution. But these algorithms utilize previous history, memory updates to mimic biological evolution and interaction. The next section discusses the brief description of these different evolutionary algorithms.

Genetic Algorithm

The genetic algorithm (GA) is introduced by Holland (Holland, 1973) using binary string representation. The evolution starts from a random generation of population of individuals. The next generation, individuals are stochastically selected (e.g., roulette wheel selection) based on fitness value. The selected pairs of current generation produce offspring using genetic operators, crossover and mutation. During crossover, m number of points is chosen at random and exchange between the parents. In mutation, the binary 1 is converted to 0 and vice-versa at one or more occurrences in random. The new population of individual is then used in the next iteration of the algorithm and the process terminates with the maximum number of iterations has been reached or desired fitness value is reached. In GA, the solution is characterised as strings.

In GA-based feature subset selection, each of the individual is represented by presence and absence of features with 1 or 0. A binary string of length equal to the number of features is considered for feature selection process. The bit 1 is to represent the selection of feature and 0 for dropping of feature in an individual representation. Each individual in the population is feature subset. The initial population size is set to random value with randomly generated individuals.

Evolutionary Strategy

Evolution strategy was invented in early 1960. In evolution strategy (ES), the population is represented as real-valued numbers. Similar to GA, random population of individual is generated (Beyer and Schwefel, 2002). Offspring are generated from the parents with high fitness value using recombination. The offspring undergo mutation and replace the parent only if fitness value of offspring is greater than the parent, in case of 1+1-ES. The iterative process terminates when the termination criteria is met. There are different types evolution strategies in considering the parents for next generation.

Evolutionary Programming

In evolutionary programming, offspring are generated only by mutation. The candidate solution is characterized as finite state machine. Finding the optimized solution is similar to ES and GA. This iterative process continues until the termination criterion is met.

Particle Swarm Optimization

Particle swarm optimization (PSO) is a stochastic, population-based computation technique inspired from the behaviour of bird flocks, fish school (Kennedy and Eberhart, 1995). Similar to evolutionary algorithm, a population of individuals (or particles) is initialized for a given problem in PSO. Each particle represents a point in multidimensional space. The population of these particles is referred as swarm. The PSO iterative program begins with random initialization of size of the swarm as well as the particle value in the swarm. Further, the boundaries of variables in particle are also necessarily to be specified with the minimum and maximum value of each variable. Each particle is evaluated with fitness function at every iteration to direct the velocity of the particle and hence the position in multidimensional search space. The particles move in the search space until the termination condition is reached.

The algorithm begins with the random initialization of particles, size of the swarm, position with zero velocity. The fitness function is evaluated and the particle's best position (p_b) or the local best (l_b), and the globally the best position (g_{be}) is updated. In the solution space, the particles local solution and or global position is updated based on the current particle performance. Further, the velocity and position of the particle is updated using the equation (7) & (8).

$$u_i^{k+1} = \alpha^k u_i^k + c_1 ran_{1,i}^k \left(pb_i^k - x_i^k \right) + c_2 ran_{2,i}^k \left(gb_i^k - x_i^k \right) \tag{7}$$

$$x_i^{k+1} = x_i^k + v_i^{k+1} \Delta t \tag{8}$$

where,

v_i^k the velocity of the particle at k^{th} iteration

pb_i^k the best position of the particle i in the search space at k^{th} iteration

gb_i^k the best position of the particle i in the search space at k^{th} iteration

x_i^k the position of the particle at k^{th} iteration

c_1 and c_2 the coefficients for cognitive and social behaviour

$ran_{1,i}^k$ and $ran_{2,i}^k$ generation of random number in the interval $\{0, 1\}$

$\Delta t = 1$

The PSO algorithm steps are given below

1. Initialize particles population, position and maximum number of iterations.
2. Evaluate the fitness function
3. Selection of best position of particle from all particles is referred as global best and from personal position of same particle is local best.
4. Update the position and velocity of the particle.
5. Repeat steps 2-4 until termination is reached

During feature selection task, the swarm is feature subset candidate. The selection of feature is based on presence or absence of bit 1 in a string from the value of fitness function. The equations (1) and (2) to be modified due to use of binary number in the particle position. The fitness value is estimation of accuracy in classification problem with the feature subset.

Ant Colony Optimization

Ant colony optimization (ACO) is another population based optimization technique introduced by Marco Dorigo and his colleague, in early 1990 (Dorigo and Caro 1999) from the inspiration of cooperative work of ant colonies. Since the introduction of algorithm, a lot of modified algorithms have been proposed to improve the solution to the problem. Typically, ants find their shortest path between food and its destination using the chemical substance called pheromone, left in trails while ants are moving. Ants are modelled as agents in optimization problem and solution are pheromone model. The concentration of pheromone guides the ants to select the path. The paths with less pheromone concentration are not the optimal path and path with higher level of concentration are considered as optimal path due to frequent traversal of ants. In case of feature selection process, features represent nodes in the path. The algorithm begins with the random initialization of number of ants and with the selection probability for the nodes as 1. The antsbeginwith solution from the randomly selected nodes. The selection measure for next node is influenced by evaluation probability of selection using equation (9).

$$P_i^k = \frac{\left(\tau_i\right)^{\beta} \left(\vartheta_i\right)^{\alpha}}{\sum_{j \notin N^k} \left(\tau_j\right)^{\beta} \left(\vartheta_j\right)^{\alpha}} \tag{9}$$

where,

$\tau_i$the level of pheromone

$\upsilon_i$is the heuristic indication of selection of feature i

N^ktheneighbouring nodes of kth ant

$gb_i^k$the best position of the particle i in the search space at k^{th} iteration

$x_i^k$the position of the particle at k^{th} iteration

$\alpha$and β parameters associated with pheromone trail and heuristic information to control the movement of ant

At the end iteration, when all ants completed the transverse movement, the strength of pheromone is updated using equation (10).

$$\tau_i = \rho\tau_i + \sum_{k=1}^{n}\Delta\tau_i^k \tag{10}$$

$n$the number of ants

ρ parameter for pheromone evaporation between 0 and 1

The algorithm steps are as follows

1. Initialize ants population, intensity of pheromone, parameters associated with pheromone trail and heuristic information and number of iterations.
2. Randomly assign nodes to the plant
3. Evaluate the movement of ant from food to destination
4. Update for globally best ant and locally best ant.
5. Update pheromone level
6. Repeat steps 3-5 until maximum iteration or termination condition is met.

Bat Algorithm

Bat algorithm is one of the recent heuristics algorithms derived from the biological behaviour of a natural system (Yang, 2010). Yang has introduced the algorithm from the inspiration of bats' echolocative behaviour. Bats are capable of tracking the food/prey using the following three rules as given by Yang (Yang, 2010). All bats use echolocation to sense distance, and they also "know" the difference between food/prey and background barriers in some magical way; A bat b_i flies randomly with velocity v_i at position x_i with a fixed frequency f_{min}, varying wavelength λ and loudness A_0 to search for prey. They can automatically adjust the wavelength (or frequency) of their emitted pulses and adjust the rate of pulse emission $r \in [0,1]$, depending on the proximity of their target; Although the loudness can vary in many ways, assume that the loudness varies from a large (positive) A_0 to a minimum constant value A_{min}.

The following steps present the Bat algorithm in finding the optimal solution for the given objective function.

1. Initialize ants population, pulse frequency, pulse rates and the loudness and number of iterations.
2. Evaluate the solution for bat using the equation (11)-(13) to update the velocity and its position.

$$f_i = f_{min} + \left(f_{min} - f_{max}\right)\beta \tag{11}$$

$$v_i^j\left(t\right) = v_i^j\left(t-1\right) + \left[\hat{x}^j - x_i^j\left(t-1\right)\right]f_i \tag{12}$$

$$x_i^j\left(t\right) = \left[x_i^j\left(t-1\right)\right] + v_i^j\left(t\right) \tag{13}$$

where,

$f_i$the pulse frequency to control the movement of bats

$v_i$is the velocity at position x_i

$x_i^j(t)$ the decision value of i^{th}bat at time t for thej^{th}variable

$\hat{x}^j$ is the global best for thej^{th}variable

β a random number

3. **If***rand*> *pulse rate$_i$***then** find global best and local best solution **end**
4. **If***rand*< A_i and $f\left(x_i\right) < f(\widehat{x})$ **then** accept the new solution. Increase *pulse rate$_i$* and reduce A_i**end**
5. Repeat steps 2-4 for all the bats and rank them to find the best solution
6. Repeat steps 3-5 until maximum iteration or termination condition is met.

In addition to above mentioned bio-inspired algorithms, there are various optimization algorithms such as Wolf search algorithm, Firefly algorithm, Monkey search algorithm, Glowworm swarm optimization, Cat swarm, Bees swarm optimization, etc. are discussed in the literature. However, the selection of appropriate algorithm for feature selection, classification which improves the accuracy of identification is a challenging task.

APPLICATION OF BIO-INSPIRED ALGORITHM IN REHABILITATION ENGINEERING

The bio-inspired techniques find application in pattern recognition for selection of subset of features from the feature space, classification of features in pattern recognition and estimation of motor parameters for development of accurate control in assistive devices. Pattern recognition (classification), maps the feature vectors into specific classes of motion. Many literatures highlight the success of neural networks (NN) and its ability to learn the distinction among different conditions in pattern recognition. The advantage of the neural network is, its ability to learn linear and non-linear relationships directly from data being modelled. Various type of neural network has been used to identify the information contained in the signals in developing real-time pattern recognition-based myoelectric control.

Kelly et al. (1990) used Hopfield neural network to calculate time-series parameter and perceptron network to classify the MES signals. In this myoelectric signal features are classified using two layer perceptron. The transfer function of hidden and output units is given below.

$$F(\alpha) = \frac{1}{\left(1 + e^{-(\alpha-\theta)}\right)} \qquad (14)$$

where,

α is the $\sum_{k=1}^{n} P_k W_k$

θ is the threshold

Hudgins et al. (1993), Tenore and Ramos (2007), Tsenov et al. (2006) used a multi-layer perceptron (MLP) neural network to classify time-domain features. Wang et al. (2005) applied back-propagation neural network (BPNN) with AR coefficients for classification. Zhao et al. (2005) applied Levenberg-Marquardt based neural network with parametric AR model and integral of EMG to control five-fingered prosthetic hand. Tsuji et al. (2000) proposed a NN that combines a common BPNN with recurrent neural filter to classify from time-series of EMG signals, rather than features. Barrero et al. (2001) discriminated EMG signals for externally controlled upper extremity prosthesis using artificial neural network (ANN).

Del and Park (1994) extracted myoelectric signal features through Fourier analysis and clustered using Fuzzy C-Means (FCM) algorithm. The EMG data have been interpreted using fuzzy clustering approach. The feature space is clustered into 9 classes with FCM technique. Three membership functions have been used to perform clustering. Data obtained by this unsupervised learning technique are then presented to MLP type NN. Khushaba et al. (2009) used evolutionary fuzzy discriminant technique for feature reduction in myoelectic control.

Jung et al. (2007) proposed linear vector quantisation (LVQ) neural network to classify spectral estimates from fourth order AR parameters of EMG signals obtained using Yule-Walker method. Guo et al. (2006) used wavelet packet transform features of EMG signals to LVQ neural network. Ito et al. (2008) proposed a multiple NN to determine the movement intended by an amputee from EMG signals. Ma et al. (2001) used NN to classify EMG signals resulting from the dynamic muscle contraction. Guo et al. (2009) used Levenberg-Marquardt algorithm to advance the training speed and accuracy compared to back-propagation algorithm for pattern recognition of human motion from AR coefficients. Matsumura et al. (2002) used NN to FFT spectra of EMG signals for recognition hand motion. Shuman (2009) performed classification using ANN, random forest (RF), one nearest-neighbour (1NN), decision tree with Boosting (DT/B), support vector machine (SVM) and decision tree (DT) and found that ANN with 6 internal nodes and 30 forest for RF resulted in the highest accuracy. Wojtczak et al. (2009) proposed an NN identification system using features based on time and energy histograms. Markou and Singh (2003) discussed various neural network based approaches for the purpose of identification of unknown data or signal.

Smith et al. (2009) studied the applicability of time delayed neural network (TDNN) to track movement of the shoulder and elbow joints. Huang et al. (2003) discriminated eight kinds of prehensile postures using cascaded architecture of neural networks with feature map (CANFM) and obtained higher discrimination rate compared to k-nearest neighbour (kNN), fuzzy kNN, and BPNN. Sebelius et al. (2005) applied a modified SOFM composed of a combination of a Kohonen network with conscience mechanism algorithm for EMG classification and found results are superior in performance than MLP. Chong and Sundaraj (2009) investigated that BPNN is well performed for fast weak and fast strong muscle activities and probabilistic neural network (PNN) is well performed for slow weak and slow strong muscle activities. Xizhi (2008) shown that EMG pattern recognized using radial basis function (RBF) neural network is higher than BPNN. Zalzala and Chaiyaratana (2000) used hybrid radial basis function multilayer perceptron (RBF-MLP) network for classification. Yuan et al. (2008) used BPNN to classify feature vector extracted from recurrence plots and recurrence quantification analysis (RQA). Yazama et al. (2004) used NN to classify the EMG signals using multidimensional directed information (MDI) for wrist motions. Du et al. (2010) recognised EMG signal patterns using grey relational analysis (GRA) and shown better performance than multi-layer neural network based classifier.

Due to the multi-channel approach used for acquisition of signals, the extracted feature vector dimension can become large. Also, wavelet transform generates many coefficients to represent time-scale features. Thus, dimensionality reduction can be achieved using either feature selection (FS) or feature projection (FP) methods. Feature selection requires a search strategy that selects a candidate subset and an objective function that evaluates these candidates.

Yazama et al. (2003) selected features using GA. The FFT have been used for the extraction of frequency distribution information from four channel EMG data. The purpose of GA is the selection of frequency band to perform classification using NN classifier. The frequency corresponding to a code 1 us utilized and 0 has been ignored. Oskoei and Hu (2006) presented feature subset selection, to find an optimal subset of myoelectric features using GA as a search strategy. In this features subset selection Davies-Bouldin index, Fishers linear discriminant index, and linear discriminant analysis (LDA) has been used as objective functions. The time frequency domain features have been used for feature subset selection. Huang et al. (2003) demonstrated reduction of feature space by Kohonen's self-organizing map. Khushaba and Al-Jumaily (2007a) selected features using particle swarm optimisation (PSO) and Khushaba et al. (2007) developed a mixture of PSO and the concept of mutual information (MI) for selection of features.

Researchers have used bio-inspired optimization techniques in different motor parameter estimation (Dupuis et al. 2004, Udomsuk et al. 2010, Huynh and Dunnigan, 2010).

FUTURE RESEARCH DIRECTIONS

Researchers are attempting to address several significant problems, like response time, computational burden etc. with the bio-inspired techniques in pattern recognition. Researchers can attempt on feature selection and classification algorithms that significantly improve the performance of assistive devices.

Further, few researchers have shown that bio-inspired algorithms have important role in selection of channels/number of electrodes in brain computer interface for the development of communication and control assistance. Similarly, in EMG based assistive devices bio-inspired based optimization techniques may be used for the choice of number of channels, eliminating number of sensors used for degree of control. Recently researchers are using bio-inspired techniques in various electrical motor parameter identification for the purposed of development of controller, fault diagnosis, etc. The appropriate identification of motor parameter enables to actuate the assistive devices with appropriate control strategy. Techniques such as, rough set classification, rough set on fuzzy approximation space, rough set on fuzzy approximation and rough set on fuzzy approximation and Bayesian classification, rough set with ANN etc. may be attempted to identify the discriminating capability with the bio-electric signals.

CONCLUSION

The processing of bioelectric signals is a challenging and heart of pattern recognition based assistive device control. The objective is achieved through the successive processing of input bioelectric signals in several combinations of intermediate stages, before the decision making/output stage. The various stages such as digital filtering, preprocessing, extraction of relevant information in the form of features, identification of the relevance of channel (channel selection)/ extracted features (feature selection), feature reduction and interpretation of the information through a classification algorithm may be included to translate the human intention in the bioelectric signals. The number of intermediate signals processing stages depends on the real-time factors such as computational complexity, time, memory, etc. Several combinations of signal processing stages and techniques have been developed and a wide application of bio-inspired techniques in rehabilitation engineering is due to the fact that big amount of data and usually introduces a time delay in continuous control. The second limitation, besides the time delay, is the computational burden in processing the features extracted from large number of data. To reduce the computational burden, researchers used bio-inspired based feature selection techniques. The performance of the classification also depends on the classifier. The bio-inspired techniques have the ability to learn from training and are used as classifier due to generalisation capability on unseen data like neural network. The identification of motor parameters in developing the controller and controller parameters, are other bio-inspired optimization research areas.

REFERENCES

Back, T. (1996). *Evolutionary Algorithms in Theory and Practice*. New York: Oxford University Press.

Barrero, V., Grisales, E. V., Rosas, F., Sanchez, C., & Leon, J. (2001). Design and implementation of an intelligent interface for myoelectric controlled prosthesis. In *Proceedings of the 23rd Annual International Conference of the IEEE*. Istanbul, Turkey: IEEE.

Beyer, H. G., & Schwefel, H. P. (2002). Evolution strategies. *Natural Computing*, *1*(1), 3–52. doi:10.1023/A:1015059928466

Chong, Y. L., & Sundaraj, K. (2009). A study of back-propagation and radial basis neural network on EMG signal classification. In *Proceedings of the 6th International Symposium* Mechatronics and its Applications ISMA '09. Sharjah: IEEE.

Del, B. A., & Park, D. C. (1994). Myoelectric signal recognition using fuzzy clustering and artificial neural networks in real time. In *Proceedings of the IEEE World Congress on Computational Intelligence and Neural Networks*. IEEE.

Dorigo, M., & Caro, G. D. (1999). Ant Colony Optimization: A New Meta-heuristic. In Proceedings of Evolutionary Computation CEC 99, Washington, DC.

Du, Y.-C., Lin, C.-H., Shyu, L.-Y., & Chen, T. (2010). Portable hand motion classifier for multi-channel surface electromyography recognition using grey relational analysis. *Journal Expert Systems with Applications*, *37*(6), 4283–4291. doi:10.1016/j.eswa.2009.11.072

Dupuis, A., Ghribi, M., & Kaddouri, A. (2004). Multi-objective genetic estimation of DC motor parameters and load torque. In *Proceedings of Industrial Technology, 2004. IEEE ICIT '04.* IEEE.

Guo, X., Yang, P., Chen, L., Wang, X., & Li, L. (2006). Study of the control mechanism of robot-prosthesis based-on the EMG processed. In *Proceedings of 6th World Congress on Intelligent Control and Automation* (pp. 9490-9493), Dalian, China: IEEE.

Guo, X., Yu, H., Zhen, G., Liu, Y., Zhang, Y., & Zhang, Y. (2009). Artificial intelligent based human motion pattern recognition and prediction for the surface electromyographic signals. In *Proceedings of Information Technology and Computer Science ITCS '09*. Ukraine: IEEE. doi:10.1109/ITCS.2009.65

Holland, J. H. (1973). Genetic algorithms and the optimal allocation of trials. *SIAM Journal on Computing*, *2*(2), 88–105. doi:10.1137/0202009

Huang, H.-P., Liu, Y.-H., Liu, L.-W., & Wong, C.-S. (2003). EMG classification for prehensile postures using cascaded architecture of neural networks with self-organizing maps. In *Proceedings of the 2006 6th World Congress on Intelligent Control and Automation*, Taipei, Taiwan: IEEE.

Hudgins, B., Parker, P., & Scott, R. N. (1993). A new strategy for multifunction myoelectric control. *IEEE Transactions on Bio-Medical Engineering*, *40*(1), 82–94. doi:10.1109/10.204774 PMID:8468080

Huynh, D. C., & Dunnigan, M. W. (2010). Parameter estimation of an induction machine using advanced particle swarm optimization algorithms. *IET Electric Power Applications*, *4*(9), 748–760. doi:10.1049/iet-epa.2009.0296

Ito, K., Tsukamoto, M., & Kondo, T. (2008). Discrimination of intended movements based on nonstationary EMG for a prosthetic hand control. In *Proceedings of Communications, Control and Signal Processing ISCCSP '08*, St. Julian's, Malta. IEEE.

Jung, K. K., Kim, J. W., Lee, H. K., Chung, S. B., & Eom, K. H. (2007). EMG pattern classification using spectral estimation and neural network. *In Proceedings of the 2007 Annual Conference*, Takamatsu, Japan. IEEE. doi:10.1109/SICE.2007.4421150

Kelly, M. F., Parker, P. A., & Scott, R. N. (1990). The application of neural networks to myoelectric signal analysis: A preliminary study. *IEEE Transactions on Bio-Medical Engineering, 37*(3), 221–230. doi:10.1109/10.52324 PMID:2328997

Kennedy, J., & Eberhart, R. C. (1995).Particle swarm optimization. In *Proceedings of the IEEE International Conference on Neural Networks*. Piscataway, NJ: IEEE. doi:10.1109/ICNN.1995.488968

Khushaba, R. N., Al-Ani, A., & Al-Jumaily, A. (2007). Swarm intelligence based dimensionality reduction for myoelectric control. In *Proceedings of Intelligent Sensors, Sensor Networks and Information ISSNIP '07*, Melbourne, QLD, Australia. IEEE. doi:10.1109/ISSNIP.2007.4496907

Khushaba, R. N., & Al-Jumaily, A. (2007a). Channel and feature selection in multifunction myoelectric control. In *Proceedings of 2007 29th Annual International Conference of the IEEE Engineering in Medicine and Biology Society*, Lyon, France. IEEE. doi:10.1109/IEMBS.2007.4353509

Khushaba, R. N., Al-Jumaily, A., & Al-Ani, A. (2009). Evolutionary fuzzy discriminant analysis feature projection technique in myoelectric control. *Pattern Recognition Letters, 30*(7), 699–707. doi:10.1016/j.patrec.2009.02.004

Kohonen, T. (1995). *Self-Organizing Maps*. Berlin/Heidelberg, Germany: Springer. doi:10.1007/978-3-642-97610-0

Ma, N., Kumar, D. K., & Pah, N. (2001). Classification of hand direction using multi-channel electromyography by neural network. In *Proceedings of The Seventh Australian and New Zealand Intelligent Information Systems Conference*, Perth, Western Australia. IEEE.

Markou, M., & Singh, S. (2003). Novelty detection: a review-part 2: neural network based approaches. *Journal of Signal Processing, 83*(12), 2499–2521. doi:10.1016/j.sigpro.2003.07.019

Matsumura, Y., Mitsukura, Y., Fukumi, M., & Akamatsu, N. (2002). Recognition of EMG signal patterns by neural networks. In *Proceedings of Neural Information Processing ICONIP '02*, Singapore, Singapore. IEEE. doi:10.1109/ICONIP.2002.1198158

Sebelius, F., Eriksson, L., Holmberg, H., Levinsson, A., Lundborg, G., Danielsen, N., & Montelius, L. et al. (2005). Classification of motor commands using a modified self-organising feature map. *Journal of Medical Engineering and Physics, 27*(5), 403–413. doi:10.1016/j.medengphy.2004.09.008 PMID:15863349

Shuman, G. (2009). Using forearm electromyograms to classify hand gestures. In Proceedings of Bioinformatics and Biomedicine BIBM '09. Washington, DC, USA.

Smith, A., Nanda, P., & Brown, E. E. (2009). Development of a myoelectric control scheme based on a time delayed neural network. In *Proceedings of 2009 Annual International Conference of the IEEE Engineering in Medicine and Biology Society*, Minneapolis, Minnesota. IEEE. doi:10.1109/IEMBS.2009.5332846

Tenore, F. V. G., Ramos, A., Fahmy, A., Acharya, S., Etienne-cummings, R., & Thakor, N. T. (2009). Decoding of individuated finger movements using surface electromyography. *IEEE Transactions on Bio-Medical Engineering, 56*(5), 1427–1434. doi:10.1109/TBME.2008.2005485 PMID:19473933

Tsenov, G., Zeghbib, A. H., Palis, F., Shoylev, N., & Mladenov, V. (2006). Neural networks for online classification of hand and finger movements using surface EMG signals. In *Proceedings of 2006 8th Seminar on Neural Network Applications in Electrical Engineering,* Belgrade, Serbia. IEEE.

Tsuji, T., Fukuda, O., Kaneko, M., & Koji, I. (2000). Pattern classification of time-series EMG signals using neural networks. *International Journal of Adaptive Control and Signal Processing, 14*(8), 829–848. doi:10.1002/1099-1115(200012)14:8<829::AID-ACS623>3.0.CO;2-L

Udomsuk, S., Areerak, K.-L., Areerak, K.-N., & Srikaew, A. (2010). Parameters identification of separately excited dc motor using adaptive tabu search technique. In *Proceedings of Advances in Energy Engineering (ICAEE).Beijling.* IEEE. doi:10.1109/ICAEE.2010.5557618

Wang, J. Z., Wang, R. C., Li, F., Jiang, M. W., & Jin, D. W. (2005). EMG signal classification for myoelectric teleoperating a dexterous robot hand. In *Proceedings of the 2005 IEEE 27th Annual Conference on Engineering in Medicine and Biology*, Shanghai, China. IEEE. doi:10.1109/IEMBS.2005.1615841

Wojtczak, P., Amaral, T. G., Dias, O. P., Wolczowski, A., & Kurzynski, M. (2009). Hand movement recognition based on biosignal analysis. *Journal of Engineering Applications of Artificial Intelligence, 22*(4-5), 608–615. doi:10.1016/j.engappai.2008.12.004

Yang, X. S. (2010). *A New Metaheuristic Bat-Inspired Algorithm. Cruz, C.; Gonz'alez, J. R.; Pelta, D. A* (G. Terrazas, Ed.). Springer Berlin.

Yazama, Y., Mistukura, Y., Fukumi, M., & Akamatsu, N. (2003). Feature analysis for the EMG signals based on the class distance. In *Proceedings of Computational Intelligence in Robotics and Automation,* Kobe, Japan. IEEE. doi:10.1109/CIRA.2003.1222292

Yazama, Y., Mitsukura, Y., Fukumi, M., & Fukumi, N. (2004). Analysis and recognition of wrist motions by using multidimensional directed information and EMG signal. In *Proceedings of IEEE Annual Meeting of the Fuzzy Information Processing NAFIPS '04*, Banff, Alberta. IEEE.

Zalzala, A. M. S., & Chaiyaratana, N. (2000). Myoelectric signal classification using evolutionary hybridRBF-MLP networks. In *Proceedings of Evolutionary Computation*, La Jolla, California. IEEE.

Zhao, J. Xie, Z. Jiang, L., Cai, H., Liu, H., & Hirzinger, G. (2005). Levenberg-Marquardt based neural network control for a five-fingered prosthetic hand. In *Proceedings of the 2005 IEEE International Conference on Robotics and Automation*, Barcelona, Spain. IEEE.

KEY TERMS AND DEFINITIONS

Classification: Identification of a category/class from the input feature vector.

Electroencephalogram (EEG): A record of the electrical activity of the brain.

Electromyogram (EMG): A record of the electrical activity of the muscle.

Feature Extraction: The process of defining meaningful and efficient information from the raw data.

Feature Reduction: The process of reducing number of extracted features to optimal numbers to identify a category/class of data using transformation.

Feature Selection: The process of selection of existing features to identify the class of data.

Neural Network: A computing system made up of a number of simple, highly interconnected processing elements which process information by their dynamic state response to external inputs.

Neuromuscular Disorder: A disorder that affects the muscles and or nerves.

Pattern Recognition: The process of identification of category/class of the pattern from the raw data.

Prosthetic Hand: An artificial hand that replaces the missing hand.

Chapter 3
Privacy Preserving Big Data Publishing:
Challenges, Techniques, and Architectures

Nancy Victor
VIT University, India

Daphne Lopez
VIT University, India

ABSTRACT

Data privacy plays a noteworthy part in today's digital world where information is gathered at exceptional rates from different sources. Privacy preserving data publishing refers to the process of publishing personal data without questioning the privacy of individuals in any manner. A variety of approaches have been devised to forfend consumer privacy by applying traditional anonymization mechanisms. But these mechanisms are not well suited for Big Data, as the data which is generated nowadays is not just structured in manner. The data which is generated at very high velocities from various sources includes unstructured and semi-structured information, and thus becomes very difficult to process using traditional mechanisms. This chapter focuses on the various challenges with Big Data, PPDM and PPDP techniques for Big Data and how well it can be scaled for processing both historical and real-time data together using Lambda architecture. A distributed framework for privacy preservation in Big Data by combining Natural language processing techniques is also proposed in this chapter.

DOI: 10.4018/978-1-5225-2863-0.ch003

INTRODUCTION

"Data is the new oil", declared Clive Humby, a Sheffield mathematician ('Tech giants may be huge, but nothing matches big data', 2013). Michael Palmer expanded the quote as: "Data is just like crude. It's valuable, but if unrefined it cannot really be used. It has to be changed into gas, plastic, chemicals etc. to create a valuable entity that drives profitable activity; so must data be broken down, analyzed for it to have value". This is true in the case of Big Data. Data is the natural resource growing bigger and bigger each and every second. Big Data is so large amount of data that cannot be processed using traditional systems. Big Data analytics is the process of generalizing values from large data sets through which hidden patterns, unknown correlations and other useful information can be uncovered ('The state of the enterprise cloud and prepping for AWS re:Invent 2013').

The main characteristics of Big Data (4 V's) are: Volume, Velocity, Variety and Veracity (The Four V's of Big Data, 2015).

- **Volume:** The word "big" in Big Data defines the volume. The various sources of Big data include sensors, social media, activity generated data, data warehouse appliances, archives, business apps etc. (The Big 9 big data sources, 2014; Top 10 categories for big data sources and mining technologies, 2012).
- **Velocity:** This refers to the speed at which the data flows in and out of the system. Some of the examples for data generation points include mobile devices, microphones, sensors, social media etc.
- **Variety:** Big Data includes structured, semi-structured and unstructured data, which is being produced from various sources.
- **Veracity:** It refers to the inconsistencies and incompleteness in data which is collected from various sources.

In order to derive value out of this massive data, it should be collected and processed efficiently. This itself brings in a lot of challenges which includes preserving the privacy of data that is collected from various data sources at very high rates, in a variety of data formats. For processing and managing Big data, various technologies are used in the Hadoop ecosystem. This includes HDFS for storage and replication, MapReduce for distributed processing, Mahout for machine learning, Pig for scripting and so on (Khan, N et al., 2014). Data publishing plays a major role in the case of Big data as the data which is collected can be publicized for use or reuse by researchers in order to obtain valuable research output. The data can then be used for performing various data mining tasks, which helps to gain better insights about the data which is collected.

The chapter is organized as follows: Section II gives an outline about the various challenges with Big Data. Section III explains the various models used for privacy preservation. Section IV focuses on privacy preserving data mining, whereas section V discusses about privacy preserving data publishing. An architecture for privacy preserving data publishing has been proposed in section VI and Section VII concludes the chapter.

CHALLENGES WITH BIG DATA

Wu et al. (2014) has considered the three tiers of a Big Data processing framework to explain the various challenges faced in the Big data domain. The three tiers include big data mining platform, big data semantics and application knowledge and big data mining algorithms. Big data mining platform mainly focuses on the difficulty in accessing, processing and computing the massive quantity of data that is clearly impossible with the existing computing facilities. MapReduce computation model plays a major role here in efficiently handling the pool of data which is being gathered from various sources at very high velocities. Big data semantics and application knowledge deals with the privacy concerns and distributing data to the public. Data privacy and location privacy is given at most importance in this case. The third tier mainly deals with various data mining algorithms. As the amount of data produced increases rapidly, it becomes difficult to extract information for mining purposes using the existing methodologies. The next few sections are entirely dedicated to explain about the privacy preserving data mining challenges and how the existing data mining algorithms are extended to work with massive quantity of data which is generated at very high velocities from various sources such as social media networks and sensors.

Preserving the privacy was not a difficult task when all the published data was in the relational data format. But, in today's digital world, the data gets published in a variety of formats and at high velocities, which makes it very difficult for the publisher to protect the privacy of the data owner. Data owner here refers to the individual whose data is collected and published. The major challenges in Big Data privacy and security domain includes infra-structure security, integrity and reactive security, data privacy and data management. A detailed survey on various Big Data security and privacy challenges can be studied in (Big Data Working Group, 2013).

Various studies have been carried out in the field of Big Data security. As big data consists of massive amount of data, it has always been a challenge to store and process it in a secured manner. Mahajan et al. (2016) discusses about the various solutions in order to achieve big data security. Thota et al. (2017) proposed an efficient meta cloud storage architecture to secure the data which is deployed in the cloud using different big data technologies. Gai et al. (2016) proposed a distributed storage architecture to secure the cloud data. Yao et al. (2016) came up with a framework which uses semantic inference and association methods for securing big data in an efficient manner. A real-time security verification model has been devised by Puthal et al. (2016). This uses a dynamic key length based approach for implementing the same. An attribute based evaluation methodology for Big data security has been proposed by Kim (2013). Zhao et al. (2014) proposed a security framework for G-Hadoop using various cryptographic approaches.

PRIVACY MODELS

"Privacy is the claim of individuals, groups or institutions to determine for themselves when, how, and to what extent information about them is communicated to others." (Alan F. Westin, 1967). Preserving the privacy of data is of great concern when it is shared among multiple parties. Anonymization techniques proves to be an efficient mechanism for privacy preservation. Anonymization refers to the process of removing Personally Identifying Information (PII) from the table to keep the identity of the individual private. There are four types of data in a data set: (i) Explicit identifiers are used to identify an individual uniquely. E.g.: name, address. (ii) Quasi Identifiers are used along with external information to identify the identity of the individual. E.g.: Date of Birth, Job. (iii) Sensitive Attributes includes the data which are sensitive. E.g.: Salary, Disease. (iv) Non-sensitive Attributes includes the data which are not sensitive. Maintaining data privacy usually relies on removing the explicit identifiers in a data set. As this alone is not sufficient for complete privacy, various privacy models have been proposed such as k-anonymity, l-diversity, t-closeness and differential privacy. Fung et al. (2010) surveyed the recent developments in privacy preserving data publishing.

Various methods have been devised for anonymizing relational data. k-anonymity approach states that at least 'k' tuples in a table should be present in an equivalence class (Sweeney, 2002). Equivalence class can be defined as the set of tuples that have the same value for quasi identifiers. For satisfying k-anonymity where k = 5, an equivalence class should have at least five rows with the same value for Quasi identifiers. One of the main attacks with k-anonymity is the homogeneity attack which happens when the sensitive attribute lacks diversity. l-diversity approach states that in every block of quasi identifiers in the table, at least 'l' different sensitive values should be present (Machanavajjhala, Ashwin, et al, 2007). An equivalence class is said to have t-closeness if the distance between the distribution of a sensitive attribute in this class and the distribution of the attribute in the whole table is no more than a threshold 't'. A table is said to have t-closeness if all equivalence classes have t-closeness (Li et al., 2007). The idea of differential privacy is to publish the results of a query by adding some noise to the data which is already available. The notion of this approach is that the risk of individual privacy should not be increased by having a record in the statistical database. This model ensures that removal or addition of a particular record in the published database does not affect the overall analysis of the data in the table (Dwork, 2011). The model is quite good in overcoming linkage attacks.

These existing privacy models were extended for preserving Big Data privacy. Some of the approaches are discussed here. SaNGreeA (Social Network Greedy Anonymization) approach was proposed by Alina Campan and Traian Marius Truta (2009) to effectively anonymize social network data based on clustering approach. FAANST is an anonymizing algorithm which is basically dedicated for working with numerical data. This is based on cluster based k-anonymity approach for anonymization (Zakerzadeh and Osborn, 2011). The method of stream k-anonymity was proposed by Li for facilitating continuous anonymization of data streams (Li et al., 2008). Airavat is a Map Reduce system which preserves the privacy of Map Reduce computations with untrusted code. This system includes an untrusted/trusted Mapper and a trusted Reducer (Roy et al., 2010). Differential privacy has been employed here to give perturbed results to the program.

As a Big Data extension to the survey done by Fung et al., privacy models for Big Data has been studied by Victor et al. (2016).

DATA MINING

Data Mining is the mining or discovery of new information in terms of patterns/rules from huge amount of data. There are mainly two categories of data mining tasks based on the kind of data to be mined: Descriptive and Predictive. Wu et al. (2008) has conducted a survey on the most influential and top ten algorithms in data mining. Figure 1 gives an overview of some of the best data mining techniques under each category.

Privacy Preserving Data Mining

Privacy Preserving Data Mining can be defined as getting valuable data mining results without revealing the underlying data values (Lindell & Pinkas, 2000). The main goal behind privacy preserving data mining is that, once privacy preserved, data can be shared freely among multiple parties and this will not involve any restrictive access controls.

Figure 1. Data mining techniques

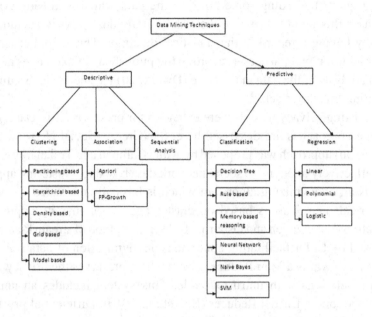

Two approaches are commonly adopted for protecting the privacy of data items that is published. One method involves restricting access to the data whereas the other technique focuses on anonymizing the data fields (Corti, Day, & Backhouse, 2000). In this section, we provide an overview of the various Data Mining techniques and privacy models used for rendering better data mining results, while preserving the privacy of individuals.

Privacy Preserving Data Mining With Big Data

Big Data is so large amount of data that cannot be processed using traditional database systems. A comprehensive study on various PPDM techniques has been done by Aldeen et al. (2015). This section focuses on extending the techniques used for relational databases to work with massive quantity of data. This section reviews the techniques adopted for privacy preserving data mining with Big Data, and can be considered as an extension to the Big Data domain. The techniques have been categorized based on classification, clustering and association approaches.

Classification Based Privacy Preserving Data Mining Techniques for Big Data

Classification predicts categorical class labels (discrete or nominal) and classifies data (constructs a model) based on the training set and the values (class labels) in a classifying attribute and uses it in classifying new data. Various techniques have been proposed for classifying Big Data (Fayyad et al., 1996).

Vaidya et al. (2014) proposed a random decision tree framework for horizontally and vertically partitioned Big Data sets using randomization and cryptographic approaches, in order to provide better security and efficiency. The method works well with semi-honest adversaries. The two basic horizontal partitioning approaches considers whether the tree structure is known to the participant or not. Secure sum protocol was used in the case where the global class distribution of each vector is known to all participants, whereas threshold encryption was used when the vector is known only to the tree owner and a combination of secure electronic voting protocol and threshold encryption was used when the vector is unknown to all participants. For vertically partitioned data sets, each random tree was split across different sites and the node statistics was updated once the tree structure was constructed. Additively homomorphic encryption was used for preventing information leakage. The prediction was computed by averaging the probability outputs from various random decision trees.

C4.5 Map Reduce computation model was proposed by Saravanan et al. (2014), which focuses on providing better prediction values without questioning the individual's privacy in any manner. Two techniques for privacy preservation are dealt in the work. One technique works by applying prediction algorithms on perturbed data and the other works on raw data which will be applied to the prediction algorithm. A combination of these techniques balances the "utility" and "privacy" of data items in an efficient manner. The proposed hybrid technique works by applying normalization on data items and performing root level perturbation, where by the privacy paradigm works perfectly with Big Data sets.

Marinchev and Agre (2015) came up with an interesting idea for speeding up the working of nearest neighbour algorithm for working with Big Data. The techniques were improved by using micro optimizations and polar orthogonalization. The classes were identified using the resultant matrix that was obtained as a result of applying polar decomposition to the items. Big Data sets can be divided into various subclasses and the algorithm can be applied efficiently.

Twitter data is one of the well-known sources for Big Data. An opinion mining strategy for mining twitter data was proposed by Bing and Chan (2014), which uses a fuzzy based approach for solving the challenges associated with the velocity and volume characteristics of massive data sets. The execution time and accuracy proved to be efficient using the matrix-based and parallel techniques adopted for implementing twitter data mining. The proposed FMM algorithm works by classifying the tweets based on sentiment levels and then converting the data set as matrices and computing the vectors using fuzzy values. This result is used as the training data for improving the classification accuracy. A parallel implementation of this technique FMM-MR, using MapReduce computation model proved that the system can scale well with Big Data sets.

A multivariate randomized response technique was proposed by Du and Zhan (2003) for implementing various data mining techniques without resulting in privacy breach. In this approach, decision trees are constructed using perturbed data. The model works by letting the user answer two different, but related questions, where the answers will be just the opposite of each other. This related question model allows the users to answer the queries to any one of the question, without letting the asker know about the question that was answered. The method uses a disguising technique during data collection and the decision tree is constructed from the modified/disguised data.

Teo et al. (2013) proposed a technique for reducing computational load while reducing privacy breach. The two approaches of THL and collusion resistant secure sum product protocol(CRSSPP) are integrated for processing cloud based big data applications. The problem with collusion is bypassed by creating a pair of keys for each party instead of using the public key that is produced by the initiator. The THL algorithm works by integrating Support Vector Machines and perturbation approaches.

Clustering Based Privacy Preserving Data Mining Techniques for Big Data

Clustering is the technique of grouping data in such a manner that similar objects will be given to the same group and will be more similar when compared with objects of other groups. The different types of clustering include partitioning-based, density-based, hierarchical-based, grid-based and model-based techniques (Popat & Emmanuel, 2014).

C-Means clustering technique which takes privacy preservation into consideration was proposed by Vashkevich and Zhukov (2015). The privacy preserving protocols that was proposed works for any number of parties and with vertically and horizontally partitioned big data sets. This is an improvement of the general k-means algorithm, where each data object belongs to each cluster in some degree. As the participating party owns a set of data in horizontally partitioned sets and is required to compute the common cluster centre jointly, secure dot protocol is used for working with multiple parties. In vertical partitioning, each party will have only a part of the dimensions and therefore cluster centres can be found out locally and is not required to share among other parties. As the membership matrix will be common for all, privacy mechanisms will be imposed in this area.

Assam and Seidl (2011) proposed an interesting privacy preservation technique using the k-anonymity privacy model for moving objects through temporal clustering techniques. The initial step of temporal clustering focuses on pruning the redundant traces and the next step finds the overlapping submission windows. Euclidean distances between the traces are determined and is compared with the threshold value. Based on this, clustering operation is performed and the similar traces are grouped into the same cluster. The traces in same clusters are given the same spatial and temporal value, checked for satisfying k-anonymity property and Quasi-identifiers are formed with the traces of the cluster. It is also shown that reoccurring anonymized trajectories cannot be detected.

Esteves (2014) came up with an idea of distributed cluster analysis of Big Data using CK-means algorithm, which alleviates the issues with serial K-means++, by parallelising the same. The MapReduce implementation of CK-Means takes as input a set of data points shuffled in a random order and the number of partitions, m. Partition the data into 'm' sets and assign a unique key to each partition. The key-value pair is supplied to the Hadoop Distributed File System. Each map function finds the set of initial centroids and a fitness score to the reducer function, which in turn chooses the fittest set of centroids. This new technique helps in performing accurate analysis on massive data sets.

Gkoulalas-Divanis and Loukides (2011) pointed out that transforming or perturbing transaction data before publishing suffers because of the trade-off between privacy and utility. Two algorithms named PCTA and UPCTA were proposed and proved that the techniques improve the utility of data in an efficient manner. Privacy Constrained Clustering-based Transaction Anonymization (PCTA) algorithm works by imposing privacy constraints one at a time, checks all possible conclusions and applies the best decision that will incur a minimum loss of utility. This is iterated until the privacy constraint condition is satisfied. Then, it goes for the next non-satisfied constraint. The Utility-guided Privacy-constrained Clustering-based Transaction Anonymization considers both privacy and utility conditions while anonymizing the data. The technique works by applying generalization and suppression operations whenever necessary by keeping an eye on utility and privacy.

Association Based Privacy Preserving Data Mining Techniques for Big Data

Association in data mining refers to the technique of identifying similar patterns and correlations among various sets of items or objects in a data set or any other information repositories. Various association based privacy preserving techniques have been proposed for Big Data sets (Aggarwal & Philip, 2008)

The parallel MASK (Mining Associations with secrecy constraints) algorithm can work well with massive data sets while preserving data privacy. Map Reduce computation model have been used here for better results. The input will be an information repository and the output will be the frequent items in the data set. Apriori algorithm is used for mining process. The general working is given below (Xie, Y.et al., 2012):

There are mainly four phases: Mapper, Combiner, Partitioner and Reducer. It is not always necessary to use combiner and partitioner. In Mapper phase, for each key, an output value of 1 will be produced. That is, the key-value pair that is generated from mapper phase will be having a value 1 for all keys. Combiner is actually a mini-reducer that runs after Map, and which operates only on data generated by one machine. The combiner will get input from Mappers, do some processing on it, and then sends the output from combiner as input to the next phase. The process of partitioning actually determines which reducer instance will receive which intermediate keys and values. Here also, the partitioner does the same job. Based on the length of the key, it is choosing the Reducer instance which should process the key-value pair. In the reducer phase, for a particular key, it will add up all the values and the support for a particular key can thus be found. The final output will be the key-value pair, which gives information about a particular key, and the number of times that particular key is repeating. For estimating the real support of the k-candidate item set, a Mapper is implemented for giving the key-value pair as output. In the Reducer phase, for each item in item[k], get the value from the map array. Now, calculate M_inverse(k,p), using the distortion probability p, for preserving the privacy while using the item sets for finding the frequent item sets. Using a combiner, combine all the values for a particular item, k. Now, for each element which is given for a combiner, for a particular item or key, support can be computed.

Finally, output the real support. This real support can be used for finding out whether a k-item set is frequent or not, using the formula: supr $\geq$ sup.

A scalable and distributed association rule mining method was proposed by Barkhordari and Niamanesh (2014) using the MapReduce computation model. This takes into account of the issues generally affecting the efficiency of Map Reduce architectures: data placement and network traffic. The input data whether it is discrete or continuous is converted into binomial format, and the resultant data is given to the layer 1 mappers. The output is fed into the layer 2 mappers and the resultant values will be given to the support and confidence calculation layer. Finally, the data is given to the combiners and reducers for computing the final results. This novel framework generates association rules directly instead of finding frequent items, hence association rules algorithms can be executed on distributable and scalable architectures.

Panackal and Pillai (2014), proposed an adaptive utility based anonymization model for addressing the quality of data mining task performed. The model takes into account of the fact that general privacy models such as k-anonymity cannot be applied to similar items since the generalization of records inversely affects the data mining task. The AUA technique involves a two-step process where the first step focuses on filtering based on association rule mining techniques to generate the quasi-identifiers as frequent and non-frequent items. The second step focuses on anonymization techniques based on the utility of data, where it anonymizes non-frequently associated attributes. Kapoor, V et al. (2006) presents a secure multiparty computation model for sequential pattern mining over distributed transactional databases. The model requires three non-colluding and semi-honest sites: data miner, non-colluding and processing sites. All parties correctly follow the protocols, but then are free to use whatever information they see during the execution of the protocols in any way. These are also referred to as honest but curious sites. The technique involves generating a set of items, and an incremental approach can be followed for the same.

The main idea behind mining frequent itemsets is to extract the data itemsets without directly accessing the original data and to make sure that the mining process does not get sufficient information to reconstruct the original data. But, the fact is that the data changes from time to time. So, if the data is not updated, there is a chance that some new frequent itemsets can occur and the itemsets which were frequent can disappear also. Here comes the importance of incremental mining. An incremental updating algorithm can update, maintain and manage the knowledge efficiently. The IPPFIM (Incremental Privacy Preserving Frequent Itemset Mining) proposed by Wang, J., Xu, C. F., & Pan, Y. H. (2006) does this database incremental updating efficiently. The algorithm is explained below:

1. Check whether the support is greater than the minimum support value. If yes, check whether the item X is present in Fp, the set of frequent itemsets in D. If yes, go to step 2. Else, go to step 5. If the support is less, go to step 3.

2. Add the item X to Fp', the set of frequent itemsets in DUd. Generate the candidate itemsets for the next pass k+1, from Fpk'. Making use of the data in distorted incremental database, d*, calculate the support of these candidate itemsets in d*. Reconstruct the support of candidate itemsets in d, the incremental

database. Repeat from the starting of the algorithm, as we need incremental mining.
3.   Check whether the item is in Fp. If yes, go to step 4. Else, reject the item.
4.   Check whether the support of the item in DUd $\geq$s. If yes, add it to Fp'. Else, reject the item.
   a.   Go to step 2.
5.Put the item X, to the temporary candidate itemset. Go to step 7.
6.   Find the support of the item using the distorted original database, D*. Go to step 8.
7.   Reconstruct the support using the original database, D.
8.   Check whether the support of the item in DUd$\geq$s. If yes, go to step 2. Else, reject the item.
   a.   Go to step 2.
      i.   End.

The focus of preserving privacy in association rule mining is to hide the most important and sensitive data in the mining process. Many algorithms have been proposed so far which works efficiently with association rule mining. The main goal is to make sure that the data is not revealed during the process. The algorithm SWTA works by combining two major algorithms in the field: PPARM and IMBA. The idea behind SWTA is that it will hide most of the sensitive data and will make the effect of non-sensitive information less (Wei, S., & Yonggui, W., 2010). In terms of the degree of data protection, this algorithm is efficient when considering privacy, validity and confidentiality. The input will be the itemsets which are sensitive, say Si, the minimum support measure minsup, the minimum confidence minconf and the original affair data set, DB. The affair data set consists of all the sensitive sets. The output will be a new affair data library D'. The IMBA algorithm is used here to make the effect of non-sensitive rules to a lesser degree. Thus, it helps to protect the non-sensitive rules in a better way.

The method for protecting privacy in the case of high dimensional correlated data is studied by Ba, H et al. (2014) where the key feature set is anonymized for protecting the individual's privacy. Two algorithms, IPFS and KIPFS are used to find the key inferring privacy feature set. After that, most of the existing privacy preserving algorithms could be directly integrated with this proposed approach. A privacy preserving apriori algorithm using MapReduce computation model was proposed by Jung, K et al. (2014), for solving privacy violation without degrading the utility of data items. The input consists of a candidate item set and the output lists the frequent item sets. At first, noise will be added in order to perturb the data and then, the apriori algorithm is run in a cloud platform. A noise filtering stage is applied after running the apriori process.

Table 1. Summarizes the various privacy preserving data mining techniques for Big Data.

Sl. No	PPDM Approach	Data Mining Technique Used	Privacy Considerations	Advantages	References
1	Random decision tree framework	Classification	randomization and cryptographic approaches	security and efficiency	Vaidya et al., 2014
2	C4.5 Map Reduce computation model		normalization on data items and root level perturbation	Provides better prediction values	Saravanan et al., 2014
3	Nearest neighbour algorithm		micro optimizations and polar orthogonalization	Speeding up nearest neighbor approach	Marinchev & Agre, 2015
4	FMM algorithm		matrix-based and parallel techniques	opinion mining strategy	Bing & Chan, 2014
5	Multivariate randomized response technique		decision tree is constructed from the modified/disguised data	Related question model	Du & Zhan, 2003
6	THL and CRSSPP		SVM with perturbation	reducing computational load	Teo et al., 2013
7	C-Means clustering	Clustering	Secure dot protocol	Works with both horizontally and vertically partitioned data sets.	Vashkevich & Zhukov, 2015
8	Temporal clustering		k-anonymity	Privacy model for moving objects	Assam & Seidl, 2011
9	CK-Means		Randomization	Distributed cluster analysis	Esteves, 2014
10	PCTA and UPCTA		Generalization Suppression Perturbation	Works with transactional data	Gkoulalas-Divanis & Loukides, 2011
11	Parallel MASK	Association	Distortion probability	Generates frequent itemsets	Xie, 2012
12	Adaptive Utility based Anonymization		Filtering and anonymization	Data mining quality	Panackal & Pillai, 2014
13	PriPSeP		secure multiparty computation	sequential pattern mining over distributed transactional databases	Kapoor et al., 2006
14	IPPFIM		Distortion	Incremental updation of database	Wang, Xu, & Pan, 2006
15	SWTA		Perturbation	Privacy Validity Confidentiality	Wei & Yonggui, 2010
16	IPFS and KIPFS		key feature set anonymization	Works with high dimensional correlated data	Ba et al., 2014
17	Privacy preserving Apriori algorithm		Noise addition	Noise filtering approach	Jung et al., 2014

PRIVACY PRESERVING DATA PUBLISHING

Data publishing plays a major role in today's digital world where data are collected at unprecedented rates from different sources in a variety of data formats. Data publishing becomes important when the personal data is needed by various organizations and researchers to identify the unusual patterns and trends availing in today's world. But, the major issue with data publishing is the privacy concerns of the data owner. This is explained in detail in section: privacy models. Data publishing becomes even more important when comes to Big Data. As discussed earlier, Big Data can be well explained by examining its characteristics: 4 V's: Volume, Velocity, Variety and Veracity. We have to consider all these characteristics when planning for an effective privacy model for Big Data. This section focuses on some of the architectures proposed for effective preservation of privacy while focusing on data characteristics. The next section proposes a privacy preserving data processing framework for dealing with both historical and real-time data. Various architectures which focuses on Big Data privacy preservation are discussed below:

Panackal et al. (2015) proposed a "Adaptive Utility-based Anonymization Model" for privacy preservation in Big Data sets. This framework mainly focuses on solving the problem of disclosure risk. The first step deals with filtering based on association mining and the second step deals with anonymization based on utility of data. Nabeel et al. (2010) proposed a framework "MASK" for policy based data publishing. This system works by limiting the information dissemination based on the role of the requester. Xu et al. (2014) discusses about privacy preserving data mining and the challenges associated with it. This paper gives at most importance to the concept of personalized privacy protection. A universal storage architecture for Big Data has been proposed by Zhang et al. (2013). Clustering techniques have been used here for clustering the nodes based on its properties. ADS-B data analytic framework was proposed by Boci et al. (2015) for supporting fast data analysis irrespective of the volume of data generated. A quality centric architecture was proposed for federated sensor services by Ramaswamy et. al (2013).

Liu et al. (2014) proposed a big data architecture for IT incident management by making use of stream computing technologies and MapReduce computation model. Hasan, O et al. (2013) reviewed the various privacy challenges in User profiling. They also explained about EEXCESS project which enables user profiling even by collecting sensitive information about the user. Cutillo et al. (2009) proposed an online social network based on a peer-to-peer architecture, which helps to avoid centralized control thereby decreasing the privacy risks associated with it.

An architecture which meets the basic privacy needs of the data owner, and at the same time that can work with streaming and batch data is proposed in the next section.

Figure 2. Privacy preserving framework for Big Data

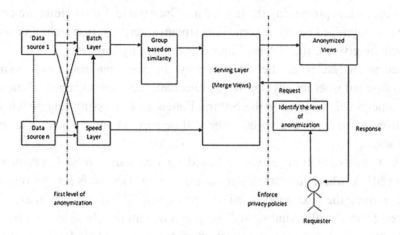

PRIVACY PRESERVING DATA PUBLISHING WITH BIG DATA

Figure 2 shows the conceptual architecture of a privacy preserving data processing framework for Big Data. This architecture is actually developed from the Lambda architecture, which was proposed by Marz (2015). The lambda architecture comprises of mainly three layers such as batch layer, speed layer and serving layer. The batch layer is used to store the non-changeable and ever growing master dataset and thereby creating views for the same. Apache Hadoop is used in this layer. The serving layer takes care of indexing the views created by the batch layer and thus makes it available when some analyst fires a query. Cloudera Impala is used in this layer. Speed layer makes it possible to deal with real-time data and it functions mostly like the batch layer. Storm and HBase can be used for implementing this layer.

As the Lambda architecture is modeled for processing batch and real-time data, the input that can be fed into the system can take any form. The input data can be in structured, semi-structured or un-structured formats. The architecture works as follows: When a new data stream enters the system, it will be fed into the batch layer and speed layer. As we are dealing with privacy preservation, the data that is fed into the batch layer will be anonymized first and the result will be given to the batch layer. This first level of anonymization should be done from the data provider side itself. Data provider here refers to the organization or individual who supplies the information about the data owner. The batch layer will create views for the entire data set and the updated views will be given to the speed layer. The speed layer will in turn submit the anonymized views to the Natural Language Processing Engine.

Data that is given to the speed layer will not be anonymized because of the delay it may cause while processing the input data. Once the real-time views are created, it will be anonymized based on some data stream anonymization technique and the result will be given to the Natural Language Processing Engine.

When an analyst/ researcher fires a query, the query auditing mechanism will work to find out whether any similar queries have reported an attack. If the query is a fair one, it will be given to the Natural Language Processing Engine where the views from batch layer and speed layer will be merged and the response will be given back.

A data anonymization technique based on t-closeness model was proposed by Cao (2011), where for each input data stream, a window is set. As one of the window moves, the next window will be processed. The tuples which are not yet published from the old window will be given as output. These are called as the expiring tuples. Anonymization is performed for each window data by comparing it with some sample. For all the data in input stream, the anonymized data is sent as the output. The sensitive attribute distribution in the equivalence class does not differ from that of all tuples by more than a threshold 't'. The window buffers first set of tuples from the input stream. When the new set arrives, the first set of tuples will get expired and will be sent as the output stream. Any stream anonymization technique can be applied for anonymizing data streams. A window based scheme can be used along with this conceptual architecture for better efficiency.

Once the data sets are anonymized and views are created, it is ready to be sent as output to the query provider. When an analyst submits a query, it will be audited based on the policies set by the data provider while publishing the data sets. Query Auditing refers to the process of inspecting past queries to determine whether they were in conformance with official policies (Motwani et al., 2008). Once the queries are audited, the system makes use of differential privacy mechanism to submit the response to the user. The basic architecture for differential privacy mechanism is shown in Figure 3 (Friedman, Arik, and Schuster, 2010, Differential Privacy for Everyone, 2012).

The analyst sends a query to the privacy guard. The privacy guard in turn gets the data from original data set. If the result of a query results in privacy breach, noise is added with the original data and the noisy response will be given to the user. Differential privacy aims in distorting the data to a small amount so that it will neither affect the analysis of the researcher nor questions the privacy of the individual.

Definition: "A randomized function K gives ϵ-differential privacy if for all data sets D and D' differing on at most one row, and all $S \subseteq$ Range(K), $Pr[K(D)\epsilon S] \leq exp(\epsilon)$ x $Pr[K(D')\epsilon S]$" (Dwork, Cynthia, 2008).

The choice of the value for 'ϵ' depends upon the context of the data and the query. This can work with both interactive and non-interactive queries. Policy

Figure 3. Differential Privacy Mechanism

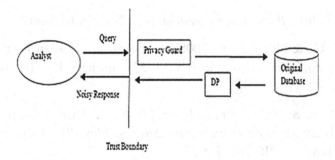

based decisions can be made by the Natural Language Processing Engine to give near exact response to the queries. Based on the policies set by the data publisher, response will be given to the analyst. The proposed framework works by making use of differential privacy mechanism to give the response to the query.

CONCLUSION

As the amount of data produced from various sensors and social networking sites increases rapidly, it clearly becomes impossible to process huge amount of data using traditional mechanisms. This chapter gave an overview about the various challenges associated with Big Data processing methodologies. The various techniques for privacy preserving data mining and privacy preserving data publishing were discussed in this chapter. A privacy preserving data processing framework for dealing with Big Data sets has been proposed here, which takes care of batch data and streaming data. Various anonymization techniques are used for anonymizing data in batch and speed layers. Query Auditing mechanisms have been proposed for auditing the queries to find out the fair queries fired by an analyst. Policy based decisions are used to determine whether the response to the queries are in conformance with the official policies set by the data publisher. The major challenge of this approach is to identify the various anonymization strategies to be followed for different types of data under consideration. Our future work focuses on implementing a recommendation system based on the proposed framework. This can be further extended by incorporating Natural language processing techniques for better efficiency.

REFERENCES

WestinA., F. (1967). *Privacy and Freedom*. New York: Atheneum.

Aggarwal, C. C., & Philip, S. Y. (2008). *A general survey of privacy-preserving data mining models and algorithms* (pp. 11–52). Springer, US. doi:10.1007/978-0-387-70992-5_2

Aldeen, Y. A. A. S., Salleh, M., & Razzaque, M. A. (2015). A comprehensive review on privacy preserving data mining. *SpringerPlus*, *4*(1), 1–36. doi:10.1186/s40064-015-1481-x PMID:26587362

Assam, R., & Seidl, T. (2011, November). Preserving privacy of moving objects via temporal clustering of spatio-temporal data streams. In *Proceedings of the 4th ACM SIGSPATIAL International Workshop on Security and Privacy in GIS and LBS* (pp. 9-16). ACM. doi:10.1145/2071880.2071883

Ba, H., Gao, X., Zhang, X., & He, Z. (2014, August). Protecting Data Privacy from Being Inferred from High Dimensional Correlated Data. In *Proceedings of the 2014 IEEE/WIC/ACM International Joint Conferences on Web Intelligence (WI) and Intelligent Agent Technologies (IAT)* (Vol. 2, pp. 495-502). IEEE. doi:10.1109/WI-IAT.2014.139

Barkhordari, M., & Niamanesh, M. (2014, August). ScadiBino: An effective MapReduce-based association rule mining method. In *Proceedings of the Sixteenth International Conference on Electronic Commerce* (p. 1). ACM. doi:10.1145/2617848.2617853

Big Data Working Group. (2013). *Cloud Security Alliance*. Expanded Top Ten Big Data Security and Privacy Challenges.

Bing, L., & Chan, K. C. (2014, December). A Fuzzy Logic Approach for Opinion Mining on Large Scale Twitter Data. In *Proceedings of the 2014 IEEE/ACM 7th International Conference on Utility and Cloud Computing* (pp. 652-657). IEEE Computer Society. doi:10.1109/UCC.2014.105

Boci, E., & Thistlethwaite, S. A novel big data architecture in support of ADS-B data analytic (2015). In *Proceedings of the 2015 Integrated Communication, Navigation and Surveillance Conference (ICNS)* (pp. C1-1). IEEE.

Campan, A., & Truta, T. M. (2009). Data and structural k-anonymity in social networks. In *Privacy, Security, and Trust in KDD* (pp. 33–54). Berlin, Heidelberg: Springer. doi:10.1007/978-3-642-01718-6_4

Cao, J., Karras, P., Kalnis, P., & Tan, K. L. (2011). SABRE: A Sensitive Attribute Bucketization and Redistribution framework for t-closeness. *The VLDB Journal*, *20*(1), 59–81. doi:10.1007/s00778-010-0191-9

Corti, L., Day, A., & Backhouse, G. (2000, December). Confidentiality and informed consent: Issues for consideration in the preservation of and provision of access to qualitative data archives. In Forum Qualitative Sozialforschung/Forum: Qualitative. *Social Research*, *1*(3).

Cutillo, L. A., Molva, R., & Strufe, T. (2009) Privacy preserving social networking through decentralization. In *Proceedings of the Sixth International Conference on Wireless On-Demand Network Systems and Services WONS '09* (pp. 145-152). IEEE. doi:10.1109/WONS.2009.4801860

Du, W., & Zhan, Z. (2003, August). Using randomized response techniques for privacy-preserving data mining. In *Proceedings of the ninth ACM SIGKDD international conference on Knowledge discovery and data mining* (pp. 505-510). ACM. doi:10.1145/956750.956810

Dwork, C. (2008). Differential privacy: A survey of results. In *Theory and Applications of Models of Computation*. Springer Berlin Heidelberg.

Dwork, C. (2011). Differential privacy. In Encyclopedia of Cryptography and Security. Springer US, pp 338-340.

Esteves, R. M., Hacker, T., & Rong, C. (2014). A new approach for accurate distributed cluster analysis for Big Data: competitive K-Means. *International Journal of Big Data Intelligence*, *5*(1-2), 50-64.

Fayyad, U. M., Piatetsky-Shapiro, G., Smyth, P., & Uthurusamy, R. (1996). Advances in knowledge discovery and data mining.

Friedman, A., & Schuster, A. (2010). Data mining with differential privacy. In *Proceedings of the 16th ACM SIGKDD international conference on Knowledge discovery and data mining*. ACM. doi:10.1145/1835804.1835868

Fung, B., Wang, K., Chen, R., & Yu, P. S. (2010). Privacy-preserving data publishing: A survey of recent developments. [CSUR]. *ACM Computing Surveys*, *42*(4), 14. doi:10.1145/1749603.1749605

Gai, K., Qiu, M., & Zhao, H. (2016, April). Security-aware efficient mass distributed storage approach for cloud systems in big data. In *Proceedings of the 2016 IEEE 2nd International Conference on Big Data Security on Cloud (BigDataSecurity), IEEE International Conference on High Performance and Smart Computing (HPSC), and IEEE International Conference on Intelligent Data and Security (IDS)* (pp. 140-145). IEEE. doi:10.1109/BigDataSecurity-HPSC-IDS.2016.68

Getelastic.com. (2014). The Big 9 big data sources [Infographic]. Retrieved 2017 from http://www.getelastic.com/big-data-infographic/

Gkoulalas-Divanis, A., & Loukides, G. (2011, March). PCTA: privacy-constrained clustering-based transaction data anonymization. In *Proceedings of the 4th International Workshop on Privacy and Anonymity in the Information Society* (p. 5). ACM.

Hasan, O., Habegger, B., Brunie, L., Bennani, N., & Damiani, E. (2013, June). A discussion of privacy challenges in user profiling with big data techniques: The excess use case. In *Proceedings of the 2013 IEEE International Congress on Big Data* (pp. 25-30). IEEE. doi:10.1109/BigData.Congress.2013.13

IBM Big Data Hub. (n. d.). The Four V's of Big Data. Retrieved 2017 from http://www.ibmbigdatahub.com/infographic/four-vs-big-data

Jung, K., Park, S., & Park, S. (2014, November). Hiding a Needle in a Haystack: Privacy Preserving Apriori algorithm inMapReduce Framework. In *Proceedings of the First International Workshop on Privacy and Security of Big Data* (pp. 11-17). ACM. doi:10.1145/2663715.2669611

Kapoor, V., Poncelet, P., Trousset, F., & Teisseire, M. (2006, November). Privacy preserving sequential pattern mining in distributed databases. In *Proceedings of the 15th ACM international conference on Information and knowledge management* (pp. 758-767). ACM. doi:10.1145/1183614.1183722

Khan, N., Yaqoob, I., Hashem, I. A. T., Inayat, Z., Mahmoud Ali, W. K., Alam, M., & Gani, A. et al. (2014). Big data: Survey, technologies, opportunities, and challenges. *TheScientificWorldJournal*. PMID:25136682

Kim, S. H., Kim, N. U., & Chung, T. M. (2013, December). Attribute relationship evaluation methodology for big data security. In *Proceedings of the 2013 International Conference on IT Convergence and Security (ICITCS)* (pp. 1-4). IEEE. doi:10.1109/ICITCS.2013.6717808

Li, J., Ooi, B. C., & Wang, W. (2008). Anonymizing streaming data for privacy protection. In *Proceedings of the IEEE 24ᵗʰ International Conference on Data Engineering ICDE '08* (pp. 1367–1369). IEEE. doi:10.1109/ICDE.2008.4497558

Li, N., Li, T., & Venkatasubramanian, S. (2007, April). t-closeness: Privacy beyond k-anonymity and l-diversity. In *Proceedings of the 2007 IEEE 23rd International Conference on Data Engineering* (pp. 106-115). IEEE.

Lindell, Y., & Pinkas, B. (2000, January). Privacy preserving data mining. In Advances in Cryptology—CRYPTO 2000 (pp. 36-54). Springer Berlin Heidelberg. doi:10.1007/3-540-44598-6_3

Liu, R., Li, Q., Li, F., Mei, L., & Lee, J. (2014, October). Big Data architecture for IT incident management. In *Proceedings of the 2014 IEEE International Conference on Service Operations and Logistics, and Informatics (SOLI)* (pp. 424-429). IEEE. doi:10.1109/SOLI.2014.6960762

Machanavajjhala, A., Kifer, D., Gehrke, J., & Venkitasubramaniam, M. (2007). l-diversity: Privacy beyond k-anonymity. *ACM Transactions on Knowledge Discovery from Data, 1*(1), 3. doi:10.1145/1217299.1217302

Mahajan, P., Gaba, G., & Chauhan, N. S. (2016). Big Data Security. *IITM Journal of Management and IT, 7*(1), 89–94.

Marinchev, I., & Agre, G. (2015, June). On speeding up the implementation of nearest neighbour search and classification. In *Proceedings of the 16th International Conference on Computer Systems and Technologies* (pp. 207-213). ACM. doi:10.1145/2812428.2812464

Marz, N., & Warren, J. (2015). *Big Data: Principles and best practices of scalable realtime data systems*. Manning Publications Co.

Microsoft Corporation. (2012). Differential Privacy for Everyone.

Motwani, R., Nabar, S. U., & Thomas, D. (2008, April). Auditing sql queries. In *Proceedings of the 2008 IEEE 24th International Conference on Data Engineering* (pp. 287-296). IEEE. doi:10.1109/ICDE.2008.4497437

Nabeel, M., Shang, N., Zage, J., & Bertino, E. (2010, June). Mask: a system for privacy-preserving policy-based access to published content. In *Proceedings of the 2010 ACM SIGMOD International Conference on Management of data* (pp. 1239-1242). ACM. doi:10.1145/1807167.1807329

Panackal, J. J., & Pillai, A. S. (2014, December). An intelligent framework for protecting privacy of individuals empirical evaluations on data mining classification. In *Proceedings of the 2014 14th International Conference on Hybrid Intelligent Systems (HIS)* (pp. 67-72). IEEE. doi:10.1109/HIS.2014.7086174

Panackal, J. J., & Pillai, A. S. (2015). Adaptive Utility-based Anonymization Model: Performance Evaluation on Big Data Sets. *Procedia Computer Science*, *50*, 347–352. doi:10.1016/j.procs.2015.04.037

Popat, S. K., & Emmanuel, M. (2014). Review and Comparative Study of Clustering Techniques. *International Journal of Computer Science and Information Technologies*, *5*(1), 805–812.

Puthal, D., Nepal, S., Ranjan, R., & Chen, J. (2016). DLSeF: A Dynamic Key-Length-Based Efficient Real-Time Security Verification Model for Big Data Stream. *ACM Transactions on Embedded Computing Systems*, *16*(2), 51. doi:10.1145/2937755

Ramaswamy, L., Lawson, V., & Gogineni, S. V. (2013, June). Towards a quality-centric big data architecture for federated sensor services. In *Proceedings of the 2013 IEEE International Congress on Big Data* (pp. 86-93). IEEE. doi:10.1109/BigData.Congress.2013.21

Roy, I., Setty, S. T., Kilzer, A., Shmatikov, V., & Witchel, E. (2010) 'Airavat: security and privacy for MapReduce. In *Proceedings of the 7th USENIX Conference on Networked Systems Design and Implementation (NSDI'10)* (Vol. 10, pp. 297–312).

Saravanan, M., Thoufeeq, A. M., Akshaya, S., & Jayasre Manchari, V. L. (2014, October). Exploring new privacy approaches in a scalable classification framework. In *Proceedings of the 2014 International Conference on Data Science and Advanced Analytics (DSAA)* (pp. 209-215). IEEE. doi:10.1109/DSAA.2014.7058075

Search Cloud Computing. (2013). The state of the enterprise cloud and prepping for AWS re:Invent 2013. Retrieved 2017 from http://searchcloudcomputing.techtarget.com/essentialguide/The-state-of-the-enterprise-cloud-and-prepping-for-AWS-reInvent-2013

Sweeney, L. (2002). k-anonymity: A model for protecting privacy. *International Journal of Uncertainty, Fuzziness and Knowledge-based Systems*, *10*(05), 557–570. doi:10.1142/S0218488502001648

Teo, S. G., Han, S., & Lee, V. (2013, December). Privacy preserving support vector machine using non-linear kernels on Hadoop Mahout. In *Proceedings of the 2013 IEEE 16th International Conference on Computational Science and Engineering (CSE)* (pp. 941-948). IEEE. doi:10.1109/CSE.2013.200

The Guardian. (2013). Tech giants may be huge, but nothing matches big data. Retrieved from https://www.theguardian.com/technology/2013/aug/23/tech-giants-data

Thota, C., Manogaran, G., Lopez, D., & Vijayakumar, V. (2017). Big Data Security Framework for Distributed Cloud Data Centers. In Cybersecurity Breaches and Issues Surrounding Online Threat Protection (pp. 288-310). Hershey, PA: IGI Global. doi:10.4018/978-1-5225-1941-6.ch012

Vaidya, J., Shafiq, B., Fan, W., Mehmood, D., & Lorenzi, D. (2014). A random decision tree framework for privacy-preserving data mining. *IEEE Transactions on Dependable and Secure Computing, 11*(5), 399–411.

Vashkevich, A. V., & Zhukov, V. G. (2015) Privacy-Preserving Clustering Using C-Means.

Victor, N., Lopez, D., & Abawajy, J. H. (2016). Privacy models for big data: A survey. *International Journal of Big Data Intelligence, 3*(1), 61–75. doi:10.1504/IJBDI.2016.073904

Wang, J., Xu, C. F., & Pan, Y. H. (2006, August). An incremental algorithm for mining privacy-preserving frequent itemsets. In *Proceedings of Fifth International Conference on Machine Learning and Cybernetics*, Dalian (Vol. 13, p. 16). doi:10.1109/ICMLC.2006.258592

Wei, S., & Yonggui, W. (2010, February). Association rule mining algorithm based on privacy preserving. In *Proceedings of the 2010 The 2nd International Conference on Computer and Automation Engineering (ICCAE)* (Vol. 4, pp. 140-143). IEEE.

Wu, X., Kumar, V., Quinlan, J. R., Ghosh, J., Yang, Q., Motoda, H., & Zhou, Z. H. et al. (2008). Top 10 algorithms in data mining. *Knowledge and Information Systems, 14*(1), 1–37. doi:10.1007/s10115-007-0114-2

Wu, X., Zhu, X., Wu, G. Q., & Ding, W. (2014). Data mining with big data. *IEEE Transactions on Knowledge and Data Engineering, 26*(1), 97–107. doi:10.1109/TKDE.2013.109

Xie, Y., Xu, Z., Zhu, X., & Xie, P. (2012, August). A parallel algorithm PMASK based on privacy-preserving data mining. In *Proceedings of the 2012 International Symposium on Instrumentation & Measurement, Sensor Network and Automation (IMSNA)* (Vol. 2, pp. 398-402). IEEE. doi:10.1109/MSNA.2012.6324604

Xu, L., Jiang, C., Wang, J., Yuan, J., & Ren, Y. (2014). Information security in big data: Privacy and data mining. *IEEE Access*, *2*, 1149–1176. doi:10.1109/ACCESS.2014.2362522

Yao, Y., Zhang, L., Yi, J., Peng, Y., Hu, W., & Shi, L. (2016, September). A Framework for Big Data Security Analysis and the Semantic Technology. In *Proceedings of the 2016 6th International Conference on IT Convergence and Security (ICITCS)* (pp. 1-4). IEEE. doi:10.1109/ICITCS.2016.7740303

Zakerzadeh, H., & Osborn, S. L. (2011). Faanst: fast anonymizing algorithm for numerical streaming data. In *Data Privacy Management and Autonomous Spontaneous Security* (pp. 36–50). Berlin, Heidelberg: Springer. doi:10.1007/978-3-642-19348-4_4

ZDnet.com. (2012). Top 10 categories for big data sources and mining technologies. Retrieved 2017 from http://www.zdnet.com/article/top-10-categories-for-big-data-sources-and-mining-technologies/

Zhang, Q., Chen, Z., Lv, A., Zhao, L., Liu, F., & Zou, J. (2013, August). A universal storage architecture for big data in cloud environment. In *Proceedings of the IEEE International Conference on Green Computing and Communications (GreenCom), and Internet of Things (iThings/CPSCom), and IEEE Cyber, Physical and Social Computing* (pp. 476-480). IEEE. doi:10.1109/GreenCom-iThings-CPSCom.2013.96

Zhao, J., Wang, L., Tao, J., Chen, J., Sun, W., Ranjan, R., & Georgakopoulos, D. et al. (2014). A security framework in G-Hadoop for big data computing across distributed Cloud data centres. *Journal of Computer and System Sciences*, *80*(5), 994–1007. doi:10.1016/j.jcss.2014.02.006

Chapter 4
Cryptography in Big Data Security

Navin Jambhekar
S. S. S. K. R. Innani Mahavidyalaya Karanja, India

Chitra Dhawale
P. R. Pote College of Engineering and Management, India

ABSTRACT

Information security is a prime goal for every individual and organization. The travelling from client to cloud server can be prone to security issues. The big data storages are available through cloud computing system to facilitate mobile client. The information security can be provided to mobile client and cloud technology with the help of integrated parallel and distributed encryption and decryption mechanism. The traditional technologies include the plaintext stored across cloud and can be prone to security issues. The solution provided by applying the encrypted data upload and encrypted search. The clouds can work in collaboration; therefore, the encryption can also be done in collaboration. Some part of encryption handle by client and other part handled by cloud system. This chapter presents the security scenario of different security algorithms and the concept of mobile and cloud computing. This chapter precisely defines the security features of existing cloud and big data system and provides the new framework that helps to improve the data security over cloud computing and big data security system.

DOI: 10.4018/978-1-5225-2863-0.ch004

1. INTRODUCTION

1.1 Background

Nowadays due to recent technological development, the amount of data generated by internet, social networking sites, sensor networks, healthcare applications, Banking Sector and many other companies, is drastically increasing day by day. All the enormous measure of data produced from various sources in multiple formats with very high speed (Bagheri & Jahanshahi, 2015) is referred as big data. The term big data (Bosch et al, 2014; Chan, 2009) is defined as "a new generation of technologies and architectures, designed to economically separate value from very large volumes of a wide variety of data, by enabling high-velocity capture, discovery and analysis".

From this definition, we can say that big data are reflected by 3V's, which are, volume, velocity and variety. A common theme of big data is that the data are diverse, i.e., they may contain text, audio, image, or video etc. This big data is stored on cloud and to attain the big data security over cloud computing, the mono encryption technique is not adequate. Because of the voluminous architecture of cloud computing system, the traditional data security systems are not adequate to provide the complete security solution.

During mobile communication, the encryption and decryption facilities are harder to implement. Clouds can work in collaboration, even if they have their own security features. Therefore, without modifying the sequence of the encryption process, the parallel and distributed encryption facilities will be available at every cloud during surfing from cloud to cloud. Every cloud manages the essential resources and allocation can be done on every request of the resource while user moves from one cloud to another. The major issues when dealing with the cloud computing system is the network and resource availability. If the resources are not allocated during cloud computing, the encryption and decryption cannot feasible and can be difficult to pursue. The cloud collaborative encryption is a technique where, various clouds can work concurrently with distributed processing facilities. Here, the security can be enhanced by implementing the homomorphic encryption.

2. BASICS OF CRYPTOGRAPHY

Data communication plays a vital role for every individual or organization all over the world. Every organization completely relies on the day-to-day data processed by their systems. Massive amount of data transferred from one location to another, contains the confidential information and must be protected from the various potential attacks occurring during network communication. Recent advances in the information technology offered new business, personal, social, educational, research opportunities to everyone.

Cryptography is the science of "Secret Writing" that helps the trusted secure communication over the non-trusted communication channel. Encryption is a technique through with the confidential data can be secure by applying the specific encryption algorithm with a combination of a key. Decryption is a technique that reverts, or extracts the original data only using the valid key used for encryption.

Encryption is used in two ways such as; one-way encryption and two-way encryption. One-way encryption is used to encrypt the unique key used for encryption and decryption to enhance the security of the key itself. This encryption key is only used for encryption and decryption of valuable information. The key itself is not required to decrypt and is worthless. Two-way encryption technique is used to encrypt the valuable information flows over the communication channel and need to protect from the potential network attacks. This encrypted information is then decrypted to get the original information. Encryption is done with the help of single and multiple keys i.e. symmetric key and asymmetric key. The symmetric key encryption is a technique where the same key is used for encryption and decryption of the original message. In case of asymmetric key, different keys are used to encrypt and decrypt the original message. Figure 1 depicts the basic encryption and decryption mechanism.

The decryption is a reverse procedure of encryption that extracts the original message processed by the cipher technique and the encryption key. For this, a key plays a very important role in decryption. Decryption process takes the cipher text and the right key and performing those operations are more mathematical until the plaintext is recovered.

Cryptography is nothing but a framework that protects the digital documents even if adversary may present at the communication channel. One cryptographic algorithm can be identified as useful by comparing its ability to protect the data against attacks, its speed, throughput, key transmission method, resources used, power consumption and the algorithm structure.

Figure 1. Encryption and Decryption Mechanism

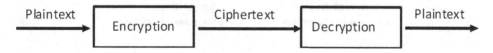

2.1 Classification of Cryptographic Algorithms

The classification of the cryptographic algorithms based on the way it uses the key agreement and exchange routines are

2.1.1 Secret Key Cryptography (SKC)

Secret Key cryptography also known as symmetric; is possible with the help of stream ciphers or block ciphers. The stream cipher uses bit or byte of information at a time and uses feedback mechanism. Therefore, the key is constantly changing.

In case of Block cipher, the secret message is divided into equal size block and the same key is used to encrypt all blocks.

2.1.2 Public Key Cryptography (PKC)

The asymmetric key cryptographic algorithm such as Public Key cryptography (PKC) was invented in 1976 by Diffie and Hellman. Here, the security has been provided during the data communication between receiver and sender without a common key agreement.

In PKC, the sender encrypts the secret message with the help of receiver's private key, known to everyone. The receiver then decrypts the secret message with the help of its private key. Here, both public and private keys are different. One algorithm is used for encryption and decryption. Here, one of the two keys must be kept secret and no one can decrypt the message without the private key. The RSA algorithm is one of the PKC algorithms.

Figure 2. Typical Secret Key Cryptography Process

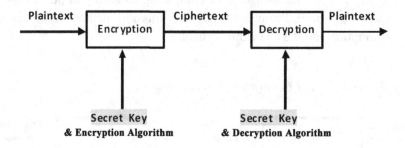

Figure 3. Typical Public Key Cryptography Process

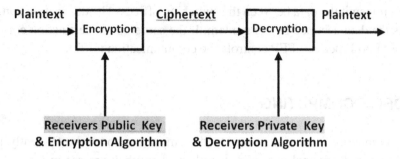

3. DATA COMMUNICATION NETWORKS

Data refers to the raw facts collected from various sources. The valuable information can be discovered from the collected data. Data communication is the transfer of valuable information between two or more different points by means of optical and electrical transmission system. This system is called as Data Communication Network. Data communication enables different organizations or individual to work remotely and controls the working from its source.

The fundamental use of a data communications system is to exchange the data between the parties engaged in the communication. The entities required for the data communication are the source, encoder, transmission system, decoder and destination.

The source device who transmits the data can be client computer and the destination becomes the server. Modem plays a role of encoder and decoder that converts digital data from a computer into a form suitable for transmission over the electrical/wired transmission network. The data transmitted from client computer to the switching

Figure 4. The common Data Communication System

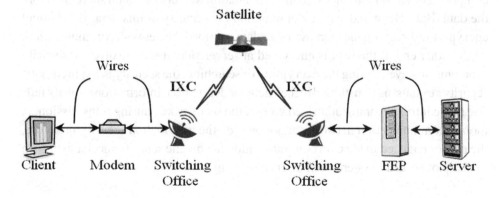

office by means of wired or wireless lines. The Inter Exchange Channel IXC plays a role to transmit the data between the switching offices. The destination computer collects the data decoded by the modem. If the server is the destination computer, the Front End Processor FEP controls the communication traffic.

4. MOBILE COMPUTING

Mobile computing gives the power to the employees to work efficiently in the remote places. Personnel can work together where they are not in a same place and can get the benefits of mobile computing feature. Mobile computing is not the essential factor for everyone, but increases use of smart phones, Personal Digital Assistant-PDA makes the mobile computing a crucial factor. Mobile computing is a great invention, but the information security of mobile communication is the biggest issue for everyone. Mobile computing is a distributed wireless computing technology that enables desktop computer users to work outside anywhere from office or home. Mobile computing enabled devices use wireless communication feature makes them accessible and present online on any remote place anywhere anytime. Mobile computing supports two advantageous entities such as mobility and computing. However, it is facing the challenges such as wireless communication bandwidth and information security.

4.1 Mobile Computing Security

Mobile networks are open to everyone and introduce various security risks. To resists from different attacks on the data transmission and the mobile computing enabled device attacks, the security protocols are strong enough that rescue the system from different attacks. Secure data transmission over the insecure network can be achieved by encryption and can be implemented by software and hardware itself. Mobile computing environment can use static and dynamic servers i.e. cloud servers to store the data. Both client and server can maintain the security of this data. If the client encrypts the data, then the increased size data overload the network communication. At the other end, if the data is encrypted at server side, it will resolve the security problem. However, during the decryption or searching, the security is required. This security key must be transmitted to the client for decryption. Information security fails due to the intrusion or unauthorized gain of the security key during transmission. A mobile communication network cannot provide the information security therefore, the parties engaged in the data communication handle the security mechanism with the help of security system such as cryptography.

4.2 Security Threats

Security plays a critical role for both the parties engaged in the sensitive data communication over the insecure communication channel. Information or network security attacks are classified as Passive and Active attacks are discussed below.

4.2.1 Passive Attacks

The motivation behind the passive attacks is to monitoring the services and communication of two parties engaged in the communication.

Two types of passive attacks are classified such as release of message contents and traffic analysis is depicted using Figure 5. The release of message contents is a type of attack that analyzes and read the message delivered between senders to receiver. Under the traffic analysis, the data transmission patterns are studied and trying to extract the original hidden data. The types of attacks are difficult to detect, because they do not reflect the presence of an intruder on the unauthorized gain of control on network traffic.

4.2.2 Active Attacks

The attacker directly involved in the attack by making his impression on the network communication. This attack includes the modification of data, hacking of resources and false replay of messages, delaying and denial of the services.

- **Masking:** Intruder gets the unauthorized access by getting the authorized permission to access the confidential information. Figure 6 depicts the masking by an intruder.

Figure 5. Traffic Analysis and Release of Message Contents

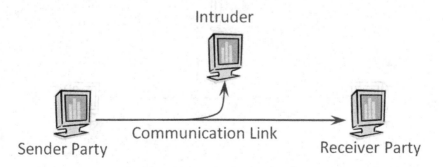

Figure 6. Masking

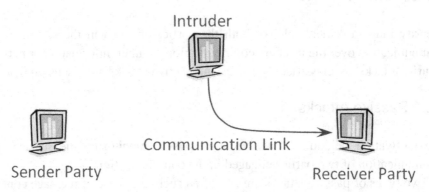

- **Hacking Resources:** Hackers get the unauthorized access of resources of both parties engaged in confidential data transmission. The resources may be a computer, network or memory device. The hacking of resources is depicted using Figure 7.
- **Unauthorized Capturing of Information:** Data flows from one party to another get access in an unauthorized way silently without giving knowledge to the original owners is depicted using Figure 7.
- **Unauthorized Modifications of Information:** Blocking the original service, accessing of information, modifying the original message and resend it is depicted using Figure 8.
- **Service Denial or Repudiation:** The traffic of the sender is completely stopped by regulating the communication resources and giving the false messages by blocking the services which is depicted using Figure 9.

Figure 7. Hacking Resources & Unauthorized Capture of Information

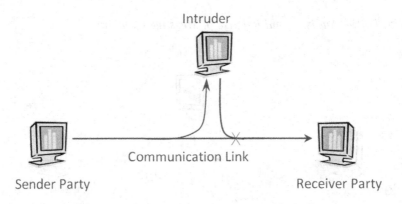

Figure 8. Modification of Message

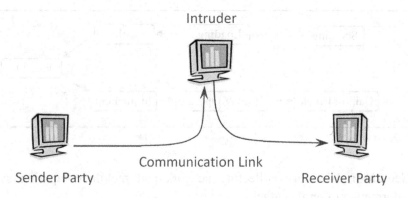

Figure 9. Service Denial

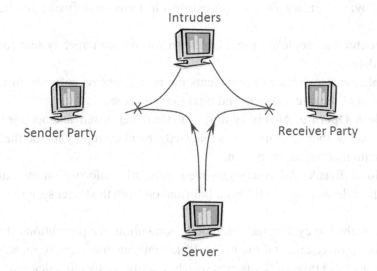

4.3 Life Cycle of Attacks on Mobile Computing

The prime goal of adversaries is to find the weak positions to attack. The weakest part of the mobile computing is the wireless network. Planning is carried out by hackers to enter into the system, spread over, collecting data and access by wireless network.

The phases of Mobile network attack life cycle are discussed below and are depicted using Figure 10.

Figure 10. Attack Life Cycle on Mobile Computing

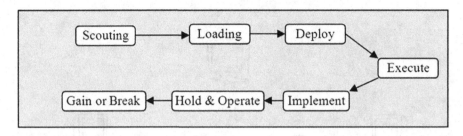

- **Scouting:** Adversary collecting network and mobile computing system information to set the attacks.
- **Loading:** Adversary assembles and ready to put the executable object on the target system.
- **Deploy:** Adversary deploy the executable tools or software to the target system.
- **Execute:** The deployed executables get run on the target system to collect the data.
- **Implement:** Adversary implements the remote access software to gain the control of the target system and bind to their servers.
- **Hold & Operate:** Adversary fully grab the target system and operate by their own way without making any acknowledgement or impression on the normal execution of the target system.
- **Gain or Break:** Adversary gets the confidential information by mailing to itself or destroy the confidential information from the target system.

To break the life cycle attack on mobile computing, the precautions should be taken at the host system and the network side information security management. Different phases of this attack life cycle can be controlled. Communication network is open to everyone, but the mobile computing device must be protected by the external firewall against the Scouting.

The external firewall can protect the mobile computing system from the adversaries to deploy the malicious tools. If the external firewall fails to protect, then the mobile computing operating system restricting to install unwanted tools and software without the permission of the user. The Operating system can play a role to protect the system by restricting the actions of unwanted software to hold the system resources and work with them. The internal firewall has an important feature that prohibits the use of network prior permission of the user. The network connection terminates only if the mail program tries to send mail without entering a password key using physically

5. CLOUD COMPUTING

Mobile computing becomes valuable because of the cloud computing by offering network and resources on demand. The resources are available on the shared pool independently. The facilities provided by the cloud computing system are the network, virtual information storages, collaborating servers, utilities and application of cloud without any efforts.

5.1 Cloud Computing Framework

Cloud computing provides various services and resources with and without demand. Figure 11 shows the data storage and cloud computing scenario. The facilities provided by various clouds are-

- **On-Demand Self Service:** Various services required for user can be available as on-demand while user connected to any cloud.
- **Heterogeneous Platforms:** Even with the heterogeneous platforms used by the user, network access can be provided by the cloud computing system.
- **Resource Sharing:** Every cloud has the resource scheduling facility to the incoming online users from other cloud. A resource bank is maintained by each cloud and allocation of resources can be done on first come and first serve basis. The cloud resources can be acts as virtual resources even if they are physical. The resources provided by the cloud systems are the virtual storages, processors and network bandwidth.

Figure 11. Big Data Security

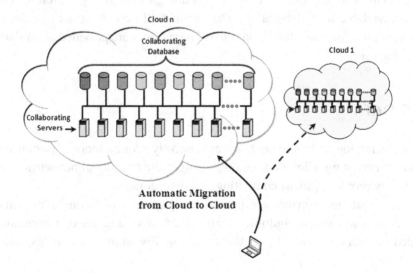

5.2 Cloud Collaboration

Collaboration of multiple clouds provides the uninterrupted services to the users connected during mobile communication.

Clouds are classified depending on the requirements by various types of users, such as:

5.2.1 Private Cloud

It is sometimes known as the intranet cloud system, limited to the campus area users with its own limited and predefined facilities provided as on-demand only.

5.2.2 Community Cloud

Multiple private clouds system are interconnected with each other to form a backbone network cloud and shared by multiple organizations within their own cloud. Each cloud connected to community cloud has its own limitations and policies.

5.2.3 Public Cloud

The public cloud is open freely to every individual user and other cloud members. All the resources of public cloud can be accessible openly without any restrictions. But the resource sharing is scheduled here by the public cloud. The public cloud sometimes owned by private or public organization. The services of public cloud can be accessible as on-demand.

- **Hybrid Cloud:** Heterogeneous technologies used by different clouds are available in collaboration. They provide different services to the users relocating from one cloud to another. The services are provided as on-demand to the users.

6. BIG DATA

Big data technology's promising features relatively acquire more importance than the cloud computing. Cloud computing changes the traditional non-virtual world to virtual by providing smart computing and data storage.

Big data is storage with massive dataset having universe of dissimilar information and facilitates to store in multiple locations. Massive amount of information is recorded on every second all over the world and disseminated. For this, massive amount of data storages should be required. The difficulties arise when, the data structure contains monolithic structure and difficult to maintain, organize, analyze, store and retrieve.

The world is moved towards the digital era. The hard-coded paper document becomes digital and paper less. The digital libraries take the place of paper and books libraries. The paperless digital libraries are more attractive due to non-requirement of physical space in a building. Due to their virtual use, any remote user can access any digital content without any limitations.

6.1 Big Data Security Challenge

A massive data stored digitally on various servers is the big data and it can be easily available through the use of cloud computing system. The smaller data can be easily secured before and during the communication and in the storage. Figure 12 shows the security of big data. Some issues arise while handling the big data such as hardware offload, security problems, data acquisition, processing workloads, operating and resource management, data analysis, data mining, cataloging, indexing, searching and dissemination. The text data is easier to process but, if the data is in the images, audio and video form then, the manipulation is difficult due to large size. The processing big data in terabytes or petabytes recorded by any organization is very harder by supercomputer or cluster machines.

6.2 Encrypted Storage

Cloud storages are frequently used by every individual or organization to save their secret information. The data stored by the clients are in the form of plain confidential information or the secured encrypted data. The data can be secured by the client

Figure 12. Big data security platform

computer prior sending to cloud or cloud server can secure the incoming data or both are engaged in the security implementation.

6.3 Encrypted Workload

The amount of data which is being secured during encryption is the workload known as payload. If larger data comes for encryption then, the workload becomes heavier for the cloud system. Client and servers works in collaboration to implement the security to the data. If client encrypts the data, then server becomes offloaded to work on other work. But the network traffic issues arise here to transfer the secured data from client to cloud server, because the data size increases after providing security. For various security issues, it is more beneficial to secure the data at its local place by client. It can solve security issues such as key maintenance, encryption, decryption and data transfer.

6.4 Decryption

If client machines are engaged in the data encryption and decryption, the cloud servers can only store the encrypted data. Cloud can perform the work to handle the secured data, storage and transfer.

6.5 Failure and Recovery

Any Database Management System (DBMS) itself is a complete software package that uses the ACID properties for the complete successful transaction processing such as Atomicity, Consistency, Isolation, and Durability. The log based recovery system is available for the failure recovery.

In big data cloud computing, the transaction failure recovery can be enforced by the log based recovery system with the enforcement of ACID properties.

The big data security is not singly controlled by the single security framework; rather it can be controlled by the integrated encryption system and collaborating encryption system. Here, the client security mechanism must be work with the collaborating cloud servers to handle the security of big data.

7. EXISTING BIG DATA SECURITY FRAMEWORK

Recently, the following security challenges arises for big data

7.1 Secure Parallel and Distributed Processing

The client's big data is divided into equal number of pats and processed in distributed and parallel way. As the data is separately used for encryption and collected, the security at each level from machine to machine must be enforced.

7.2 Secured Data Storage and Retrieval

However, the size of big data storages increases tremendously from cloud to cloud, availability and scalability is a major issue during the maintenance of massive data.

7.3 Source Input Validation

Massive data comes to the cloud storage from variety of clients. Here, it is not possible to ensure the data coming from trusted sources or not. It must be required to ensure the validation of the incoming data to store over the cloud.

7.4 Active Monitoring

The active monitoring of the big data is a major challenge for every cloud. As the data is massive, several extra cloud servers are required to monitor the security threats of the incoming real time data flow incoming from other cloud servers and storages.

7.5 Privacy Preserving

Different cloud servers are required to store the massive amount of big data. The transaction log plays a vital role to keep track the privacy leakage of the big data. The major issue which must be handle by the cloud servers is to keep track the access of confidential information and its storage form other clouds.

7.6 Secure Communication

The data secure prior communication from client to cloud server preserves the insecure data communication and restricts the security flaws of communication.

7.7 Access Control

No access other valid sources must be restricted to preserve the security of the data. The access to the original source by identifying its authentication restricts the malicious users. This can be possible by maintaining the metadata about the user and their access. Other resources are restricted to access the secured data from cloud storages. The access must be granted to the original and valid sources by identifying their authentication and restrict the unwanted users. This can be possible by using the secured front end processors before cloud and maintain the metadata for the big data its users and their access.

8. BIG DATA SECURITY

The security is harder for the bigger data stored on the cloud. Weaker security is a bottleneck for the big data and the cloud computing. The following section explores the big data platform.

8.1 Big Data Platform

Not all the data is useful and scientists do the work to refine the useful data across the big data store on cloud storages. The specialized architecture is essential for the Big Data that can handle the storage, move and integrate massive data with greater accuracy and speed. The only solution is to convert the unstructured Big Data to a structured form using complex structured database management system. Figure 13 shows the essential Big Data security platform.

Number of large storages is required to keep the massive huge data. As the huge clients' increases, big number of storages is required. Due to massive data, a single store point is not adequate; therefore, parallel storages must in collaboration to perform the big data storage.

8.1.2 Communication and Distribution

Massive data is moving from server to server and client to servers need huge amount of communication and distribution capacity with the requirement of agility and speed.

8.1.3 Structuring of Unstructured Data

The structure data is valuable and unstructured data must be omitted that occupy large storage space. The incoming unstructured data must be transformed into structured form and this work requires processing, large hardware and networking cost.

8.1.4 Metadata Management

The metadata becomes bigger for the voluminous data stored over the cloud storage. The unstructured data cannot provide the right metadata. The structured data and its metadata is useful in searching the right information.

8.2 Big Data Processing

The data processing cost for the big data is heavier. The required cost of storage, hardware, software and networking is bigger to process the voluminous data.

- **Sharing:** Data sharing across cloud to cloud, servers to servers and client to servers is a time-consuming job. The security trouble arises during the data sharing. The data security and confidentiality is a prime goal of every individual, organization and the big data cloud also.
- **Transition:** The conversion of unstructured data into structured form solves the ordering, indexing and recognizing issues.
- **Retrieval:** The complex query processing architecture is essential to retrieve the useful part of data across the massive data storage. The well-structured and well-organized data preserves the cloud resources and easy for searching. As client increases, the communication, sharing and retrieval speed declines.
- **Query Processing and Views:** The fruitful views are produced for the clients by using the complex query processing for the huge data. The collaborating function and distributed query processing for multiple clouds and its multiple servers and storages helps to gain the valuable information across the massive data.

Figure 13.

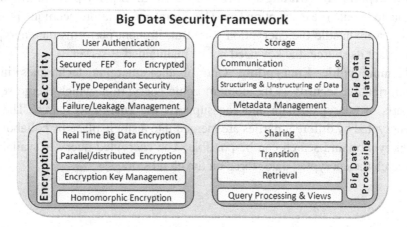

87

Security:

- **User/Administrator Authentication:** The metadata for the guest, registered users and administrators is required for their authentication. The security is provided by the Front End Processor machine on every single door of every cloud.
- **Secured Front End Processors for encrypted search:** The encrypted search plays a vital role to provide the security in the big data security system. The front-end processor with its secured software and hardware support plays a great role in the big data security.
- **Type Dependent Security:** Different type of digital data comes to the cloud require different security. The cryptographic algorithms are used to secure the text data while images, audio and video security are handle by the different steganographic techniques.
- **Failure/Leakage Management:** The log based recovery is essential in maintaining the failure of transaction over cloud. The big data leakage can be maintained efficiently by the Two-Phase-Locking protocol.
- **Encryption:** The basic to big security can be available through the different encryption techniques such as AES, TDES to secure the big data.
- **Real Time Big Data Encryption:** The local encryption known as offline encryption is feasible for the small data stored in client machine. However, the huge data moves from client to cloud must be secured by real time encryption. This can be possible by capture the incoming data from client to cloud and encrypt it before store.
- **Parallel/Distributed Encryption:** If cloud handles the security task of huge data, it can be effectively handled by the parallel and distributed encryption technique. The collaboration encryption can be effectively handled by multiple servers across different clouds.
- **Encryption Key Management:** The trusted third party plays an important role to handle the encryption key. The digital certification technique is useful if servers handle the encryption part. But, if client performs the encryption work at its source, the key need not be maintained at server.
- **Homomorphic Encryption:** One of the emerging techniques in the information security is the homomorphic encryption, which merge several parts of encrypted data and can supports the encrypted search. The data encrypted by different parties are merged into a single place by collaborating encryption and search can be possible. The encrypted query is available to search the encrypted data stored on the cloud storage.

9. LIMITATIONS AND CHALLENGES TO BIG DATA SECURITY

Till now companies were using ordinary security measures to secure their data; however, with the increased use of web-based, mobile and cloud-based applications, sensitive data has become accessible from different platforms. These platforms are highly vulnerable to hacking, especially if they are low-cost or free.

Nowadays, organizations are collecting and processing massive amounts of information. The more data is stored, the more vital it is to ensure its security. A lack of data security can lead to great financial losses and reputational damage for a company. As far as Big Data is concerned, losses due to poor IT security can exceed even the worst expectations.

Almost all data security issues are caused by the lack of effective measures provided by antivirus software and firewalls. These systems were developed to protect the limited scope of information stored on the hard disk, but Big Data goes beyond hard disks and isolated systems.

9.1 Big Data Security Challenges

- Unethical IT specialists practicing information mining can gather personal data without asking users for permission or notifying them.
- Access control encryption and connections security can become dated and inaccessible to the IT specialists who rely on it.
- Recommended detailed audits are not routinely performed on Big Data due to the huge amount of information involved.
- Most distributed systems' computations have only a single level of protection, which is not recommended.
- Non-relational databases (NoSQL) are actively evolving, making it difficult for security solutions to keep up with demand.
- Automated data transfer requires additional security measures, which are often not available.
- When a system receives a large amount of information, it should be validated to remain trustworthy and accurate; this practice doesn't always occur, however.
- Due to the size of Big Data, its origins are not consistently monitored and tracked.

9.2 Need for Big Data Security Be Improved?

Cloud computing experts believe that the most reasonable way to improve the security of Big Data is through the continual expansion of the antivirus industry. A multitude of antivirus vendors, offering a variety of solutions, provides a better defense against Big Data security threats. Refreshingly, the antivirus industry is often touted for its openness. Antivirus software providers freely exchange information about current Big Data security threats, and industry leaders often work together to cope with new malicious software attacks, providing maximum gains in Big Data security.

Here are some additional recommendations to strengthen Big Data security:

- Focus on application security, rather than device security.
- Isolate devices and servers containing critical data.
- Introduce real-time security information and event management.
- Provide reactive and proactive protection.

10. FUTURE RECOMMENDATION

Companies using big data should allocate top most to the security of cloud-based systems. Intel Security has recently published the McAfee Labs' Threat Predictions Report that contains their expectations for the near-future of data security. Of particular concern in this report is the supposition that legitimate cloud file hosting services such as Dropbox, Box, and Stream Nation, are at risk of being used as control servers in upcoming cyber espionage campaigns. If targeted, these popular cloud services could enable the malware to transfer commands without raising suspicion.

11. SUMMARY

The mobile computing with the security threats and the type of security attacks with their life cycle has been discussed in this chapter. The collaborating network and encryption technique discussed in this chapter facilitates the network users to keep their information and database safe. The mobile computing environment requires the rapid encryption and decryption system that keep the sensitive information safe. In this chapter, the preliminary analysis has been conducted on the fundamental issues such as data communication, mobile computing, information security, attacks and their types. The most tedious part of the security for cloud big data is the practical implementation of security mechanism. The present cryptosystem and its single algorithm are not suitable to provide the full security. The encrypted data stored across various cloud data servers cannot search by the traditional encryption techniques. This chapter presents the real-time encryption system scenario for the flowing data over the cloud. Major technology changes occurred in a few years where formal encryption techniques are not suitable to fulfill the security requirements. In this chapter, the concept of parallel and distributed encryption technique is introduced to overcome the confidentiality and data security issues.

REFERENCES

Ahmed, S. T., & Loguinov, D. (2014). On the performance of MapReduce: A stochastic approach. In *Proceedings of IEEE International Conference on Big Data (Big Data)* (pp. 49-54). doi:10.1109/BigData.2014.7004212

Alguliyev, R., & Imamverdiyev, Y. (2014). Big Data: Big Promises for Information Security. In *Proceedings of IEEE 8th International Conference on Application of Information and Communication Technologies (AICT)* (pp. 1-4). doi:10.1109/ICAICT.2014.7035946

Bagheri, R. & Jahanshahi, M. (2015). Scheduling Workflow Applications on the Heterogeneous Cloud Resources. *Indian Journal of Science and Technology, 8*(12), doi:10.17485/ijst/2015/v8i12/57984

Bosch, C., Peter, A., Leenders, B., Lim, H. W., Tang, Q., Wang, H., & Jonker, W. et al. (2014). Distributed Searchable Symmetric Encryption. In *Proceedings of Twelfth Annual International Conference on Privacy, Security and Trust (PST)* (pp. 330-337). doi:10.1109/PST.2014.6890956

Chan, A. C.-F. (2009). Symmetric-Key Homomorphic Encryption for Encrypted Data Processing. In *Proceedings of IEEE International Conference on Communications ICC '09*. doi:10.1109/ICC.2009.5199505

Chen, X.-W., & Lin, X. (2014). Big Data Deep Learning: Challenges and Perspectives. *IEEE Access, 2*, 214–225.

Dev, D., & Baishnab, K. L. (2014). A Review and Research Towards Mobile Cloud Computing. *Proceedings of 2nd IEEE International Conference on Mobile Cloud Computing, Services and Engineering (MobileCloud)* (pp. 252-255). doi:10.1109/MobileCloud.2014.41

Dong, X., Li, R., He, H., Zhou, W., Xue, Z., & Wu, H. (2015). Secure sensitive data sharing on a big data platform. *Tsinghua Science and Technology, 20*(1), 72–80. doi:10.1109/TST.2015.7040516

Hu, H., Wen, Y., Chua, T.-S., & Li, X. (2014). Toward Scalable Systems for Big Data Analytics: A Technology Tutorial. *IEEE Access*, *2*, 652–687. doi:10.1109/ACCESS.2014.2332453

Hwang, Y. H., Seo, J. W., & Kim, I. J. (2014). Encrypted Keyword Search Mechanism Based on Bitmap Index for Personal Storage Services. In *Proceedings of IEEE 13th International Conference on Trust, Security and Privacy in Computing and Communications (TrustCom)* (pp. 140-147). doi:10.1109/TrustCom.2014.22

Jasmine, R.M. & Nishibha, G.M. (2015). Public Cloud Secure Group Sharing and Accessing in Cloud Computing. *Indian Journal of Science and Technology,* 8(15). doi:10.17485/ijst/2015/v8i15/75177

Jeuk, S., Szefer, J., & Zhou, S. (2014). Towards Cloud, Service and Tenant Classification for Cloud Computing. In *Proceedings of 14th IEEE/ACM International Symposium on Cluster, Cloud and Grid Computing (CCGrid)* (pp. 792-801). doi:10.1109/CCGrid.2014.71

Ji, C., Li, Y., Qiu, W., Awada, U., & Li, K. (2012). Big Data Processing in Cloud Computing Environments. In *Proceedings of the 12th International Symposium on Pervasive Systems. Algorithms and Networks (ISPAN)* (pp. 17-23).

Kalpana, V. & Meena, V. (2015). Study on Data Storage Correctness Methods in Mobile Cloud Computing. *Indian Journal of Science and Technology.* doi:10.17485/ijst/2015/v8i6/70094

Kirubakaramoorthi, R., Arivazhagan, D. & Helen, D. (2015). Analysis of Cloud Computing Technology. *Indian Journal of Science and Technology,* 8(21). doi:10.17485/ijst/2015/v8i21/79144

Lee, J.-Y. (2015). A Study on the Use of Secure Data in Cloud Storage for Collaboration. *Indian Journal of Science and Technology,* 8(S5), Doi no:.10.17485/ijst/2015/v8iS5/61462

Marchal, S., Jiang, X., State, R., & Engel, T. (2014). A Big Data Architecture for Large Scale Security Monitoring. In *Proceedings of IEEE International Congress on Big Data (Big Data Congress)* (Vol. 2, pp. 56-63). doi:10.1109/BigData.Congress.2014.18

Matturdi, B., Xianwei, Z., Shuai, L., & Fuhong, L. (2014). Big Data security and privacy: A review. *China Communications*, *11*(14), 135–145. doi:10.1109/CC.2014.7085614

Murthy, P. K. (2014). Top ten challenges in Big Data security and privacy. In *Proceedings of IEEE International Test Conference (ITC)*. doi:10.1109/TEST.2014.7035307

Pal, A.S. & Pattnaik, B.P. (2013). Classification of Virtualization Environment for Cloud Computing. *Indian Journal of Science and Technology, 6*(1). doi:10.17485/ijst/2013/v6i1/30572

Parthiban, P. & Selvakumar, S. (2016). Big Data Architecture for Capturing, Storing, Analyzing and Visualizing of Web Server Logs. *Indian Journal of Science and Technology, 9*(4). Doi:10.17485/ijst/2016/v9i4/84173

Rajathi, A. & Saravanan, N. (2013). A Survey on Secure Storage in Cloud Computing. *Indian Journal of Science and Technology, 6*(4). doi:10.17485/ijst/2013/v6i4/31871

Ranjan, R. (2014). Streaming Big Data Processing in Datacenter Clouds. *IEEE Cloud Computing, 1*(1), 78–83. doi:10.1109/MCC.2014.22

Ren, D.-Q., & Wei, Z. (2013). A Failure Recovery Solution for Transplanting High-Performance Data-Intensive Algorithms from the Cluster to the Cloud. In *Proceedings of IEEE International Conference on High Performance Computing and Communications & IEEE 10th International Conference on Embedded and Ubiquitous Computing (HPCC & EUC)* (pp. 1463-1468). doi:10.1109/HPCC.and.EUC.2013.207

Shyamala, K. & Sunitha Rani, T. (2015). An Analysis on Efficient Resource Allocation Mechanisms in Cloud Computing. *Indian Journal of Science and Technology, 8*(9). doi:10.17485/ijst/2015/v8i9/50180

Singh, J. (2014). Real time BIG data analytic: Security concern and challenges with Machine Learning algorithm. In *Proceedings of Conference on IT in Business, Industry and Government (CSIBIG)*. doi:10.1109/CSIBIG.2014.7056985

Stallings, W. (2011). *Cryptography and Network Security: Principles and Practice* (5th ed.). Pearson Education.

Tan, Z., Nagar, U. T., He, X., Nanda, P., Liu, R. P., Wang, S., & Hu, J. (2014). Enhancing Big Data Security with Collaborative Intrusion Detection. *IEEE Cloud Computing, 1*(3), 27–33. doi:10.1109/MCC.2014.53

Xiang, G., Yu, B., & Zhu, P. (2012). A algorithm of fully homomorphic encryption. In *Proceedings of 9th International Conference on Fuzzy Systems and Knowledge Discovery (FSKD)* (pp. 2030-2033).

Xu, L., Jiang, C., Wang, J., Yuan, J., & Ren, Y. (2014). Information Security in Big Data: Privacy and Data Mining. *IEEE Access*, *2*, 1149–1176. doi:10.1109/ACCESS.2014.2362522

Zhao, F., Li, C., & Liu, C. F. (2014). A cloud computing security solution based on fully homomorphic encryption. In *Proceedings of 16th International Conference on Advanced Communication Technology (ICACT)* (pp. 485-488). doi:10.1109/ICACT.2014.6779008

Chapter 5

A Survey of Big Data Analytics Using Machine Learning Algorithms

Usha Moorthy
Vellore Institute of Technology, India

Usha Devi Gandhi
Vellore Institute of Technology, India

ABSTRACT

Big data is information management system through the integration of various traditional data techniques. Big data usually contains high volume of personal and authenticated information which makes privacy as a major concern. To provide security and effective processing of collected data various techniques are evolved. Machine Learning (ML) is considered as one of the data technology which handles one of the central and hidden parts of collected data. Same like ML algorithm Deep Learning (DL) algorithm learn program automatically from the data it is considered to enhance the performance and security of the collected massive data. This paper reviewed security issues in big data and evaluated the performance of ML and DL in a critical environment. At first, this paper reviewed about the ML and DL algorithm. Next, the study focuses towards issues and challenges of ML and their remedies. Following, the study continues to investigate DL concepts in big data. At last, the study figures out methods adopted in recent research trends and conclude with a future scope.

DOI: 10.4018/978-1-5225-2863-0.ch005

1. INTRODUCTION

Big data analytics is the vast level investigation and preparing of data in dynamic utilize in a few fields and, as of late, has pulled in light of a legitimate concern for the security group for its guaranteed capacity to dissect and correspond security related data effectively and at phenomenal scale (Shirudkar et al., 2015). Separating between customary data examination and enormous data investigation for security is, in any case, not clear (Imperva, 2015). All things considered, the data security group has been utilizing the investigation of system movement, framework logs, and other data sources to recognize dangers and identify noxious exercises for over 10 years, and it's not clear how these customary methodologies vary from big data (Mulanee et al., 2015). "Big Data Analytics for Security Intelligence," concentrates on big data's part insecurity (Raja et al., 2014). In advanced world, data are produced from different sources and the quick move from computerized innovations has prompted the development of enormous data (Suryawanshi et al., 2015). It gives transformative leaps forward in numerous fields with an accumulation of vast datasets. When all is said in done, it alludes to the accumulation of extensive and complex datasets which are hard to process utilizing customary database administration instruments or data handling applications (UK Data Archive, 2011). These are accessible in the organized, semi-organized, and unstructured organization in peta bytes and past (Tsai et al., 2015). Some of these extraction strategies for acquiring accommodating data were examined by Gandomi and Haider (Gandomi et al., 2015). The, however, correct definition for big data is not characterized, and there is trusted that it is issue particular. This will help us in getting upgraded basic leadership, knowledge disclosure, and advancement while being inventive and financially savvy (Kaur and Kaur, 2016). Extensive scale data sets are gathered and examined in various spaces, from designing sciences to interpersonal organizations, trade, bimolecular examination, and security (Tsai et al., 2015). Especially, advanced data produced from an assortment of computerized gadgets, and are developing at amazing rates. As per Gandomi and Haider (2015), in 2011, computerized data is grown nine times in volume in only 5years, and its sum on the planet will be reached 35 trillion gigabytes by 2020 (Lynch, 2008). In this manner, the expression "Enormous Data" was begotten to catch the significant importance of this data blast pattern (Qiu et al., 2016).

The aim of Machine Learning (ML) is to empower a framework to gain from the past or present and utilize that data to settle on expectations or choices with respect to obscure future occasions (Rajkumar et al., 2016). In the broadest terms, the work process for an administered ML errand comprises of three stages: manufacture the model, assess and tune the model, and afterward put the model into creation

(Natarajan et al., 2012). The multiplication of big data has constrained us to reexamine data preparing systems, as well as usage of ML algorithms too. Picking the fitting apparatuses for a specific errand or environment can overwhelm for two reasons. To start with, the expanding multifaceted nature of ML venture necessities and additionally of the data itself may require distinctive sorts of arrangements. Second, frequently engineers will discover the determination of devices accessible to be unsuitable; however, as opposed to adding to existing open source ventures, they start one of their own (Mani et al., 1998). This has prompted a lot of discontinuity among existing big data stages (Kashyap et al., 2014). Both of these issues can add to the trouble of building a learning situation, the same number of alternatives have covering use cases, yet separate in imperative regions. Since there is no single device or system that covers all or even the larger part of normal assignments, one must consider the exchange offs that exist between ease of use, execution, and calculation choice while inspecting diverse arrangements. There is an absence of extensive examination of a large number of them, in spite of being generally utilized on an undertaking level and there is no present industry standard (Landset et al., 2015).

2.1 Review of Big Data Processing

In recent world processing of a large amount of data is difficult task which makes big data processing more complex. This section provides a detailed review of challenges facing by various big data processing mechanisms.

2.1.1. Learning of Large Scale Data

- The solution to overcoming the learning of large data set is considering alternating direction method (ADMM) of multipliers which serves as computing framework (Hu et al., 2014)
- This framework is used to develop convex optimizing, scalable and distributed algorithms in both distributed and parallel data processing.
- ADMM has capacity to part or decouple numerous variables in improvement issues, which empowers individual, discover an answer for an extensive scale worldwide advancement issue by organizing answers for littler sub-issues.
- For the most part, ADMM is united for raised enhancement, yet it is the absence of a meeting, and hypothetical execution ensures for non-convex improvement. It is immeasurable trial proof in the writing bolsters experimental merging and great execution of ADM (Boyd et al., 2010).

2.1.2. Learning of Different Types of Data

- The effective key to concentrate on the problem of data integration is to obtain a proper data representation since the one to present in the data source.
- These data sources are then integrated to various features from the different levels (Hinton, 2012). and hence learning is considered to this problem
- In Wu (2013), the authors proposed a data combination hypothesis given actual learning for the 2D range different data. Moreover, Deep Learning (DL) strategies have likewise been appeared to be extremely compelling in incorporating data from various sources.

2.1.3. Learning for High-Speed Streaming Data

- Online learning approach is considered as one of the optimal solutions for the problem of learning such as very high velocity of data
- Online learning (Shalev-Shwartz, 2011; Wang et al., 2014; Bilenko et al., 2005) is a created learning worldview whose methodology is learning a example at once, rather than in a disconnected or bunch learning design, which needs to gather the full data of preparing data.
- This chronological learning instrument functions admirably for enormous data as present machines can't hold the whole dataset in process.
- To speed up adapting, as of late, a fresh algorithm for single concealed layer sustain forward neural systems (SLFNs) named amazing learning machine (ELM) (Huang et al., 2006) was proposed.
- ELM gives amazingly speedier learning speed, better speculation execution, and with slightest human intercession than some other customary learning calculations (Ding et al., 2014) Hence, ELM has solid preferences in managing the high speed of data.

2.1.4. Learning for Uncertain and Incomplete Data

- Uncertainty data are a unique sort of data reality where data readings and accumulations are no more deterministic however are liable to some arbitrary or likelihood disseminations.
- In numerous applications, data instability is basic. For instance, in remote systems, some range data are. Naturally, indeterminate came about because of omnipresent commotion, blurring, and shadowing, and the innovation obstruction of the GPS sensor hardware additionally confines the exactness of the data to specific levels.

- For indeterminate data, the significant test is that the data highlight or property is caught not by a solitary point esteem but rather spoke to as test disseminations (Wu et al., 2014). A basic approach to handling data instability is to apply synopsis insights, for example, means and differences to extract test appropriations.
- Another methodology is to use the complete data conveyed by the likelihood dispersions to develop a choice tree, which is called dissemination based methodology in (Tsang et al., 2011).

2.1.5. Learning for Data With Low-Value Density and Meaning Diversity

- To handle the problem the solution that used is data mining technologies and knowledge discovery in databases (KDD) (Wu et al., Fayyad et al., 1996; Tsai et al., 2014), this provides a solution with data hidden in the massive data.
- In Tsai et al., the authors looked into studies on applying data mining and KDD innovations to the IoT. Especially, using grouping, characterization, and continuous examples innovations to mine quality from enormous data in IoT, from bases and the viewpoint of administrations were talked about in subtle element.
- In Wu et al., Wu et al. described the components of the big data transformation and proposed big data preparing techniques with ML and data mining calculations.

3.0. OVERVIEW OF ML

ML could be a field of examination that formally concentrates on the hypothesis, execution, and properties of learning frameworks and algorithms (Domingos, 2012). It is an exceptionally interdisciplinary field expanding upon thoughts from various

Table 1. ML and data types

ML Technique	Data Type
Alternating Direction Method (ADMM)	Large Scale Data
Data combination hypothesis for two-dimensional range heterogeneous data	Different Data Type
Sustain forward neural systems (SLFNs)	High-speed streaming data
Knowledge discovery in databases (KDD)	Data with low-value density and meaning diversity

sorts of fields of research (Pawlak, 1982; Molodtsov 1999; Peters, 2007; Wille, 2005). Due to its execution in an extensive variety of utilizations, ML has secured practically every logical area, that has brought incredible effect on the science and society (Jolliffe, 2002). It has been utilized on an assortment of issues, including suggestion motors, acknowledgment frameworks, informatics and data mining, and self-governing control frameworks (Al-Jarrah et al., 2015).

For the most part, the area of ML has three subdomains: managed learning, unsupervised learning, and support learning (Changwon et al., 2014). Quickly, directed learning needs preparing with named data which has independent variables whereas craved yields. Interestingly with the directed learning, unsupervised learning doesn't need marked preparing data and nature just gives inputs without fancied targets (Bengio et al., 2014). Fortification taking in empowers gaining from input got through connections with an outer situation. Given these three crucial learning ideal models, a great deal of hypothesis components and application administrations have been proposed for managing data undertakings (Singh et al., 2014; Jacob et al., 2009; Zhu et al., 2015). For instance, in (Singh, 2014), Google implements ML algorithms to monstrous lumps of muddled data got since the Internet for Google's interpreter, Google's road view, Android's voice acknowledgment, and picture web crawler. The "Data Processing Tasks" segment of the table provides the issues that should be understood, and the "Learning Algorithms" segment depicts the techniques which might be utilized. A rundown, since data preparing point of view, directed learning and unsupervised adapting, for the most part, concentrate on data investigation while support learning is favored for basic leadership issues (Alsheikh 2014). An additional point, is that most conventional machine-learning based frameworks are planned with the suspicion that all the gathered data would be totally stacked into memory for incorporated handling (Nithya, 2016). In any case, as the data continues getting greater and greater, the current ML systems experience incredible troubles when they are needed to hold the phenomenal quantity of data. These days, an awesome necessitate to create productively and practicality learning strategies to adapt to expectations data handling requests (Setia, 2008).

In the common emphasis of ML is the illustration of the info data and speculation of the educated examples for utilize on expectations concealed data. The integrity of the data representation largely affects the execution of machine learners on the data: a poor data representation is prone to diminish the execution of even a propelled, complex machine learner, while a decent data representation can prompt superior for a moderately less complex machine learner. Along these lines, highlight building, which concentrates on developing components and data representations from crude data (Domingos, 2012), is a critical component of ML. Highlight designing devours an expensive bit of the exertion in a ML assignment, and is ordinarily very space particular and includes extensive human info (Najafabadi, 2015).

3.1. Various ML Algorithms

Several algorithms were differentiated before in the assessment of the extensive data set experience the diverse work done to hold Big Data. Before all else diverse Decision Tree Learning was used before to divide the big data. This section provides extensive analysis of existing ML algorithm for data processing in the cloud. In work done by Hall et al. (Hall, 1998), there is characterized a methodology for shaping taking in the standards of the substantial arrangement of preparing data. The methodology is to have a solitary choice framework produced from an extensive and free n subset of data. Patil et al., utilizes a cross breed approach joining both hereditary calculation and choice tree to make a streamlined choice tree in this manner enhancing proficiency and execution of calculation (Patil, 2006). At that point, bunching systems appeared. Distinctive grouping procedures were being utilized to dissect the data sets.

The above Table 2 describes various ML types and its corresponding functionality on collected big data for analysis. The observed ML techniques are used in the second stage of the hierarchical method of data processing as defined in Figure 2. Another calculation called GLC++ was created for substantially blended data set not at all like calculation which manages Whereas Koyuturk et al. Characterized another procedure PROXIMUS for the pressure of exchange sets, quickens the affiliation

Table 2. ML types and functionality

ML Types [6]	Functionality
Representation Learning	• Feature Selection • Feature Extraction • Dimensionality Reduction
DL	• Learning Deep Architectures
Distributed and Parallel Learning	• Parallel and Distributed Computing • Scalable Learning
Transfer Learning	• Knowledge Transfer • Multi-domain Learning
Active Learning	• Query Strategies and resampling • Labeling Patterns
Kernel-based learning	• Nonlinear data processing • High-dimensional mapping
Online Learning	• Streaming Processing • Sequential Learning
Extreme Learning Machine	• Fast Learning Speed • Good Generalization Performance • Less human intervention

mining guideline, and a proficient strategy for bunching and the revelation of examples in a substantial dataset (Koyuturk et al., 2005).With the developing learning in the field of enormous data, the different strategies for data investigation auxiliary coding, frequencies, co-event and diagram hypothesis, data diminishment systems, progressive bunching procedures, multidimensional scaling were characterized in Data Reduction Techniques for Large Qualitative Data Sets. It depicted that the requirement for the specific methodology emerge with the kind of dataset and the way the example is to be broke down (Namey et al., 2007).

Through the analysis of existing research articles related to ML approaches certain drawbacks challenges has been identified. The Table 2 defines challenges that exist in big data (UK Data Archive, 2011) and its impacts like insufficient volume for a large dataset, lack of variety identification regarding nonlinear, high-dimensional and heterogeneous data. Due to lack of incomplete and uncertainty veracity is also exists in cloud data and other problems like value get reduced for diverse data (Dragicevic et al., 2015)

The review of traditional researches related to ML provides certain limitation and drawbacks as stated in Table 2 also due to structural drawback it faces certain drawbacks. Due to drawbacks in existing traditional approaches Advanced Streaming Hierarchical Clustering for Concept Mining has been characterized for semantic substance from the expansive dataset (Looks et al., 2007).. The calculation was intended to be actualized in equipment, to handle data at high ingestion rates (Looks et al., 2007).In thecase of Hierarchical Artificial Neural Networks for Recognizing High Similar Large Data Sets., portrayed the procedures of SOM (self-arranging highlight map) system and learning vector quantization (LVQ) systems for regulated learning. It classifies vast data set into smaller in this way enhancing the general calculation time expected to prepare the extensive dataset (Lu et al., 2007). At that point change in the methodology for mining online data originates from Archana et al. suggested that the web mining affiliation tenets were characterized to mine the data to evacuate the excess principles. The result appeared through a diagram that the quantity of hubs in this chart is less as contrasted and the grid (Singh, 2014].

Table 3. Impact of big data challenges

Big Data Challenges (UK Data Archive, 2011)	Impact
Volume	Large Scale
Variety	Heterogeneous, High-Dimensional, Nonlinear
Velocity	Real Time, Streams, High Speed
Veracity	Uncertain and Incomplete
Value	Low value density, Diverse data mining

Figure 1 pictorially illustrates various types of ML methods and their technique for data processing. In same Figure 1 data security challenges observed from existing research articles.

At that point after the procedures of the choice tree and grouping, there came a strategy of maximal data coefficient (MIC) was characterized, which is maximal reliance between the pair of variables of different non-direct connections of data (Reshef et al., 2015). Advancement of different methodologies through hierarchical framework discovered more productive in distinguishing the reliance and affiliation (Dong et al., 2016; Vadivel et al., 2014). But developed faces certain limitations like it has low power and accordingly as a result of it doesn't fulfill the property of evenhandedness for substantial dataset (Reshef et al., 2011). At that point Wang (2012) utilizes the idea of Physical Science, the Data field to produce collaboration between among articles and after that gathering them into bunches. This calculation was contrasted and K-Means, CURE, BIRCH, and CHAMELEON and was observed to be a great deal more productive than them (Wang et al., 2011). To overcome

Figure 1.

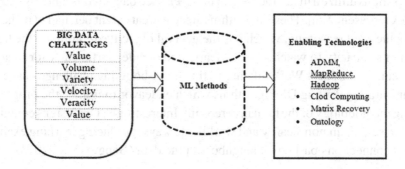

Figure 2.

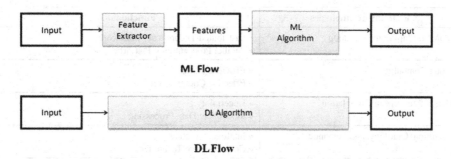

existing challenges in data mining, various technologies are evolved stated in Table 3 like cloud computing, ADMM, cognition, and matrix recovery as stated below.

To Investigate big biological datasets with affiliation system" to change numerical and ostensible data gathered in tables, data processing was carried out through study structures, polls or sort esteem explanation records into systems of affiliations (ANets) and afterward producing Association manages (A Rules) (Kalanat et al, 2015). After processing of data through A Netsany perception or grouping calculation can be connected to them. It experienced the downside that the configuration of the dataset ought to be linguistically and semantically right to get the outcome (Karpinets et al., 2012).

Later, in Survey of Different Issues of Different Clustering Algorithms utilized as a part of Large Data Sets groups distinctive DL algorithms and gives a review of various grouping calculation utilized as a part of extensive datasets (Vijayalakshmi, 2012)

3.2 Relationship Between ML and DL Techniques

The principle idea in DL algorithms is mechanizing the extraction of representations (deliberations) from the data (Le Callet et al., 2006; Wu et al., 2016; Ali et al., 2016). DL algorithms utilize a major measure of unsupervised data to consequently extricate complex representation. These algorithms are to a great extent persuaded in the field of computerized reasoning, which has the general objective of copying the human cerebrum's capacity to watch, dissect, learn, and decide, particularly for to a great degree complex issues. Work relating to this mind-boggling challenges have been a key inspiration driving DL algorithms which endeavor to imitate the progressive learning methodology of the human cerebrum. Interestingly, DL designs contain the ability, to sum up in non-nearby and worldwide ways, producing learning examples whereas connections past quick neighbors in the data (Bengio et al., 2013).

Table 4. Emerging technologies and its function

Enabling Technologies	Functionality
ADMM, MapReduce, Hadoop	• Distributed Theoretical Framework • Parallel Programming Platform
Cloud Computing	• Efficient Storage • Effective Computation
Matrix Recovery or Completion	• Uncertainty • Incomplete Data Processing
Cognition, Ontology, and Semantic	• Intelligent Techniques • Context-aware Techniques

Table 5. Review of ML methodology

Author	Method	Advantages	Research Gap
Hall, 1998	Creation of large dataset using Clustering	Proposed framework is most extensive and free n subset of data	This research does not concentrate on non-stationary datasets
Patil et al., 2007	Cross breed approach	The incorporation of Cross breed approach enhances the proficiency and execution of calculation in the cloud data.	The evaluation is not examined for particular data applications
Koyuturk et al., 2005	PROXIMUS for the pressure of exchange sets	Quickens the affiliation mining guideline, and a proficient strategy for bunching and the revelation for datasets.	This research does not focus on computational time.
Looks et al., 2015	Streaming Hierarchical Clustering	The calculation was intended to be actualized in equipment, to handle data at high ingestion rates	The computational complexity of the proposed approach is not examined.
Lu & Fahn, 2014	SOM (self-arranging highlight map) system and learning vector quantization (LVQ) systems	It classifies vast data set into littler in this way enhancing the general calculation time expected to prepare the extensive dataset.	Computational time is high
Reshef et al., 2014	Maximal data coefficient (MIC)	Methodologies were discovered more productive in distinguishing the reliance and affiliation.	The proposed approach is not examined for specific data set applications.

A key idea is hidden DL strategies is conveyed representation of the data, in which countless designs of the dynamic components of the info data are possible, taking into consideration (Fent, 2015).Taking note of that the watched data was created through connections of a few known/obscure components, and in this manner when a data example is acquired through a few designs of learned variables, extra (concealed) data examples can likely be depicted through new arrangements of the learned elements (Le Callet et al., 2006; Wu et al., 2016). This algorithm may lead to abstract samples of more dynamic representations are regularly developed in light of less conceptual ones (Najafabadi et al., 2015). An imperative favorable position of more theoretical representations is that they can be invariant to the neighborhood changes in the data. The genuine data utilized as a part of AI-related errands, for the most part, emerge from confounded connections of numerous sources. For instance, a picture is made out of various wellsprings of varieties such as light, protest shapes, and question materials. The dynamic representations gave by profound learning algorithms can isolate the diverse wellsprings of varieties in data (Goodfellow et al., 2015).

The DL algorithm is deep structures of back to back layers. Every layer applies a non-linear change in its data whereas gives a sample in its yield (Sivarajah et al., 2016). The goal is to take in a confounded and theoretical sample of the data in a progressive way by going the data through various change levels. The tangible data which means pixels in a picture is sustained to the principal level. Therefore, the yield of every level is given as a contribution to its next level (Najafabadi et al., 2015). The principle contrast between ML and profound learning calculations is in the element building. In ML calculations, we have to hand-make the components. By difference, in DL calculations, highlight building is done consequently by the calculation. Highlight building is troublesome, tedious and requires space mastery. The guarantee of profound learning is more exact ML calculations contrasted with ML with less or no component building.

4.0. ML APPROACH THROUGH DL PROCESSING

The framework can prepare 1 billion framework systems on only 3 machines in a few days, and it can scale to systems with more than 11 billion frameworks utilizing only 16 machines and where the adaptability is equivalent to that of DistBelief. In contrast with the manipulational assets utilized by DistBelief, the circulated framework system given COTS HPC is all the more for the most part accessible to a bigger gathering of people, making it a sensible option for other DL specialists investigating extensive scale models. Overall review of DL algorithm and it methodologiesare tabulated in Table 5.

4.1 Application of ANN in DL Algorithm

Artificial neural systems (ANNs) are a group of ML models motivated by natural neural systems. Natural Neurons are the center parts of the human cerebrum. A neuron comprises a cell body, dendrites, and an axon. It forms and transmitsdata to different neurons by radiating electrical signs. Every neuron gets info signals from its dendrites and produces yield signals along its axon. The axon branches out and interfaces using neurotransmitters to dendrites of different neurons as described in Figure 3. Counterfeit neurons are enlivened by Biological neurons, and attempt to define the model clarified above in a computational structure. An Artifical neuron has a limited number of inputs with weights related to them, and an initiation capacity (likewise called exchange capacity).

Feedforward Neural Networks are the most straightforward type of Artificial Neural Networks graphically illustrated in Figure 4. These systems have 3 sorts of layers: anInput layer, shrouded layer, and yield layer (Yu et al., 2011). In these

Table 6. Review of DL approach

Authors	Learning Approach	Outcome	Problem Identified
Zhou et al., 2012	DL technique using autoencoders	In a denoising autoencoder, there is one concealed layer which removes highlights, with the quantity of hubs in this shrouded layer at first being the same as the quantity of elements that would be separated.	Not Identified
Calandra et al., 2012	DL for online non-stationary and spilling data	The approaching this research specimen and examined tests are utilized to take in the new Deep convection system which has adjusted to the recently watched data.	Developed have a drawback of a versatile Deep convection system is the prerequisite for consistent memory utilization.
Chen et al., n. d.	Minimized stacked denoising autoencoders (mSDAs)	Methodology framed in this research underestimates clamor in SDA and generates stochastic slope for other improved algorithms to learn parameters.	The capacity of the proposed approach is not sufficient for the vast amount of data for ML and data mining approach.
Coates and Ng, 2011	Commodity-Off-The-Shelf High Performance Computing (COTS HPC)	The framework can prepare 1 billion parameter systems on only 3 machines in a few days, and it can scale to systems with more than 11 billion parameters utilizing only 16 machines using DistBelief.	This proposed framework COTS HPC is accessible to a bigger gathering of people alone which means for huge dataset,

Figure 3.

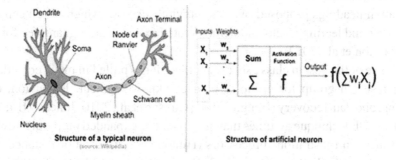

Structure of a typical neuron (source: Wikipedia)

Structure of artificial neuron

systems, data moves from the info layer through the shrouded hubs (assuming any) and to the yield hubs. The following is a case of a completely associated feedforward neural system with 2shrouded layers. "Completely associated" implies that every hubis associated with every one of the hubs in the following layer. Note that, the quantity of shrouded layers and their size are the main free parameters. The bigger and more profound the shrouded layers, the more perplexing examples we can demonstrate in principle (Arel, 2010).

Figure 4.

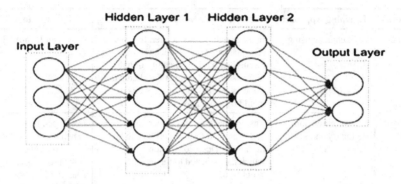

4.1.1 Implementation Challenges in DL

Now a days, there is most likely profound learning is one of the most blazing examination patterns in ML field. DL technique utilizes regulated and unsupervised procedures in profound designs to naturally learn various leveled representations (Bengio, et al., 2009). DL designs can regularly catch more confused, progressively propelled measurable examples of inputs for accomplishing to be versatile to new zones than conventional learning techniques and frequently beat best in class accomplished by hand-made elements (Collobert et al., 2011). DL based network(DBNs) (Bengio 2009; Le Callet et al., 2006) and Convolutional Neural Systems (CNNs) (Chen et al., 2014; Dahl et al., 2012) are two standard profound learning methodologies and exploration headings proposed over the previous decade, which have been settled in the profound learning field and demonstrated extraordinary guarantee for future work (Hinton et al., 2012)

Because of the best in class execution of DL, it has pulled in much consideration among research group for group discourse acknowledgment, PC vision, dialect handling, and data recovery (Bengio, 2009; Ciresan et al., 2010; Jones, 2014; Wange t al, 2011). DL technique assumes that huge data sets expanded preparing power and the advances in illustrations processors (Hinton et al 2012).. For instance, IBM's cerebrum like PC (Bengio et al., 2007; Baker, 2016) and Microsoft's continuous dialect interpretation in Bing's voice seek (Baker 2016) have utilized strategies like DL out how to influence big data for theupper hand.

DL algorithms utilizea gigantic measure of unsupervised data to consequently separate complex representation. These algorithms are to a great extent inspired by the field of computerized reasoning.Conversely, DL designs have the capacity, to sum up in non-nearby and worldwide ways, creating learning examples and connections past quick neighbors in the data (Bengio et al., 2013). DL is, indeed, a critical stride toward computerized reasoning. It not just gives complex representations of data which are appropriate for AI assignments additionally makes the machines free of human learning which is a definitive objective of AI. It removes representations specifically from unsupervised data without human obstruction.DL alludes to a class of Artifical Neural Systems (ANNs) made out of numerous handling layers (Bengio et al., 2013). ANNs existed for a long time, yet endeavors at preparing profound designs of ANNs fizzled until Geoffrey Hinton's leap forward work of the mid-2000s. Notwithstanding algorithmic advancements, the expansion in processing abilities utilizing GPUs and the gathering of bigger datasets are all figures that helped the late surge of profound learning (Wadhwa et al., 2014).

4.2 Application of DL in Big Data

As expressed already, DL algorithms remove significant dynamic representations of the crude data using a progressive multi-level learning approach. While DL can be connected to gain from named data on the off chance that it is accessible inadequately substantial sums, it is principally alluring for gaining a lot of unlabeled/ unsupervised data (Bengio et al., 2013; Wu et al., 2016; Ali et al., 2016)., making it appealing for removing significant representations and examples from Big Data. DL algorithms are appeared to perform better at removing non-nearby and worldwide connections, and examples in the data, contrasted with generally shallow learning models (Bengio et al., 2014). Other helpful qualities of the learnt conceptual representations by DL include:

1. Generally basic straight models can work viably with the data acquired from the more mind boggling and more theoretical data representations,
2. Expanded computerization of data representation extraction from unsupervised data empowers its wide application to various data sorts.,
3. Social and semantic learning can be gotten at the more elevated amounts of reflection and representation of the crude data.

Considering each of the four Vs. of Big Data attributes, i.e., Volume, Variety, Velocity, and Veracity, DL algorithms and models are all the more apropos suited to deliver issues identified with Volume and Variety of Big Data Analytics (Deng, 2915). DL characteristically abuses the accessibility of enormous measures of data, i.e. Volume in Big Data, where algorithms with shallow learning chains of importance neglect to investigate and comprehend the higher complexities of data examples. Besides, since DL manages data reflection and representations, it is entirely likely suited for investigating crude data displayed in various arrangements and/or from various sources, i.e. Assortment in Big Data, and may minimize the requirement for contribution from human specialists to concentrate highlights from each new data sort saw in Big Data (Abdarbo et al., 2016). While displaying distinctive difficulties for more traditional data investigation approaches, Big Data Analytics presents an essential open door for creating novel algorithms and models to deliver particular issues identified with Big Data. For instance, the removed representations by DL can be considered as a pragmatic wellspring of data for basic leadership, semantic indexing, data recovery, and for different purposes in Big Data Analytics, and furthermore, straightforward, direct displaying procedures can be considered for Big Data Analytics when complex data is spoken to in higher types of deliberation (Najafabadi et al., 2015).

5.0 CHALLENGING IN MACHINE LEARNING WITH CORRESPONDING TO BIG DATA

In this present section, we present discussion about the issues of ML approaches with corresponding for the five different perspective (Hu et al., 2015) which has been explained in Figure 5 that includes learning of large-scale data, learning of different data types, learning of high-speed data streaming, learning of incomplete and uncertain data and learning of extracting the data that are valuable from the amount of data set.

The Table 6 defines challenges that are related to big data analytics that observed from the existing literature. Through the observation of existing literatures challenges like processing of large datasets, uncertain datasets, high dimensional data, non-stationary difficulties are identified.

5.2. Implementation Challenge of DL in Big Data

This segment exhibits a few ranges of Big Data where DL needs encourage investigation, particularly, learning with spilling data, managing high-dimensional

Figure 5.

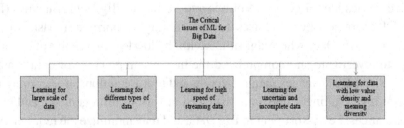

Table 7. Challenges in big data analytics

Critical Parameters	Author Name	Drawbacks
Large Dataset (2015)	Wang et al., 2015	Taking just the computerized data as an example, consistently, Google alone needs to prepare around 24 petabytes. Also, on the off chance, it encourages other data sources, the data scale will turn out to be much greater.
Different data type (2011)	UK Archive, 2011	The tremendous assortment of data is the second measurement that makes enormous data both intriguing and testing. Learning with such a dataset, the colossal test is detectable, and the level of intricacy is not in any case believable before we profoundly arrive
High-speed streaming data (2015)	Gandomi and Haider, 2015	For huge dataset rate or learning rate or speed truly matters, which is another rising test for learning. The preparing results turn out to be less profitable or even useless. In these time-touchy cases, the potential estimation of data relies on upon data freshness that should be handled in a continuous way.
Learning for Uncertain and incomplete data	UK Archive, 2011	ML algorithms were regularly encouraged with generally exact data from surely understood and very restricted sources, so the learning results have a tendency to be unerring. The significance of tending to and dealing with the vulnerability and inadequacy on data quality.
Data with low-value density and meaning diversity	Wang et al., 2015; Vincent et al., 2010	Abusing an assortment of learning techniques to investigate enormous datasets, the last design is to concentrate significant data from monstrous measures of data as profound understanding or business advantages.
Incremental learning for non-stationary data	Vadivel et al., 2014; Reshef et al., 2011; Wang et al., 2011	This incremental component learning and mapping can enhance the discriminative or generative target capacity; be that as it may, monotonically adding elements can prompt having a considerable measure of excess elements and overfitting of data.
High-dimensional data	Kalanat et al., 2015	The utilization of DL algorithms for Big Data Analytics including high dimensional data remains to a great extent unexplored, and warrants advancement of DL based arrangements that either adjust approaches like the ones introduced above or create novel answers for tending to the high-dimensionality found in some Big Data areas.
Large-scale models	Coates, 2011	The system bolsters model parallelism both inside a machine (by means of multi-threading), and crosswise over machines (through message going), with the points of interest of parallelism, synchronization, and correspondence oversaw by DistBelief.

data, the versatility of models, and dispersed processing (Huang et al., 2006). The major challenges of the DL are (Ding et al., 2014)

- Incremental learning for non-stationary data
- High-dimensional data
- Large-scale models

5.2.1. Incremental Learning for Non-Stationary Data

One of the testing perspectives in Big Data Analytics is managing spilling and quick moving info data. Such data investigation is valuable in observing errands, for example, extortion location. It is imperative to adjust DL to handle gushing data, as there is a requirement for algorithms that can manage a lot of nonstop info data. In this area, we talk about a few works connected with DL and spilling data, including incremental element learning and extraction (Shou et al., 2012), denoising autoencoders (Vincent et al., 2008), and profound conviction systems (Chen et al., n. d.). Zhou et al. (2012) portray how a DL calculation can be utilized for incremental component learning on big datasets, utilizing denoising autoencoders (Vincent et al., 2008). Denoising Autoencoders are a variation of autoencoders which extricate highlights from adulterated info, where the separated components are powerful to boisterous data and useful for order purposes. Zhou et al. show that the incremental element learning strategy rapidly localizes to the ideal number of components in a substantial scale web setting. This sort of incremental component extraction is helpful in applications where the conveyance of data changes as for time in monstrous online data streams. Incremental element learning and extraction can be summed up for other DL algorithms, for example, RBM (Wu et al., 2014), and makes it conceivable to adjust to anew approaching stream of online expansive scale data. In addition, it maintains a strategic distance from costly cross-acceptance investigation in selecting the quantity of components in expansive scale datasets. Calandra et al. (2012) present versatile profound conviction systems which exhibit how DL can be summed up to gain from online non-stationary and gushing data (Chen, n. d.). Their study abuses the generative property of profound conviction systems to emulate the specimens from the first data, where these examples and the new watched tests are utilized to take in the new profound conviction system which has adjusted to the recently watched data. Be that as it may, a drawback of a versatile profound conviction system is the prerequisite for consistent memory utilization.

5.2.2. High-Dimensional Data

Some DL algorithms can turn out to be restrictively computationally-costly when managing high-dimensional data, for example, pictures, likely because of the frequently moderate learning process connected with a profoundly layered chain of command of taking in data deliberations and representations from a lower-level layer to a more elevated amount layer. That is to say; these DL algorithms can be hindered when working with Big Data that shows big Volume, one of the four Vs connected with Big Data Analytics. A high-dimensional data source contributes intensely to the volume of the crude data, notwithstanding entangling gaining from the data. Chen et al. (nd) present minimized stacked denoising autoencoders (mSDAs) which scale successfully for high-dimensional data and is computationally quicker than standard stacked denoising autoencoders (SDAs). The quick preparing time, the capacity to scale to expansive scale and high dimensional data, and execution effortlessness make mSDA a promising technique with speak to a substantial group of onlookers in data mining and ML.

CNNs are another strategy which scales up adequately on high dimensional data. Analysts have taken preferences of CNNs on Image Net dataset with 256×256 RGB pictures to accomplish best in class results (Tsang et al., 2011; Fayyad et al., 1996). In CNNs, the neurons in the concealed layers units don't should be associated with the greater part of the hubs in the past layer, however just to the neurons that are in the same spatial zone. The utilization of DL algorithms for Big Data Analytics including high dimensional data remains to a great extent unexplored, and warrants advancement of DL based arrangements that either adjust approaches like the ones introduced above or create novel answers for tending to the high-dimensionality found out some Big Data areas.

5.2.3. Large-Scale Models

Dean et al. (2012) consider the issue of preparing a DL neural system with billions of parameters utilizing countless CPU centers, with regards to discourse acknowledgment and PC vision. A product system, DistBelief, is created that can use figuring bunches with a big number of machines to prepare extensive scale models. The system bolsters model parallelism both inside a machine (by means of multi-threading), and crosswise over machines (through message going), with the points of interest of parallelism, synchronization, and correspondence oversaw by DistBelief. What's more, the system additionally bolsters data parallelism, where numerous copies of a model are utilized to enhance a solitary goal (Hu, 2015). With a specific end goal to make vast scale appropriated preparing conceivable an offbeat SGD and additionally a dispersed cluster improvement methodology is produced that incorporates a disseminated usage of L-BFGS (Limited-memory Broyden-Fletcher-GoldfarbShanno, a semi Newton technique for unconstrained advancement). Coates et al. (2013) influence the moderately modest registering force of a bunch of GPU servers. All the more particularly, they build up their own particular framework (utilizing neural systems) taking into account Commodity-Off-The-Shelf High Performance Computing (COTS HPC) Innovation and present a fast correspondence foundation to arrange appropriated algorithms. The framework can prepare 1 billion parameter systems on only 3 machines in a few days, and it can scale to systems with more than 11 billion parameters utilizing only 16 machines and where the versatility is practically identical to that of DistBelief (Lopez-Moreno, 2016).

In contrast with the computational assets utilized by DistBelief, the appropriated framework system taking into account COTS HPC is all the more for the most part accessible to a bigger group of onlookers, making it a sensible option for other DL specialists investigating extensive scale models.

Same like ML approach certain DL mechanisms were examined for its own functionality to its corresponding data type. The table 8 provides types of DL techniques and its corresponding supportable data type for analysis of data. From the review, it is observed that DDM technique will be applicable for high-dimensional dataset and large scale data will be analyzed using deep scaling models.

6. CONCLUSION

ML and DL has the leverage of possibly giving an answer for the location the data investigation and learning issues found in gigantic volumes of data. Both ML and DL techniques help in consequently extricating difficult data representations from vast volumes of unsupervised data. This makes it a significant instrument for big data analytics, which includes data examination from huge accumulations of crude data that is, for the most part, unsupervised and unsorted. The present study began to explain with a description of ML algorithm followed by issues faced in the ML algorithm and its possible remedies. Then it discusses the DL relationship between DL and ML and deep applications with that of the big data. At last, the challenges faced by the DL in the research trends have been discussed. Also, the present study aimed to implement a solution for particular issue i.e. Uncertain and incomplete dataset using the solution learning of uncertain and incomplete dataset with the use of Parkinson telecommunication dataset. In future, it would be more interesting in concentrating towards the trend one or a greater amount of these issues frequently seen in big data, hence accumulation the DL and big data analytics research corpus.

7. FUTURE SCOPE

This review article provides the detailed description of the application of ML approach to big data analytics. Specifically, this research concentrates on DL algorithm implementation in big data analytics. Further, this research provides implementation difficulties of the machine and DL algorithm in big data analytics. This research suggested that ML through DL approach enhances to medical data processing where it is described as Parkinson dataset. Usually, Parkinson dataset contains a large number of medical records which can be examined using Hadoop platform in future.

REFERENCES

Aakash, P. K., & Pushpalatha, S. (2016). A Survey on Applications of Artificial Neural Networks in Data Mining, Int. *J. Sci. Eng. Technol. Res.*, *5*, 1470–1473.

Abdrabo, M., Elmogy, M., Eltaweel, G., & Barakat, S., & (2016Enhancing Big Data Value Using Knowledge Discovery Techniques, I.*J. Inf. Technol. Comput. Sci.*, *8*, 1–12. Retrieved from http://www.mecs-press.org/ijitcs/ijitcs-v8-n8/IJITCS-V8-N8-1.pdf

Al-Jarrah, O. Y., Yoo, P. D., Muhaidat, S., Karagiannidis, G. K., & Taha, K. (2015). Efficient ML for Big Data: A Review. *Big Data Res.*, *2*(3), 87–93. doi:10.1016/j.bdr.2015.04.001

Ali, A., Qadir, J., Rasool, R., Sathiaseelan, A., Zwitter, A., & Crowcroft, J. (2016). Big data for development: Applications and techniques. *Big Data Anal.*, *1*(1), 2. doi:10.1186/s41044-016-0002-4

Alsheikh, M. A., Lin, S., Niyato, D., & Tan, H.-P. (2014). ML in Wireless Sensor Networks: Algorithms, Strategies, and Applica. *IEEE Communications Surveys and Tutorials*, *16*(4), 1996–2018. doi:10.1109/COMST.2014.2320099

Arel, I., Rose, D., & Karnowski, T. (2010). Deep ML-A new frontier in artificial intelligence research. *IEEE Computational Intelligence Magazine*, *5*(4), 13–18. doi:10.1109/MCI.2010.938364

Baker, J. (2016). Artificial Neural Networks and DL, Lancaster. Retrieved September 27, 2016 from http://www.lancaster.ac.uk/pg/bakerj1/pdfs/ANNs/Artificial_neural_networks-poster.pdf

Bengio, Y. (2009). Learning Deep Architectures for AI, Found. Trends. *Machine Learning*, *2*(1), 1–127. doi:10.1561/2200000006

Bengio, Y., Courville, A., & Vincent, P. (2013). Representation learning: A review and new perspectives. *IEEE Transactions on Pattern Analysis and Machine Intelligence*, *35*(8), 1798–1828. doi:10.1109/TPAMI.2013.50 PMID:23787338

Bengio, Y., Courville, A., & Vincent, P. (2014). Representation Learning: A Review and New Perspectives. *IEEE Transactions on Pattern Analysis and Machine Intelligence*, *35*(8), 1798–1828. doi:10.1109/TPAMI.2013.50 PMID:23787338

Bengio, Y., & LeCun, Y. (2007). Scaling learning algorithms towards. In S. K. M. Large (Ed.), *L. Bottou, O. Chapelle, D. DeCoste, J. Weston* (pp. 321–360). Cambridge, MA: MIT Press.

Bengio Y. (2013) Deep Learning of Representations: Looking Forward. In A.H. Dediu, C. Martín-Vide, R. Mitkov et al., (Eds.), Statistical Language and Speech Processing, LNCS (Vol. 7978). Springer. doi:10.1007/978-3-642-39593-2_1

Boyd, S., Parikh, N., Chu, E., Peleato, B., & Eckstein, J. (2010). Distributed Optimization and Statistical Learning via the Alternating Direction Method of Multipliers, Found. *Machine Learning, 3*(1), 1–122. doi:10.1561/2200000016

Calandra, R., Raiko, T., Deisenroth, M. P., & Pouzols, F. M. (2012). Learning deep belief networks from non-stationary streams. In Artificial Neural Networks and Machine Learning–ICANN 2012, LNCS (Vol. 7553, pp. 379–386). doi:10.1007/978-3-642-33266-1_47

Changwon, Y., & Ramirez, L. (2014). Juan. Liuzzi, Big data analysis using modern statistical and ML methods in medicine. *Int. Neurourol. J., 18*, 50–57. doi:10.5213/inj.2014.18.2.50 PMID:24987556

M. Chen, Z. Xu, K. Weinberger, F. Sha, Marginalized denoising autoencoders for domain

Chen, X., & Lin, X. (2014). Big Data Deep Learning: Challenges and Perspectives. *IEEE Access, 2*, 514–525. doi:10.1109/ACCESS.2014.2325029 PMID:24963700

Ciresan, D. C., Meier, U., Gambardella, L. M., & Schmidhuber, J. (2010). Deep Big Simple Neural Nets Excel on Handwritten Digit Recognition. *Neural Computation, 22*(12), 1–14. doi:10.1162/NECO_a_00052 PMID:19842986

Coates, A., Huval, B., Wang, T., Wu, D. J., Ng, A. Y., & Catanzaro, B. (2013). DL with COTS HPC systems. In Proc. of the 30th Int. Conf. Mach. Learn., Atlanta, Georgia. Retrieved from http://www.jmlr.org/proceedings/papers/v28/coates13.pdf

Coates, A., & Ng, A. (2011). The importance of encoding versus training with sparse coding and vector quantization. In *Proc. of the 28th Int. Conf. Mach. Learn* (pp. 921–928). Omnipress.

Collobert, R., Weston, J., Bottou, L., Karlen, M., Kavukcuoglu, K., & Kuksa, P. (2011). Natural language processing (almost) from scratch. *Journal of Machine Learning Research, 12*(August), 2493–2537.

Dahl, G. E., Yu, D., Deng, L., & Acero, A. (2012). Context-dependent pre-trained deep neural networks for large-vocabulary speech recognition. *IEEE Trans. Audio, Speech Lang. Process., 20*(1), 30–42. doi:10.1109/TASL.2011.2134090

Dean, J., Corrado, G., Monga, R., Chen, K., Devin, M., & Le, Q. et al.. (2012). In P. Bartlett, F. Pereira, C. Burges, L. Bottou, & K. Weinberger (Eds.), *Large scale distributed deep network* (pp. 1232–1240). Retrieved from http://papers.nips.cc/book/advances-in-neural-information-processing-systems-25-2012

Deng, L., & Togneri, R. (2015). Deep Dynamic Models for Learning Hidden Representations of Speech Features. In Speech Audio Process. Coding, Enhanc. Recognit. (pp. 153–195). Springer. doi:10.1007/978-1-4939-1456-2_6

Ding, S. F., Xu, X. Z., & Nie, R. (2014). Extreme learning machine and its applications. *Neural Computing & Applications*, *25*(3-4), 549–556. doi:10.1007/s00521-013-1522-8

Domingos, P. (2012). A few useful things to know about ML. *Communications of the ACM*, *55*(10), 78–87. doi:10.1145/2347736.2347755

Dong, L., Lin, Z., Liang, Y., He, L., Zhang, N., & Chen, Q. et al. (2016). A Hierarchical Distributed Processing Framework for Big Image Data. *J. Latex Cl. Files.*, *20*, 1–13.

Fayyad, U., Piatetsky-Shapiro, G., & Smyth, P. (1996). From Data Mining to Knowledge Discovery in Databases. *AI Magazine*, *17*, 37–54. doi:10.1609/aimag.v17i3.1230

Feng, J., & Darrell, T. (2015). Learning the Structure of Deep Convolutional Networks. In *Proceedings of the 2015 IEEE Int. Conf. Comput. Vis.* (pp. 2749–2757). doi:10.1109/ICCV.2015.315

Gandomi, A., & Haider, M. (2015). Beyond the hype: Big data concepts, methods, and analytics. *International Journal of Information Management*, *35*(2), 137–144. doi:10.1016/j.ijinfomgt.2014.10.007

Goodfellow, I. J., Erhan, D., Luc Carrier, P., Courville, A., Mirza, M., Hamner, B., & Bengio, Y. et al. (2015). Challenges in representation learning: A report on three ML contests. *Neural Networks*, *64*, 59–63. doi:10.1016/j.neunet.2014.09.005 PMID:25613956

Heger, D. A. (n. d.). An Introduction to Artificial Neural Networks (ANN) - Methods, Abstraction, and Usage. Retrieved from http://www.dhtusa.com/media/NeuralNetworkIntro.pdf

Hinton, G., Deng, L., Yu, D., Dahl, G., Mohamed, A. R., Jaitly, N., & Kingsbury, B. et al. (2012). Deep neural networks for acoustic modeling in speech recognition: The shared views of four research groups. *IEEE Signal Processing Magazine*, *29*(6), 82–97. doi:10.1109/MSP.2012.2205597

Hinton, G. E., Osindero, S., & Teh, Y.-W. Y. (2006). A fast learning algorithm for deep belief nets. *Neural Computation, 18*(7), 1527–1554. doi:10.1162/neco.2006.18.7.1527 PMID:16764513

Hu, W., Qian, Y., Soong, F. K., & Wang, Y. (2015). Improved mispronunciation detection with deep neural network trained acoustic models and transfer learning based logistic regression classifiers. *Speech Communication, 67*, 154–166. doi:10.1016/j.specom.2014.12.008

Huang, G.-B., Zhu, Q., & Siew, C. (2006). Extreme learning machine: Theory and applications. *Neurocomputing, 70*(1-3), 489–501. doi:10.1016/j.neucom.2005.12.126

Imperva. (2015). Top Ten Database Threats. Retrieved from https://www.imperva.com/docs/gated/WP_TopTen_Database_Threats.pdf

Jacob, A. (2009). The pathologies of big data. *Communications of the ACM, 52*(8), 36–44. doi:10.1145/1536616.1536632

Jolliffe, I. T. (2002). *Principal Component Analysis*. New York: Springer.

Jones, N. (2014). The learning machines. *Nature, 505*(7482), 146–148. doi:10.1038/505146a PMID:24402264

Kalanat, N., & Kangavari, M. R. (2015). Data Mining Methods for Rule Designing and Rule Triggering in Active Database Systems. *Int. J. Database Theory Appl., 8*(1), 39–44. doi:10.14257/ijdta.2015.8.1.05

Karpinets, T. V., Park, B. H., & Uberbacher, E. C. (2012). Analyzing large biological datasets with association networks. *Nucleic Acids Research, 40*(17), e131. doi:10.1093/nar/gks403 PMID:22638576

Kashyap, H., Ahmed, H. A., Hoque, N., Roy, S., & Bhattacharyya, D. K. (2014). Big Data Analytics in Bioinformatics: A ML Perspective. *J. LATEX Cl. FILES., 13*, 1–20.

Kaur, P., & Kaur, P. (2016). A Review on Cloud Computing: Backbone Technologies, Fundaments & Challenges. *Int. J. Eng. Appl. Sci. Technol., 1*, 123–129.

Koyuturk, M., Grama, A., & Ramakrishnan, N. (2005). Compression, clustering, and pattern discovery in very high-dimensional discrete-attribute data sets. *IEEE Transactions on Knowledge and Data Engineering, 17*(4), 447–461. doi:10.1109/TKDE.2005.55

L. 0. Hall, N. Chawla, K.W. Bowyer, Decision Tree Learning on Very Large Data Sets, IEEE, 1998.

Landset, S., Khoshgoftaar, T. M., Richter, A. N., & Hasanin, T. (2015). A survey of open source tools for ML with big data in the Hadoop ecosystem. *J. Big Data.*, *2*(1), 24. doi:10.1186/s40537-015-0032-1

Le Callet, P., Viard-Gaudin, C., & Barba, D. (2006). A convolutional neural network approach for objective video quality assessment. *IEEE Transactions on Neural Networks*, *17*(5), 1316–1327. doi:10.1109/TNN.2006.879766 PMID:17001990

Li, S., Dragicevic, S., Anton, F., Sester, M., Winter, S., Coltekin, A., ... (2015). Geospatial Big Data Handling Theory and Methods: A Review and Research Challenges. Retrieved from https://arxiv.org/ftp/arxiv/papers/1511/1511.03010.pdf

Looks, M., Levine, A., Covington, G. A., Loui, R. P., Lockwood, J. W., & Cho, Y. H. (2007). *Streaming Hierarchical Clustering for Concept Mining. In Proceedings of the 2007 IEEE Aerosp. Conf.* (pp. 1–12). IEEE. doi:10.1109/AERO.2007.352792

Lopez-Moreno, I., Gonzalez-Dominguez, J., Martinez, D., Plchot, O., Gonzalez-Rodriguez, J., & Moreno, P. J. (2016). On the use of deep feedforward neural networks for automatic language identification. *Computer Speech & Language*, *40*, 46–59. doi:10.1016/j.csl.2016.03.001

Lu, Y.-L., & Fahn, C.-S. (2007). Hierarchical Artificial Neural Networks for Recognizing High Similar Large Data Sets. In *Proceedings of the 2007 Int. Conf. Mach. Learn. Cybern.* (pp. 1930–1935). doi:10.1109/ICMLC.2007.4370463

Lynch, C. (2008). Big data: How do your data grow? *Nature*, *455*(7209), 28–29. doi:10.1038/455028a PMID:18769419

Mani, S., Shankle, W. R., Dick, M. B., & Pazzani, M. J. (1998). Two-Stage ML Model for Guideline Development. Retrieved from http://www.ics.uci.edu/~pazzani/Publications/two_stage_ml.pdf

Molodtsov, D. (1999). Soft set theory—First results. *Computers & Mathematics with Applications (Oxford, England)*, *37*(4-5), 19–31. doi:10.1016/S0898-1221(99)00056-5

Moujahid, A. (2016). A Practical Introduction to DL with Caffe and Python. Retrieved August 27, 2016 from http://adilmoujahid.com/posts/2016/06/introduction-deep-learning-python-caffe/

Mulanee, A., Shaikh, A., Dhavale, H., Lambate, S., & Teke, A. R. (2015). Database Security Against Intrusion. *Int. J. Adv. Eng. Glob. Technol.*, *3*, 560–566. http://ijaegt.com/wp-content/uploads/2014/12/409440-pp-560-566-shaik.pdf

Najafabadi, M. M., Villanustre, F., Khoshgoftaar, T. M., Seliya, N., Wald, R., & Muharemagic, E. (2015). DL applications and challenges in big data analytics. *J. Big Data.*, *2*(1), 1–21. doi:10.1186/s40537-014-0007-7

Namey, E., Guest, G., Thairu, L., & Johnson, L. (2007). Data Reduction Techniques for Large Qualitative Data Sets. In G. Guest & K. M. MacQueen (Eds.), *Handbook for team-based qualitative research* (pp. 137–163). Rowman Altamira, United kingdom: Team-Based Qual. Res.

Natarajan, S., Joshi, S., Saha, B., Edwards, A., Khot, T., Moody, E., ... (2012). A ML Pipeline for Three-way Classification of Alzheimer Patients from Structural Magnetic Resonance Images of the Brain. *Int. J. Mach. Learn. Cybern.*, *5*, 659–669. Retrieved from http://pages.cs.wisc.edu/~tushar/papers/icmla12.pdf

Nithya, B. (2016). An Analysis on Applications of ML Tools, Techniques and Practices in Health Care System. *Int. J. Adv. Res. Comput. Sci. Softw. Eng.*, *6*(6), 1–8.

Patil, D. V., & Bichkar, R. S. (2006). A Hybrid Evolutionary Approach To Construct Optimal Decision Trees With Large Data Sets. In *Proceedings of the 2006 IEEE Int. Conf. Ind. Technol.* (pp. 429–433). doi:10.1109/ICIT.2006.372250

Pawlak, Z. (1982). Rough sets. *Int. J. Comput. Inf. Sci.*, *11*(5), 341–356. doi:10.1007/BF01001956

Peters, J. F. (2007). Near Sets. General Theory About Nearness of Objects. *Appl. Math. Sci.*, *1*, 2609–2629.

Qiu, J., Wu, Q., Ding, G., Xu, Y., & Feng, S. (2016). A survey of ML for big data processing. doi:.10.1186/s13634-016-0355-x

Raja, C., & Rabbani, M. A. (2014). Big Data Analytics Security Issues in Data Driven Information System. *Int. J. Innov. Res. Comput. Commun. Eng.*, *2*, 6132–6135.

Rajkumar, D., & Usha, S. (2016). A Survey on Big Data Mining Platforms, Algorithms and Handling Techniques. Int. J. Res. Emerg. Sci. Technol., 3, 50–55. Retrieved from http://ijrest.net/downloads/volume-3/special-issue/ncrtct-16/pid-ijrest-3s1ncrtct2016018.pdf

Reshef, Y. A., Reshef, D. N., Sabeti, P. C., & Mitzenmacher, M. (2015). Theoretical Foundations of Equitability and the Maximal Information Coefficient. Retrieved from https://arxiv.org/pdf/1408.4908.pdf

Reshef, D. N., Reshef, Y. A., Finucane, H. K., Grossman, S. R., McVean, G., Turnbaugh, P. J., ... & Sabeti, P. C. (2011). Detecting novel associations in large data sets. *science*, *334*(6062), 1518-1524. doi:.10.1126/science.1205438

Setia, L. (2008). Strategies for Content Based Image Retrieval. Albert-Ludwigs-University. Retrieved from https://www.freidok.uni-freiburg.de/fedora/objects/freidok:6150/datastreams/FILE1/content

Shirudkar, K., & Motwani, D. (2015). Big-Data Security. *Int. J. Adv. Res. Comput. Sci. Softw. Eng.*, *5*, 1100–1109.

Singh, A., Chaudhary, M., Rana, A., & Dubey, G. (2011). Online Mining of data to generate association rule mining in large databases. In *Proceedings of the 2011 Int. Conf. Recent Trends Inf. Syst.* (pp. 126–131). doi:10.1109/ReTIS.2011.6146853

Singh, P., & Suri, B. (2014). Quality assessment of data using statistical and ML methods. In L. C. Jain, H. S. Behera, J. K. Mandal, & D. P. Mohapatra (Eds.), *Comput* (2nd ed., pp. 89–97). Intell. Data Min.

Sivarajah, U., Kamal, M. M., Irani, Z., & Weerakkody, V. (2016). Critical analysis of Big Data challenges and analytical methods. *Journal of Business Research*. doi:10.1016/j.jbusres.2016.08.001

Suryawanshi, S. S., Mulani, T., Zanjurne, S., Inarkar, K., & Jambhulkar, A. (2015). Database Intrusion Detection and Protection System Using Log Mining and Forensic Analysis. *Int. J. Comput. Sci. Inf. Technol.*, *6*, 5059–5061.

Tsai, C., Lai, C., Chiang, M., & Yang, L. (2014). Data mining for internet of things: A survey. *IEEE Communications Surveys and Tutorials*, *16*(1), 77–97. doi:10.1109/SURV.2013.103013.00206

Tsai, C. W., La, C. F., Chao, H. C., & Vasilakos, A. V. (2015). Big data analytics: A survey. *J. Big Data.*, *2*(1), 1–32. doi:10.1186/s40537-015-0030-3 PMID:26191487

Tsai, C. W., La, C. F., Chao, H. C., & Vasilakos, A. V. (2015). Big data analytics: A survey. *J. Big Data.*, *2*(1), 1–32. doi:10.1186/s40537-015-0030-3 PMID:26191487

Tsang, S., Kao, B., Yip, K. Y., Ho, W. S., & Lee, S. D. (2011). Decision trees for uncertain data. *Knowl. Data Eng. IEEE Trans.*, *23*(1), 64–78. doi:10.1109/TKDE.2009.175

Tulasi, B., Wagh, R. S., & Balaji, S. (2015). High Performance Computing and Big Data Analytics – Paradigms and Challenges. *International Journal of Computers and Applications*, *116*(2), 28–33. doi:10.5120/20311-2356

UK Data Archive. (2011). Managing and Sharing Data. Retrieved from http://www.data-archive.ac.uk/media/2894/managingsharing.pdf

Vadivel, M., & Raghunath, V. (2014). Enhancing Map-Reduce Framework for Bigdata with Hierarchical Clustering. *Int. J. Innov. Res. Comput. Commun. Eng.*, *2*, 490–498.

Vijayalakshmi, M., & Devi, M. R. (2012). A Survey of Different Issue of Different clustering Algorithms Used in Large Data sets. *Int. J. Adv. Res. Comput. Sci. Softw. Eng.*, *2*(3), 304–307. Retrieved fromhttp://www.ijarcsse.com/docs/papers/March2012/volume_2_Issue_3/V2I300137.pdf

Vincent, P., Larochelle, H., Bengio, Y., & Manzagol, P.-A. (2008). Extracting and composing robust features with denoising autoencoders. In Proc. of the 25th Int. Conf. Mach. Learn. ICML '08 (pp. 1096–1103). New York, NY: ACM. doi:10.1145/1390156.1390294

Wadhwa, A., & Madhow, U. (2014). Bottom-up DL using the Hebbian Principle. Retrieved from http://www.ece.ucsb.edu/wcsl/people/aseem/Aseem_stuff/hebbian_preprint.pdf

Wang, L., Wang, G., & Sng, D. (2015). DL Algorithms with Applications to Video Analytics for A Smart City: A Survey.

Wang, S., Gan, W., Li, D., & Li, D. (2011). Data Field for Hierarchical Clustering. *International Journal of Data Warehousing and Mining*, *7*(4), 43–63. doi:10.4018/jdwm.2011100103

Wang, Y., Yu, D., Ju, Y., & Acero, A. (2011). Voice search. In *Lang. Underst. Syst. Extr. Semant. Inf. from Speech*. New York: Wiley. doi:10.1002/9781119992691.ch5

Wille, R. (2005). Formal concept analysis as mathematical theory of concept and concept hierarchies. In Form. Concept Anal. Springer. doi:10.1007/11528784_1

Wu, C., Buyya, R., & Ramamohanarao, K. (2016). Big Data Analytics = ML + Cloud Computing. Retrieved from https://arxiv.org/ftp/arxiv/papers/1601/1601.03115.pdf

Wu, Q., Ding, G., Wang, J., & Yao, Y. D. (2013). Spatial-temporal opportunity detection for spectrum-heterogeneous cognitive radio networks: Two-dimensional sensing. *IEEE Transactions on Wireless Communications*, *12*(2), 516–526. doi:10.1109/TWC.2012.122212.111638

Wu, X., Zhu, X., Wu, G. Q., & Ding, W. (2014). Data mining with big data. *IEEE Transactions on Knowledge and Data Engineering*, *26*(1), 97–107. doi:10.1109/TKDE.2013.109

Yu, D., & Deng, L. (2011). DL and Its Applications to Signal and Information Processing. *IEEE Signal Processing Magazine*, *28*, 145–150. doi:10.1109/MSP.2010.939038

Zhou, G., Sohn, K., & Lee, H. (2012). Online incremental feature learning with denoising autoencoders. In Proceedings of the Int. Conf. Artif. Intell. Stat. (pp. 1453–1461).

Zhu, H., Xu, Z., & Huang, Y. (2015). Research on the security technology of big data information. In *Proceedings of the Int. Conf. Inf. Technol. Manag. Innov.* (pp. 1041–1044).

Chapter 6
Big Data Analytics:
An Expedition Through Rapidly Budding Data Exhaustive Era

Sreenu G.
Muthoot Institute of Technology and Science, India

M.A. Saleem Durai
VIT University, India

ABSTRACT

Advances in recent hardware technology have permitted to document transactions and other pieces of information of everyday life at an express pace. In addition of speed up and storage capacity, real-life perceptions tend to transform over time. However, there are so much prospective and highly functional values unseen in the vast volume of data. For this kind of applications conventional data mining is not suitable, so they should be tuned and changed or designed with new algorithms. Big data computing is inflowing to the category of most hopeful technologies that shows the way to new ways of thinking and decision making. This epoch of big data helps users to take benefit out of all available data to gain more precise systematic results or determine latent information, and then make best possible decisions. Depiction from a broad set of workloads, the author establishes a set of classifying measures based on the storage architecture, processing types, processing techniques and the tools and technologies used.

DOI: 10.4018/978-1-5225-2863-0.ch006

INTRODUCTION

Big data is a latest happening with the potential to trans-form the values of products and services in industry and business. A definition for big data is given by ("Big Data," n. d.) as "Big data is high-volume, high-velocity, and high-variety information assets that demand cost-effective, innovative forms of information processing for enhanced insight and decision making."

Rapid advancements in technical knowledge and networking lead to tremendous growth of information in all fields such as education, health science and business. The materialization of novel technologies such as Internet, Network-of-Things and large scale wireless sensor systems facilitates the gathering of data from an increasing volume, velocity and variety of networked sensors for analysis. Data volume corresponds to the magnitude of data that can be warehoused and evaluated. Data velocity symbolizes the speed of data aggregation and streaming. Data variety point towards various sources of data's such as images, audio, text, video, etc. Veracity refers to disorderliness or reliability of data.

The progresses of computer systems as well as internet technologies as per Moore's law witnessed the fact that the difficulties of managing the extensive data still occur at the age of big data. Heterogeneous nature of data leads to the classification such as structured and unstructured data. The fact that science is lagging behind the real world in the proficiencies of handling large volume of data and realizing useful facts from immense volume of data. Techniques to develop architecture capable of handling massive volume of data comprise various hardware capabilities and various programming models.

The enormous growth of data needs enhancement from old-fashioned data processing solutions to systems which handles a constant stream of real time data. Several distributed stream processing engines are also taken for a review. Applications which need valuable analyses of huge datasets are widely increasing nowadays. As a result, data evolution will primarily outperform expected improvements in the cost and concentration of storage technologies, the reachable computational power for processing it, and the connected energy path. Discussion of these methods is described in following section of this chapter. The data processing section will analyze various mining techniques developed for processing big data. Various tools used to make the big data processing easier will be discussed.

ORGANIZATION OF BIG DATA

The way of capturing and storing data has been changed by the arrival of big data. Disk access latencies are reduced by the introduction of storage technologies like solid state drive (SSD) (Hutchinson, 2012) and phase-change memory (PCM) (Pirovano et al., 2003). But these technologies are not good enough by having lot of draw backs and limitations.

In a nutshell managing big data means having an infrastructure which is scalable, able to handle large volume of multi-formatted data and fault tolerant with a high degree of parallelism and a distributed data processing. According to Brewer's CAP (Brewer, 2000) theorem it is impossible to assurance steadiness along with high availability in the presence of partitions. Due to the presence of large number of replicas, any modification made in data should reflect that in all available copies to ensure consistency. Depending on the application the consistency level varies. Sensitive information like electronic medical records, bank accounts should be consistent.

TECHNIQUES AND TECHNOLOGIES FOR HANDLING BIG DATA

The various techniques involved in big data scenario covers various arenas including statistics, data mining, machine learning, neural networks and optimization methods. Statistical techniques explore the correlation and causal relationship between different objectives. Data mining techniques extract valuable pattern from data through clustering, classification, regression and association rules. Big data mining techniques extend the existing algorithms to deal with huge amount of data. The main feature of machine learning is to absorb information and construct intellectual conclusions automatically.

Technology Innovation Leads to Software Approaches like Map Reduce, No SQL

In conjunction with evolved storage architecture, the data processing techniques are to be advanced furthermore. Current technology focuses on three classes of data processing, namely, batch processing, stream processing and interactive processing. Resource utilization is enhanced due to the increasing gap between magnitude of data and compute power. Datacenters having very huge clusters of commodity hardware and the technology of cloud computing are already existing solutions. Distributed software running on clustered architectures is capable to with strand failures through the presence of replicas.

Handling structured data comprises two parts, one is a schema to store the data set, and other is a relational database for data retrieval. Data warehouses and data marts are two popular approaches for structured data. Unstructured data can be modeled using NoSQL (Han et al., 2011) data base. No SQL data base can be classified into different categories like Key-value, Graph database, Document-oriented and Column family. Horizontal scalability is not possible in relational data base. Big data distributed across nodes in a distributed system must ensure horizontal scalability. That is one of the features of NoSQL database.

Multi core processors also challenged to handle big data which introduced parallel computing. Google's Map Reduce (Dean et al, 2004) is one data processing model which efficiently developed applications on distributed systems which are both scalable and fault tolerant. Map Reduce and its open-source version Hadoop (Dean et al, 2004) are popular in the big-data analysis because of its minimalism and ease-of-programming. Optimization of data and optimization of memory access patterns are also required before entering into Map Reduce program.

Big Data Optimization

Different techniques like simulated annealing (Chen et al, 2014), quantum annealing and adaptive simulated annealing are strategies used for handling optimization problems in various fields. Genetic algorithms, which are naturally lending to parallelism, can be highly proficient. The specific techniques which are inspired by nature like stochastic optimization, together with genetic programming, evolutionary programming, plus particle swarm optimization are advantageous in various fields. Real-time optimization namely WSNs and ITSs are required in any big data applications. Other techniques like are Data reduction and parallelization are also alternative approaches in optimization problems.

Architecture Behind Batch Processing

1.   Apache Hadoop

Data-rich distributed applications can be organized very well using the Apache Hadoop software. From data acquisition to data analysis data management can be done through a variety of tools. Majority of these tools are components of Apache projects and they are built around the Hadoop. One of the main components in Apache Hadoop platform is distributed file system (HDFS). The Hadoop Distributed File System (HDFS) is a distributed file system intended to run on commodity hardware. HDFS is extremely fault tolerant, having high throughput access to data.

MapReduce job accepts as input a list of key value pairs and put on a programmer-defined function on each pair in the list. The intermediate output contains list of keys and their associated value lists. The reduce phase of the MapReduce job uses this intermediary output data as input and perform another user defined function on each combination of key and value list. Figure1 gives an overview about MapReduce.

Figure 1. MapReduce overview: Map/reduce overview: solid arrows are for Map flows, and feint arrows are for reduce flows (Dean et al, 2014)

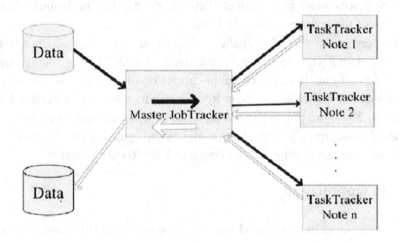

2.   Dryad

Dryad (Isard et al., 2007) bases on dataflow graph processing model. The model can be scaled from a very small cluster to a large cluster for implementing parallel and distributed programs. Dryad offers a number of functionalities consist of generating the job graph, scheduling the processes on the existing machines, managing transient failures in the cluster, gathering performance metrics, picturing the job, invoking user defined policies and dynamically informing the job graph in response to these policy decisions, without attentiveness of the semantics of the vertices. Figure 2 explains the implementation diagram of Dryad. The centralized job manager present in Dryad supervises every Dryad job and that applies a small set of cluster services to control the execution of the vertices on the cluster.

Architecture Behind Stream Processing

Applications like processing log files, sensor data and telematics wants real-time reply for processing huge amount of stream data. Stream data is another category of big data. Stream data flow in and out of a computer system constantly and with fluctuating update rates. They are temporally ordered. Since Map/Reduce framework has to face lot of challenges when data streams in real time gets processed. Consequently, the real-time Big Data platforms, such as, Storm (2012), SQLstream (sqlstream, 2012) are designed particularly for real-time stream data analytics. A stream is a series of abundant tuples of the form $(a_1, a_2, a_3, ..., a_n, t)$ generated continuously in

Figure 2. The structure of dryad jobs (Dean et al, 2014)

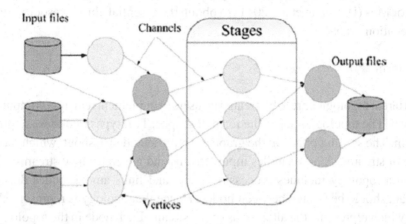

time. Here a_i denotes an attribute and t denotes the time. Stream processing absorbs processing data before storing and Hadoop like batch systems process after storing.

The requirements of a distributed stream processing engine can be listed as Data Mobility, High availability and data processing guarantees, Data Partitioning, Data Querying, Deterministic or non-deterministic processing, Data storage and Handling stream imperfections. The distributed streaming applications are arranged in DSPFs running on big clusters. Figure 3 shows the architecture. The top layer describes the user APIs where a streaming application is defined as a graph. The events stream through the edges of this graph and processing takes place at the nodes. The user graph is then transformed to an execution graph and components of this are distributed to a set of workers/executors across a cluster of nodes. Network communications are stable among the workers to complete the graph. The bottom three layers can

Figure 3. DSPF Layered architecture (Hjelmervik et al., 2016)

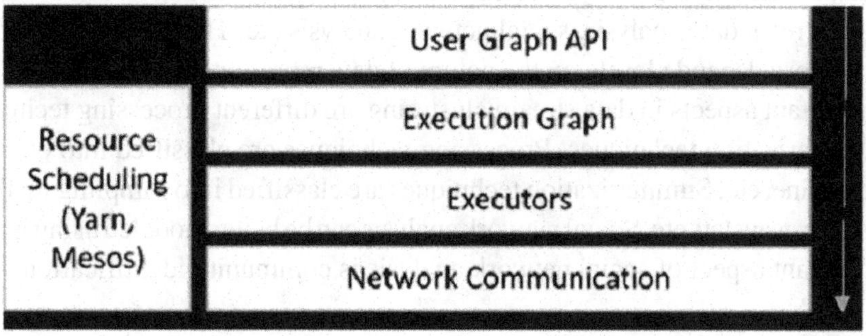

Resource Scheduling (Yarn, Mesos)	User Graph API
	Execution Graph
	Executors
	Network Communication

work with a resource management layer such as Apache Yarn (Vavilapalli et al., 2013) or Mes (Hindman et al., 2011) to obtain the essential cluster resources to run the execution graph.

1.   Storm

Different topologies are to be created by users to implement real time computation on storm. The topologies are in the form of graphs. Two types of nodes are present in storm. The starting points in the graph are represented by a spout, which indicate source of streams. A bolt handles input streams and generates new streams. Every node in a topology includes processing logic, and links among nodes designate how data should be treated between nodes. Hence the topology is represented as a graph which represents the alterations of the stream. Each node in the topology can be executed in parallel. Storm cluster includes one master node and several worker nodes. Two types of daemons namely Nimbus and Supervisor are implemented by master node and worker node respectively. Nimbus will recognize failures in the network and re execute the corresponding job. The supervisor obeys the tasks assigned by nimbus.

2.   SQL Stream

NoDatabase technology or in-memory processing are employed in SQL stream. Using streaming SQL queries the stream data is processed in memory. Intelligent and automatic operations are performed using SQL stream. The data is not stored in disks. The technology is really fast due to the memory nature.

INNOVATIVE TECHNIQUES FOR ANALYSING BIG DATA IN VARIOUS FIELDS TO GENERATE USEFUL PATTERNS

The chapter classifying analysis techniques into different categories like big data analysis, stream data analysis, social network analysis etc. The methods adopted in each category depend closely on the nature of data representation in each category. The important aspects in data stream clustering are different processing techniques and summarization techniques. Processing techniques are classified into one pass, online offline, etc. Summarization techniques are classified into sampling methods, histograms, wavelets etc. Social network analysis can be better modeled using graphs. An important aspect of social network analysis is community identification.

The nodes represent entities and edges represent the relationship between nodes. The labeled edges represent the degree of relationship. Social network graphs can be undirected like Facebook friends graph and can be directed graphs like graphs of followers on Twitter. The solutions provided for each category are discussed below briefly.

Interactive Exploration of Big Scientific Data: New Representations and Techniques (Hjelmervik et al, 2016)

Group of new generation techniques are required to allow truly interactive techniques for huge scientific data visualization. Those techniques stabilize the use of up to date technologies from high-performance computing towards pixel-accurate rendering on thin clients. Set of new representations which suits different architectures and data types are needed. The paper investigates use of splines for producing higher-order representations to trimly represent dense data. CAD technology is using splines for long years. Recent research results show that splines are going to play effective role in big data exploration techniques.

Existing methods like finite-element meshes or voxel grids are too fussy to be transmitted over a network. Techniques that are adaptable to GPU's are needed. One solution is to use higher-order representations that are able to compactly represent dense data. Smooth representations do need more computations, but GPUs are improved at doing computations than moving data.

An Efficient and Fine-grained Big Data Access Control Scheme With Privacy-Preserving Policy (Yang et al, 2016)

When big data are warehoused in the cloud the main challenging issue is data security through access control. Ciphertext-Policy Attribute based Encryption (CP-ABE) is a hopeful encryption method that allows end-users to encrypt their data below the access policies. The attribute values are partially hidden in existing methods. This paper suggests a well-organized and fine-gained big data access control method with privacy-preserving strategy. Rather than the attribute values, complete attributes are concealed in the access policy. An Attribute Bloom Filter is designed to assess whether an attribute is in the access policy and trace the exact position. The method contains four phases namely System Setup, Key Generation, Data Encryption and Data Decryption.

A Cloud Reservation System for Big Data Applications (Marinescu et al., 2016)

Upcoming Big Data applications more and more require resources further than those available from a single server and may be articulated as a complex workflow of many components in a cloud environment. These kinds of applications can be expressed as a resource management problem in cloud. This paper suggests a protocol having two stages. The first stage will form rack-level coalitions of servers to execute a work flow component. We also presume that all servers in a rack are identical from one another, but different in each rack. The second stage builds a package of these coalitions, which are designed to support all the components in the complete workflow. The advantage over existing models is that lower overhead for resource aggregation. A comparative analysis is made between two strategies namely history based and just in time. The results show that History-based strategy performs much better at high system load than the Just-in-time one.

SeLINA: A Self-Learning Insightful Network Analyzer (Apiletti et al., 2016)

SeLINA can be easily exploited to investigate excessive collections of network data. Evaluating the behavior of a network from a large-scale traffic dataset is a demanding problem. Big data frameworks suggest scalable algorithms to extract information from raw data, but necessitate a complicated fine-tuning and a thorough knowledge of machine learning algorithms. To reorganize this process, the paper proposes self-learning insightful network analyzer (SeLINA), a simple tool to dig out knowledge from network traffic dimensions. SeLINA provides self-learning abilities to modern scalable approaches. The paper combines both unsupervised and supervised methodologies to mine data with a scalable tactic. The method implants procedures to evaluate whether the data fits the model, if not start model rebuilding. SeLINA currently implemented on Apache Spark. The experimental results established the ability of SeLINA to provide insight and perceive changes in the data which recommend advance analyses.

A Parallel Random Forest Algorithm for Big Data in a Spark Cloud Computing Environment (Chen et al., 2016)

The paper suggests a Parallel Random Forest (PRF) algorithm meant for big data on the Apache Spark platform. Data-parallel and task-parallel optimizations are used to optimize the PRF algorithm based on a hybrid approach. A vertical data-partitioning technique is executed to lessen the data communication cost. As part of task parallel optimization task Directed Acyclic Graph (DAG) is created according to the parallel training process of PRF and the requirement of the Resilient Distributed Datasets (RDD) objects. Different task schedulers are then summoned for the tasks in the DAG.A dimension-reduction method in the training process and a weighted voting method in the prediction process are applied before parallelization to progress the algorithm's correctness for high-dimensional and noisy data.

Heterogeneous Cooperative Co-evolution Memetic Differential Evolution Algorithms for Big Data Optimisation Problems (Sabar et al., 2016)

Evolutionary algorithms (EAs) are proposed as candidate for solving big data optimization problems. When handling big data EA's have scalability issues. It is difficult to design a single EA which outstrips all other methods. The paper suggests the cooperative co-evolution technique to divide the big problem into small sub-problems in order to broaden the competence of the solving process. Different memetic algorithms are used to solve the sub problems. The framework suggested in the paper adaptively assigns, for each solution, different operators and parameter values. Experimental results reveal that the projected algorithm performs better than algorithms without cooperative co-evolution method.

Solutions for Processing Data Streams

1. A fast density-based data stream clustering algorithm with cluster centers self-determined for mixed data (Chen et al., 2016)

Most data streams come across in real life are data objects with diverse attributes. Currently most data stream algorithms have insufficiencies including little clustering quality, difficulties in defining cluster centers, poor capacity for dealing with outliers. Mixed data sets are trooped into three types based on data attribute relationships analysis. The outliers of the graph can be spotted through linear regression model and residuals analysis which are centered on field intensity-distance distribution graph for each data object. Once the cluster center is established all objects can be clustered according to their distance with center. Two stages of processing namely online/offline processing are adopted by the algorithm. The data objects arriving are preserved by two-stage processing framework, and a new micro cluster characteristic vector.

2. Penalty parameter selection for hierarchical data stream clustering (AmolBhagat et al., 2016)

Recognizing the number of clusters necessary for the accurate clustering of data streams is an open research area. This paper reviews the hierarchical data stream clustering algorithms. Besides that, it also compares the performance analysis of the different hierarchical clustering techniques for data streams. Different data clustering tools are enlightened and compared in the paper. These papers deal with the issue of identifying the number of clusters through proposed penalty parameter selection approach. The penalty parameters are identified by analyzing performance parameters used in various hierarchical clustering techniques. The performance parameters used in the paper are precision, recall, purity, G-precision and G-Recall.

3.   Micro-Batching Growing Neural Gas for Clustering Data Streams using Spark Streaming (Ghesmoune et al., 2015)

The proposed MBG-Stream is a proficient method for topological clustering on a developing data stream in an online manner. Here the nodes are weighted by a fading function and the edges by an exponential function. MBG-Stream is executed on a distributed streaming platform based on the micro-batching processing model. The effectiveness and proficiency of MBG-Stream in discovering clusters of random shape is demonstrated by experimental assessment over a number of real and synthetic data sets. MBG-Stream is apprehended on a distributed streaming platform based on the micro batching processing model, i.e., the Spark Streaming API. A graph is used to represent the topological structure. Each node represents a cluster, and neighboring nodes (clusters) are connected by edges. The graph size develops through each iteration. The method suggests an exponential fading function to reduce the impact of old data whose importance reduces over time. The links between nodes are also weighted by an exponential function.

Solutions for Social Network Analysis

1.   Graphical Evolutionary Game for Information Diffusion Over Social Networks (Chen et al., 2014)

The crucial challenge in managing social network analysis is the tremendous information flow. In such a situation, understanding information circulation over social networks has become an important research issue. Majority works on information dissemination analysis are based on either network structure modeling or experimental approach with dataset mining. In addition to that the information diffusion is heavily influenced by network users' choices, activities and their social connections. This paper proposes an evolutionary game theoretic framework to characterize the dynamic information dispersal process in social networks. Experiments show that the proposed work is effective and functional in modeling the social network user's information forwarding manners. The information diffusion ideas come from the research of spreading computer virus/epidemic over network. The basic idea employed is same as the idea behind game theory. The customary analysis of game theory is that a game with some particular rule is played among a group of static players and a static Nash equilibrium (NE) can be attained by evaluating the players' payoff, utility function and the game rule.

2.   **CAP:** Community Activity Prediction Based on Big Data Analysis (Zhang et al., 2014)

Crowd sensing attaches the power of the crowd by accumulating a large number of users carrying numerous mobile and networked devices to collect data with the intrinsic multi-modal and large-volume features. It is difficult to scrutinize the huge data volume created by crowd sensing. Still there are several individual approaches; the common features of individual activity have not been fully analyzed. This paper offers a new community-centric framework for community activity forecast based on big data analysis. Specifically, the method is to take out community activity patterns by examining the big data collected from both the physical world and virtual social space. The community detection is accomplished in the paper based on singular value decomposition and clustering, and community activity modeling based on tensors.

3.   **Friendbook:** A Semantic-Based Friend Recommendation System for Social Networks (Wang et al, 2015)

This system recommends friends to users not based on the social graph but based on their life style. By using of sensor-rich smart phones, the method learns life styles of users from user-centric sensor data, evaluate the similarity of life styles between users, and recommends friends to users if their life styles have high similarity. Motivation from text mining is used to model a user's daily life as life documents, from which his/her life styles are extracted by using the Latent Dirichlet Allocation algorithm. A similarity metric is proposed to measure the similarity of life styles between users, and calculate users' impact in terms of life styles with a friend-matching graph. After receiving a request, Friendbook returns a list of people with highest recommendation scores to the query user. Finally, assimilates a feedback mechanism to improve the accuracy of recommendations.

CONCLUSION

The term Big Data has been used to represent an era of data deluge. This chapter defines and differentiates the concept of Big Data along with a chain of technologies. Distributed storage systems are the result of these recent advancements in technology side. Various application specific optimization techniques are needed in future as the data sizes remain to grow and the areas of these applications diverge. This situation can be handled by discharging some of the computation to the sources itself to avoid the costly data movement costs. Recent hardware progresses have played a major role in appreciating the distributed software platforms desired for big-data analytics. The chapter classifies the area of big data into two different sub sections like big data organization and big data processing techniques. Recent solutions published under the field of big data are also discussed.

REFERENCES

Apiletti, D., Baralis, E., Cerquitelli, T., Garza, P., Giordano, D., Mellia, M., & Venturini, L. (2016). *SeLINA: A Self-Learning Insightful Network Analyzer*. IEEE.

Bhagat, A., Kshirsagar, N., Khodke, P., Dongre, K., & Ali, S. (2016). Penalty parameter selection for hierarchical data stream clustering.

Brewer, E. A. (2000). Towards robust distributed systems. In *Proc. 19th Annual ACM Symposium on Principles of Distributed Computing*.

Chen, C. P., & Zhang, C. Y. (2014). Data-intensive applications, challenges, techniques and technologies: A survey on Big Data. Elsevier.

Chen, J., Li, K., Tang, Z., Bilal, K., Yu, S., Weng, C., & Li, K. (2016). A Parallel Random Forest Algorithm for Big Data in a Spark Cloud Computing Environment.

Chen, J.Y., & He, H.H. (2016). A fast density-based data stream clustering algorithm with cluster centers self-determined for mixed data.

Dean, J., & Ghemawat, S. (2004). MapReduce: simplified data processing on large clusters.

Gartner. (n. d.). IT Glossary: Big Data. Retrieved from http://www.gartner.com/it-glossary/big-data

Ghesmoune, M., Lebbah, M., & Azzag, H. (2015). Micro-batching growing neural gas for clustering data streams using spark streaming.

Han, J., Haihong, E., Le, G., & Du, J. (2011). Survey on nosql database. In *Proceedings of the 2011 6th International Conference on Pervasive Computing and Applications*.

Hindman, B., Konwinski, A., Zaharia, M., Ghodsi, A., Joseph, A. D., Katz, R. H., ... & Stoica, I. (2011). Mesos: A Platform for Fine Grained Resource Sharing in the Data Center. In *NSDI* (Vol. 11, pp. 22-22).

Hjelmervik, J. M., & Barrowclough, O. J. D. (2016). *Interactive Exploration of Big Scientific Data: New Representations and Techniques*. IEEE.

Hutchinson, L. (2012). Solid-state revolution: in-depth on how ssds really work. ArsTechnica.

Isard, M., Budiu, M., Yu, Y., Birrell, A., & Fetterly, D. (2007). Dryad: distributed data-parallel programs from sequential building blocks. In *Proceedings of the 2nd ACM SIGOPS/EuroSys European Conference on Computer Systems EuroSys '07*.

Jiang, C., Chen, Y., & Ray Liu, K. J. (2014). *Graphical Evolutionary Game for Information Diffusion Over Social Networks*.

Kamburugamuve, S., & Fox, G. (2016). *Survey of Distributed Stream Processing*. Bloomington, IN: Indiana University.

Marinescu, D. C., Paya, A., & Morrison, J. P. (2016). A Cloud Reservation System for Big Data Applications.

Pirovano, A., Lacaita, A. L., Benvenuti, A., Pellizzer, F., Hudgens, S., & Bez, R. (2003). Scaling analysis of phase-change memory technology. In *Proceedings of the IEEE Int. Electron Dev. Meeting* (pp. 29.6.1–29.6.4).

Sabar, N. R., Abawajy, J., & Yearwood, J. (2016). Heterogeneous Cooperative Co-evolution Memetic Differential Evolution Algorithms for Big Data Optimisation Problems.

Sqlstream. (2012). Retrieved from http://www.sqlstream.com/products/server/

Storm. (2012). Retrieved from http://storm-project.net/

Vavilapalli, V. K., Murthy, A. C., Douglas, C., Agarwal, S., Konar, M., Evans, R., ... & Saha, B. (2013). Apache hadoop yarn: Yet another resource negotiator. In *Proceedings of the 4th annual Symposium on Cloud Computing* (p. 5). doi:10.1145/2523616.2523633

Wang, Z., Liao, J., Cao, Q., Qi, H., & Wang, Z. (2015). Friendbook: A Semantic-Based Friend Recommendation System for Social Networks.

Yang, K., Han, Q., Li, H., Zheng, K., Su, Z., & Shen, X. (2016). An Efficient and Fine-grained Big Data Access Control Scheme with Privacy-preserving Policy.

Zhang, Y., Chen, M., Mao, S., Hu, L., & Leung, V. C. M. (2014). *CAP: Community Activity Prediction Based on Big Data Analysis*.

Chapter 7
Prediction of Cancer Disease Using Classification Techniques in Map Reduce Programming Model

M. A. Saleem Durai
VIT University, India

Anbarasi M.
VIT University, India

Jaiti Handa
VIT University, India

ABSTRACT

As the volume of data is increasing with time the primary issue is how to store and process such data and get useful information out of it. Analysis of classification algorithms and MapReduce programming model has led to the conclusion that the distributed file system and parallel computing attributes of MapReduce are good for designing classifier model. The major reason for it is parallel processing of data in which data is divided and processed in parallel and the output from each is reduced further for a single output. In this paper, we are going to study how to use MapReduce model to build classifier model. We are using cancer dataset to predict if a person has cancer or not by using Naive Bayes and KNN classification algorithms. We have compared them on the basis on computational time and the factors like sensitivity, specificity, and accuracy. In the end, we would be able to compare these two algorithms and tell which one works better on MapReduce programming model

DOI: 10.4018/978-1-5225-2863-0.ch007

1. INTRODUCTION

"The amount of data that was generated during the last couple of years accounts to 95% of the total data" With the advancement of new technologies, increased usage of social networking sites, need of storing the data for analysis purpose is of utmost importance. Until yesterday the data you stored on the servers in your company was simply data, then suddenly a term emerges Big Data; this term refers to each and every bit of data you have stored till date. It includes even the URL's you have been marking till date. In short, every piece of data doesn't matter if it is structured or unstructured is collectively big data.

1.1 What Contributes to Big Data?

Data stored in Black Box: It is deployed in aircrafts. It keeps a record of all conversations of the crew, also records the information about the performance of the aircraft time to time. Data generated by social media: People on social networking sites share pictures, messages, voice messages, every second post has been generated and all such information needs to be stored. Stock Exchange: The stock market takes a new turn every minute, all the information regarding the "buying" and "selling" of shares needs to tracked and stored. It further allows us to understand the market well.

1.2 Uses of Big Data

Understanding the Market and Customer Requirements: It is one of the biggest areas where big data is used. The market researchers will understand the market and help big firms and business act according to the trends in the market and the customer requirements for example it may help Wal-Mart to estimate which product to sell and at what cost according to the need and demand in the market.

Improve quality of healthcare service: Big data can be used to predict certain diseases like cancer, heart attacks etc. This will further assist our doctors to help provide quality of services (Ebenezer et al., 2015). It has the power to decode a DNA in seconds and help us to understand disease patterns.

Helps sportsperson to understand better and perform better: there are certain tools that use analytics using videos to understand how each player performs and to understand pattern each player follows. Such tools have already been used in analyzing performance of players in basketball, tennis.

Weather forecasting as well as disaster forecasting: Analytics has been used to forecast the weather conditions using big data. It is been also used by scientists to predict disasters which further helps in saving human lives and prepare for such disasters in advance.

Helps in development of smart devices and to increase their performance: recently invented the Google's self-driving car uses big data to operate and understand what should be done at certain circumstances; it uses big data to identify humans, cars, buildings and to act according to the situation.

1.3 Big Data Technologies

In order to have accurate analysis and concrete decision we need to know the big data technologies which will in turn reduce the operation cost and efficiencies (Beakta et al., 2015; Lakshmi et al., 2016). Different vendors provide various technologies which include the once provided by IBM, Amazon, etc. Operational Big Data Systems like Mongo DB come under this that provides operational capabilities. The cloud computing architectures came into existence, help in huge computations with higher efficiency and lowering the cost. The systems like NoSQL take advantage of it.

1.3.1 Analytical Big Data

Analytical big data is the method of analyzing big data that may include understanding of market, demand and trends and help business to increase profit, quality of customer services as they are able to understand customers' needs and demands. The basic advantage of it is to help organizations to make good business decisions. The data scientists can understand the huge transactional data.

2. LITERATURE SURVEY

In olden days as the volume of data was less RDMS was capable of handling it but with the increase in volume of data it has become impossible for it. In S.Vikram ("MapReduce Model" 2014) he clearly told the definition of big data, what led to big data, how it is useful for analytics and decision making etc. it describes clearly hadoop architecture its main components like namenode, datanode, secondary namenode, job tracker, task tracker also stating advantages of big data in healthcare, aircrafts, stock market etc. Kiran Kumara ("Comparative Study" 2013) further enhanced our information about big data by clearly explaining what is structured data, un-structured data and semi structured data. He gave suggestions regarding the usage of some models during the transfer of data of the networks and to take care of things like security. Wei Fan and ashish they both have put some light on big data mining ("A survey" 2014; Patokar, 2016) and how storing of such data is of utmost importance and classification algorithms can be used to extract useful information from such data. He also proposed the consequences of using classification algorithms for large datasets and the need of using parallel and distributed programming method to overcome the problem of cost and time. Yingyi Bu ("Map Reduce: Simplified" n. d.) introduced a new method called HaLoop which he called new version of Hadoop. Map Reduce is not good for iterative applications; Haloop can do that using the already implemented features of Hadoop which in turn has led to improvement of efficiency.

3. HADOOP VS. CONVENTIONAL DATABASES

The most important difference is that Hadoop is "Write once, read many times" i.e. once you have entered the data it can only be read and deleted in future you can't write or modify it whereas in conventional database you can write multiple times, for example a table containing information regarding the cost, revenue and production of a company. A simple example of Hadoop database may be the ''The Black box data of an Aircraft" which contains information regarding all the conversions in the cockpit and the performance status of the aircraft time to time.

Another difference is that the conventional database uses Structured query language (SQL) to interact with the database while Hadoop doesn't use SQL, since Hadoop database is distributed SQL doesn't support it, SQL works well when the data is stored on a single machine and we need to retrieve that data, but if data is distributed over cluster of machines then SQL fails.

In Figure 1 shows with the increase in volume of data the performance of relational database decreases while for NoSQL databases it remains constant whatever may be the volume of data. In Figure 2 specify the modules of hadoop. HDFS design to run on large clusters of commodity hardware based on google file system(GFS).

3.1 Hadoop Architecture

- **HDFS:** Is a specially designed file system designed is such a way that deployment can be done on low cost hardware. Basically, it is a file system bases on Java that can be used for storing data that is huge in volume and size. Reliability and scalability are its basic attributes as well as distributed storage. It has its command interface which acts as intermediate to interact with HDFS
- **YARN:** It responsible for management of resources and scheduling the jobs to different clusters.

Figure 1.

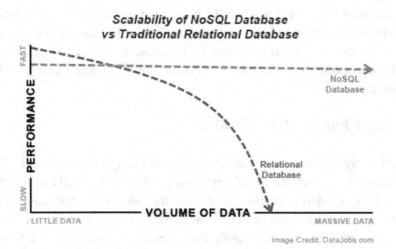

Figure 2.

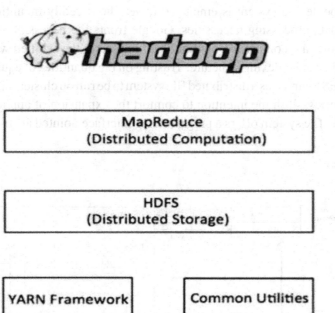

- **Map Reduce:** With the increasing size of data to be processed it uses the concept of distributed and parallel processing of data. The data is divided to different clusters which compute the results parallel and individually and in the end their results are combined by the reducer to reach to final result.
- **Hadoop Common:** These include certain libraries and jar files that Hadoop requires

3.2 Google File System (GFS)

Google File System is a trademarked distributed file system invented by Google and specifically deliberated to deliver resourceful, steadfast right to use data by means of bulky clusters of product servers. Figure 3 shows the architecture for GFS. Files are separated into portions of 64 megabytes, and are customarily affixed to or read and only exceptionally hardly ever overwritten or contracted. Compared with outmoded file systems, GFS is intended and augmented to run on data hubs to deliver tremendously great data amounts, little dormancy and endure singular server let downs.

The Google file system is employed to see the speedily mounting hassles of Google's data processing necessities. Google fronts the necessities to cope huge volumes of data – comprising but not being limited to the scuttled web content to be handled by the indexing structure. Trusting on big quantities of equivalent trivial servers, GFS is aimed as a distributed file system to be run on clusters up to thousands of machineries. With the intention to comfort the expansion of applications based on GFS, the file system offers a programming interface pointed at abstracting from

Figure 3.

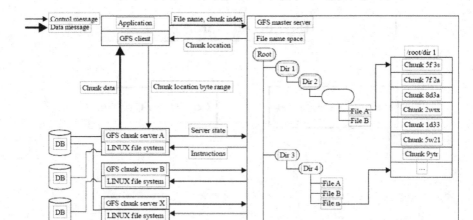

these distribution and management facets. Running on product hardware, GFS is not only confronted by supervision distribution, it also has to deal with the enlarged threat of hardware errors. As a result, one of the conventions through in the project of GFS is to reflect disk errors, machine errors in addition to network errors as being the standard instead of the exemption.

Safeguarding well-being of data as well as being capable of clambering up to thousands of computers while handling numerous terabytes of data can thus have thought to be one of the crucial encounters confronted by GFS. Having sanitized the goals and non-goals of a potential file system in detail, Google has chosen not to use a prevailing distributed file system. In its place, it decided to advance a new file system. GFS has been entirely tailored to complement Google's requirements. This specialism consents the project of the file system to refrain from several negotiations made by other file systems. For instance, a file system aiming universal applicability is anticipated to be able to proficiently handle files with dimensions stretching from very trivial (i.e. few bytes) to outsized (i.e. gigabyte to multi-terabyte). GFS, nevertheless, being directed at a specific customary of usage situations, is augmented for usage of bulky files only with space productivity being of insignificant standing. Furthermore, GFS files are generally amended by affixing data, while alterations at subjective file counterbalances are infrequent. The mainstream of files can thus, in severe dissimilarity to other file systems, be reflected as being append-only or even incontrovertible (write once, read many). Impending along with being augmented for bulky files and interim as the basis for large-volume data handling systems, the design of GFS has been enhanced for outsized streaming reads and usually favours throughput over dormancy. GFS implements a copyrighted interface that applications can utilize.

3.3 Google File System (GFS) Architecture

The GFS is encompassed of clusters. A cluster is a set of networked processors. GFS clusters comprise three kinds of mutually dependent units which are: Client, master and chunk server. Clients could be: Computers or applications deploying prevailing files or generating fresh files on the system. The master server is the orchestrator or administrator of the cluster coordination that conserve the operation log. Operation log possesses track of the undertakings made by the master itself which benefits in dropping the service disruptions to a least level. At startup, master server retrieves data about contents and inventories from chunk servers. Then after, the master server retains tracks of the whereabouts of the chunks with the cluster. The GFS architecture retains the communications that the master server propels and accepts very small. The master server itself doesn't handle file data at all, this is accomplished by chunk servers. Chunk servers are the principal engine of the

GFS. They stockpile file chunks of 64 MB size. Chunk servers harmonize with the master server and direct entreated chunks to clients directly.

3.4 Hadoop's Distributed File System (HDFS)

The Hadoop is an open-source distributed computing framework and delivered by Apache. Grounded on three white papers published by Google, which are: "Google file system", "MapReduce: Simplified data processing on large clusters" and "Bigtable: A distributed storage system for structured data", Apache industrialized Apache HDFS, Apache MapReduce and Apache HBase, correspondingly. Nearly 95% of the structural design styled in these three white papers is executed in Apache ventures with some trifling alterations. Google released these white papers with no code. So, it was up to engineers and scientists at Apache to plan and accomplish the structural design. HDFS architecture stipulates in Figure 4 and more comprehensive given in (Borthakur et al., 2008; Zhou et al., 2011). Hadoop is exploited in many of the world's leading online media corporations like Yahoo, LinkedIn, Twitter, Facebook, eBay, Amazon, Adobe, Fox interactive media etc.

- **Namenode:** The namenode is the commodity hardware that contains the GNU/Linux operating system and the namenode software. It is software that can be run on commodity hardware. The system having the namenode acts as the master server and it does the following tasks:

Figure 4.

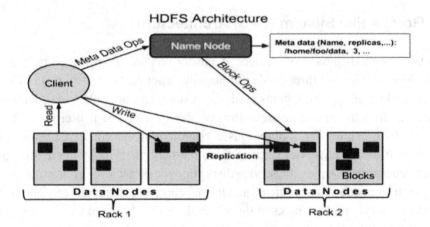

Manages the file system namespace regulates client's access to files. It also executes file system operations such as renaming, closing, and opening files and directories.

- **Datanode:** The datanode is a commodity hardware having the GNU/Linux operating system and datanode software. For every node (Commodity hardware/System) in a cluster, there will be a datanode. These nodes manage the data storage of their system. Datanodes perform read-write operations on the file systems, as per client request. They also perform operations such as block creation, deletion, and replication according to the instructions of the namenode.
- **Block:** Generally, the user data is stored in the files of HDFS. The file in a file system will be divided into one or more segments and/or stored in individual data nodes. These file segments are called as blocks. In other words, the minimum amount of data that HDFS can read or write is called a Block. The default block size is 64MB, but it can be increased as per the need to change in HDFS configuration

3.5 Comparison of GFS and HDFS

Utilization

Since GFS is trademarked file system and private to Google only, it cannot be used by any other corporation.

In contrast, HDFS grounded on Apache Hadoop ("Apache Hadoop" n. d.) open-source project can be deployed and used by any corporation keen to accomplish and process big data. Hadoop is used in several of the world's leading online media corporations like Yahoo, LinkedIn, Twitter, Facebook, eBay, Amazon, Adobe, Fox interactive media etc. (Ganes et al., 2014) map reduce is a minimization technique which makes use of file indexing with mapping, sorting, shuffling and finally reducing and it has used in data mining algorithms (Kumar et al., n. d.). In (Gamayel et al., 2016) author analysed in detailed about GFS and HDFS and compared in (Vijayakumari et al., 2014).

Processes

In GFS, the processes are commenced in Master and chunk server.

In HDFS, Name node and Data node are where processes are taken care.

File Allocation

In GFS, files are distributed into divisions called chunks of static proportions. Chunk dimension is 64 MB and can be warehoused on diverse nodes in cluster for load balancing and performance requirements.

In Hadoop, HDFS file system distributes the files into entities called blocks of 128 MB in size. Block dimension can be modifiable based on the size of data.

Cache Management

In GFS, cache metadata are hoarded in client memory. Chunk server does not requisite cache file data. Linux system running on the chunk server caches regularly retrieved data in memory.

The HDFS devours "Distributed Cache". Distributed Cache is amenity delivered by the MapReduce to allocate application-precise, large, read-only files resourcefully. It also stockpiles files such as text, archives (zip, tar, tgz and tar.gz) and containers desired by applications.

Internal Communication

Communication amongst chucks and clusters in the interior of GFS is made over and done with TCP networks. For data transmission, pipelining is used over TCP associates.

The equivalent technique is in HDFS, but Remote Procedure Call (RPC) is used to conduct peripheral communication amongst clusters and blocks.

Files Security and Authorization

Suite briar-Google partner remarks in its security study exploration that GFS separates files up and stocks it in numerous fragments on several machineries. File designations have unsystematic terms and are not human understandable. Files are obscured over algorithms that undergo alteration relentlessly.

The HDFS gears POSIX-like mode authorization for files and directories. All files and directories are related with an owner and an assemblage with distinct clearances for consumers who are owners, for consumers that are associates of the assemblage and for all other users.

Replication Approach

The GFS has two replicas: Primary replicas and secondary replicas. A primary replica is the data chunk that a chunk server sends to a client. Secondary replicas assist as backups on other chunk servers. Handler can stipulate the quantity of replicas to be upheld.

The HDFS has an involuntary replication support centered structure. By default, two copies of each block are warehoused by dissimilar Data Nodes in the identical rack and a third copy is stowed on a Data Node on a diverse rack.

3.6 MapReduce Model

Hadoop **MapReduce** is a software framework for easily writing applications which process big amounts of data in-parallel on large clusters (thousands of nodes) of commodity hardware in a reliable, fault-tolerant manner. The term MapReduce actually refers to the following two different tasks that Hadoop programs perform and MapReduce model specifies in Figure 5.

- **The Map Task:** This is the first task, which takes input data and converts it into a set of data, where individual elements are broken down into tuples (key/value pairs).
- **The Reduce Task:** This task takes the output from a map task as input and combines those data tuples into a smaller set of tuples. The reduce task is always performed after the map task.

Figure 5.

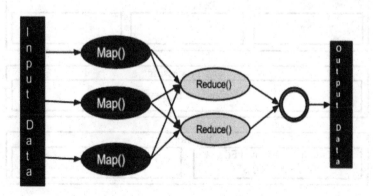

Typically, both the input and the output are stored in a file-system. The framework takes care of scheduling tasks, monitoring them and re-executes the failed tasks.

The MapReduce framework consists of a single master JobTracker and one slave TaskTracker per cluster-node. The master is responsible for resource management, tracking resource consumption/availability and scheduling the jobs component tasks on the slaves, monitoring them and re-executing the failed tasks. The slaves TaskTracker execute the tasks as directed by the master and provide task-status information to the master periodically. The JobTracker is a single point of failure for the Hadoop MapReduce service which means if JobTracker goes down, all running jobs are halted.

Hadoop Components

Figure 6 shows the hadoop components and explanations are given below:

- **Zookeeper:** A centralized amenity for upholding structure statistics, nomenclature, giving distributed harmonization and providing group facilities.

Figure 6.

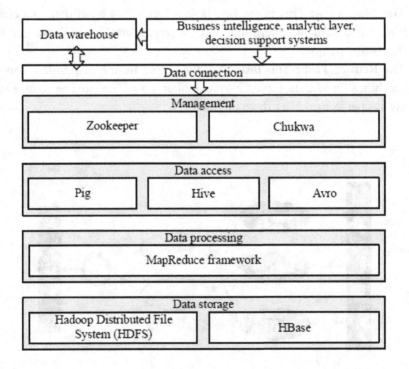

- **Chukwa:** An open source data assemblage structure for checking bulky distributed systems. Chukwa is fabricated on top of the Hadoop Distributed File System (HDFS) and MapReduce framework and takes over Hadoop's scalability and sturdiness.

- **Pig:** A podium for scrutinizing hefty data sets that comprises of a high-level language for conveying data analysis programs, together with substructure for assessing these programs.

- **Hive:** The Apache Hive data warehouse software enables interrogating and handling bulky datasets vesting in distributed storage. Hive offers a contrivance to venture structure onto this data and query the data by means of an SQL-like language called HiveQL.

- **Avro:** Apache Avro is a data serialization system. It has rich data structures. A compacted, speedy and binary data format. It acts as a container file, to stockpile persistent information. It also delivers simple incorporation with dynamic languages.

- **MapReduce:** Hadoop MapReduce has the identical structural design and functionality of Google MapReduce but the variance is that Hadoop MapReduce was written in Java and GFS MapReduce was written in C++. Furthermore, not to overlook that Google's original version of MapReduce works only with GFS file system but Hadoop's version can work with various file systems since it was embraced by Apache open-source mission henceforth used in many structural designs.

- **HBase:** Apache HBase is the Hadoop database, a disseminated, ascendable and big data stockpile.

- **HDFS:** Hadoop file system is a central module in the Hadoop architecture. The HDFS stands in the data storage stratum in Hadoop.

- **Underlying File System:** The HDFS is the distributed file system of Hadoop. What HDFS ensures is to generate an abstract level over a basic prevailing file systems running on the machine. Underlying file systems could be ext3, ext4 or xfs.

- **Hadoop Architecture:** Since Hadoop originates from Google white papers, it has the equivalent master/slave architecture but in altered execution. Therefore, all methods or amenities in the Hadoop file system are categorized as slave or master.

4. DATA MINING ALGORITHMS FOR BIG DATA ANALYSIS

In simple terms, Big Data – when united with Data Science – permit executives to quantify and evaluate considerably extra information about the intricacies of their industries, and to utilize the data in building more intellectual judgements. The Big Data revolution has perhaps delivered a further authoritative data groundwork than any aforementioned digital innovation. A variation of Machine Learning and data mining algorithms are accessible for crafting treasured analytic platforms. Several algorithms have been industrialized to contract precisely with commercial complications.

4.1 Classification Methods

As we all know classification name itself tells grouping or categorizing of things/ people according to their similarities that means grouping things which are alike together based on the training data. There are many algorithms available for it but in this paper we are going to focus on

1.   Naive Bayes
2.   KNN (K Nearest Neighbors)

First let's take a look at basics of Naïve Bayes using this example

In Figure 7 there are two types of data one represented by CIRCLES and other by SQUARES, now suppose a new object arrives we need to classify weather it belongs to circle category or the square category. By looking at the diagram one may think that the number of squares are twice as many the no of circles hence the new object is twice likely to be a square then the circle. This is known as prior probability (pp) they are based on previous data available.

Figure 7.

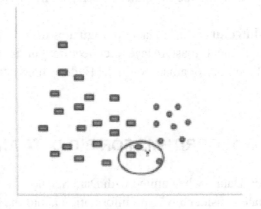

PP of squares = No. of squares / Total no. of (Squares + Circles)

PP of circles = No. of circles / Total no. of (Squares + Circles)

PP of Squares = 20/30

PP of Circles = 10/30

Now let us consider a new object represented by Y arrives, we need to identify if it is a circle or square.

Likelihood of Y given square = No of squares in the vicinity of Y / Total no. of squares

Likelihood of Y given circle = No of circles in the vicinity of Y / Total no of circles

Probability of Y given square propositional to 1/20

Probability of Y given circle propositional to 3/10

Posterior probability of Y being square = 2/3 * 1/20

Posterior probability of Y being circle = 1/3 * 3/10

Finally, we can conclude that Y is classified as a circle because the posterior probability of it is more.

KNN algorithm

1. First define the value of K for the algorithm
2. The query dataset will be given for which we need to identify the class
3. Calculate the Euclidian distance between each values of query and each value of the training dataset
4. You will get distance for each row, ow sort them in ascending order of the distance value
5. See the value of K
6. For example, if the value of K is 3, use the topmost 3 values for classification
7. Find out the majority and use it to predict the class to which it belongs

Consider the following classification example in Table 1.

Table 1. Classification example

Y1 = Durability	Y2 = Strength	Class
6	6	A
6	3	A
2	3	B
1	3	B

First define the value of K for the algorithm K=3

The query dataset will be given for which we need to identify the class

Now a new object has come with values Y1 =3 Y2 =7

Calculate the Euclidian distance between each value given in Table 2 of query and each value of the training dataset you will get distance for each row; now sort them in ascending order of the distance value

Find out the majority and use it to predict the class to which it belongs. In Table 3 we have 1 A and 2 B since 2>1 we conclude that the new object Y1 =3 and Y2=7 belongs to class B.

Table 2. Euclidian distance between two objects

Y1 = Durability	Y2 = Strength	Class
6	6	(6-3) * (6-3) + (6-7) * (6-7) = 10
6	3	(6-3) * (6-3) + (3-7) * (3-7) = 25
2	3	(2-3) * (2-3) + (3-7) * (3-7) = 17
1	3	(1-3) *(1-3) + (3-7) * (3-7) = 20

Table 3. Rank minimum distance

Y1	Y2	Rank Minimum Distance
6	6	1
6	3	4
2	3	2
1	3	3

5. RESULTS AND DISCUSSION

Compare Time Taken by Naïve Bayes and MapReduce

Below is the table which is given as Input to the classifier Model. Here in Table 4 we have R1, R2 …….. R10 represents 10 Records given as input and A1, A2 …, A9 represent 9 attributes. We already know that which record belongs to which class. We are going to see the computation time for each record and compare for Naïve Bayes and KNN to find out which computes faster using MapReduce programming model.

From Table 5 we can clearly see that time taken by KNN is less than time taken by Naive Bayes.

Table 4. Testing data, data given as input

	A1	A2	A3	A4	A5	A6	A7	A8	A9
R1	5	1	1	1	2	1	3	1	1
R2	5	4	4	5	7	10	3	2	1
R3	3	1	1	1	2	2	3	1	1
R4	6	8	8	1	3	4	3	7	1
R5	4	1	1	3	2	1	3	1	1
R6	6	10	2	8	10	2	7	8	10
R7	10	6	4	1	3	4	3	2	3
R8	8	10	10	8	7	10	9	7	1
R9	8	7	5	10	7	9	5	5	4
R10	7	4	6	4	6	1	4	3	1

Table 5. Time taken by MapReduce and KNNSo

Record	Time Taken By MapReduce(sec)	Time Taken By KNN(sec)
R1	154	59
R2	154	56
R3	153	55
R4	158	61
R5	152	60
R6	156	54
R7	155	62
R8	154	63
R9	157	65
R10	154	62

Compare on the Basis of Sensitivity, Specificity and Accuracy

$$\text{Sensitivity} = \frac{\text{Number of True Positives}}{\text{Number of False Negatives} + \text{Number of True Positives}}$$

$$\text{Specificity} = \frac{\text{Number of True Negatives}}{\text{Number of False Positives} + \text{Number of True Negatives}}$$

$$\text{Accuracy} = \frac{TP + TN}{TP + TN + FP + FN}$$

Results for MapReduce:

R1 Benign correctly identified as Benign
R2 Benign incorrectly identified as Malignant
R3 Benign correctly identified as Benign
R4 Benign incorrectly identified as Malignant
R5 Benign correctly identified as Benign
R6 Malignant correctly identified as Malignant
R7 Malignant correctly identified as Malignant
R8 Malignant correctly identified as Malignant
R9 Malignant correctly identified as Malignant
R10 Malignant incorrectly identified as Benign
TP = 4
FP = 2
TN= 3
FN = 1
Sensitivity = 4/5 = 0.8
Specificity = 3/5= 0.6

Results for KNN:

R1 Benign correctly identified as Benign
R2 Benign correctly identified as Benign
R3 Benign correctly identified as Benign
R4 Benign correctly identified as Benign
R5 Benign correctly identified as Benign
R6 Malignant correctly identified as Malignant

R7 Malignant correctly identified as Malignant
R8 Malignant correctly identified as Malignant
R9 Malignant correctly identified as Malignant
R10 Malignant correctly identified as Malignant
TP = 5
TN = 5
FN = 0
FP = 0
Sensitivity = 5/5=1
Specificity = 5/5=1

6. CONCLUSION AND FUTURE WORK

Hence KNN has more Specificity and Sensitivity than Naïve Bayes and takes less time for execution. So, we can say that in our approach KNN is taking significantly less time compared to Naïve Bayes. However, for large datasets accuracy of Naïve Bayes might be more. So in future we can take real world large datasets with comparatively large number of attributes to process it and compare the accuracy of both algorithms. Also, we can take more algorithms and implement them using MapReduce too.

REFERENCES

Patokar, A.A., & Patil, V.M. (2016). Efficient Analysis of Big Data by using Hadoop in Cloud Computing by Map Reducing. *National Conference on Innovative Trends in Science and Engineering*, *4*(7), 378 – 381.

B., A., & Jagani, J.M. (2014). A survey: classification of huge cloud Datasets with efficient Map - Reduce policy. *International Journal of Engineering Trends and Technology*, *18*(2). Retrieved from http://www.ijettjournal.org

Beakta, R. (2015). Big Data And Hadoop: A Review Paper.

Ebenezer, J. G. A., & Durga, S. (2015). Big Data Analytics In Healthcare: A Survey. *Journal of Engineering and Applied Sciences (Asian Research Publishing Network)*, *10*(8), 3645–3650.

Borthakur, D. (2008). HDFS Architecture Guide. *The apache software foundation*.

Dean, J., & Ghemawat, S. (n. d.). MapReduce: Simplified Data Processing on Large Clusters.

Garg, D., Trivedi, K., & Panchal, B. B. (2013, October). A comparative study of clustering algorithms using mapreduce in hadoop. *International Journal of Engineering Research and Technology*, 2(10).

Gemayel, N. (2016Analyzing Google File System and Hadoop Distributed File System. *Journal of Information Technology*, 8(3), 66–74. doi:10.3923/rjit.2016.66.74

Apache. (n. d.). Hadoop. Retrieved from http://hadoop.apache.org

Lakshmi, C., & Nagendra Kumar, V.V. (2016, August). Survey Paper on Big Data. *International Journal of Advanced Research in Computer Science and Software Engineering*, 6(8).

Zhou, P., Lei, J., & Ye, W. (2011). Large-Scale Data Sets Clustering Based on MapReduce and Hadoop. *Journal of Computer Information Systems*, 7(16), 5956–5963.

Manikandan, S. G., & Ravi, S. (2014). Big Data Analysis using Apache Hadoop.

Nandakumar, D. R. A. N., & Yambem, N. (2014). A Survey on Data Mining Algorithms on Apache Hadoop Platform. *International Journal of Emerging Technology and Advanced Engineering*, 4(1), 563-565.

Pakize, S. R., & Gandomi, A. (2014). Comparative study of classification algorithms based On MapReduce Model. *International Journal of Innovative Research in Advanced Engineering*, 1(7).

Vijayakumari, R., Kirankumar, R., & Gangadhara Rao, K. (2014). Comparative analysis of Google File System and Hadoop Distributed File System. *International Journal of Advanced Trends in Computer Science and Engineering*, 3(1), 553–558.

Chapter 8
Case Studies in Amalgamation of Deep Learning and Big Data

Balajee Jeyakumar
VIT University, India

M.A. Saleem Durai
VIT University, India

Daphne Lopez
VIT University, India

ABSTRACT

Deep learning is now more popular research domain in machine learning and pattern recognition in the world. It is widely success in the far-reaching area of applications such as Speech recognition, Computer vision, Natural language processing and Reinforcement learning. With the absolute amount of data accessible nowadays, big data brings chances and transformative possible for several sectors, on the other hand, it also performs on the unpredicted defies to connecting data and information. The size of the data is getting larger, and deep learning is imminent to play a vital role in big data predictive analytics solutions. In this paper, we make available a brief outline of deep learning and focus recent research efforts and the challenges in the fields of science, medical and water resource system.

DOI: 10.4018/978-1-5225-2863-0.ch008

INTRODUCTION

Big data and Deep learning are the two hottest topics rising quickly in the real world. While the big data has defined in many ways, it raised to becoming more growth and excellent accessibility of digital data in shapes and size, is increasing at beyond belief rates (Lopez et al., 2016). This detonation of digital data gets big chances and transformative possible for numerous sectors such as enterprises, healthcare industry manufacturing, and educational services (Lopez & Gunasekaran, 2015). Big data suggestions great potential for developing all features of our humanity, gathering of valued information from big data is not such an easy task. The significant and rapid growing of hidden information in the unmatched capacities of non-traditional data needs together with the improvement of innovative technologies and relating to more than one branch of knowledge in close by collaboration (Lopez & Sekaran, 2016).

Currently, machine learning techniques, organized with improvements in available computational control, have come to play a dynamic role in Big Data analytics and knowledge discovery (Lopez et al., 2016). In compare to best conventional learning methods, which are well thought-out using shallow-structured learning architectures, deep learning refers to machine learning techniques that practice supervised and unsupervised approaches to spontaneously learn hierarchical representations in deep architectures for classification (Parimala & Lopez, 2015).

Deep learning successfully implemented in industry domains that perform very well on an enormous amount of ordinal data (Boobalan et al., 2016). Firms similar to Facebook, Apple, and Google gather and explore massive volumes of data each and every day, violently insistent to deep learning associated projects (Manogaran et al., 2016). Apple Siri, is one of the examples for computer-generated personal assistant in iPhones, provides wide-ranging facilities containing sports news, reminders, answers to user's questions and weather reports by making use of deep learning and more data collected by Apple services.

BACKGROUND

2. Overview of Big Data

Big data defined as datasets size is away from the capacity of the usual database, capture by software tools, store, manage, and analyze. Handling the data is not easy, and analysis in the standard database likes SQL. The data is too outsized, moves very quick, or it is not related to the structure of database architectures (Parimala & Lopez, 2016).

The key fact of V-based characterization is to focus the big data's maximum thoughtful challenges are capture, cleaning, curation, integration, storage, processing, indexing, search, sharing, transfer, mining, analysis and visualization of huge sizes of rapid moving high complex data (Manogaran et al., 2016). Big data can be categorized as 10 V's (Figure 1) are Volume, Variety, Velocity, Veracity, Validity, Value, Variability, Venue, Vocabulary, and Vagueness.

2.1 Big Data Technologies

The several tools used in big data from data acquisition to data analysis are measures of Apache projects about the standard one is Hadoop. It is developed by Java and created by Doug Cutting. Hadoop brings easy process on huge volume of data, regardless of its structure (Manogaran et al., 2017). Hadoop is made up of two projects,

- Hadoop distributed file system (HDFS)
- Map / Reduce

Figure 1. 10 V's of big data

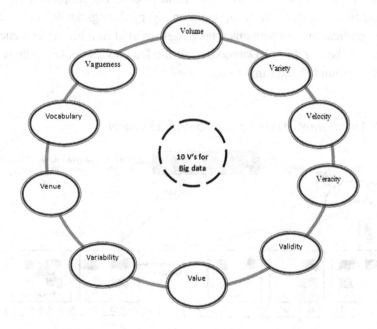

2.2 HDFS

Hadoop distributed file system intended to run on massive clusters of service hardware based on Google File System (GFS) (Manogaran & Lopez, 2016). Google file system provides as previously distributed file systems do like reliability, availability, performance and scalability. This file system successfully does the need for storage. It stores large datasets and to stream datasets at high bandwidth to user applications. GFS arrange for an acquainted file system interface, and yet a standard API is not applied as per POSIX. In directories, the files prearranged in hierarchically, and path names identified clearly. The regular operations like create, delete, open, close, read, and write files it supports. GFS be responsible for a locality independent namespace which permits data to move visibly for load balance or fault tolerance. It determines the qualities needed for large-scale data handling (Manogaran & Lopez, 2016) workloads on service hardware. It is one of the important tools to modernize and outbreak problems on the measure of the entire web.

The HDFS is the pattern after UNIX file system, and it performs by using batch processing rather than interactive use by users. In this, the data once were written, and it is accessed more times, in high throughput (Manogaran & Lopez, 2016). In HDFS file system metadata are stored in the server called Name Node and the application data in another server called Data Nodes. The major role in HDFS is to find and handle failures at the application layer (Manogaran & Lopez, 2016). It processes replication mechanisms where files divided into blocks and each block replicated on the number of Datanodes; all the Datanodes contains the replica of the block not found in the same rack.

Figure 2. Architecture of hadoop distributed file system

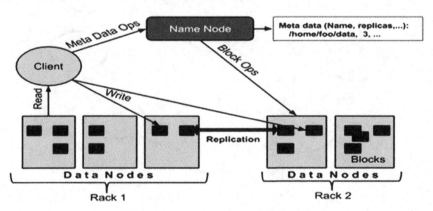

2.3 Map / Reduce

Google endorsed a Map Reduce programming framework based on functional programming. The structure splits the work into independent tasks and parallelizes the computational flow across large-scale clusters of machines, taking steps for communications between them and possible failures and efficiently controls network bandwidth and disk usage (Singh & Reddy, 2014). MapReduce splits the computational flow into two phases: Map and Reduce. By using the Map and Reduce functions the user can implement parallel algorithms that handle across very clusters.

MapReduce is carrying out settings that execute a user program; it divides the dataset into independent splits that can process in parallel by different machines. The framework of MapReduce starts up many replicas of the user program on the machine cluster. One of the copy denoted as master, it plans and handles tasks inside the cluster. The others are named workers. The master allocates a map task or a reduce task to any model worker (Singh & Reddy, 2014). A map task allotted to a worker, it reads the content of the corresponding input split, parses the <key, value> pair as input data and permits the computational flow to the user defined map function. The map function intakes a single <key, value> pair as input and creates a list of intermediate <key, value> pairs as output. Workers from time to time store in the native disk the intermediate values created by the map functions, and partition the values into regions. As a final point, the worker departure back the result to the master (Singh & Reddy, 2014). The key is taken by reduce function and the list of associated value as input and produces a list of new values as output. At last, the reduce function output is add on to the output file.

It was earlier initiated by Google and developed by Yahoo for resolving the search creation problem for web indexing. Map/reduce is based on the divide and conquer method and works by breaking down the difficult problem into many subproblems until these sub-problems is accessible for resolving directly. The solutions of the subproblems are then joined to give a solution to the new issue (Victor, N et al., 2016). The input data formed in map reduce framework is suitable for semi-structured and unstructured data.

In most recent years, more open source projects developed to a pact with big data, given by companies like Facebook, Yahoo! Moreover, Twitter. Some of these are, Spark is for faster and general engine to deal with large scale data processing, Apache S4 for handling continuous data streams, Storm for data-intensive distributed applications in streaming S4 (Victor et al., 2016). Dremel and Apache Drill are for scalable, collaborative low latency ad-hoc query systems to analysis read-only nested data.

Figure 3. Diagram of map / reduce

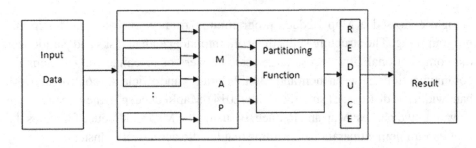

The well-known implementation environment for the MapReduce programming model has been Apache Hadoop, and now Apache Spark is getting further popular of its enhanced flexibility and efficiency. Hadoop lets the implementation of custom applications that quickly process big data sets stored in distributed file system (Thilagavathi et al., 2014). Mahout provides data mining tools for big data and most familiar machine learning library running on the top of the Hadoop. It provides an extensive collection of machine learning and data mining algorithms for clustering, classification problems, and frequent pattern mining. The MLib library supports equivalent features on Spark.

3. OUTLINE OF DEEP LEARNING

Machine-learning systems are used to detect objects in images, transliterate speech into text, contest news items, posts or products with user's benefits, and select related results of the search. Moreover, these applications make a practice of a class of methods called deep learning. Deep learning is a very early field, where theories not solidly established, and views quickly change (Manogaran & Lopez, 2017). Deep learning is on the way, most popular nowadays. It is renovating the industries, as computer instructs themselves all sorts of well-ordered tricks that have not thought about a few years ago. (Rajeshwari et al., 2013) Matlab is used to provide tools for deep learning methods to analyze and interpret the results in good manner.

Deep learning usually related to machine learning techniques that learn multiple levels of representations in deep architectures. In this segment, we will present a brief summary of three well-established deep architectures: deep belief networks (DBNs), convolutional neural networks (CNNs) and recursive neural networks.

3.1 Deep Belief Networks (DBN)

In present nonparametric machine learning algorithms that are kernel machines like graph-based manifold, support vector machines (SVMs) and semi-supervised learning algorithms put forward significant restrictions of some learning algorithms (Parimala et al., 2011). In kernel machines, the Shallow architecture (not in local kernel) only two levels of data dependent computational elements efficiently used, this correct for feed-forward neural networks with a single hidden layer. The biggest problem in shallow architecture it is in vain when regarding the number of computational units (base and hidden units), and the only way to represent few parameters with the alignment of numerous non-linear is deep architecture.

To train deep multi-layer neural networks is difficult, so just introduced a greedy layer-wise unsupervised learning algorithm for Deep belief networks (DBN) a propagative model of several layers with hidden cause variables. DBN performs approach with three aspects are essential first, pre-training one layer with greedy way; second, to realm data from input using unsupervised learning at each layer and third, fine tuning the complete network with standard interest.

3.2 Convolutional Neural Networks (CNN)

Convolutional Neural Networks (CNN) is a typical deep learning architecture stimulated by standard optical insight mechanism of living creatures. A Convolutional Neural Network (CNN) covered with one or more convolutional layers and then trailed

Figure 4. Architecture of Deep Belief Networks (DBN)

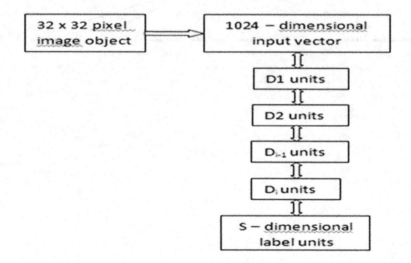

by one or more fully connected layers as in a standard multilayer neural network (Lopez & Raja, 2009). The architecture of a CNN is considered to take benefit of the 2D structure of an input image and succeeded by with local connections and tied weights followed by some form of pooling which results in translation invariant features. An additional benefit of CNNs is that they are at ease to train and have various fewer parameters than fully connected networks with the same number of hidden units.

Around many modifications of CNN architectures in the works. Though, their simple modules are very alike. Take the well-known LeNet-5 one of the example; it contains three types of layers specifically convolutional, pooling, and fully-connected layers.

3.3 Recursive Neural Networks (RNN)

A recursive neural network (RNN) is a type of deep neural network designed by relating the identical set of weights recursively above structure, to create a structured prediction above variable-size input structures or a scalar prediction over it, by traversing a known structure in topological order (Lopez & Raja, 2009). RNNs have remained popular for example in learning order and tree structures in natural language processing, mostly phrase and continuous sentence representations based on word entrenching.

Figure 5. Categorized structure of CNN

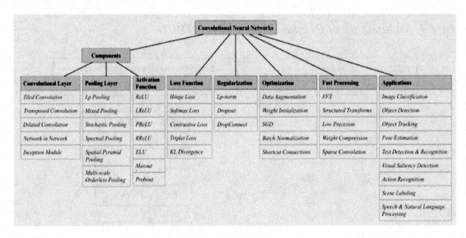

3.4 Autoencoders

One of the first important results in Deep Learning since early 2000 was the use of Deep Belief Networks to pretrain deep networks. This approach is based on the observation that random initialization is a bad idea, and that pretraining each layer with an unsupervised learning algorithm can allow for better initial weights. Examples of such unsupervised algorithms are Deep Belief Networks, which are based on Restricted Boltzmann Machines, and Deep Autoencoders, which are based on Autoencoders. Although the first breakthrough result is related to Deep Belief Networks, similar gains can also be obtained later by Autoencoders. In the following section, I will only describe the Autoencoder algorithm because it is simpler to understand. Autoencoders have many interesting applications, such as data compression, visualization, etc. It could be used as a way to "pretrain" neural networks.

4. BIG DATA DEEP LEARNING IN ELECTRONIC HEALTHCARE

Nowadays, People are now turning over the highest importance to their health. They assume the highest level of precaution and service unrelatedly to cost and further expressive almost to this field on refining the health of residents, dropping the cost of care and improving the patient experience.

(Ranjith et al., 2016) In medical imaging field, machine learning is used for numerous services like computer-aided diagnosis, image segmentation, image registration, image annotation, and image –guided therapy. Deep learning methods are usual of algorithms in machine learning. These algorithms are intended for automatically study multiple levels of representation and abstraction, which supports in making sense of data.

(Saleem Durai & Sriman Narayana Iyengar, 2010) Expertise is now concentrating on computing deep learning methods in the medical domain. Big data and Deep learning are the two hottest topics rising quickly in the real world. While the big data has defined in many ways, it raised to becoming more growth and excellent accessibility of digital data in shapes and size, is increasing at beyond belief rates. Currently, machine learning techniques, organized with improvements in available computational control, have come to play a dynamic role in Big Data analytics and knowledge discovery (Xue-wen Chen & Xiaotong Lin, 2014).

Deep learning implemented successfully in industry domains that perform very well on an enormous amount of ordinal data (Manogaran et al., 2017). Firms similar to MRIs, CT scans, and X-rays gather and explore massive volumes of images each and every day, violently insistent to deep learning associated projects (Manogaran & Lopez, 2016). To influence innovative analytics to develop new insights from data sets with the objective of improving diagnostics and enhanced predicting outcomes machine learning and deep learning turned out the health systems in the field of healthcare.

5. BIG DATA DEEP LEARNING IN DRUG DISCOVERY

The design implementation is to evaluate and make use of large volumes of data to develop the performance of the machines. Deep learning algorithms are mostly handled by Amazon, Google, Facebook, LinkedIn, IBM and Netflix to give suggestions and recommendations of one's preferences to examine user's activities. Deep learning utilized in many ways by computers to read and write. When it is accompanying with machine to perform and understand images has reduced to 6% that is improved than humans.

Figure 6. Theoretical framework of electronic health data processing using deep learning

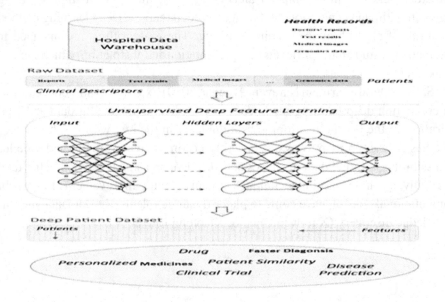

(Anbarasi & Saleem Durai, 2015) The technology is sightseen through several areas of applications, especially in the field of healthcare, much ingenuity is certified by medical data in healthcare standards. In detail, the growth of medical big data is dramatically increased to 25,000 petabytes by 2020.

The present background and upcoming point of view is growing area of deep learning solutions within the healthcare domain. Mostly driven by the big data revolution, deep learning algorithms have emerged as a novel solution to generate relevant insights from medical data. The major idea of this study was to identify the various deep learning solutions that are currently available and being developed to supply to unmet medical needs, and also evaluate the future prospects of deep learning within the healthcare industry (Manogaran & Lopez, 2016). The solutions are predicted to open up significant opportunities in the field of drug discovery and diagnostics as the healthcare industry gradually shifts towards digital solutions.

There two major categories of ligand-based and structure-based methods for the prediction of biological activities of chemical compounds, namely quantitative structure-activity relationship (QSAR) analysis and docking-based scoring.

QSAR methods are endowed with robustness and good ranking ability when applied to the prediction of the activity of closely related analogs. However, their great dependence on training sets significantly limits their applicability to the evaluation of diverse compounds.

Deep learning can predict

- Cross-reactive
- Side effect
- Toxicity

Figure 7. Big data deep learning in Drug discovery

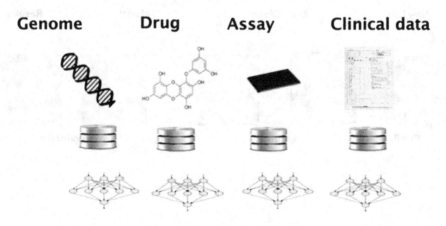

from their structures and known experimental result.

6. BIG DATA DEEP LEARNING IN WATER RESOURCE MANAGEMENT

(Parimala & Lopez, 2016) The Deep learning can automate, simplify and improve many aspects of water monitoring including

- Improving modeling and analysis
- Detecting and correcting equipment malfunctioning
- Detecting environmental anomalies
- Predicting the effect of policies decisions
- Automating and controlling allocation of distribution

(Lavanya el al., 2015) The environmental times series in general are complex in water and hard to model because of the following problems:

- Highly- non-stationary
- Highly non-linear
- Many changes in dynamics
- Can contain outliers, anomalies and gaps, etc.

Our model for water monitoring system using deep learning may provide general, flexible and robust. It is easily interpretable and fast efficient for real-time applications.

Figure 8. Big data deep learning in water resource management

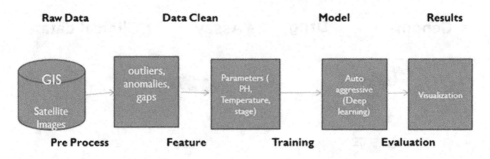

7. CONCLUSION

Big Data presents important tasks to deep learning, including large scale, heterogeneity, noisy labels, and non-stationary distribution, among many others. In order to understand the full potential of Big Data, we need to address these nominal challenges with new ways of thinking and transformative solutions. We are certain of that these research challenges pretended by Big Data are not only timely, but will also bring ample opportunities for deep learning. Together, they will provide major advances in science, medicine, and water resources system.

REFRENCES

Anbarasi, M., & Saleem Durai, M.A. (2015) A study on predicting protein secondary structure using various data mining approaches. *International Journal of Pharma and Bio Sciences (B)*, 6(3), 549-B561.

Thota, C., Manogaran, G., & Sundarsekar, R. (in press). Architecture for Big Data Storage in Different Cloud Deployment Models. In R.S. Segall, J.S. Cook & N. Gupta (Eds.), Big Data Storage and Visualization Techniques. Hershey, PA: IGI Global.

Boobalan, M. P., Lopez, D., & Gao, X. Z. (2016). Graph clustering using k-Neighbourhood Attribute Structural similarity. *Applied Soft Computing*, 47(C), 216-223.

Durai, M. S., & Iyengar, N. C. S. N. (2010). Secure medical diagnosis using rule based mining. In *Proceedings of the International Conference on Advances in Information Technology* (pp. 34-42). Springer.

Manogaran, G., & Lopez, D. (in press). Spatial cumulative sum algorithm with big data analytics for climate change detection. *Computers & Electrical Engineering*. doi:10.1016/j.compeleceng.2017.04.006

Kumar, S., & Lopez, D. (2015). Feature Selection used for Wind Speed Forecasting with Data Driven Approaches. *Journal of Engineering Science and Technology Review*, 8(5), 124 - 127.

Lavanya, K., Durai, M. S., & Iyengar, N. C. S. (2015). Site specific soil fertility ranking and seasonal paddy variety selection: An intuitionistic fuzzy rough set and fuzzy Bayesian based decision model. *International Journal of Multimedia and Ubiquitous Engineering, 10*(6), 311-328.

Lopez, D., & Gunasekaran, M. (2015). Assessment of vaccination strategies using fuzzy multi-criteria decision making. In *Proceedings of the Fifth International Conference on Fuzzy and Neuro Computing (FANCCO-2015)* (pp. 195-208). Switzerland: Springer.

Lopez, D., & Manogaran, G. (2016). Big data architecture for climate change and disease dynamics. In G.S. Tomar, N.S. Chaudhari, R.S. Bhadoria et al. (Eds.), *The Human Element of Big Data: Issues, Analytics, and Performance*. FL: CRC Press.

Lopez, D., & Raja, S. K. (2009, January 3-6). Virtual Time Fair Queuing Algorithm for a Computational Grid. In *Proceedings of the 10th International Conference on Distributed Computing and Networking*, Hyderabad, India (Vol. 5408, p. 468-474). Springer.

Lopez, D., & Sekaran, G. (2016). Climate change and disease dynamics-A big data perspective. *International Journal of Infectious Diseases, 45*, 23-24.

Lopez, D., Gunasekaran, M., Murugan, B. S., Kaur, H., & Abbas, K. M. (2014). Spatial big data analytics of influenza epidemic in Vellore, India. In *Proceedings of the IEEE International Conference on Big Data (Big Data)* (pp. 19-24). IEEE.

Manogaran, G., & Lopez, D. (2016). A survey of big data architectures and machine learning algorithms in healthcare. *International Journal of Biomedical Engineering and Technology, 23*(4), 1-27.

Manogaran, G., & Lopez, D. (2016). Disease surveillance system for big climate data processing and dengue transmission. *International Journal of Ambient Computing and Intelligence, 8*(2), 88-105.

Manogaran, G., & Lopez, D. (2016). Health data analytics using scalable logistic regression with stochastic gradient descent. *International Journal of Advanced Intelligence Paradigms, 9*(1), 1-18.

Manogaran, G., & Lopez, D. (2016). Health data analytics using scalable logistic regression with stochastic gradient descent. *International Journal of Advanced Intelligence Paradigms, 9*(1), 1-18.

Manogaran, G., Lopez, D., Thota, C., Abbas, K. M., Pyne, S., & Sundarasekar, R. (2017). Big Data Analytics in Healthcare Internet of Things. In *Innovative Healthcare Systems for the 21st Century* (pp. 263-284). Springer International Publishing.

Manogaran, G., Thota, C., & Kumar, M. V. (2016). MetaCloudDataStorage architecture for big data security in cloud computing. *Procedia Computer Science, 87,* 128-133.

Manogaran, G., Thota, C., Lopez, D., & Sundarasekar, R. (2017). Big Data Security Intelligence for Healthcare Industry 4.0. In *Cybersecurity for Industry 4.0* (pp. 103-126).

Manogaran, G., Thota, C., Lopez, D., Vijayakumar, V., Abbas, K. M., & Sundarsekar, R. (2017). Big data knowledge system in healthcare. In C. Bhatt, N. Dey & A. Ashour (Eds.), *Internet of Things and Big Data Technologies in Next Generation Healthcare.* Springer International Publishing.

Parimala, M., & Lopez, D. (2015). K-Neighbourhood Structural Similarity Approach for Spatial Clustering. *Indian Journal of Science and Technology, 8*(23).

Parimala, M., & Lopez, D. (2016). Spatio-temporal graph clustering algorithm based on attribute and structural similarity. *International Journal of Knowledge-based and Intelligent Engineering Systems, 20*(3), 149-160.

Parimala, M., Lopez, D., & Senthilkumar, N. C. (2011). A survey on density based clustering algorithms for mining large spatial databases. *International Journal of Advanced Science and Technology, 31*(1), 59-66.

Rajeshwari, A., Prathna, T. C., Balajee, J., Chandrasekaran, N., Mandal, A. B., & Mukherjee, A. (2013). Computational approach for particle size measurement of silver nanoparticle from electron microscopic image. *International Journal of Pharmacy and Pharmaceutical Sciences, 5*(2 Suppl.), 619-623.

Ranjith, D., Balajee, J., & Kumar, C. (2016). In premises of cloud computing and models. *International Journal of Pharmacy and Technology, 8*(3), 4685-4695.

Singh, D., & Reddy, C. K. (2014). A survey on platforms for Big Data analytics. *Journal of Big Data, 2*(1), 8.

Thilagavathi, M., Lopez, D., & Murugan, B. S. (2014). Middleware for Preserving Privacy in Big Data. In *Handbook of Research on Cloud Infrastructures for Big Data Analytics* (pp. 419-443). Hershey, PA: IGI Global.

Thota, C., Manogaran, G., Lopez, D., & Vijayakumar, V. (2017). Big data security framework for distributed cloud data centers. In M. Moore (Eds.), *Cybersecurity Breaches and Issues Surrounding Online Threat Protection*. Hershey, PA: IGI Global.

Thota, C., Sundarsekar, R., Manogaran, G., R., V., & M.K., P. (in press). Centralized Fog Computing Security Platform for IoT and Cloud in Healthcare System. In *Exploring the Convergence of Big Data and the Internet of Things*. Hershey, PA: IGI Global.

Victor, N., Lopez, D., & Abawajy, J. H. (2016). Privacy models for big data: a survey. *Int. J. Big Data Intelligence*, *3*(1), 61.

Related References

To continue our tradition of advancing information science and technology research, we have compiled a list of recommended IGI Global readings. These references will provide additional information and guidance to further enrich your knowledge and assist you with your own research and future publications.

Acharjya, D. P., & Mary, A. G. (2014). Privacy preservation in information system. In B. Tripathy & D. Acharjya (Eds.), *Advances in secure computing, internet services, and applications* (pp. 49–72). Hershey, PA: IGI Global. doi:10.4018/978-1-4666-4940-8.ch003

Agamba, J., & Keengwe, J. (2012). Pre-service teachers perceptions of information assurance and cyber security. *International Journal of Information and Communication Technology Education*, 8(2), 94–101. doi:10.4018/jicte.2012040108

Aggarwal, R. (2013). Dispute settlement for cyber crimes in India: An analysis. In R. Khurana & R. Aggarwal (Eds.), *Interdisciplinary perspectives on business convergence, computing, and legality* (pp. 160–171). Hershey, PA: IGI Global. doi:10.4018/978-1-4666-4209-6.ch015

Agwu, E. (2013). Cyber criminals on the internet super highways: A technical investigation of different shades and colours within the Nigerian cyber space. *International Journal of Online Marketing*, 3(2), 56–74. doi:10.4018/ijom.2013040104

Ahmad, A. (2012). Security assessment of networks. In *Wireless technologies: Concepts, methodologies, tools and applications* (pp. 208–224). Hershey, PA: IGI Global. doi:10.4018/978-1-61350-101-6.ch111

Ahmed, N., & Jensen, C. D. (2012). Security of dependable systems. In L. Petre, K. Sere, & E. Troubitsyna (Eds.), *Dependability and computer engineering: Concepts for software-intensive systems* (pp. 230–264). Hershey, PA: IGI Global. doi:10.4018/978-1-60960-747-0.ch011

Al, M., & Yoshigoe, K. (2012). Security and attacks in wireless sensor networks. In *Wireless technologies: Concepts, methodologies, tools and applications* (pp. 1811–1846). Hershey, PA: IGI Global. doi:10.4018/978-1-61350-101-6.ch706

Al-Ahmad, W. (2011). Building secure software using XP. *International Journal of Secure Software Engineering*, 2(3), 63–76. doi:10.4018/jsse.2011070104

Al-Bayatti, A. H., & Al-Bayatti, H. M. (2012). Security management and simulation of mobile ad hoc networks (MANET). In H. Al-Bahadili (Ed.), *Simulation in computer network design and modeling: Use and analysis* (pp. 297–314). Hershey, PA: IGI Global. doi:10.4018/978-1-4666-0191-8.ch014

Al-Bayatti, A. H., Zedan, H., Cau, A., & Siewe, F. (2012). Security management for mobile ad hoc network of networks (MANoN). In I. Khalil & E. Weippl (Eds.), *Advancing the next-generation of mobile computing: Emerging technologies* (pp. 1–18). Hershey, PA: IGI Global. doi:10.4018/978-1-4666-0119-2.ch001

Al-Hamdani, W. A. (2011). Three models to measure information security compliance. In H. Nemati (Ed.), *Security and privacy assurance in advancing technologies: New developments* (pp. 351–373). Hershey, PA: IGI Global. doi:10.4018/978-1-60960-200-0.ch022

Al-Hamdani, W. A. (2014). Secure e-learning and cryptography. In K. Sullivan, P. Czigler, & J. Sullivan Hellgren (Eds.), *Cases on professional distance education degree programs and practices: Successes, challenges, and issues* (pp. 331–369). Hershey, PA: IGI Global. doi:10.4018/978-1-4666-4486-1.ch012

Al-Jaljouli, R., & Abawajy, J. H. (2012). Security framework for mobile agents-based applications. In A. Kumar & H. Rahman (Eds.), *Mobile computing techniques in emerging markets: Systems, applications and services* (pp. 242–269). Hershey, PA: IGI Global. doi:10.4018/978-1-4666-0080-5.ch009

Al-Jaljouli, R., & Abawajy, J. H. (2014). Mobile agent's security protocols. In *Crisis management: Concepts, methodologies, tools and applications* (pp. 166–202). Hershey, PA: IGI Global. doi:10.4018/978-1-4666-4707-7.ch007

Al-Suqri, M. N., & Akomolafe-Fatuyi, E. (2012). Security and privacy in digital libraries: Challenges, opportunities and prospects. *International Journal of Digital Library Systems*, 3(4), 54–61. doi:10.4018/ijdls.2012100103

Alavi, R., Islam, S., Jahankhani, H., & Al-Nemrat, A. (2013). Analyzing human factors for an effective information security management system. *International Journal of Secure Software Engineering, 4*(1), 50–74. doi:10.4018/jsse.2013010104

Alazab, A., Abawajy, J. H., & Hobbs, M. (2013). Web malware that targets web applications. In L. Caviglione, M. Coccoli, & A. Merlo (Eds.), *Social network engineering for secure web data and services* (pp. 248–264). Hershey, PA: IGI Global. doi:10.4018/978-1-4666-3926-3.ch012

Alazab, A., Hobbs, M., Abawajy, J., & Khraisat, A. (2013). Malware detection and prevention system based on multi-stage rules. *International Journal of Information Security and Privacy, 7*(2), 29–43. doi:10.4018/jisp.2013040102

Alazab, M., Venkatraman, S., Watters, P., & Alazab, M. (2013). Information security governance: The art of detecting hidden malware. In D. Mellado, L. Enrique Sánchez, E. Fernández-Medina, & M. Piattini (Eds.), *IT security governance innovations: Theory and research* (pp. 293–315). Hershey, PA: IGI Global. doi:10.4018/978-1-4666-2083-4.ch011

Alhaj, A., Aljawarneh, S., Masadeh, S., & Abu-Taieh, E. (2013). A secure data transmission mechanism for cloud outsourced data. *International Journal of Cloud Applications and Computing, 3*(1), 34–43. doi:10.4018/ijcac.2013010104

Ali, M., & Jawandhiya, P. (2012). Security aware routing protocols for mobile ad hoc networks. In K. Lakhtaria (Ed.), *Technological advancements and applications in mobile ad-hoc networks: Research trends* (pp. 264–289). Hershey, PA: IGI Global. doi:10.4018/978-1-4666-0321-9.ch016

Ali, S. (2012). Practical web application security audit following industry standards and compliance. In J. Zubairi & A. Mahboob (Eds.), *Cyber security standards, practices and industrial applications: Systems and methodologies* (pp. 259–279). Hershey, PA: IGI Global. doi:10.4018/978-1-60960-851-4.ch013

Aljawarneh, S. (2013). Cloud security engineering: Avoiding security threats the right way. In S. Aljawarneh (Ed.), *Cloud computing advancements in design, implementation, and technologies* (pp. 147–153). Hershey, PA: IGI Global. doi:10.4018/978-1-4666-1879-4.ch010

Alshaer, H., Muhaidat, S., Shubair, R., & Shayegannia, M. (2014). Security and connectivity analysis in vehicular communication networks. In D. Rawat, B. Bista, & G. Yan (Eds.), *Security, privacy, trust, and resource management in mobile and wireless communications* (pp. 83–107). Hershey, PA: IGI Global. doi:10.4018/978-1-4666-4691-9.ch005

Alzamil, Z. A. (2012). Information security awareness at Saudi Arabians organizations: An information technology employees perspective. *International Journal of Information Security and Privacy*, 6(3), 38–55. doi:10.4018/jisp.2012070102

Anyiwo, D., & Sharma, S. (2011). Web services and e-business technologies: Security issues. In O. Bak & N. Stair (Eds.), *Impact of e-business technologies on public and private organizations: Industry comparisons and perspectives* (pp. 249–261). Hershey, PA: IGI Global. doi:10.4018/978-1-60960-501-8.ch015

Apostolakis, I., Chryssanthou, A., & Varlamis, I. (2011). A holistic perspective of security in health related virtual communities. In *Virtual communities: Concepts, methodologies, tools and applications* (pp. 1190–1204). Hershey, PA: IGI Global. doi:10.4018/978-1-60960-100-3.ch406

Arnett, K. P., Templeton, G. F., & Vance, D. A. (2011). Information security by words alone: The case for strong security policies. In H. Nemati (Ed.), *Security and privacy assurance in advancing technologies: New developments* (pp. 154–159). Hershey, PA: IGI Global. doi:10.4018/978-1-60960-200-0.ch011

Arogundade, O. T., Akinwale, A. T., Jin, Z., & Yang, X. G. (2011). A unified use-misuse case model for capturing and analysing safety and security requirements. *International Journal of Information Security and Privacy*, 5(4), 8–30. doi:10.4018/jisp.2011100102

Arshad, J., Townend, P., Xu, J., & Jie, W. (2012). Cloud computing security: Opportunities and pitfalls. *International Journal of Grid and High Performance Computing*, 4(1), 52–66. doi:10.4018/jghpc.2012010104

Asim, M., & Petkovic, M. (2012). Fundamental building blocks for security interoperability in e-business. In E. Kajan, F. Dorloff, & I. Bedini (Eds.), *Handbook of research on e-business standards and protocols: Documents, data and advanced web technologies* (pp. 269–292). Hershey, PA: IGI Global. doi:10.4018/978-1-4666-0146-8.ch013

Askary, S., Goodwin, D., & Lanis, R. (2012). Improvements in audit risks related to information technology frauds. *International Journal of Enterprise Information Systems*, 8(2), 52–63. doi:10.4018/jeis.2012040104

Aurigemma, S. (2013). A composite framework for behavioral compliance with information security policies. *Journal of Organizational and End User Computing*, 25(3), 32–51. doi:10.4018/joeuc.2013070103

Avalle, M., Pironti, A., Pozza, D., & Sisto, R. (2011). JavaSPI: A framework for security protocol implementation. *International Journal of Secure Software Engineering*, 2(4), 34–48. doi:10.4018/jsse.2011100103

Axelrod, C. W. (2012). A dynamic cyber security economic model: incorporating value functions for all involved parties. In M. Gupta, J. Walp, & R. Sharman (Eds.), *Threats, countermeasures, and advances in applied information security* (pp. 462–477). Hershey, PA: IGI Global. doi:10.4018/978-1-4666-0978-5.ch024

Ayanso, A., & Herath, T. (2012). Law and technology at crossroads in cyberspace: Where do we go from here? In A. Dudley, J. Braman, & G. Vincenti (Eds.), *Investigating cyber law and cyber ethics: Issues, impacts and practices* (pp. 57–77). Hershey, PA: IGI Global. doi:10.4018/978-1-61350-132-0.ch004

Baars, T., & Spruit, M. (2012). Designing a secure cloud architecture: The SeCA model. *International Journal of Information Security and Privacy*, 6(1), 14–32. doi:10.4018/jisp.2012010102

Bachmann, M. (2011). Deciphering the hacker underground: First quantitative insights. In T. Holt & B. Schell (Eds.), *Corporate hacking and technology-driven crime: Social dynamics and implications* (pp. 105–126). Hershey, PA: IGI Global. doi:10.4018/978-1-61692-805-6.ch006

Bachmann, M., & Smith, B. (2012). Internet fraud. In Z. Yan (Ed.), *Encyclopedia of cyber behavior* (pp. 931–943). Hershey, PA: IGI Global. doi:10.4018/978-1-4666-0315-8.ch077

Bai, Y., & Khan, K. M. (2011). Ell secure information system using modal logic technique. *International Journal of Secure Software Engineering*, 2(2), 65–76. doi:10.4018/jsse.2011040104

Bandeira, G. S. (2014). Criminal liability of organizations, corporations, legal persons, and similar entities on law of Portuguese cybercrime: A brief discussion on the issue of crimes of "false information," the "damage on other programs or computer data," the "computer-software sabotage," the "illegitimate access," the "unlawful interception," and "illegitimate reproduction of the protected program". In I. Portela & F. Almeida (Eds.), *Organizational, legal, and technological dimensions of information system administration* (pp. 96–107). Hershey, PA: IGI Global. doi:10.4018/978-1-4666-4526-4.ch006

Barjis, J. (2012). Software engineering security based on business process modeling. In K. Khan (Ed.), *Security-aware systems applications and software development methods* (pp. 52–68). Hershey, PA: IGI Global. doi:10.4018/978-1-4666-1580-9.ch004

Bedi, P., Gandotra, V., & Singhal, A. (2013). Innovative strategies for secure software development. In H. Singh & K. Kaur (Eds.), *Designing, engineering, and analyzing reliable and efficient software* (pp. 217–237). Hershey, PA: IGI Global. doi:10.4018/978-1-4666-2958-5.ch013

Belsis, P., Skourlas, C., & Gritzalis, S. (2011). Secure electronic healthcare records management in wireless environments. *Journal of Information Technology Research*, *4*(4), 1–17. doi:10.4018/jitr.2011100101

Bernik, I. (2012). Internet study: Cyber threats and cybercrime awareness and fear. *International Journal of Cyber Warfare & Terrorism*, *2*(3), 1–11. doi:10.4018/ijcwt.2012070101

Bhatia, M. S. (2011). World war III: The cyber war. *International Journal of Cyber Warfare & Terrorism*, *1*(3), 59–69. doi:10.4018/ijcwt.2011070104

Blanco, C., Rosado, D., Gutiérrez, C., Rodríguez, A., Mellado, D., Fernández-Medina, E., & Piattini, M. et al. (2011). Security over the information systems development cycle. In H. Mouratidis (Ed.), *Software engineering for secure systems: Industrial and research perspectives* (pp. 113–154). Hershey, PA: IGI Global. doi:10.4018/978-1-61520-837-1.ch005

Bobbert, Y., & Mulder, H. (2012). A research journey into maturing the business information security of mid market organizations. In W. Van Grembergen & S. De Haes (Eds.), *Business strategy and applications in enterprise IT governance* (pp. 236–259). Hershey, PA: IGI Global. doi:10.4018/978-1-4666-1779-7.ch014

Boddington, R. (2011). Digital evidence. In D. Kerr, J. Gammack, & K. Bryant (Eds.), *Digital business security development: Management technologies* (pp. 37–72). Hershey, PA: IGI Global. doi:10.4018/978-1-60566-806-2.ch002

Bossler, A. M., & Burruss, G. W. (2011). The general theory of crime and computer hacking: Low self-control hackers? In T. Holt & B. Schell (Eds.), *Corporate hacking and technology-driven crime: Social dynamics and implications* (pp. 38–67). Hershey, PA: IGI Global. doi:10.4018/978-1-61692-805-6.ch003

Bouras, C., & Stamos, K. (2011). Security issues for multi-domain resource reservation. In D. Kar & M. Syed (Eds.), *Network security, administration and management: Advancing technology and practice* (pp. 38–50). Hershey, PA: IGI Global. doi:10.4018/978-1-60960-777-7.ch003

Bracci, F., Corradi, A., & Foschini, L. (2014). Cloud standards: Security and interoperability issues. In H. Mouftah & B. Kantarci (Eds.), *Communication infrastructures for cloud computing* (pp. 465–495). Hershey, PA: IGI Global. doi:10.4018/978-1-4666-4522-6.ch020

Brodsky, J., & Radvanovsky, R. (2011). Control systems security. In T. Holt & B. Schell (Eds.), *Corporate hacking and technology-driven crime: Social dynamics and implications* (pp. 187–204). Hershey, PA: IGI Global. doi:10.4018/978-1-61692-805-6.ch010

Brooks, D. (2013). Security threats and risks of intelligent building systems: Protecting facilities from current and emerging vulnerabilities. In C. Laing, A. Badii, & P. Vickers (Eds.), *Securing critical infrastructures and critical control systems: Approaches for threat protection* (pp. 1–16). Hershey, PA: IGI Global. doi:10.4018/978-1-4666-2659-1.ch001

Bülow, W., & Wester, M. (2012). The right to privacy and the protection of personal data in a digital era and the age of information. In C. Akrivopoulou & N. Garipidis (Eds.), *Human rights and risks in the digital era: Globalization and the effects of information technologies* (pp. 34–45). Hershey, PA: IGI Global. doi:10.4018/978-1-4666-0891-7.ch004

Canongia, C., & Mandarino, R. (2014). Cybersecurity: The new challenge of the information society. In Crisis management: Concepts, methodologies, tools and applications (pp. 60-80). Hershey, PA: IGI Global. doi:10.4018/978-1-4666-4707-7.ch003

Cao, X., & Lu, Y. (2011). The social network structure of a computer hacker community. In H. Nemati (Ed.), *Security and privacy assurance in advancing technologies: New developments* (pp. 160–173). Hershey, PA: IGI Global. doi:10.4018/978-1-60960-200-0.ch012

Cardholm, L. (2014). Identifying the business value of information security. In T. Tsiakis, T. Kargidis, & P. Katsaros (Eds.), *Approaches and processes for managing the economics of information systems* (pp. 157–180). Hershey, PA: IGI Global. doi:10.4018/978-1-4666-4983-5.ch010

Cardoso, R. C., & Gomes, A. (2012). Security issues in massively multiplayer online games. In M. Cruz-Cunha (Ed.), *Handbook of research on serious games as educational, business and research tools* (pp. 290–314). Hershey, PA: IGI Global. doi:10.4018/978-1-4666-0149-9.ch016

Carpen-Amarie, A., Costan, A., Leordeanu, C., Basescu, C., & Antoniu, G. (2012). Towards a generic security framework for cloud data management environments. *International Journal of Distributed Systems and Technologies*, *3*(1), 17–34. doi:10.4018/jdst.2012010102

Caushaj, E., Fu, H., Sethi, I., Badih, H., Watson, D., Zhu, Y., & Leng, S. (2013). Theoretical analysis and experimental study: Monitoring data privacy in smartphone communications. *International Journal of Interdisciplinary Telecommunications and Networking*, *5*(2), 66–82. doi:10.4018/jitn.2013040106

Cepheli, Ö., & Kurt, G. K. (2014). Physical layer security in wireless communication networks. In D. Rawat, B. Bista, & G. Yan (Eds.), *Security, privacy, trust, and resource management in mobile and wireless communications* (pp. 61–81). Hershey, PA: IGI Global. doi:10.4018/978-1-4666-4691-9.ch004

Chakraborty, P., & Raghuraman, K. (2013). Trends in information security. In K. Buragga & N. Zaman (Eds.), *Software development techniques for constructive information systems design* (pp. 354–376). Hershey, PA: IGI Global. doi:10.4018/978-1-4666-3679-8.ch020

Chandrakumar, T., & Parthasarathy, S. (2012). Enhancing data security in ERP projects using XML. *International Journal of Enterprise Information Systems*, *8*(1), 51–65. doi:10.4018/jeis.2012010104

Chapple, M. J., Striegel, A., & Crowell, C. R. (2011). Firewall rulebase management: Tools and techniques. In M. Quigley (Ed.), *ICT ethics and security in the 21st century: New developments and applications* (pp. 254–276). Hershey, PA: IGI Global. doi:10.4018/978-1-60960-573-5.ch013

Chen, L., Hu, W., Yang, M., & Zhang, L. (2011). Security and privacy issues in secure e-mail standards and services. In H. Nemati (Ed.), *Security and privacy assurance in advancing technologies: new developments* (pp. 174–185). Hershey, PA: IGI Global. doi:10.4018/978-1-60960-200-0.ch013

Chen, L., Varol, C., Liu, Q., & Zhou, B. (2014). Security in wireless metropolitan area networks: WiMAX and LTE. In D. Rawat, B. Bista, & G. Yan (Eds.), *Security, privacy, trust, and resource management in mobile and wireless communications* (pp. 11–27). Hershey, PA: IGI Global. doi:10.4018/978-1-4666-4691-9.ch002

Cherdantseva, Y., & Hilton, J. (2014). Information security and information assurance: Discussion about the meaning, scope, and goals. In I. Portela & F. Almeida (Eds.), *Organizational, legal, and technological dimensions of information system administration* (pp. 167–198). Hershey, PA: IGI Global. doi:10.4018/978-1-4666-4526-4.ch010

Cherdantseva, Y., & Hilton, J. (2014). The 2011 survey of information security and information assurance professionals: Findings. In I. Portela & F. Almeida (Eds.), *Organizational, legal, and technological dimensions of information system administration* (pp. 243–256). Hershey, PA: IGI Global. doi:10.4018/978-1-4666-4526-4.ch013

Chowdhury, M. U., & Ray, B. R. (2013). Security risks/vulnerability in a RFID system and possible defenses. In N. Karmakar (Ed.), *Advanced RFID systems, security, and applications* (pp. 1–15). Hershey, PA: IGI Global. doi:10.4018/978-1-4666-2080-3.ch001

Cofta, P., Lacohée, H., & Hodgson, P. (2011). Incorporating social trust into design practices for secure systems. In H. Mouratidis (Ed.), *Software engineering for secure systems: Industrial and research perspectives* (pp. 260–284). Hershey, PA: IGI Global. doi:10.4018/978-1-61520-837-1.ch010

Conway, M. (2012). What is cyberterrorism and how real is the threat? A review of the academic literature, 1996 – 2009. In P. Reich & E. Gelbstein (Eds.), *Law, policy, and technology: Cyberterrorism, information warfare, and internet immobilization* (pp. 279–307). Hershey, PA: IGI Global. doi:10.4018/978-1-61520-831-9.ch011

Corser, G. P., Arslanturk, S., Oluoch, J., Fu, H., & Corser, G. E. (2013). Knowing the enemy at the gates: Measuring attacker motivation. *International Journal of Interdisciplinary Telecommunications and Networking*, 5(2), 83–95. doi:10.4018/jitn.2013040107

Crosbie, M. (2013). Hack the cloud: Ethical hacking and cloud forensics. In K. Ruan (Ed.), *Cybercrime and cloud forensics: Applications for investigation processes* (pp. 42–58). Hershey, PA: IGI Global. doi:10.4018/978-1-4666-2662-1.ch002

Curran, K., Carlin, S., & Adams, M. (2012). Security issues in cloud computing. In L. Chao (Ed.), *Cloud computing for teaching and learning: Strategies for design and implementation* (pp. 200–208). Hershey, PA: IGI Global. doi:10.4018/978-1-4666-0957-0.ch014

Czosseck, C., Ottis, R., & Talihärm, A. (2011). Estonia after the 2007 cyber attacks: Legal, strategic and organisational changes in cyber security. *International Journal of Cyber Warfare & Terrorism*, 1(1), 24–34. doi:10.4018/ijcwt.2011010103

Czosseck, C., & Podins, K. (2012). A vulnerability-based model of cyber weapons and its implications for cyber conflict. *International Journal of Cyber Warfare & Terrorism*, 2(1), 14–26. doi:10.4018/ijcwt.2012010102 da Silva, F. A., Moura, D. F., & Galdino, J. F. (2012). Classes of attacks for tactical software defined radios. *International Journal of Embedded and Real-Time Communication Systems*, 3(4), 57–82. doi:10.4018/jertcs.2012100104

Dabcevic, K., Marcenaro, L., & Regazzoni, C. S. (2013). Security in cognitive radio networks. In T. Lagkas, P. Sarigiannidis, M. Louta, & P. Chatzimisios (Eds.), *Evolution of cognitive networks and self-adaptive communication systems* (pp. 301–335). Hershey, PA: IGI Global. doi:10.4018/978-1-4666-4189-1.ch013

Dahbur, K., Mohammad, B., & Tarakji, A. B. (2013). Security issues in cloud computing: A survey of risks, threats and vulnerabilities. In S. Aljawarneh (Ed.), *Cloud computing advancements in design, implementation, and technologies* (pp. 154–165). Hershey, PA: IGI Global. doi:10.4018/978-1-4666-1879-4.ch011

Dark, M. (2011). Data breach disclosure: A policy analysis. In M. Dark (Ed.), *Information assurance and security ethics in complex systems: Interdisciplinary perspectives* (pp. 226–252). Hershey, PA: IGI Global. doi:10.4018/978-1-61692-245-0.ch011

Das, S., Mukhopadhyay, A., & Bhasker, B. (2013). Today's action is better than tomorrows cure - Evaluating information security at a premier Indian business school. *Journal of Cases on Information Technology*, 15(3), 1–23. doi:10.4018/jcit.2013070101

Dasgupta, D., & Naseem, D. (2014). A framework for compliance and security coverage estimation for cloud services: A cloud insurance model. In S. Srinivasan (Ed.), *Security, trust, and regulatory aspects of cloud computing in business environments* (pp. 91–114). Hershey, PA: IGI Global. doi:10.4018/978-1-4666-5788-5.ch005

De Fuentes, J. M., González-Tablas, A. I., & Ribagorda, A. (2011). Overview of security issues in vehicular ad-hoc networks. In M. Cruz-Cunha & F. Moreira (Eds.), *Handbook of research on mobility and computing: Evolving technologies and ubiquitous impacts* (pp. 894–911). Hershey, PA: IGI Global. doi:10.4018/978-1-60960-042-6.ch056

De Groef, W., Devriese, D., Reynaert, T., & Piessens, F. (2013). Security and privacy of online social network applications. In L. Caviglione, M. Coccoli, & A. Merlo (Eds.), *Social network engineering for secure web data and services* (pp. 206–221). Hershey, PA: IGI Global. doi:10.4018/978-1-4666-3926-3.ch010

Denning, D. E. (2011). Cyber conflict as an emergent social phenomenon. In T. Holt & B. Schell (Eds.), *Corporate hacking and technology-driven crime: Social dynamics and implications* (pp. 170–186). Hershey, PA: IGI Global. doi:10.4018/978-1-61692-805-6.ch009

Desai, A. M., & Mock, K. (2013). Security in cloud computing. In A. Bento & A. Aggarwal (Eds.), *Cloud computing service and deployment models: Layers and management* (pp. 208–221). Hershey, PA: IGI Global. doi:10.4018/978-1-4666-2187-9.ch011

Dionysiou, I., & Ktoridou, D. (2012). Enhancing dynamic-content courses with student-oriented learning strategies: The case of computer security course. *International Journal of Cyber Ethics in Education, 2*(2), 24–33. doi:10.4018/ijcee.2012040103

Disterer, G. (2012). Attacks on IT systems: Categories of motives. In T. Chou (Ed.), *Information assurance and security technologies for risk assessment and threat management: Advances* (pp. 1–16). Hershey, PA: IGI Global. doi:10.4018/978-1-61350-507-6.ch001

Dougan, T., & Curran, K. (2012). Man in the browser attacks. *International Journal of Ambient Computing and Intelligence, 4*(1), 29–39. doi:10.4018/jaci.2012010103

Dubey, R., Sharma, S., & Chouhan, L. (2013). Security for cognitive radio networks. In M. Ku & J. Lin (Eds.), *Cognitive radio and interference management: Technology and strategy* (pp. 238–256). Hershey, PA: IGI Global. doi:10.4018/978-1-4666-2005-6.ch013

Dunkels, E., Frånberg, G., & Hällgren, C. (2011). Young people and online risk. In E. Dunkels, G. Franberg, & C. Hallgren (Eds.), *Youth culture and net culture: Online social practices* (pp. 1–16). Hershey, PA: IGI Global. doi:10.4018/978-1-60960-209-3.ch001

Dunkerley, K., & Tejay, G. (2012). The development of a model for information systems security success. In Z. Belkhamza & S. Azizi Wafa (Eds.), *Measuring organizational information systems success: New technologies and practices* (pp. 341–366). Hershey, PA: IGI Global. doi:10.4018/978-1-4666-0170-3.ch017

Dunkerley, K., & Tejay, G. (2012). Theorizing information security success: Towards secure e-government. In V. Weerakkody (Ed.), *Technology enabled transformation of the public sector: Advances in e-government* (pp. 224–235). Hershey, PA: IGI Global. doi:10.4018/978-1-4666-1776-6.ch014

Eisenga, A., Jones, T. L., & Rodriguez, W. (2012). Investing in IT security: How to determine the maximum threshold. *International Journal of Information Security and Privacy, 6*(3), 75–87. doi:10.4018/jisp.2012070104

Eyitemi, M. (2012). Regulation of cybercafés in Nigeria. In *Cyber crime: Concepts, methodologies, tools and applications* (pp. 1305–1313). Hershey, PA: IGI Global. doi:10.4018/978-1-61350-323-2.ch606

Ezumah, B., & Adekunle, S. O. (2012). A review of privacy, internet security threat, and legislation in Africa: A case study of Nigeria, South Africa, Egypt, and Kenya. In J. Abawajy, M. Pathan, M. Rahman, A. Pathan, & M. Deris (Eds.), *Internet and distributed computing advancements: Theoretical frameworks and practical applications* (pp. 115–136). Hershey, PA: IGI Global. doi:10.4018/978-1-4666-0161-1.ch005

Farooq-i-Azam, M., & Ayyaz, M. N. (2014). Embedded systems security. In *Software design and development: Concepts, methodologies, tools, and applications* (pp. 980–998). Hershey, PA: IGI Global. doi:10.4018/978-1-4666-4301-7.ch047

Fauzi, A. H., & Taylor, H. (2013). Secure community trust stores for peer-to-peer e-commerce applications using cloud services. *International Journal of E-Entrepreneurship and Innovation*, *4*(1), 1–15. doi:10.4018/jeei.2013010101

Fenz, S. (2011). E-business and information security risk management: Challenges and potential solutions. In E. Kajan (Ed.), *Electronic business interoperability: Concepts, opportunities and challenges* (pp. 596–614). Hershey, PA: IGI Global. doi:10.4018/978-1-60960-485-1.ch024

Fernandez, E. B., Yoshioka, N., Washizaki, H., Jurjens, J., VanHilst, M., & Pernu, G. (2011). Using security patterns to develop secure systems. In H. Mouratidis (Ed.), *Software engineering for secure systems: Industrial and research perspectives* (pp. 16–31). Hershey, PA: IGI Global. doi:10.4018/978-1-61520-837-1.ch002

Flores, A. E., Win, K. T., & Susilo, W. (2011). Secure exchange of electronic health records. In A. Chryssanthou, I. Apostolakis, & I. Varlamis (Eds.), *Certification and security in health-related web applications: Concepts and solutions* (pp. 1–22). Hershey, PA: IGI Global. doi:10.4018/978-1-61692-895-7.ch001

Fonseca, J., & Vieira, M. (2014). A survey on secure software development lifecycles. In *Software design and development: Concepts, methodologies, tools, and applications* (pp. 17–33). Hershey, PA: IGI Global. doi:10.4018/978-1-4666-4301-7.ch002

Fournaris, A. P., Kitsos, P., & Sklavos, N. (2013). Security and cryptographic engineering in embedded systems. In M. Khalgui, O. Mosbahi, & A. Valentini (Eds.), *Embedded computing systems: Applications, optimization, and advanced design* (pp. 420–438). Hershey, PA: IGI Global. doi:10.4018/978-1-4666-3922-5.ch021

Franqueira, V. N., van Cleeff, A., van Eck, P., & Wieringa, R. J. (2013). Engineering security agreements against external insider threat. *Information Resources Management Journal, 26*(4), 66–91. doi:10.4018/irmj.2013100104

French, T., Bessis, N., Maple, C., & Asimakopoulou, E. (2012). Trust issues on crowd-sourcing methods for urban environmental monitoring. *International Journal of Distributed Systems and Technologies, 3*(1), 35–47. doi:10.4018/jdst.2012010103

Fu, Y., Kulick, J., Yan, L. K., & Drager, S. (2013). Formal modeling and verification of security property in Handel C program. *International Journal of Secure Software Engineering, 3*(3), 50–65. doi:10.4018/jsse.2012070103

Furnell, S., von Solms, R., & Phippen, A. (2011). Preventative actions for enhancing online protection and privacy. *International Journal of Information Technologies and Systems Approach, 4*(2), 1–11. doi:10.4018/jitsa.2011070101

Gaivéo, J. (2011). SMEs e-business security issues. In M. Cruz-Cunha & J. Varajão (Eds.), *Innovations in SMEs and conducting e-business: Technologies, trends and solutions* (pp. 317–337). Hershey, PA: IGI Global. doi:10.4018/978-1-60960-765-4.ch018

Gaivéo, J. M. (2013). Security of ICTs supporting healthcare activities. In M. Cruz-Cunha, I. Miranda, & P. Gonçalves (Eds.), *Handbook of research on ICTs for human-centered healthcare and social care services* (pp. 208–228). Hershey, PA: IGI Global. doi:10.4018/978-1-4666-3986-7.ch011

Gelbstein, E. E. (2013). Designing a security audit plan for a critical information infrastructure (CII). In C. Laing, A. Badii, & P. Vickers (Eds.), *Securing critical infrastructures and critical control systems: Approaches for threat protection* (pp. 262–285). Hershey, PA: IGI Global. doi:10.4018/978-1-4666-2659-1.ch011

Gódor, G., & Imre, S. (2012). Security aspects in radio frequency identification systems. In D. Saha & V. Sridhar (Eds.), *Next generation data communication technologies: Emerging trends* (pp. 187–225). Hershey, PA: IGI Global. doi:10.4018/978-1-61350-477-2.ch009

Gogolin, G. (2011). Security and privacy concerns of virtual worlds. In B. Ciaramitaro (Ed.), *Virtual worlds and e-commerce: Technologies and applications for building customer relationships* (pp. 244–256). Hershey, PA: IGI Global. doi:10.4018/978-1-61692-808-7.ch014

Gogoulos, F. I., Antonakopoulou, A., Lioudakis, G. V., Kaklamani, D. I., & Venieris, I. S. (2014). Trust in an enterprise world: A survey. In M. Cruz-Cunha, F. Moreira, & J. Varajão (Eds.), *Handbook of research on enterprise 2.0: Technological, social, and organizational dimensions* (pp. 199–219). Hershey, PA: IGI Global. doi:10.4018/978-1-4666-4373-4.ch011

Goldman, J. E., & Ahuja, S. (2011). Integration of COBIT, balanced scorecard and SSE-CMM as an organizational & strategic information security management (ISM) framework. In M. Quigley (Ed.), *ICT ethics and security in the 21st century: New developments and applications* (pp. 277–309). Hershey, PA: IGI Global. doi:10.4018/978-1-60960-573-5.ch014

Goldschmidt, C., Dark, M., & Chaudhry, H. (2011). Responsibility for the harm and risk of software security flaws. In M. Dark (Ed.), *Information assurance and security ethics in complex systems: Interdisciplinary perspectives* (pp. 104–131). Hershey, PA: IGI Global. doi:10.4018/978-1-61692-245-0.ch006

Grahn, K., Karlsson, J., & Pulkkis, G. (2011). Secure routing and mobility in future IP networks. In M. Cruz-Cunha & F. Moreira (Eds.), *Handbook of research on mobility and computing: Evolving technologies and ubiquitous impacts* (pp. 952–972). Hershey, PA: IGI Global. doi:10.4018/978-1-60960-042-6.ch059

Greitzer, F. L., Frincke, D., & Zabriskie, M. (2011). Social/ethical issues in predictive insider threat monitoring. In M. Dark (Ed.), *Information assurance and security ethics in complex systems: Interdisciplinary perspectives* (pp. 132–161). Hershey, PA: IGI Global. doi:10.4018/978-1-61692-245-0.ch007

Grobler, M. (2012). The need for digital evidence standardisation. *International Journal of Digital Crime and Forensics, 4*(2), 1–12. doi:10.4018/jdcf.2012040101

Guo, J., Marshall, A., & Zhou, B. (2014). A multi-parameter trust framework for mobile ad hoc networks. In D. Rawat, B. Bista, & G. Yan (Eds.), *Security, privacy, trust, and resource management in mobile and wireless communications* (pp. 245–277). Hershey, PA: IGI Global. doi:10.4018/978-1-4666-4691-9.ch011

Gururajan, R., & Hafeez-Baig, A. (2011). Wireless handheld device and LAN security issues: A case study. In D. Kerr, J. Gammack, & K. Bryant (Eds.), *Digital business security development: Management technologies* (pp. 129–151). Hershey, PA: IGI Global. doi:10.4018/978-1-60566-806-2.ch006

Ha, H. (2012). Online security and consumer protection in ecommerce an Australian case. In K. Mohammed Rezaul (Ed.), *Strategic and pragmatic e-business: Implications for future business practices* (pp. 217–243). Hershey, PA: IGI Global. doi:10.4018/978-1-4666-1619-6.ch010

Hagen, J. M. (2012). The contributions of information security culture and human relations to the improvement of situational awareness. In C. Onwubiko & T. Owens (Eds.), *Situational awareness in computer network defense: Principles, methods and applications* (pp. 10–28). Hershey, PA: IGI Global. doi:10.4018/978-1-4666-0104-8.ch002

Hai-Jew, S. (2011). The social design of 3D interactive spaces for security in higher education: A preliminary view. In A. Rea (Ed.), *Security in virtual worlds, 3D webs, and immersive environments: Models for development, interaction, and management* (pp. 72–96). Hershey, PA: IGI Global. doi:10.4018/978-1-61520-891-3.ch005

Halder, D., & Jaishankar, K. (2012). Cyber crime against women and regulations in Australia. In *Cyber crime: Concepts, methodologies, tools and applications* (pp. 757–764). Hershey, PA: IGI Global. doi:10.4018/978-1-61350-323-2.ch404

Halder, D., & Jaishankar, K. (2012). Cyber victimization of women and cyber laws in India. In *Cyber crime: Concepts, methodologies, tools and applications* (pp. 742–756). Hershey, PA: IGI Global. doi:10.4018/978-1-61350-323-2.ch403

Halder, D., & Jaishankar, K. (2012). Definition, typology and patterns of victimization. In *Cyber crime: Concepts, methodologies, tools and applications* (pp. 1016–1042). Hershey, PA: IGI Global. doi:10.4018/978-1-61350-323-2.ch502

Hamlen, K., Kantarcioglu, M., Khan, L., & Thuraisingham, B. (2012). Security issues for cloud computing. In H. Nemati (Ed.), *Optimizing information security and advancing privacy assurance: New technologies* (pp. 150–162). Hershey, PA: IGI Global. doi:10.4018/978-1-4666-0026-3.ch008

Harnesk, D. (2011). Convergence of information security in B2B networks. In E. Kajan (Ed.), *Electronic business interoperability: Concepts, opportunities and challenges* (pp. 571–595). Hershey, PA: IGI Global. doi:10.4018/978-1-60960-485-1.ch023

Harnesk, D., & Hartikainen, H. (2011). Multi-layers of information security in emergency response. *International Journal of Information Systems for Crisis Response and Management*, *3*(2), 1–17. doi:10.4018/jiscrm.2011040101

Hawrylak, P. J., Hale, J., & Papa, M. (2013). Security issues for ISO 18000-6 type C RFID: Identification and solutions. In *Supply chain management: Concepts, methodologies, tools, and applications* (pp. 1565–1581). Hershey, PA: IGI Global. doi:10.4018/978-1-4666-2625-6.ch093

He, B., Tran, T. T., & Xie, B. (2014). Authentication and identity management for secure cloud businesses and services. In S. Srinivasan (Ed.), *Security, trust, and regulatory aspects of cloud computing in business environments* (pp. 180–201). Hershey, PA: IGI Global. doi:10.4018/978-1-4666-5788-5.ch011

Henrie, M. (2012). Cyber security in liquid petroleum pipelines. In J. Zubairi & A. Mahboob (Eds.), *Cyber security standards, practices and industrial applications: Systems and methodologies* (pp. 200–222). Hershey, PA: IGI Global. doi:10.4018/978-1-60960-851-4.ch011

Herath, T., Rao, H. R., & Upadhyaya, S. (2012). Internet crime: How vulnerable are you? Do gender, social influence and education play a role in vulnerability? In *Cyber crime: Concepts, methodologies, tools and applications* (pp. 1–13). Hershey, PA: IGI Global. doi:10.4018/978-1-61350-323-2.ch101

Hilmi, M. F., Pawanchik, S., Mustapha, Y., & Ali, H. M. (2013). Information security perspective of a learning management system: An exploratory study. *International Journal of Knowledge Society Research*, 4(2), 9–18. doi:10.4018/jksr.2013040102

Hommel, W. (2012). Security and privacy management for learning management systems. In *Virtual learning environments: Concepts, methodologies, tools and applications* (pp. 1151–1170). Hershey, PA: IGI Global. doi:10.4018/978-1-4666-0011-9.ch602

Hoops, D. S. (2012). Lost in cyberspace: Navigating the legal issues of e-commerce. *Journal of Electronic Commerce in Organizations*, 10(1), 33–51. doi:10.4018/jeco.2012010103

Houmb, S., Georg, G., Petriu, D., Bordbar, B., Ray, I., Anastasakis, K., & France, R. (2011). Balancing security and performance properties during system architectural design. In H. Mouratidis (Ed.), *Software engineering for secure systems: Industrial and research perspectives* (pp. 155–191). Hershey, PA: IGI Global. doi:10.4018/978-1-61520-837-1.ch006

Huang, E., & Cheng, F. (2012). Online security cues and e-payment continuance intention. *International Journal of E-Entrepreneurship and Innovation*, 3(1), 42–58. doi:10.4018/jeei.2012010104

Ifinedo, P. (2011). Relationships between information security concerns and national cultural dimensions: Findings in the global financial services industry. In H. Nemati (Ed.), *Security and privacy assurance in advancing technologies: New developments* (pp. 134–153). Hershey, PA: IGI Global. doi:10.4018/978-1-60960-200-0.ch010

Inden, U., Lioudakis, G., & Rückemann, C. (2013). Awareness-based security management for complex and internet-based operations management systems. In C. Rückemann (Ed.), *Integrated information and computing systems for natural, spatial, and social sciences* (pp. 43–73). Hershey, PA: IGI Global. doi:10.4018/978-1-4666-2190-9.ch003

Islam, S., Mouratidis, H., Kalloniatis, C., Hudic, A., & Zechner, L. (2013). Model based process to support security and privacy requirements engineering. *International Journal of Secure Software Engineering, 3*(3), 1–22. doi:10.4018/jsse.2012070101

Itani, W., Kayssi, A., & Chehab, A. (2012). Security and privacy in body sensor networks: Challenges, solutions, and research directions. In M. Watfa (Ed.), *E-healthcare systems and wireless communications: Current and future challenges* (pp. 100–127). Hershey, PA: IGI Global. doi:10.4018/978-1-61350-123-8.ch005

Jansen van Vuuren, J., Grobler, M., & Zaaiman, J. (2012). Cyber security awareness as critical driver to national security. *International Journal of Cyber Warfare & Terrorism, 2*(1), 27–38. doi:10.4018/ijcwt.2012010103

Jansen van Vuuren, J., Leenen, L., Phahlamohlaka, J., & Zaaiman, J. (2012). An approach to governance of CyberSecurity in South Africa. *International Journal of Cyber Warfare & Terrorism, 2*(4), 13–27. doi:10.4018/ijcwt.2012100102

Jensen, J., & Groep, D. L. (2012). Security and trust in a global research infrastructure. In J. Leng & W. Sharrock (Eds.), *Handbook of research on computational science and engineering: Theory and practice* (pp. 539–566). Hershey, PA: IGI Global. doi:10.4018/978-1-61350-116-0.ch022

Johnsen, S. O. (2014). Safety and security in SCADA systems must be improved through resilience based risk management. In *Crisis management: Concepts, methodologies, tools and applications* (pp. 1422–1436). Hershey, PA: IGI Global. doi:10.4018/978-1-4666-4707-7.ch071

Johnston, A. C., Wech, B., & Jack, E. (2012). Engaging remote employees: The moderating role of remote status in determining employee information security policy awareness. *Journal of Organizational and End User Computing, 25*(1), 1–23. doi:10.4018/joeuc.2013010101

Jung, C., Rudolph, M., & Schwarz, R. (2013). Security evaluation of service-oriented systems using the SiSOA method. In K. Khan (Ed.), *Developing and evaluating security-aware software systems* (pp. 20–35). Hershey, PA: IGI Global. doi:10.4018/978-1-4666-2482-5.ch002

Kaiya, H., Sakai, J., Ogata, S., & Kaijiri, K. (2013). Eliciting security requirements for an information system using asset flows and processor deployment. *International Journal of Secure Software Engineering, 4*(3), 42–63. doi:10.4018/jsse.2013070103

Kalloniatis, C., Kavakli, E., & Gritzalis, S. (2011). Designing privacy aware information systems. In H. Mouratidis (Ed.), *Software engineering for secure systems: Industrial and research perspectives* (pp. 212–231). Hershey, PA: IGI Global. doi:10.4018/978-1-61520-837-1.ch008

Kamoun, F., & Halaweh, M. (2012). User interface design and e-commerce security perception: An empirical study. *International Journal of E-Business Research, 8*(2), 15–32. doi:10.4018/jebr.2012040102

Kamruzzaman, J., Azad, A. K., Karmakar, N. C., Karmakar, G., & Srinivasan, B. (2013). Security and privacy in RFID systems. In N. Karmakar (Ed.), *Advanced RFID systems, security, and applications* (pp. 16–40). Hershey, PA: IGI Global. doi:10.4018/978-1-4666-2080-3.ch002

Kaosar, M. G., & Yi, X. (2011). Privacy preserving data gathering in wireless sensor network. In D. Kar & M. Syed (Eds.), *Network security, administration and management: Advancing technology and practice* (pp. 237–251). Hershey, PA: IGI Global. doi:10.4018/978-1-60960-777-7.ch012

Kar, D. C., Ngo, H. L., Mulkey, C. J., & Sanapala, G. (2011). Advances in security and privacy in wireless sensor networks. In H. Nemati (Ed.), *Security and privacy assurance in advancing technologies: New developments* (pp. 186–213). Hershey, PA: IGI Global. doi:10.4018/978-1-60960-200-0.ch014

Karadsheh, L., & Alhawari, S. (2011). Applying security policies in small business utilizing cloud computing technologies. *International Journal of Cloud Applications and Computing, 1*(2), 29–40. doi:10.4018/ijcac.2011040103

Karokola, G., Yngström, L., & Kowalski, S. (2012). Secure e-government services: A comparative analysis of e-government maturity models for the developing regions–The need for security services. *International Journal of Electronic Government Research, 8*(1), 1–25. doi:10.4018/jegr.2012010101

Kassim, N. M., & Ramayah, T. (2013). Security policy issues in internet banking in Malaysia. In *IT policy and ethics: Concepts, methodologies, tools, and applications* (pp. 1274–1293). Hershey, PA: IGI Global. doi:10.4018/978-1-4666-2919-6.ch057

Kayem, A. V. (2013). Security in service oriented architectures: Standards and challenges. In *Digital rights management: Concepts, methodologies, tools, and applications* (pp. 50–73). Hershey, PA: IGI Global. doi:10.4018/978-1-4666-2136-7.ch004

K.C., A., Forsgren, H., Grahn, K., Karvi, T., & Pulkkis, G. (2013). Security and trust of public key cryptography for HIP and HIP multicast. *International Journal of Dependable and Trustworthy Information Systems, 2*(3), 17–35. doi:10.4018/jdtis.2011070102

Kelarev, A. V., Brown, S., Watters, P., Wu, X., & Dazeley, R. (2011). Establishing reasoning communities of security experts for internet commerce security. In J. Yearwood & A. Stranieri (Eds.), *Technologies for supporting reasoning communities and collaborative decision making: Cooperative approaches* (pp. 380–396). Hershey, PA: IGI Global. doi:10.4018/978-1-60960-091-4.ch020

Kerr, D., Gammack, J. G., & Boddington, R. (2011). Overview of digital business security issues. In D. Kerr, J. Gammack, & K. Bryant (Eds.), *Digital business security development: Management technologies* (pp. 1–36). Hershey, PA: IGI Global. doi:10.4018/978-1-60566-806-2.ch001

Khan, K. M. (2011). A decision support system for selecting secure web services. In *Enterprise information systems: Concepts, methodologies, tools and applications* (pp. 1113–1120). Hershey, PA: IGI Global. doi:10.4018/978-1-61692-852-0.ch415

Khan, K. M. (2012). Software security engineering: Design and applications. *International Journal of Secure Software Engineering, 3*(1), 62–63. doi:10.4018/jsse.2012010104

Kilger, M. (2011). Social dynamics and the future of technology-driven crime. In T. Holt & B. Schell (Eds.), *Corporate hacking and technology-driven crime: Social dynamics and implications* (pp. 205–227). Hershey, PA: IGI Global. doi:10.4018/978-1-61692-805-6.ch011

Kirwan, G., & Power, A. (2012). Hacking: Legal and ethical aspects of an ambiguous activity. In A. Dudley, J. Braman, & G. Vincenti (Eds.), *Investigating cyber law and cyber ethics: Issues, impacts and practices* (pp. 21–36). Hershey, PA: IGI Global. doi:10.4018/978-1-61350-132-0.ch002

Kline, D. M., He, L., & Yaylacicegi, U. (2011). User perceptions of security technologies. *International Journal of Information Security and Privacy, 5*(2), 1–12. doi:10.4018/jisp.2011040101

Kolkowska, E., Hedström, K., & Karlsson, F. (2012). Analyzing information security goals. In M. Gupta, J. Walp, & R. Sharman (Eds.), *Threats, countermeasures, and advances in applied information security* (pp. 91–110). Hershey, PA: IGI Global. doi:10.4018/978-1-4666-0978-5.ch005

Korhonen, J. J., Hiekkanen, K., & Mykkänen, J. (2012). Information security governance. In M. Gupta, J. Walp, & R. Sharman (Eds.), *Strategic and practical approaches for information security governance: Technologies and applied solutions* (pp. 53–66). Hershey, PA: IGI Global. doi:10.4018/978-1-4666-0197-0.ch004

Korovessis, P. (2011). Information security awareness in academia. *International Journal of Knowledge Society Research, 2*(4), 1–17. doi:10.4018/jksr.2011100101

Koskosas, I., & Sariannidis, N. (2011). Project commitment in the context of information security. *International Journal of Information Technology Project Management, 2*(3), 17–29. doi:10.4018/jitpm.2011070102

Kotsonis, E., & Eliakis, S. (2013). Information security standards for health information systems: The implementer's approach. In *User-driven healthcare: Concepts, methodologies, tools, and applications* (pp. 225–257). Hershey, PA: IGI Global. doi:10.4018/978-1-4666-2770-3.ch013

Krishna, A. V. (2014). A randomized cloud library security environment. In S. Dhamdhere (Ed.), *Cloud computing and virtualization technologies in libraries* (pp. 278–296). Hershey, PA: IGI Global. doi:10.4018/978-1-4666-4631-5.ch016

Kruck, S. E., & Teer, F. P. (2011). Computer security practices and perceptions of the next generation of corporate computer users. In H. Nemati (Ed.), *Pervasive information security and privacy developments: Trends and advancements* (pp. 255–265). Hershey, PA: IGI Global. doi:10.4018/978-1-61692-000-5.ch017

Kumar, M., Sareen, M., & Chhabra, S. (2011). Technology related trust issues in SME B2B E-Commerce. *International Journal of Information Communication Technologies and Human Development, 3*(4), 31–46. doi:10.4018/jicthd.2011100103

Kumar, P., & Mittal, S. (2012). The perpetration and prevention of cyber crime: An analysis of cyber terrorism in India. *International Journal of Technoethics, 3*(1), 43–52. doi:10.4018/jte.2012010104

Kumar, P. S., Ashok, M. S., & Subramanian, R. (2012). A publicly verifiable dynamic secret sharing protocol for secure and dependable data storage in cloud computing. *International Journal of Cloud Applications and Computing, 2*(3), 1–25. doi:10.4018/ijcac.2012070101

Kumar, S., & Dutta, K. (2014). Security issues in mobile ad hoc networks: A survey. In D. Rawat, B. Bista, & G. Yan (Eds.), *Security, privacy, trust, and resource management in mobile and wireless communications* (pp. 176–221). Hershey, PA: IGI Global. doi:10.4018/978-1-4666-4691-9.ch009

Lawson, S. (2013). Motivating cybersecurity: Assessing the status of critical infrastructure as an object of cyber threats. In C. Laing, A. Badii, & P. Vickers (Eds.), *Securing critical infrastructures and critical control systems: Approaches for threat protection* (pp. 168–189). Hershey, PA: IGI Global. doi:10.4018/978-1-4666-2659-1.ch007

Leitch, S., & Warren, M. (2011). The ethics of security of personal information upon Facebook. In M. Quigley (Ed.), *ICT ethics and security in the 21st century: New developments and applications* (pp. 46–65). Hershey, PA: IGI Global. doi:10.4018/978-1-60960-573-5.ch003

Li, M. (2013). Security terminology. In A. Miri (Ed.), *Advanced security and privacy for RFID technologies* (pp. 1–13). Hershey, PA: IGI Global. doi:10.4018/978-1-4666-3685-9.ch001

Ligaarden, O. S., Refsdal, A., & Stølen, K. (2013). Using indicators to monitor security risk in systems of systems: How to capture and measure the impact of service dependencies on the security of provided services. In D. Mellado, L. Enrique Sánchez, E. Fernández-Medina, & M. Piattini (Eds.), *IT security governance innovations: Theory and research* (pp. 256–292). Hershey, PA: IGI Global. doi:10.4018/978-1-4666-2083-4.ch010

Lim, J. S., Chang, S., Ahmad, A., & Maynard, S. (2012). Towards an organizational culture framework for information security practices. In M. Gupta, J. Walp, & R. Sharman (Eds.), *Strategic and practical approaches for information security governance: Technologies and applied solutions* (pp. 296–315). Hershey, PA: IGI Global. doi:10.4018/978-1-4666-0197-0.ch017

Lin, X., & Luppicini, R. (2011). Socio-technical influences of cyber espionage: A case study of the GhostNet system. *International Journal of Technoethics, 2*(2), 65–77. doi:10.4018/jte.2011040105

Lindström, J., & Hanken, C. (2012). Security challenges and selected legal aspects for wearable computing. *Journal of Information Technology Research, 5*(1), 68–87. doi:10.4018/jitr.2012010104

Maheshwari, H., Hyman, H., & Agrawal, M. (2012). A comparison of cyber-crime definitions in India and the United States. In *Cyber crime: Concepts, methodologies, tools and applications* (pp. 714–726). Hershey, PA: IGI Global. doi:10.4018/978-1-61350-323-2.ch401

Malcolmson, J. (2014). The role of security culture. In I. Portela & F. Almeida (Eds.), *Organizational, legal, and technological dimensions of information system administration* (pp. 225–242). Hershey, PA: IGI Global. doi:10.4018/978-1-4666-4526-4.ch012

Mantas, G., Lymberopoulos, D., & Komninos, N. (2011). Security in smart home environment. In A. Lazakidou, K. Siassiakos, & K. Ioannou (Eds.), *Wireless technologies for ambient assisted living and healthcare: Systems and applications* (pp. 170–191). Hershey, PA: IGI Global. doi:10.4018/978-1-61520-805-0.ch010

Maple, C., Short, E., Brown, A., Bryden, C., & Salter, M. (2012). Cyberstalking in the UK: Analysis and recommendations. *International Journal of Distributed Systems and Technologies, 3*(4), 34–51. doi:10.4018/jdst.2012100104

Maqousi, A., & Balikhina, T. (2011). Building security awareness culture to serve e-government initiative. In A. Al Ajeeli & Y. Al-Bastaki (Eds.), *Handbook of research on e-services in the public sector: E-government strategies and advancements* (pp. 304–311). Hershey, PA: IGI Global. doi:10.4018/978-1-61520-789-3.ch024

Martin, N., & Rice, J. (2013). Spearing high net wealth individuals: The case of online fraud and mature age internet users. *International Journal of Information Security and Privacy, 7*(1), 1–15. doi:10.4018/jisp.2013010101

Martino, L., & Bertino, E. (2012). Security for web services: Standards and research issues. In L. Jie-Zhang (Ed.), *Innovations, standards and practices of web services: Emerging research topics* (pp. 336–362). Hershey, PA: IGI Global. doi:10.4018/978-1-61350-104-7.ch015

Massonet, P., Michot, A., Naqvi, S., Villari, M., & Latanicki, J. (2013). Securing the external interfaces of a federated infrastructure cloud. In *IT policy and ethics: Concepts, methodologies, tools, and applications* (pp. 1876–1903). Hershey, PA: IGI Global. doi:10.4018/978-1-4666-2919-6.ch082

Maumbe, B., & Owei, V. T. (2013). Understanding the information security landscape in South Africa: Implications for strategic collaboration and policy development. In B. Maumbe & C. Patrikakis (Eds.), *E-agriculture and rural development: Global innovations and future prospects* (pp. 90–102). Hershey, PA: IGI Global. doi:10.4018/978-1-4666-2655-3.ch009

Mazumdar, C. (2011). Enterprise information system security: A life-cycle approach. In *Enterprise information systems: Concepts, methodologies, tools and applications* (pp. 154–168). Hershey, PA: IGI Global. doi:10.4018/978-1-61692-852-0.ch111

McCune, J., & Haworth, D. A. (2012). Securing America against cyber war. *International Journal of Cyber Warfare & Terrorism*, 2(1), 39–49. doi:10.4018/ijcwt.2012010104

Melvin, A. O., & Ayotunde, T. (2011). Spirituality in cybercrime (Yahoo Yahoo) activities among youths in south west Nigeria. In E. Dunkels, G. Franberg, & C. Hallgren (Eds.), *Youth culture and net culture: Online social practices* (pp. 357–380). Hershey, PA: IGI Global. doi:10.4018/978-1-60960-209-3.ch020

Miller, J. M., Higgins, G. E., & Lopez, K. M. (2013). Considering the role of e-government in cybercrime awareness and prevention: Toward a theoretical research program for the 21st century. In *Digital rights management: Concepts, methodologies, tools, and applications* (pp. 789–800). Hershey, PA: IGI Global. doi:10.4018/978-1-4666-2136-7.ch036

Millman, C., Whitty, M., Winder, B., & Griffiths, M. D. (2012). Perceived criminality of cyber-harassing behaviors among undergraduate students in the United Kingdom. *International Journal of Cyber Behavior, Psychology and Learning*, 2(4), 49–59. doi:10.4018/ijcbpl.2012100104

Minami, N. A. (2012). Employing dynamic models to enhance corporate IT security policy. *International Journal of Agent Technologies and Systems*, 4(2), 42–59. doi:10.4018/jats.2012040103

Mirante, D. P., & Ammari, H. M. (2014). Wireless sensor network security attacks: A survey. In *Crisis management: Concepts, methodologies, tools and applications* (pp. 25–59). Hershey, PA: IGI Global. doi:10.4018/978-1-4666-4707-7.ch002

Mishra, A., & Mishra, D. (2013). Cyber stalking: A challenge for web security. In J. Bishop (Ed.), *Examining the concepts, issues, and implications of internet trolling* (pp. 32–42). Hershey, PA: IGI Global. doi:10.4018/978-1-4666-2803-8.ch004

Mishra, S. (2011). Wireless sensor networks: Emerging applications and security solutions. In D. Kar & M. Syed (Eds.), *Network security, administration and management: Advancing technology and practice* (pp. 217–236). Hershey, PA: IGI Global. doi:10.4018/978-1-60960-777-7.ch011

Mitra, S., & Padman, R. (2012). Privacy and security concerns in adopting social media for personal health management: A health plan case study. *Journal of Cases on Information Technology*, 14(4), 12–26. doi:10.4018/jcit.2012100102

Modares, H., Lloret, J., Moravejosharieh, A., & Salleh, R. (2014). Security in mobile cloud computing. In J. Rodrigues, K. Lin, & J. Lloret (Eds.), *Mobile networks and cloud computing convergence for progressive services and applications* (pp. 79–91). Hershey, PA: IGI Global. doi:10.4018/978-1-4666-4781-7.ch005

Mohammadi, S., Golara, S., & Mousavi, N. (2012). Selecting adequate security mechanisms in e-business processes using fuzzy TOPSIS. *International Journal of Fuzzy System Applications*, 2(1), 35–53. doi:10.4018/ijfsa.2012010103

Mohammed, L. A. (2012). ICT security policy: Challenges and potential remedies. In *Cyber crime: Concepts, methodologies, tools and applications* (pp. 999–1015). Hershey, PA: IGI Global. doi:10.4018/978-1-61350-323-2.ch501

Molok, N. N., Ahmad, A., & Chang, S. (2012). Online social networking: A source of intelligence for advanced persistent threats. *International Journal of Cyber Warfare & Terrorism*, 2(1), 1–13. doi:10.4018/ijcwt.2012010101

Monteleone, S. (2011). Ambient intelligence: Legal challenges and possible directions for privacy protection. In C. Akrivopoulou & A. Psygkas (Eds.), *Personal data privacy and protection in a surveillance era: Technologies and practices* (pp. 201–221). Hershey, PA: IGI Global. doi:10.4018/978-1-60960-083-9.ch012

Moralis, A., Pouli, V., Grammatikou, M., Kalogeras, D., & Maglaris, V. (2012). Security standards and issues for grid computing. In N. Preve (Ed.), *Computational and data grids: Principles, applications and design* (pp. 248–264). Hershey, PA: IGI Global. doi:10.4018/978-1-61350-113-9.ch010

Mouratidis, H., & Kang, M. (2011). Secure by design: Developing secure software systems from the ground up. *International Journal of Secure Software Engineering*, 2(3), 23–41. doi:10.4018/jsse.2011070102

Murthy, A. S., Nagadevara, V., & De', R. (2012). Predictive models in cybercrime investigation: An application of data mining techniques. In J. Wang (Ed.), *Advancing the service sector with evolving technologies: Techniques and principles* (pp. 166–177). Hershey, PA: IGI Global. doi:10.4018/978-1-4666-0044-7.ch011

Nabi, S. I., Al-Ghmlas, G. S., & Alghathbar, K. (2012). Enterprise information security policies, standards, and procedures: A survey of available standards and guidelines. In M. Gupta, J. Walp, & R. Sharman (Eds.), *Strategic and practical approaches for information security governance: Technologies and applied solutions* (pp. 67–89). Hershey, PA: IGI Global. doi:10.4018/978-1-4666-0197-0.ch005

Nachtigal, S. (2011). E-business and security. In O. Bak & N. Stair (Eds.), *Impact of e-business technologies on public and private organizations: Industry comparisons and perspectives* (pp. 262–277). Hershey, PA: IGI Global. doi:10.4018/978-1-60960-501-8.ch016

Namal, S., & Gurtov, A. (2012). Security and mobility aspects of femtocell networks. In R. Saeed, B. Chaudhari, & R. Mokhtar (Eds.), *Femtocell communications and technologies: Business opportunities and deployment challenges* (pp. 124–156). Hershey, PA: IGI Global. doi:10.4018/978-1-4666-0092-8.ch008

Naqvi, D. E. (2011). Designing efficient security services infrastructure for virtualization oriented architectures. In H. Nemati (Ed.), *Pervasive information security and privacy developments: Trends and advancements* (pp. 149–171). Hershey, PA: IGI Global. doi:10.4018/978-1-61692-000-5.ch011

Neto, A. A., & Vieira, M. (2011). Security gaps in databases: A comparison of alternative software products for web applications support. *International Journal of Secure Software Engineering*, 2(3), 42–62. doi:10.4018/jsse.2011070103

Ngugi, B., Mana, J., & Segal, L. (2011). Evaluating the quality and usefulness of data breach information systems. *International Journal of Information Security and Privacy*, 5(4), 31–46. doi:10.4018/jisp.2011100103

Nhlabatsi, A., Bandara, A., Hayashi, S., Haley, C., Jurjens, J., & Kaiya, H. ... Yu, Y. (2011). Security patterns: Comparing modeling approaches. In H. Mouratidis (Ed.), Software engineering for secure systems: Industrial and research perspectives (pp. 75-111). Hershey, PA: IGI Global. doi:10.4018/978-1-61520-837-1.ch004

Nicho, M. (2013). An information governance model for information security management. In D. Mellado, L. Enrique Sánchez, E. Fernández-Medina, & M. Piattini (Eds.), *IT security governance innovations: Theory and research* (pp. 155–189). Hershey, PA: IGI Global. doi:10.4018/978-1-4666-2083-4.ch007

Nicho, M., Fakhry, H., & Haiber, C. (2011). An integrated security governance framework for effective PCI DSS implementation. *International Journal of Information Security and Privacy*, 5(3), 50–67. doi:10.4018/jisp.2011070104

Nobelis, N., Boudaoud, K., Delettre, C., & Riveill, M. (2012). Designing security properties-centric communication protocols using a component-based approach. *International Journal of Distributed Systems and Technologies*, 3(1), 1–16. doi:10.4018/jdst.2012010101

Ohashi, M., & Hori, M. (2011). Security management services based on authentication roaming between different certificate authorities. In M. Cruz-Cunha & J. Varajao (Eds.), *Enterprise information systems design, implementation and management: Organizational applications* (pp. 72–84). Hershey, PA: IGI Global. doi:10.4018/978-1-61692-020-3.ch005

Okubo, T., Kaiya, H., & Yoshioka, N. (2012). Analyzing impacts on software enhancement caused by security design alternatives with patterns. *International Journal of Secure Software Engineering, 3*(1), 37–61. doi:10.4018/jsse.2012010103

Oost, D., & Chew, E. K. (2012). Investigating the concept of information security culture. In M. Gupta, J. Walp, & R. Sharman (Eds.), *Strategic and practical approaches for information security governance: Technologies and applied solutions* (pp. 1–12). Hershey, PA: IGI Global. doi:10.4018/978-1-4666-0197-0.ch001

Otero, A. R., Ejnioui, A., Otero, C. E., & Tejay, G. (2013). Evaluation of information security controls in organizations by grey relational analysis. *International Journal of Dependable and Trustworthy Information Systems, 2*(3), 36–54. doi:10.4018/jdtis.2011070103

Ouedraogo, M., Mouratidis, H., Dubois, E., & Khadraoui, D. (2011). Security assurance evaluation and IT systems context of use security criticality. *International Journal of Handheld Computing Research, 2*(4), 59–81. doi:10.4018/jhcr.2011100104

Pal, S. (2013). Cloud computing: Security concerns and issues. In A. Bento & A. Aggarwal (Eds.), *Cloud computing service and deployment models: Layers and management* (pp. 191–207). Hershey, PA: IGI Global. doi:10.4018/978-1-4666-2187-9.ch010

Palanisamy, R., & Mukerji, B. (2012). Security and privacy issues in e-government. In M. Shareef, N. Archer, & S. Dutta (Eds.), *E-government service maturity and development: Cultural, organizational and technological perspectives* (pp. 236–248). Hershey, PA: IGI Global. doi:10.4018/978-1-60960-848-4.ch013

Pan, Y., Yuan, B., & Mishra, S. (2011). Network security auditing. In D. Kar & M. Syed (Eds.), *Network security, administration and management: Advancing technology and practice* (pp. 131–157). Hershey, PA: IGI Global. doi:10.4018/978-1-60960-777-7.ch008

Patel, A., Taghavi, M., Júnior, J. C., Latih, R., & Zin, A. M. (2012). Safety measures for social computing in wiki learning environment. *International Journal of Information Security and Privacy, 6*(2), 1–15. doi:10.4018/jisp.2012040101

Pathan, A. K. (2012). Security management in heterogeneous distributed sensor networks. In S. Bagchi (Ed.), *Ubiquitous multimedia and mobile agents: Models and implementations* (pp. 274–294). Hershey, PA: IGI Global. doi:10.4018/978-1-61350-107-8.ch012

Paul, C., & Porche, I. R. (2011). Toward a U.S. army cyber security culture. *International Journal of Cyber Warfare & Terrorism, 1*(3), 70–80. doi:10.4018/ijcwt.2011070105

Pavlidis, M., Mouratidis, H., & Islam, S. (2012). Modelling security using trust based concepts. *International Journal of Secure Software Engineering, 3*(2), 36–53. doi:10.4018/jsse.2012040102

Pendegraft, N., Rounds, M., & Stone, R. W. (2012). Factors influencing college students' use of computer security. In H. Nemati (Ed.), *Optimizing information security and advancing privacy assurance: New technologies* (pp. 225–234). Hershey, PA: IGI Global. doi:10.4018/978-1-4666-0026-3.ch013

Petkovic, M., & Ibraimi, L. (2011). Privacy and security in e-health applications. In C. Röcker & M. Ziefle (Eds.), *E-health, assistive technologies and applications for assisted living: Challenges and solutions* (pp. 23–48). Hershey, PA: IGI Global. doi:10.4018/978-1-60960-469-1.ch002

Picazo-Sanchez, P., Ortiz-Martin, L., Peris-Lopez, P., & Hernandez-Castro, J. C. (2013). Security of EPC class-1. In P. Lopez, J. Hernandez-Castro, & T. Li (Eds.), *Security and trends in wireless identification and sensing platform tags: Advancements in RFID* (pp. 34–63). Hershey, PA: IGI Global. doi:10.4018/978-1-4666-1990-6.ch002

Pieters, W., Probst, C. W., Lukszo, Z., & Montoya, L. (2014). Cost-effectiveness of security measures: A model-based framework. In T. Tsiakis, T. Kargidis, & P. Katsaros (Eds.), *Approaches and processes for managing the economics of information systems* (pp. 139–156). Hershey, PA: IGI Global. doi:10.4018/978-1-4666-4983-5.ch009

Pirim, T., James, T., Boswell, K., Reithel, B., & Barkhi, R. (2011). Examining an individual's perceived need for privacy and security: Construct and scale development. In H. Nemati (Ed.), *Pervasive information security and privacy developments: Trends and advancements* (pp. 1–13). Hershey, PA: IGI Global. doi:10.4018/978-1-61692-000-5.ch001

Podhradsky, A., Casey, C., & Ceretti, P. (2012). The bluetooth honeypot project: Measuring and managing bluetooth risks in the workplace. *International Journal of Interdisciplinary Telecommunications and Networking, 4*(3), 1–22. doi:10.4018/jitn.2012070101

Pomponiu, V. (2011). Security in e-health applications. In C. Röcker & M. Ziefle (Eds.), *E-health, assistive technologies and applications for assisted living: Challenges and solutions* (pp. 94–118). Hershey, PA: IGI Global. doi:10.4018/978-1-60960-469-1.ch005

Pomponiu, V. (2014). Securing wireless ad hoc networks: State of the art and challenges. In *Crisis management: Concepts, methodologies, tools and applications* (pp. 81–101). Hershey, PA: IGI Global. doi:10.4018/978-1-4666-4707-7.ch004

Pope, M. B., Warkentin, M., & Luo, X. R. (2012). Evolutionary malware: Mobile malware, botnets, and malware toolkits. *International Journal of Wireless Networks and Broadband Technologies*, 2(3), 52–60. doi:10.4018/ijwnbt.2012070105

Prakash, S., Vaish, A., Coul, N. G. S., Srinidhi, T., & Botsa, J. (2013). Child security in cyberspace through moral cognition. *International Journal of Information Security and Privacy*, 7(1), 16–29. doi:10.4018/jisp.2013010102

Pye, G. (2011). Critical infrastructure systems: Security analysis and modelling approach. *International Journal of Cyber Warfare & Terrorism*, 1(3), 37–58. doi:10.4018/ijcwt.2011070103

Rahman, M. M., & Rezaul, K. M. (2012). Information security management: Awareness of threats in e-commerce. In M. Gupta, J. Walp, & R. Sharman (Eds.), *Threats, countermeasures, and advances in applied information security* (pp. 66–90). Hershey, PA: IGI Global. doi:10.4018/978-1-4666-0978-5.ch004

Rak, M., Ficco, M., Luna, J., Ghani, H., Suri, N., Panica, S., & Petcu, D. (2012). Security issues in cloud federations. In M. Villari, I. Brandic, & F. Tusa (Eds.), *Achieving federated and self-manageable cloud infrastructures: Theory and practice* (pp. 176–194). Hershey, PA: IGI Global. doi:10.4018/978-1-4666-1631-8.ch010

Ramachandran, M., & Mahmood, Z. (2011). A framework for internet security assessment and improvement process. In M. Ramachandran (Ed.), *Knowledge engineering for software development life cycles: Support technologies and applications* (pp. 244–255). Hershey, PA: IGI Global. doi:10.4018/978-1-60960-509-4.ch013

Ramachandran, S., Mundada, R., Bhattacharjee, A., Murthy, C., & Sharma, R. (2011). Classifying host anomalies: Using ontology in information security monitoring. In R. Santanam, M. Sethumadhavan, & M. Virendra (Eds.), *Cyber security, cyber crime and cyber forensics: Applications and perspectives* (pp. 70–86). Hershey, PA: IGI Global. doi:10.4018/978-1-60960-123-2.ch006

Ramamurthy, B. (2014). Securing business IT on the cloud. In S. Srinivasan (Ed.), *Security, trust, and regulatory aspects of cloud computing in business environments* (pp. 115–125). Hershey, PA: IGI Global. doi:10.4018/978-1-4666-5788-5.ch006

Raspotnig, C., & Opdahl, A. L. (2012). Improving security and safety modelling with failure sequence diagrams. *International Journal of Secure Software Engineering, 3*(1), 20–36. doi:10.4018/jsse.2012010102

Reddy, A., & Prasad, G. V. (2012). Consumer perceptions on security, privacy, and trust on e-portals. *International Journal of Online Marketing, 2*(2), 10–24. doi:10.4018/ijom.2012040102

Richet, J. (2013). From young hackers to crackers. *International Journal of Technology and Human Interaction, 9*(3), 53–62. doi:10.4018/jthi.2013070104

Rjaibi, N., Rabai, L. B., Ben Aissa, A., & Mili, A. (2013). Mean failure cost as a measurable value and evidence of cybersecurity: E-learning case study. *International Journal of Secure Software Engineering, 4*(3), 64–81. doi:10.4018/jsse.2013070104

Roberts, L. D. (2012). Cyber identity theft. In *Cyber crime: Concepts, methodologies, tools and applications* (pp. 21–36). Hershey, PA: IGI Global. doi:10.4018/978-1-61350-323-2.ch103

Rodríguez, J., Fernández-Medina, E., Piattini, M., & Mellado, D. (2011). A security requirements engineering tool for domain engineering in software product lines. In N. Milanovic (Ed.), *Non-functional properties in service oriented architecture: Requirements, models and methods* (pp. 73–92). Hershey, PA: IGI Global. doi:10.4018/978-1-60566-794-2.ch004

Roldan, M., & Rea, A. (2011). Individual privacy and security in virtual worlds. In A. Rea (Ed.), *Security in virtual worlds, 3D webs, and immersive environments: Models for development, interaction, and management* (pp. 1–19). Hershey, PA: IGI Global. doi:10.4018/978-1-61520-891-3.ch001

Rowe, N. C., Garfinkel, S. L., Beverly, R., & Yannakogeorgos, P. (2011). Challenges in monitoring cyberarms compliance. *International Journal of Cyber Warfare & Terrorism, 1*(2), 35–48. doi:10.4018/ijcwt.2011040104

Rwabutaza, A., Yang, M., & Bourbakis, N. (2012). A comparative survey on cryptology-based methodologies. *International Journal of Information Security and Privacy, 6*(3), 1–37. doi:10.4018/jisp.2012070101

Sadkhan, S. B., & Abbas, N. A. (2014). Privacy and security of wireless communication networks. In J. Rodrigues, K. Lin, & J. Lloret (Eds.), *Mobile networks and cloud computing convergence for progressive services and applications* (pp. 58–78). Hershey, PA: IGI Global. doi:10.4018/978-1-4666-4781-7.ch004

Saedy, M., & Mojtahed, V. (2011). Machine-to-machine communications and security solution in cellular systems. *International Journal of Interdisciplinary Telecommunications and Networking*, 3(2), 66–75. doi:10.4018/jitn.2011040105

San Nicolas-Rocca, T., & Olfman, L. (2013). End user security training for identification and access management. *Journal of Organizational and End User Computing*, 25(4), 75–103. doi:10.4018/joeuc.2013100104

Satoh, F., Nakamura, Y., Mukhi, N. K., Tatsubori, M., & Ono, K. (2011). Model-driven approach for end-to-end SOA security configurations. In N. Milanovic (Ed.), *Non-functional properties in service oriented architecture: Requirements, models and methods* (pp. 268–298). Hershey, PA: IGI Global. doi:10.4018/978-1-60566-794-2.ch012

Saucez, D., Iannone, L., & Bonaventure, O. (2014). The map-and-encap locator/identifier separation paradigm: A security analysis. In M. Boucadair & D. Binet (Eds.), *Solutions for sustaining scalability in internet growth* (pp. 148–163). Hershey, PA: IGI Global. doi:10.4018/978-1-4666-4305-5.ch008

Schell, B. H., & Holt, T. J. (2012). A profile of the demographics, psychological predispositions, and social/behavioral patterns of computer hacker insiders and outsiders. In *Cyber crime: Concepts, methodologies, tools and applications* (pp. 1461–1484). Hershey, PA: IGI Global. doi:10.4018/978-1-61350-323-2.ch705

Schmidt, H. (2011). Threat and risk-driven security requirements engineering. *International Journal of Mobile Computing and Multimedia Communications*, 3(1), 35–50. doi:10.4018/jmcmc.2011010103

Schmidt, H., Hatebur, D., & Heisel, M. (2011). A pattern-based method to develop secure software. In H. Mouratidis (Ed.), *Software engineering for secure systems: Industrial and research perspectives* (pp. 32–74). Hershey, PA: IGI Global. doi:10.4018/978-1-61520-837-1.ch003

Seale, R. O., & Hargiss, K. M. (2011). A proposed architecture for autonomous mobile agent intrusion prevention and malware defense in heterogeneous networks. *International Journal of Strategic Information Technology and Applications*, 2(4), 44–54. doi:10.4018/jsita.2011100104

Sen, J. (2013). Security and privacy challenges in cognitive wireless sensor networks. In N. Meghanathan & Y. Reddy (Eds.), *Cognitive radio technology applications for wireless and mobile ad hoc networks* (pp. 194–232). Hershey, PA: IGI Global. doi:10.4018/978-1-4666-4221-8.ch011

Sen, J. (2014). Security and privacy issues in cloud computing. In A. Ruiz-Martinez, R. Marin-Lopez, & F. Pereniguez-Garcia (Eds.), *Architectures and protocols for secure information technology infrastructures* (pp. 1–45). Hershey, PA: IGI Global. doi:10.4018/978-1-4666-4514-1.ch001

Sengupta, A., & Mazumdar, C. (2011). A mark-up language for the specification of information security governance requirements. *International Journal of Information Security and Privacy, 5*(2), 33–53. doi:10.4018/jisp.2011040103

Shaqrah, A. A. (2011). The influence of internet security on e-business competence in Jordan: An empirical analysis. In *Global business: Concepts, methodologies, tools and applications* (pp. 1071–1086). Hershey, PA: IGI Global. doi:10.4018/978-1-60960-587-2.ch413

Shareef, M. A., & Kumar, V. (2012). Prevent/control identity theft: Impact on trust and consumers purchase intention in B2C EC. *Information Resources Management Journal, 25*(3), 30–60. doi:10.4018/irmj.2012070102

Sharma, K., & Singh, A. (2011). Biometric security in the e-world. In H. Nemati & L. Yang (Eds.), *Applied cryptography for cyber security and defense: Information encryption and cyphering* (pp. 289–337). Hershey, PA: IGI Global. doi:10.4018/978-1-61520-783-1.ch013

Sharma, R. K. (2014). Physical layer security and its applications: A survey. In D. Rawat, B. Bista, & G. Yan (Eds.), *Security, Privacy, Trust, and Resource Management in Mobile and Wireless Communications* (pp. 29–60). Hershey, PA: IGI Global. doi:10.4018/978-1-4666-4691-9.ch003

Shaw, R., Keh, H., & Huang, N. (2011). Information security awareness on-line materials design with knowledge maps. *International Journal of Distance Education Technologies, 9*(4), 41–56. doi:10.4018/jdet.2011100104

Shebanow, A., Perez, R., & Howard, C. (2012). The effect of firewall testing types on cloud security policies. *International Journal of Strategic Information Technology and Applications, 3*(3), 60–68. doi:10.4018/jsita.2012070105

Shen, Y., Li, Y., Wu, L., Liu, S., & Wen, Q. (2014). Data protection in the cloud era. In Y. Shen, Y. Li, L. Wu, S. Liu, & Q. Wen (Eds.), *Enabling the new era of cloud computing: Data security, transfer, and management* (pp. 132–154). Hershey, PA: IGI Global. doi:10.4018/978-1-4666-4801-2.ch007

Shen, Y., Li, Y., Wu, L., Liu, S., & Wen, Q. (2014). Enterprise security monitoring with the fusion center model. In Y. Shen, Y. Li, L. Wu, S. Liu, & Q. Wen (Eds.), *Enabling the new era of cloud computing: Data security, transfer, and management* (pp. 116–131). Hershey, PA: IGI Global. doi:10.4018/978-1-4666-4801-2.ch006

Shore, M. (2011). Cyber security and anti-social networking. In *Virtual communities: Concepts, methodologies, tools and applications* (pp. 1286–1297). Hershey, PA: IGI Global. doi:10.4018/978-1-60960-100-3.ch412

Siddiqi, J., Alqatawna, J., & Btoush, M. H. (2011). Do insecure systems increase global digital divide? In *Global business: Concepts, methodologies, tools and applications* (pp. 2102–2111). Hershey, PA: IGI Global. doi:10.4018/978-1-60960-587-2.ch717

Simpson, J. J., Simpson, M. J., Endicott-Popovsky, B., & Popovsky, V. (2012). Secure software education: A contextual model-based approach. In K. Khan (Ed.), *Security-aware systems applications and software development methods* (pp. 286–312). Hershey, PA: IGI Global. doi:10.4018/978-1-4666-1580-9.ch016

Singh, S. (2012). Security threats and issues with MANET. In K. Lakhtaria (Ed.), *Technological advancements and applications in mobile ad-hoc networks: Research trends* (pp. 247–263). Hershey, PA: IGI Global. doi:10.4018/978-1-4666-0321-9. ch015

Sockel, H., & Falk, L. K. (2012). Online privacy, vulnerabilities, and threats: A manager's perspective. In *Cyber crime: Concepts, methodologies, tools and applications* (pp. 101–123). Hershey, PA: IGI Global. doi:10.4018/978-1-61350-323-2.ch108

Spruit, M., & de Bruijn, W. (2012). CITS: The cost of IT security framework. *International Journal of Information Security and Privacy, 6*(4), 94–116. doi:10.4018/jisp.2012100105

Srinivasan, C., Lakshmy, K., & Sethumadhavan, M. (2011). Complexity measures of cryptographically secure boolean functions. In R. Santanam, M. Sethumadhavan, & M. Virendra (Eds.), *Cyber security, cyber crime and cyber forensics: Applications and perspectives* (pp. 220–230). Hershey, PA: IGI Global. doi:10.4018/978-1-60960-123-2.ch015

Srivatsa, M., Agrawal, D., & McDonald, A. D. (2012). Security across disparate management domains in coalition MANETs. In *Wireless technologies: Concepts, methodologies, tools and applications* (pp. 1494–1518). Hershey, PA: IGI Global. doi:10.4018/978-1-61350-101-6.ch521

Stojanovic, M. D., Acimovic-Raspopovic, V. S., & Rakas, S. B. (2013). Security management issues for open source ERP in the NGN environment. In *Enterprise resource planning: Concepts, methodologies, tools, and applications* (pp. 789–804). Hershey, PA: IGI Global. doi:10.4018/978-1-4666-4153-2.ch046

Stoll, M., & Breu, R. (2012). Information security governance and standard based management systems. In M. Gupta, J. Walp, & R. Sharman (Eds.), *Strategic and practical approaches for information security governance: Technologies and applied solutions* (pp. 261–282). Hershey, PA: IGI Global. doi:10.4018/978-1-4666-0197-0.ch015

Sundaresan, M., & Boopathy, D. (2014). Different perspectives of cloud security. In S. Srinivasan (Ed.), *Security, trust, and regulatory aspects of cloud computing in business environments* (pp. 73–90). Hershey, PA: IGI Global. doi:10.4018/978-1-4666-5788-5.ch004

Takabi, H., Joshi, J. B., & Ahn, G. (2013). Security and privacy in cloud computing: Towards a comprehensive framework. In X. Yang & L. Liu (Eds.), *Principles, methodologies, and service-oriented approaches for cloud computing* (pp. 164–184). Hershey, PA: IGI Global. doi:10.4018/978-1-4666-2854-0.ch007

Takabi, H., Zargar, S. T., & Joshi, J. B. (2014). Mobile cloud computing and its security and privacy challenges. In D. Rawat, B. Bista, & G. Yan (Eds.), *Security, privacy, trust, and resource management in mobile and wireless communications* (pp. 384–407). Hershey, PA: IGI Global. doi:10.4018/978-1-4666-4691-9.ch016

Takemura, T. (2014). Unethical information security behavior and organizational commitment. In T. Tsiakis, T. Kargidis, & P. Katsaros (Eds.), *Approaches and processes for managing the economics of information systems* (pp. 181–198). Hershey, PA: IGI Global. doi:10.4018/978-1-4666-4983-5.ch011

Talib, S., Clarke, N. L., & Furnell, S. M. (2011). Establishing a personalized information security culture. *International Journal of Mobile Computing and Multimedia Communications*, 3(1), 63–79. doi:10.4018/jmcmc.2011010105

Talukder, A. K. (2011). Securing next generation internet services. In R. Santanam, M. Sethumadhavan, & M. Virendra (Eds.), *Cyber security, cyber crime and cyber forensics: Applications and perspectives* (pp. 87–105). Hershey, PA: IGI Global. doi:10.4018/978-1-60960-123-2.ch007

Tchepnda, C., Moustafa, H., Labiod, H., & Bourdon, G. (2011). Vehicular networks security: Attacks, requirements, challenges and current contributions. In K. Curran (Ed.), *Ubiquitous developments in ambient computing and intelligence: Human-centered applications* (pp. 43–55). Hershey, PA: IGI Global. doi:10.4018/978-1-60960-549-0.ch004

Tereshchenko, N. (2012). US foreign policy challenges of non-state actors cyber terrorism against critical infrastructure. *International Journal of Cyber Warfare & Terrorism*, 2(4), 28–48. doi:10.4018/ijcwt.2012100103

Thurimella, R., & Baird, L. C. (2011). Network security. In H. Nemati & L. Yang (Eds.), *Applied cryptography for cyber security and defense: Information encryption and cyphering* (pp. 1–31). Hershey, PA: IGI Global. doi:10.4018/978-1-61520-783-1.ch001

Thurimella, R., & Mitchell, W. (2011). Cloak and dagger: Man-in-the-middle and other insidious attacks. In H. Nemati (Ed.), *Security and privacy assurance in advancing technologies: New developments* (pp. 252–270). Hershey, PA: IGI Global. doi:10.4018/978-1-60960-200-0.ch016

Tiwari, S., Singh, A., Singh, R. S., & Singh, S. K. (2013). Internet security using biometrics. In *IT policy and ethics: Concepts, methodologies, tools, and applications* (pp. 1680–1707). Hershey, PA: IGI Global. doi:10.4018/978-1-4666-2919-6.ch074

Tomaiuolo, M. (2012). Trust enforcing and trust building, different technologies and visions. *International Journal of Cyber Warfare & Terrorism*, 2(4), 49–66. doi:10.4018/ijcwt.2012100104

Tomaiuolo, M. (2014). Trust management and delegation for the administration of web services. In I. Portela & F. Almeida (Eds.), *Organizational, legal, and technological dimensions of information system administration* (pp. 18–37). Hershey, PA: IGI Global. doi:10.4018/978-1-4666-4526-4.ch002

Touhafi, A., Braeken, A., Cornetta, G., Mentens, N., & Steenhaut, K. (2011). Secure techniques for remote reconfiguration of wireless embedded systems. In M. Cruz-Cunha & F. Moreira (Eds.), *Handbook of research on mobility and computing: Evolving technologies and ubiquitous impacts* (pp. 930–951). Hershey, PA: IGI Global. doi:10.4018/978-1-60960-042-6.ch058

Traore, I., & Woungang, I. (2013). Software security engineering – Part I: Security requirements and risk analysis. In K. Buragga & N. Zaman (Eds.), *Software development techniques for constructive information systems design* (pp. 221–255). Hershey, PA: IGI Global. doi:10.4018/978-1-4666-3679-8.ch012

Tripathi, M., Gaur, M., & Laxmi, V. (2014). Security challenges in wireless sensor network. In D. Rawat, B. Bista, & G. Yan (Eds.), *Security, privacy, trust, and resource management in mobile and wireless communications* (pp. 334–359). Hershey, PA: IGI Global. doi:10.4018/978-1-4666-4691-9.ch014

Trösterer, S., Beck, E., Dalpiaz, F., Paja, E., Giorgini, P., & Tscheligi, M. (2012). Formative user-centered evaluation of security modeling: Results from a case study. *International Journal of Secure Software Engineering, 3*(1), 1–19. doi:10.4018/jsse.2012010101

Tsiakis, T. (2013). The role of information security and cryptography in digital democracy: (Human) rights and freedom. In C. Akrivopoulou & N. Garipidis (Eds.), *Digital democracy and the impact of technology on governance and politics: New globalized practices* (pp. 158–174). Hershey, PA: IGI Global. doi:10.4018/978-1-4666-3637-8.ch009

Tsiakis, T., Kargidis, T., & Chatzipoulidis, A. (2013). IT security governance in e-banking. In D. Mellado, L. Enrique Sánchez, E. Fernández-Medina, & M. Piattini (Eds.), *IT security governance innovations: Theory and research* (pp. 13–46). Hershey, PA: IGI Global. doi:10.4018/978-1-4666-2083-4.ch002

Turgeman-Goldschmidt, O. (2011). Between hackers and white-collar offenders. In T. Holt & B. Schell (Eds.), *Corporate hacking and technology-driven crime: Social dynamics and implications* (pp. 18–37). Hershey, PA: IGI Global. doi:10.4018/978-1-61692-805-6.ch002

Tvrdíková, M. (2012). Information system integrated security. In M. Gupta, J. Walp, & R. Sharman (Eds.), *Strategic and practical approaches for information security governance: Technologies and applied solutions* (pp. 158–169). Hershey, PA: IGI Global. doi:10.4018/978-1-4666-0197-0.ch009

Uffen, J., & Breitner, M. H. (2013). Management of technical security measures: An empirical examination of personality traits and behavioral intentions. *International Journal of Social and Organizational Dynamics in IT, 3*(1), 14–31. doi:10.4018/ijsodit.2013010102

Vance, A., & Siponen, M. T. (2012). IS security policy violations: A rational choice perspective. *Journal of Organizational and End User Computing, 24*(1), 21–41. doi:10.4018/joeuc.2012010102

Veltsos, C. (2011). Mitigating the blended threat: Protecting data and educating users. In D. Kar & M. Syed (Eds.), *Network security, administration and management: Advancing technology and practice* (pp. 20–37). Hershey, PA: IGI Global. doi:10.4018/978-1-60960-777-7.ch002

Venkataraman, R., Pushpalatha, M., & Rao, T. R. (2014). Trust management and modeling techniques in wireless communications. In D. Rawat, B. Bista, & G. Yan (Eds.), *Security, privacy, trust, and resource management in mobile and wireless communications* (pp. 278–294). Hershey, PA: IGI Global. doi:10.4018/978-1-4666-4691-9.ch012

Venkataraman, R., & Rao, T. R. (2012). Security issues and models in mobile ad hoc networks. In K. Lakhtaria (Ed.), *Technological advancements and applications in mobile ad-hoc networks: Research trends* (pp. 219–227). Hershey, PA: IGI Global. doi:10.4018/978-1-4666-0321-9.ch013

Viney, D. (2011). Future trends in digital security. In D. Kerr, J. Gammack, & K. Bryant (Eds.), *Digital business security development: Management technologies* (pp. 173–190). Hershey, PA: IGI Global. doi:10.4018/978-1-60566-806-2.ch009

Vinod, P., Laxmi, V., & Gaur, M. (2011). Metamorphic malware analysis and detection methods. In R. Santanam, M. Sethumadhavan, & M. Virendra (Eds.), *Cyber security, cyber crime and cyber forensics: Applications and perspectives* (pp. 178–202). Hershey, PA: IGI Global. doi:10.4018/978-1-60960-123-2.ch013

von Solms, R., & Warren, M. (2011). Towards the human information security firewall. *International Journal of Cyber Warfare & Terrorism*, *1*(2), 10–17. doi:10.4018/ijcwt.2011040102

Wall, D. S. (2011). Micro-frauds: Virtual robberies, stings and scams in the information age. In T. Holt & B. Schell (Eds.), *Corporate hacking and technology-driven crime: Social dynamics and implications* (pp. 68–86). Hershey, PA: IGI Global. doi:10.4018/978-1-61692-805-6.ch004

Wang, H., Zhao, J. L., & Chen, G. (2012). Managing data security in e-markets through relationship driven access control. *Journal of Database Management*, *23*(2), 1–21. doi:10.4018/jdm.2012040101

Warren, M., & Leitch, S. (2011). Protection of Australia in the cyber age. *International Journal of Cyber Warfare & Terrorism*, *1*(1), 35–40. doi:10.4018/ijcwt.2011010104

Weber, S. G., & Gustiené, P. (2013). Crafting requirements for mobile and pervasive emergency response based on privacy and security by design principles. *International Journal of Information Systems for Crisis Response and Management*, *5*(2), 1–18. doi:10.4018/jiscrm.2013040101

Wei, J., Lin, B., & Loho-Noya, M. (2013). Development of an e-healthcare information security risk assessment method. *Journal of Database Management*, *24*(1), 36–57. doi:10.4018/jdm.2013010103

Weippl, E. R., & Riedl, B. (2012). Security, trust, and privacy on mobile devices and multimedia applications. In *Cyber crime: Concepts, methodologies, tools and applications* (pp. 228–244). Hershey, PA: IGI Global. doi:10.4018/978-1-61350-323-2.ch202

White, G., & Long, J. (2012). Global information security factors. In H. Nemati (Ed.), *Optimizing information security and advancing privacy assurance: New technologies* (pp. 163–174). Hershey, PA: IGI Global. doi:10.4018/978-1-4666-0026-3.ch009

White, S. C., Sedigh, S., & Hurson, A. R. (2013). Security concepts for cloud computing. In X. Yang & L. Liu (Eds.), *Principles, methodologies, and service-oriented approaches for cloud computing* (pp. 116–142). Hershey, PA: IGI Global. doi:10.4018/978-1-4666-2854-0.ch005

Whyte, B., & Harrison, J. (2011). State of practice in secure software: Experts' views on best ways ahead. In H. Mouratidis (Ed.), *Software engineering for secure systems: Industrial and research perspectives* (pp. 1–14). Hershey, PA: IGI Global. doi:10.4018/978-1-61520-837-1.ch001

Wu, Y., & Saunders, C. S. (2011). Governing information security: Governance domains and decision rights allocation patterns. *Information Resources Management Journal, 24*(1), 28–45. doi:10.4018/irmj.2011010103

Yadav, S. B. (2011). SEACON: An integrated approach to the analysis and design of secure enterprise architecture–based computer networks. In H. Nemati (Ed.), *Pervasive information security and privacy developments: Trends and advancements* (pp. 309–331). Hershey, PA: IGI Global. doi:10.4018/978-1-61692-000-5.ch020

Yadav, S. B. (2012). A six-view perspective framework for system security: Issues, risks, and requirements. In H. Nemati (Ed.), *Optimizing information security and advancing privacy assurance: New technologies* (pp. 58–90). Hershey, PA: IGI Global. doi:10.4018/978-1-4666-0026-3.ch004

Yamany, H. F., Allison, D. S., & Capretz, M. A. (2013). Developing proactive security dimensions for SOA. In *IT policy and ethics: Concepts, methodologies, tools, and applications* (pp. 900–922). Hershey, PA: IGI Global. doi:10.4018/978-1-4666-2919-6.ch041

Yan, G., Rawat, D. B., Bista, B. B., & Chen, L. (2014). Location security in vehicular wireless networks. In D. Rawat, B. Bista, & G. Yan (Eds.), *Security, privacy, trust, and resource management in mobile and wireless communications* (pp. 108–133). Hershey, PA: IGI Global. doi:10.4018/978-1-4666-4691-9.ch006

Yaokumah, W. (2013). Evaluating the effectiveness of information security governance practices in developing nations: A case of Ghana. *International Journal of IT/ Business Alignment and Governance, 4*(1), 27–43. doi:10.4018/jitbag.2013010103

Yates, D., & Harris, A. (2011). International ethical attitudes and behaviors: Implications for organizational information security policy. In M. Dark (Ed.), *Information assurance and security ethics in complex systems: Interdisciplinary perspectives* (pp. 55–80). Hershey, PA: IGI Global. doi:10.4018/978-1-61692-245-0.ch004

Yau, S. S., Yin, Y., & An, H. (2011). An adaptive approach to optimizing tradeoff between service performance and security in service-based systems. *International Journal of Web Services Research, 8*(2), 74–91. doi:10.4018/jwsr.2011040104

Zadig, S. M., & Tejay, G. (2012). Emerging cybercrime trends: Legal, ethical, and practical issues. In A. Dudley, J. Braman, & G. Vincenti (Eds.), *Investigating cyber law and cyber ethics: Issues, impacts and practices* (pp. 37–56). Hershey, PA: IGI Global. doi:10.4018/978-1-61350-132-0.ch003

Zafar, H., Ko, M., & Osei-Bryson, K. (2012). Financial impact of information security breaches on breached firms and their non-breached competitors. *Information Resources Management Journal, 25*(1), 21–37. doi:10.4018/irmj.2012010102

Zapata, B. C., & Alemán, J. L. (2013). Security risks in cloud computing: An analysis of the main vulnerabilities. In D. Rosado, D. Mellado, E. Fernandez-Medina, & M. Piattini (Eds.), *Security engineering for cloud computing: Approaches and tools* (pp. 55–71). Hershey, PA: IGI Global. doi:10.4018/978-1-4666-2125-1.ch004

Zboril, F., Horacek, J., Drahansky, M., & Hanacek, P. (2012). Security in wireless sensor networks with mobile codes. In M. Gupta, J. Walp, & R. Sharman (Eds.), *Threats, countermeasures, and advances in applied information security* (pp. 411–425). Hershey, PA: IGI Global. doi:10.4018/978-1-4666-0978-5.ch021

Zhang, J. (2012). Trust management for VANETs: Challenges, desired properties and future directions. *International Journal of Distributed Systems and Technologies, 3*(1), 48–62. doi:10.4018/jdst.2012010104

Zhang, Y., He, L., Shu, L., Hara, T., & Nishio, S. (2012). Security issues on outlier detection and countermeasure for distributed hierarchical wireless sensor networks. In A. Pathan, M. Pathan, & H. Lee (Eds.), *Advancements in distributed computing and internet technologies: Trends and issues* (pp. 182–210). Hershey, PA: Information Science Publishing. doi:10.4018/978-1-61350-110-8.ch009

Related References

Zheng, X., & Oleshchuk, V. (2012). Security enhancement of peer-to-peer session initiation. In M. Gupta, J. Walp, & R. Sharman (Eds.), *Threats, countermeasures, and advances in applied information security* (pp. 281–308). Hershey, PA: IGI Global. doi:10.4018/978-1-4666-0978-5.ch015

Zineddine, M. (2012). Is your automated healthcare information secure? In M. Watfa (Ed.), *E-healthcare systems and wireless communications: Current and future challenges* (pp. 128–142). Hershey, PA: IGI Global. doi:10.4018/978-1-61350-123-8.ch006

Compilation of References

Aakash, P. K., & Pushpalatha, S. (2016). A Survey on Applications of Artificial Neural Networks in Data Mining, Int. *J. Sci. Eng. Technol. Res.*, *5*, 1470–1473.

Abdrabo, M., Elmogy, M., Eltaweel, G., & Barakat, S., & (2016Enhancing Big Data Value Using Knowledge Discovery Techniques, I.*J. Inf. Technol. Comput. Sci.*, *8*, 1–12. Retrieved from http://www.mecs-press.org/ijitcs/ijitcs-v8-n8/IJITCS-V8-N8-1.pdf

Acharjya, D. P., & Mary, A. G. (2014). Privacy preservation in information system. In B. Tripathy & D. Acharjya (Eds.), *Advances in secure computing, internet services, and applications* (pp. 49–72). Hershey, PA: IGI Global. doi:10.4018/978-1-4666-4940-8.ch003

Agamba, J., & Keengwe, J. (2012). Pre-service teachers perceptions of information assurance and cyber security. *International Journal of Information and Communication Technology Education*, *8*(2), 94–101. doi:10.4018/jicte.2012040108

Aggarwal, C. C., & Philip, S. Y. (2008). *A general survey of privacy-preserving data mining models and algorithms* (pp. 11–52). Springer, US. doi:10.1007/978-0-387-70992-5_2

Aggarwal, R. (2013). Dispute settlement for cyber crimes in India: An analysis. In R. Khurana & R. Aggarwal (Eds.), *Interdisciplinary perspectives on business convergence, computing, and legality* (pp. 160–171). Hershey, PA: IGI Global. doi:10.4018/978-1-4666-4209-6.ch015

Agwu, E. (2013). Cyber criminals on the internet super highways: A technical investigation of different shades and colours within the Nigerian cyber space. *International Journal of Online Marketing*, *3*(2), 56–74. doi:10.4018/ijom.2013040104

Ahmad, A. (2012). Security assessment of networks. In *Wireless technologies: Concepts, methodologies, tools and applications* (pp. 208–224). Hershey, PA: IGI Global. doi:10.4018/978-1-61350-101-6.ch111

Ahmed, N., & Jensen, C. D. (2012). Security of dependable systems. In L. Petre, K. Sere, & E. Troubitsyna (Eds.), *Dependability and computer engineering: Concepts for software-intensive systems* (pp. 230–264). Hershey, PA: IGI Global. doi:10.4018/978-1-60960-747-0.ch011

Ahmed, S. T., & Loguinov, D. (2014). On the performance of MapReduce: A stochastic approach. In *Proceedings of IEEE International Conference on Big Data (Big Data)* (pp. 49-54). doi:10.1109/BigData.2014.7004212

Al-Ahmad, W. (2011). Building secure software using XP. *International Journal of Secure Software Engineering*, 2(3), 63–76. doi:10.4018/jsse.2011070104

Alavi, R., Islam, S., Jahankhani, H., & Al-Nemrat, A. (2013). Analyzing human factors for an effective information security management system. *International Journal of Secure Software Engineering*, 4(1), 50–74. doi:10.4018/jsse.2013010104

Alazab, A., Abawajy, J. H., & Hobbs, M. (2013). Web malware that targets web applications. In L. Caviglione, M. Coccoli, & A. Merlo (Eds.), *Social network engineering for secure web data and services* (pp. 248–264). Hershey, PA: IGI Global. doi:10.4018/978-1-4666-3926-3.ch012

Alazab, A., Hobbs, M., Abawajy, J., & Khraisat, A. (2013). Malware detection and prevention system based on multi-stage rules. *International Journal of Information Security and Privacy*, 7(2), 29–43. doi:10.4018/jisp.2013040102

Alazab, M., Venkatraman, S., Watters, P., & Alazab, M. (2013). Information security governance: The art of detecting hidden malware. In D. Mellado, L. Enrique Sánchez, E. Fernández-Medina, & M. Piattini (Eds.), *IT security governance innovations: Theory and research* (pp. 293–315). Hershey, PA: IGI Global. doi:10.4018/978-1-4666-2083-4.ch011

Al-Bayatti, A. H., & Al-Bayatti, H. M. (2012). Security management and simulation of mobile ad hoc networks (MANET). In H. Al-Bahadili (Ed.), *Simulation in computer network design and modeling: Use and analysis* (pp. 297–314). Hershey, PA: IGI Global. doi:10.4018/978-1-4666-0191-8.ch014

Al-Bayatti, A. H., Zedan, H., Cau, A., & Siewe, F. (2012). Security management for mobile ad hoc network of networks (MANoN). In I. Khalil & E. Weippl (Eds.), *Advancing the next-generation of mobile computing: Emerging technologies* (pp. 1–18). Hershey, PA: IGI Global. doi:10.4018/978-1-4666-0119-2.ch001

Aldeen, Y. A. A. S., Salleh, M., & Razzaque, M. A. (2015). A comprehensive review on privacy preserving data mining. *SpringerPlus*, 4(1), 1–36. doi:10.1186/s40064-015-1481-x PMID:26587362

Alguliyev, R., & Imamverdiyev, Y. (2014). Big Data: Big Promises for Information Security. In *Proceedings of IEEE 8th International Conference on Application of Information and Communication Technologies (AICT)* (pp. 1-4). doi:10.1109/ICAICT.2014.7035946

Alhaj, A., Aljawarneh, S., Masadeh, S., & Abu-Taieh, E. (2013). A secure data transmission mechanism for cloud outsourced data. *International Journal of Cloud Applications and Computing*, 3(1), 34–43. doi:10.4018/ijcac.2013010104

Al-Hamdani, W. A. (2011). Three models to measure information security compliance. In H. Nemati (Ed.), *Security and privacy assurance in advancing technologies: New developments* (pp. 351–373). Hershey, PA: IGI Global. doi:10.4018/978-1-60960-200-0.ch022

Al-Hamdani, W. A. (2014). Secure e-learning and cryptography. In K. Sullivan, P. Czigler, & J. Sullivan Hellgren (Eds.), *Cases on professional distance education degree programs and practices: Successes, challenges, and issues* (pp. 331–369). Hershey, PA: IGI Global. doi:10.4018/978-1-4666-4486-1.ch012

Ali, A., Qadir, J., Rasool, R., Sathiaseelan, A., Zwitter, A., & Crowcroft, J. (2016). Big data for development: Applications and techniques. *Big Data Anal.*, *1*(1), 2. doi:10.1186/s41044-016-0002-4

Ali, M., & Jawandhiya, P. (2012). Security aware routing protocols for mobile ad hoc networks. In K. Lakhtaria (Ed.), *Technological advancements and applications in mobile ad-hoc networks: Research trends* (pp. 264–289). Hershey, PA: IGI Global. doi:10.4018/978-1-4666-0321-9.ch016

Ali, S. (2012). Practical web application security audit following industry standards and compliance. In J. Zubairi & A. Mahboob (Eds.), *Cyber security standards, practices and industrial applications: Systems and methodologies* (pp. 259–279). Hershey, PA: IGI Global. doi:10.4018/978-1-60960-851-4.ch013

Al-Jaljouli, R., & Abawajy, J. H. (2012). Security framework for mobile agents-based applications. In A. Kumar & H. Rahman (Eds.), *Mobile computing techniques in emerging markets: Systems, applications and services* (pp. 242–269). Hershey, PA: IGI Global. doi:10.4018/978-1-4666-0080-5.ch009

Al-Jaljouli, R., & Abawajy, J. H. (2014). Mobile agent's security protocols. In *Crisis management: Concepts, methodologies, tools and applications* (pp. 166–202). Hershey, PA: IGI Global. doi:10.4018/978-1-4666-4707-7.ch007

Al-Jarrah, O. Y., Yoo, P. D., Muhaidat, S., Karagiannidis, G. K., & Taha, K. (2015). Efficient ML for Big Data: A Review. *Big Data Res.*, *2*(3), 87–93. doi:10.1016/j.bdr.2015.04.001

Aljawarneh, S. (2013). Cloud security engineering: Avoiding security threats the right way. In S. Aljawarneh (Ed.), *Cloud computing advancements in design, implementation, and technologies* (pp. 147–153). Hershey, PA: IGI Global. doi:10.4018/978-1-4666-1879-4.ch010

Al, M., & Yoshigoe, K. (2012). Security and attacks in wireless sensor networks. In *Wireless technologies: Concepts, methodologies, tools and applications* (pp. 1811–1846). Hershey, PA: IGI Global. doi:10.4018/978-1-61350-101-6.ch706

Alshaer, H., Muhaidat, S., Shubair, R., & Shayegannia, M. (2014). Security and connectivity analysis in vehicular communication networks. In D. Rawat, B. Bista, & G. Yan (Eds.), *Security, privacy, trust, and resource management in mobile and wireless communications* (pp. 83–107). Hershey, PA: IGI Global. doi:10.4018/978-1-4666-4691-9.ch005

Alsheikh, M. A., Lin, S., Niyato, D., & Tan, H.-P. (2014). ML in Wireless Sensor Networks: Algorithms, Strategies, and Applica. *IEEE Communications Surveys and Tutorials*, *16*(4), 1996–2018. doi:10.1109/COMST.2014.2320099

Al-Suqri, M. N., & Akomolafe-Fatuyi, E. (2012). Security and privacy in digital libraries: Challenges, opportunities and prospects. *International Journal of Digital Library Systems*, *3*(4), 54–61. doi:10.4018/ijdls.2012100103

Alzamil, Z. A. (2012). Information security awareness at Saudi Arabians organizations: An information technology employees perspective. *International Journal of Information Security and Privacy*, *6*(3), 38–55. doi:10.4018/jisp.2012070102

Anbarasi, M., & Saleem Durai, M.A. (2015) A study on predicting protein secondary structure using various data mining approaches. *International Journal of Pharma and Bio Sciences (B)*, *6*(3), 549-B561.

Anyiwo, D., & Sharma, S. (2011). Web services and e-business technologies: Security issues. In O. Bak & N. Stair (Eds.), *Impact of e-business technologies on public and private organizations: Industry comparisons and perspectives* (pp. 249–261). Hershey, PA: IGI Global. doi:10.4018/978-1-60960-501-8.ch015

Apache. (n. d.). Hadoop. Retrieved from http://hadoop.apache.org

Apiletti, D., Baralis, E., Cerquitelli, T., Garza, P., Giordano, D., Mellia, M., & Venturini, L. (2016). *SeLINA: A Self-Learning Insightful Network Analyzer*. IEEE.

Apostolakis, I., Chryssanthou, A., & Varlamis, I. (2011). A holistic perspective of security in health related virtual communities. In *Virtual communities: Concepts, methodologies, tools and applications* (pp. 1190–1204). Hershey, PA: IGI Global. doi:10.4018/978-1-60960-100-3.ch406

Arel, I., Rose, D., & Karnowski, T. (2010). Deep ML-A new frontier in artificial intelligence research. *IEEE Computational Intelligence Magazine*, *5*(4), 13–18. doi:10.1109/MCI.2010.938364

Arnett, K. P., Templeton, G. F., & Vance, D. A. (2011). Information security by words alone: The case for strong security policies. In H. Nemati (Ed.), *Security and privacy assurance in advancing technologies: New developments* (pp. 154–159). Hershey, PA: IGI Global. doi:10.4018/978-1-60960-200-0.ch011

Arogundade, O. T., Akinwale, A. T., Jin, Z., & Yang, X. G. (2011). A unified use-misuse case model for capturing and analysing safety and security requirements. *International Journal of Information Security and Privacy*, *5*(4), 8–30. doi:10.4018/jisp.2011100102

Arshad, J., Townend, P., Xu, J., & Jie, W. (2012). Cloud computing security: Opportunities and pitfalls. *International Journal of Grid and High Performance Computing*, *4*(1), 52–66. doi:10.4018/jghpc.2012010104

Asim, M., & Petkovic, M. (2012). Fundamental building blocks for security interoperability in e-business. In E. Kajan, F. Dorloff, & I. Bedini (Eds.), *Handbook of research on e-business standards and protocols: Documents, data and advanced web technologies* (pp. 269–292). Hershey, PA: IGI Global. doi:10.4018/978-1-4666-0146-8.ch013

Askary, S., Goodwin, D., & Lanis, R. (2012). Improvements in audit risks related to information technology frauds. *International Journal of Enterprise Information Systems*, *8*(2), 52–63. doi:10.4018/jeis.2012040104

Assam, R., & Seidl, T. (2011, November). Preserving privacy of moving objects via temporal clustering of spatio-temporal data streams. In *Proceedings of the 4th ACM SIGSPATIAL International Workshop on Security and Privacy in GIS and LBS* (pp. 9-16). ACM. doi:10.1145/2071880.2071883

Aurigemma, S. (2013). A composite framework for behavioral compliance with information security policies. *Journal of Organizational and End User Computing*, *25*(3), 32–51. doi:10.4018/joeuc.2013070103

Avalle, M., Pironti, A., Pozza, D., & Sisto, R. (2011). JavaSPI: A framework for security protocol implementation. *International Journal of Secure Software Engineering*, *2*(4), 34–48. doi:10.4018/jsse.2011100103

Axelrod, C. W. (2012). A dynamic cyber security economic model: incorporating value functions for all involved parties. In M. Gupta, J. Walp, & R. Sharman (Eds.), *Threats, countermeasures, and advances in applied information security* (pp. 462–477). Hershey, PA: IGI Global. doi:10.4018/978-1-4666-0978-5.ch024

Ayanso, A., & Herath, T. (2012). Law and technology at crossroads in cyberspace: Where do we go from here? In A. Dudley, J. Braman, & G. Vincenti (Eds.), *Investigating cyber law and cyber ethics: Issues, impacts and practices* (pp. 57–77). Hershey, PA: IGI Global. doi:10.4018/978-1-61350-132-0.ch004

B., A., & Jagani, J.M. (2014). A survey: classification of huge cloud Datasets with efficient Map - Reduce policy. *International Journal of Engineering Trends and Technology*, *18*(2). Retrieved from http://www.ijettjournal.org

Ba, H., Gao, X., Zhang, X., & He, Z. (2014, August). Protecting Data Privacy from Being Inferred from High Dimensional Correlated Data. In *Proceedings of the 2014 IEEE/WIC/ACM International Joint Conferences on Web Intelligence (WI) and Intelligent Agent Technologies (IAT)* (Vol. 2, pp. 495-502). IEEE. doi:10.1109/WI-IAT.2014.139

Baars, T., & Spruit, M. (2012). Designing a secure cloud architecture: The SeCA model. *International Journal of Information Security and Privacy*, *6*(1), 14–32. doi:10.4018/jisp.2012010102

Bachmann, M. (2011). Deciphering the hacker underground: First quantitative insights. In T. Holt & B. Schell (Eds.), *Corporate hacking and technology-driven crime: Social dynamics and implications* (pp. 105–126). Hershey, PA: IGI Global. doi:10.4018/978-1-61692-805-6.ch006

Bachmann, M., & Smith, B. (2012). Internet fraud. In Z. Yan (Ed.), *Encyclopedia of cyber behavior* (pp. 931–943). Hershey, PA: IGI Global. doi:10.4018/978-1-4666-0315-8.ch077

Back, T. (1996). *Evolutionary Algorithms in Theory and Practice.* New York: Oxford University Press.

Bagheri, R. & Jahanshahi, M. (2015). Scheduling Workflow Applications on the Heterogeneous Cloud Resources. *Indian Journal of Science and Technology,* 8(12), doi:10.17485/ijst/2015/v8i12/57984

Bai, Y., & Khan, K. M. (2011). Ell secure information system using modal logic technique. *International Journal of Secure Software Engineering,* 2(2), 65–76. doi:10.4018/jsse.2011040104

Baker, J. (2016). Artificial Neural Networks and DL, Lancaster. Retrieved September 27, 2016 from http://www.lancaster.ac.uk/pg/bakerj1/pdfs/ANNs/Artificial_neural_networks-poster.pdf

Bandeira, G. S. (2014). Criminal liability of organizations, corporations, legal persons, and similar entities on law of Portuguese cybercrime: A brief discussion on the issue of crimes of "false information," the "damage on other programs or computer data," the "computer-software sabotage," the "illegitimate access," the "unlawful interception," and "illegitimate reproduction of the protected program". In I. Portela & F. Almeida (Eds.), *Organizational, legal, and technological dimensions of information system administration* (pp. 96–107). Hershey, PA: IGI Global. doi:10.4018/978-1-4666-4526-4.ch006

Barjis, J. (2012). Software engineering security based on business process modeling. In K. Khan (Ed.), *Security-aware systems applications and software development methods* (pp. 52–68). Hershey, PA: IGI Global. doi:10.4018/978-1-4666-1580-9.ch004

Barkhordari, M., & Niamanesh, M. (2014, August). ScadiBino: An effective MapReduce-based association rule mining method. In *Proceedings of the Sixteenth International Conference on Electronic Commerce* (p. 1). ACM. doi:10.1145/2617848.2617853

Barrero, V., Grisales, E. V., Rosas, F., Sanchez, C., & Leon, J. (2001). Design and implementation of an intelligent interface for myoelectric controlled prosthesis. In *Proceedings of the 23rd Annual International Conference of the IEEE.* Istanbul, Turkey: IEEE.

Beakta, R. (2015). Big Data And Hadoop: A Review Paper.

Bedi, P., Gandotra, V., & Singhal, A. (2013). Innovative strategies for secure software development. In H. Singh & K. Kaur (Eds.), *Designing, engineering, and analyzing reliable and efficient software* (pp. 217–237). Hershey, PA: IGI Global. doi:10.4018/978-1-4666-2958-5.ch013

Belsis, P., Skourlas, C., & Gritzalis, S. (2011). Secure electronic healthcare records management in wireless environments. *Journal of Information Technology Research,* 4(4), 1–17. doi:10.4018/jitr.2011100101

Bengio Y. (2013) Deep Learning of Representations: Looking Forward. In A.H. Dediu, C. Martín-Vide, R. Mitkov et al., (Eds.), Statistical Language and Speech Processing, LNCS (Vol. 7978). Springer. doi:10.1007/978-3-642-39593-2_1

Bengio, Y. (2009). Learning Deep Architectures for AI, Found. Trends. *Machine Learning, 2*(1), 1–127. doi:10.1561/2200000006

Bengio, Y., Courville, A., & Vincent, P. (2013). Representation learning: A review and new perspectives. *IEEE Transactions on Pattern Analysis and Machine Intelligence, 35*(8), 1798–1828. doi:10.1109/TPAMI.2013.50 PMID:23787338

Bengio, Y., & LeCun, Y. (2007). Scaling learning algorithms towards. In S. K. M. Large (Ed.), *L. Bottou, O. Chapelle, D. DeCoste, J. Weston* (pp. 321–360). Cambridge, MA: MIT Press.

Bernik, I. (2012). Internet study: Cyber threats and cybercrime awareness and fear. *International Journal of Cyber Warfare & Terrorism, 2*(3), 1–11. doi:10.4018/ijcwt.2012070101

Beyer, H. G., & Schwefel, H. P. (2002). Evolution strategies. *Natural Computing, 1*(1), 3–52. doi:10.1023/A:1015059928466

Bhagat, A., Kshirsagar, N., Khodke, P., Dongre, K., & Ali, S. (2016). Penalty parameter selection for hierarchical data stream clustering.

Bhatia, M. S. (2011). World war III: The cyber war. *International Journal of Cyber Warfare & Terrorism, 1*(3), 59–69. doi:10.4018/ijcwt.2011070104

Big Data Working Group. (2013). *Cloud Security Alliance*. Expanded Top Ten Big Data Security and Privacy Challenges.

Bing, L., & Chan, K. C. (2014, December). A Fuzzy Logic Approach for Opinion Mining on Large Scale Twitter Data. In *Proceedings of the 2014 IEEE/ACM 7th International Conference on Utility and Cloud Computing* (pp. 652-657). IEEE Computer Society. doi:10.1109/UCC.2014.105

Blanco, C., Rosado, D., Gutiérrez, C., Rodríguez, A., Mellado, D., Fernández-Medina, E., & Piattini, M. et al. (2011). Security over the information systems development cycle. In H. Mouratidis (Ed.), *Software engineering for secure systems: Industrial and research perspectives* (pp. 113–154). Hershey, PA: IGI Global. doi:10.4018/978-1-61520-837-1.ch005

Bobbert, Y., & Mulder, H. (2012). A research journey into maturing the business information security of mid market organizations. In W. Van Grembergen & S. De Haes (Eds.), *Business strategy and applications in enterprise IT governance* (pp. 236–259). Hershey, PA: IGI Global. doi:10.4018/978-1-4666-1779-7.ch014

Boci, E., & Thistlethwaite, S. A novel big data architecture in support of ADS-B data analytic (2015). In *Proceedings of the 2015 Integrated Communication, Navigation and Surveillance Conference (ICNS)* (pp. C1-1). IEEE.

Boddington, R. (2011). Digital evidence. In D. Kerr, J. Gammack, & K. Bryant (Eds.), *Digital business security development: Management technologies* (pp. 37–72). Hershey, PA: IGI Global. doi:10.4018/978-1-60566-806-2.ch002

Boobalan, M. P., Lopez, D., & Gao, X. Z. (2016). Graph clustering using k-Neighbourhood Attribute Structural similarity. *Applied Soft Computing, 47*(C), 216-223.

Borthakur, D. (2008). HDFS Architecture Guide. *The apache software foundation.*

Bosch, C., Peter, A., Leenders, B., Lim, H. W., Tang, Q., Wang, H., & Jonker, W. et al. (2014). Distributed Searchable Symmetric Encryption. In *Proceedings of Twelfth Annual International Conference on Privacy, Security and Trust (PST)* (pp. 330-337). doi:10.1109/PST.2014.6890956

Bossler, A. M., & Burruss, G. W. (2011). The general theory of crime and computer hacking: Low self-control hackers? In T. Holt & B. Schell (Eds.), *Corporate hacking and technology-driven crime: Social dynamics and implications* (pp. 38–67). Hershey, PA: IGI Global. doi:10.4018/978-1-61692-805-6.ch003

Bouras, C., & Stamos, K. (2011). Security issues for multi-domain resource reservation. In D. Kar & M. Syed (Eds.), *Network security, administration and management: Advancing technology and practice* (pp. 38–50). Hershey, PA: IGI Global. doi:10.4018/978-1-60960-777-7.ch003

Boyd, S., Parikh, N., Chu, E., Peleato, B., & Eckstein, J. (2010). Distributed Optimization and Statistical Learning via the Alternating Direction Method of Multipliers, Found. *Machine Learning*, *3*(1), 1–122. doi:10.1561/2200000016

Bracci, F., Corradi, A., & Foschini, L. (2014). Cloud standards: Security and interoperability issues. In H. Mouftah & B. Kantarci (Eds.), *Communication infrastructures for cloud computing* (pp. 465–495). Hershey, PA: IGI Global. doi:10.4018/978-1-4666-4522-6.ch020

Brewer, E. A. (2000). Towards robust distributed systems. In *Proc. 19th Annual ACM Symposium on Principles of Distributed Computing.*

Brodsky, J., & Radvanovsky, R. (2011). Control systems security. In T. Holt & B. Schell (Eds.), *Corporate hacking and technology-driven crime: Social dynamics and implications* (pp. 187–204). Hershey, PA: IGI Global. doi:10.4018/978-1-61692-805-6.ch010

Brooks, D. (2013). Security threats and risks of intelligent building systems: Protecting facilities from current and emerging vulnerabilities. In C. Laing, A. Badii, & P. Vickers (Eds.), *Securing critical infrastructures and critical control systems: Approaches for threat protection* (pp. 1–16). Hershey, PA: IGI Global. doi:10.4018/978-1-4666-2659-1.ch001

Bülow, W., & Wester, M. (2012). The right to privacy and the protection of personal data in a digital era and the age of information. In C. Akrivopoulou & N. Garipidis (Eds.), *Human rights and risks in the digital era: Globalization and the effects of information technologies* (pp. 34–45). Hershey, PA: IGI Global. doi:10.4018/978-1-4666-0891-7.ch004

Byrd, R. J., Steinhubl, S. R., Sun, J., Ebadollahi, S., & Stewart, W. F. (2014). Automatic identification of heart failure diagnostic criteria, using text analysis of clinical notes from electronic health records. *International Journal of Medical Informatics*, *83*(12), 983–992. doi:10.1016/j.ijmedinf.2012.12.005 PMID:23317809

Calandra, R., Raiko, T., Deisenroth, M. P., & Pouzols, F. M. (2012). Learning deep belief networks from non-stationary streams. In Artificial Neural Networks and Machine Learning–ICANN 2012, LNCS (Vol. 7553, pp. 379–386). doi:10.1007/978-3-642-33266-1_47

Campan, A., & Truta, T. M. (2009). Data and structural k-anonymity in social networks. In *Privacy, Security, and Trust in KDD* (pp. 33–54). Berlin, Heidelberg: Springer. doi:10.1007/978-3-642-01718-6_4

Canongia, C., & Mandarino, R. (2014). Cybersecurity: The new challenge of the information society. In Crisis management: Concepts, methodologies, tools and applications (pp. 60-80). Hershey, PA: IGI Global. doi:10.4018/978-1-4666-4707-7.ch003

Cao, J., Karras, P., Kalnis, P., & Tan, K. L. (2011). SABRE: A Sensitive Attribute Bucketization and Redistribution framework for t-closeness. *The VLDB Journal*, *20*(1), 59–81. doi:10.1007/s00778-010-0191-9

Cao, X., & Lu, Y. (2011). The social network structure of a computer hacker community. In H. Nemati (Ed.), *Security and privacy assurance in advancing technologies: New developments* (pp. 160–173). Hershey, PA: IGI Global. doi:10.4018/978-1-60960-200-0.ch012

Cardholm, L. (2014). Identifying the business value of information security. In T. Tsiakis, T. Kargidis, & P. Katsaros (Eds.), *Approaches and processes for managing the economics of information systems* (pp. 157–180). Hershey, PA: IGI Global. doi:10.4018/978-1-4666-4983-5.ch010

Cardoso, R. C., & Gomes, A. (2012). Security issues in massively multiplayer online games. In M. Cruz-Cunha (Ed.), *Handbook of research on serious games as educational, business and research tools* (pp. 290–314). Hershey, PA: IGI Global. doi:10.4018/978-1-4666-0149-9.ch016

Carpen-Amarie, A., Costan, A., Leordeanu, C., Basescu, C., & Antoniu, G. (2012). Towards a generic security framework for cloud data management environments. *International Journal of Distributed Systems and Technologies*, *3*(1), 17–34. doi:10.4018/jdst.2012010102

Caushaj, E., Fu, H., Sethi, I., Badih, H., Watson, D., Zhu, Y., & Leng, S. (2013). Theoretical analysis and experimental study: Monitoring data privacy in smartphone communications. *International Journal of Interdisciplinary Telecommunications and Networking*, *5*(2), 66–82. doi:10.4018/jitn.2013040106

Cepheli, Ö., & Kurt, G. K. (2014). Physical layer security in wireless communication networks. In D. Rawat, B. Bista, & G. Yan (Eds.), *Security, privacy, trust, and resource management in mobile and wireless communications* (pp. 61–81). Hershey, PA: IGI Global. doi:10.4018/978-1-4666-4691-9.ch004

Chakraborty, P., & Raghuraman, K. (2013). Trends in information security. In K. Buragga & N. Zaman (Eds.), *Software development techniques for constructive information systems design* (pp. 354–376). Hershey, PA: IGI Global. doi:10.4018/978-1-4666-3679-8.ch020

Chan, A. C.-F. (2009). Symmetric-Key Homomorphic Encryption for Encrypted Data Processing. In *Proceedings of IEEE International Conference on Communications ICC '09*. doi:10.1109/ICC.2009.5199505

Chandrakumar, T., & Parthasarathy, S. (2012). Enhancing data security in ERP projects using XML. *International Journal of Enterprise Information Systems*, 8(1), 51–65. doi:10.4018/jeis.2012010104

Changwon, Y., & Ramirez, L. (2014). Juan. Liuzzi, Big data analysis using modern statistical and ML methods in medicine. *Int. Neurourol. J.*, *18*, 50–57. doi:10.5213/inj.2014.18.2.50 PMID:24987556

Chapple, M. J., Striegel, A., & Crowell, C. R. (2011). Firewall rulebase management: Tools and techniques. In M. Quigley (Ed.), *ICT ethics and security in the 21st century: New developments and applications* (pp. 254–276). Hershey, PA: IGI Global. doi:10.4018/978-1-60960-573-5.ch013

Chen, C. P., & Zhang, C. Y. (2014). Data-intensive applications, challenges, techniques and technologies: A survey on Big Data. Elsevier.

Chen, J., Li, K., Tang, Z., Bilal, K., Yu, S., Weng, C., & Li, K. (2016). A Parallel Random Forest Algorithm for Big Data in a Spark Cloud Computing Environment.

Chen, J.Y., & He, H.H. (2016). A fast density-based data stream clustering algorithm with cluster centers self-determined for mixed data.

Chen, L., Hu, W., Yang, M., & Zhang, L. (2011). Security and privacy issues in secure e-mail standards and services. In H. Nemati (Ed.), *Security and privacy assurance in advancing technologies: new developments* (pp. 174–185). Hershey, PA: IGI Global. doi:10.4018/978-1-60960-200-0.ch013

Chen, L., Varol, C., Liu, Q., & Zhou, B. (2014). Security in wireless metropolitan area networks: WiMAX and LTE. In D. Rawat, B. Bista, & G. Yan (Eds.), *Security, privacy, trust, and resource management in mobile and wireless communications* (pp. 11–27). Hershey, PA: IGI Global. doi:10.4018/978-1-4666-4691-9.ch002

Chen, X., & Lin, X. (2014). Big Data Deep Learning: Challenges and Perspectives. *IEEE Access*, *2*, 514–525. doi:10.1109/ACCESS.2014.2325029 PMID:24963700

Chen, X.-W., & Lin, X. (2014). Big Data Deep Learning: Challenges and Perspectives. *IEEE Access*, *2*, 214–225.

Cherdantseva, Y., & Hilton, J. (2014). Information security and information assurance: Discussion about the meaning, scope, and goals. In I. Portela & F. Almeida (Eds.), *Organizational, legal, and technological dimensions of information system administration* (pp. 167–198). Hershey, PA: IGI Global. doi:10.4018/978-1-4666-4526-4.ch010

Cherdantseva, Y., & Hilton, J. (2014). The 2011 survey of information security and information assurance professionals: Findings. In I. Portela & F. Almeida (Eds.), *Organizational, legal, and technological dimensions of information system administration* (pp. 243–256). Hershey, PA: IGI Global. doi:10.4018/978-1-4666-4526-4.ch013

Chong, Y. L., & Sundaraj, K. (2009). A study of back-propagation and radial basis neural network on EMG signal classification. In *Proceedings of the 6th International Symposium* Mechatronics and its Applications ISMA '09. Sharjah: IEEE.

Chowdhury, M. U., & Ray, B. R. (2013). Security risks/vulnerability in a RFID system and possible defenses. In N. Karmakar (Ed.), *Advanced RFID systems, security, and applications* (pp. 1–15). Hershey, PA: IGI Global. doi:10.4018/978-1-4666-2080-3.ch001

Ciresan, D. C., Meier, U., Gambardella, L. M., & Schmidhuber, J. (2010). Deep Big Simple Neural Nets Excel on Handwritten Digit Recognition. *Neural Computation, 22*(12), 1–14. doi:10.1162/NECO_a_00052 PMID:19842986

Coates, A., & Ng, A. (2011). The importance of encoding versus training with sparse coding and vector quantization. In *Proc. of the 28th Int. Conf. Mach. Learn* (pp. 921–928). Omnipress.

Coates, A., Huval, B., Wang, T., Wu, D. J., Ng, A. Y., & Catanzaro, B. (2013). DL with COTS HPC systems. In Proc. of the 30th Int. Conf. Mach. Learn., Atlanta, Georgia. Retrieved from http://www.jmlr.org/proceedings/papers/v28/coates13.pdf

Cofta, P., Lacohée, H., & Hodgson, P. (2011). Incorporating social trust into design practices for secure systems. In H. Mouratidis (Ed.), *Software engineering for secure systems: Industrial and research perspectives* (pp. 260–284). Hershey, PA: IGI Global. doi:10.4018/978-1-61520-837-1.ch010

Collobert, R., Weston, J., Bottou, L., Karlen, M., Kavukcuoglu, K., & Kuksa, P. (2011). Natural language processing (almost) from scratch. *Journal of Machine Learning Research, 12*(August), 2493–2537.

Conway, M. (2012). What is cyberterrorism and how real is the threat? A review of the academic literature, 1996 – 2009. In P. Reich & E. Gelbstein (Eds.), *Law, policy, and technology: Cyberterrorism, information warfare, and internet immobilization* (pp. 279–307). Hershey, PA: IGI Global. doi:10.4018/978-1-61520-831-9.ch011

Corser, G. P., Arslanturk, S., Oluoch, J., Fu, H., & Corser, G. E. (2013). Knowing the enemy at the gates: Measuring attacker motivation. *International Journal of Interdisciplinary Telecommunications and Networking, 5*(2), 83–95. doi:10.4018/jitn.2013040107

Corti, L., Day, A., & Backhouse, G. (2000, December). Confidentiality and informed consent: Issues for consideration in the preservation of and provision of access to qualitative data archives. In Forum Qualitative Sozialforschung/Forum: Qualitative. *Social Research, 1*(3).

Crosbie, M. (2013). Hack the cloud: Ethical hacking and cloud forensics. In K. Ruan (Ed.), *Cybercrime and cloud forensics: Applications for investigation processes* (pp. 42–58). Hershey, PA: IGI Global. doi:10.4018/978-1-4666-2662-1.ch002

Curran, K., Carlin, S., & Adams, M. (2012). Security issues in cloud computing. In L. Chao (Ed.), *Cloud computing for teaching and learning: Strategies for design and implementation* (pp. 200–208). Hershey, PA: IGI Global. doi:10.4018/978-1-4666-0957-0.ch014

Cutillo, L. A., Molva, R., & Strufe, T. (2009) Privacy preserving social networking through decentralization. In *Proceedings of the Sixth International Conference on Wireless On-Demand Network Systems and Services WONS '09* (pp. 145-152). IEEE. doi:10.1109/WONS.2009.4801860

Czosseck, C., Ottis, R., & Talihärm, A. (2011). Estonia after the 2007 cyber attacks: Legal, strategic and organisational changes in cyber security. *International Journal of Cyber Warfare & Terrorism, 1*(1), 24–34. doi:10.4018/ijcwt.2011010103

Czosseck, C., & Podins, K. (2012). A vulnerability-based model of cyber weapons and its implications for cyber conflict. *International Journal of Cyber Warfare & Terrorism, 2*(1), 14–26. doi:10.4018/ijcwt.2012010102

da Silva, F. A., Moura, D. F., & Galdino, J. F. (2012). Classes of attacks for tactical software defined radios. *International Journal of Embedded and Real-Time Communication Systems, 3*(4), 57–82. doi:10.4018/jertcs.2012100104

Dabcevic, K., Marcenaro, L., & Regazzoni, C. S. (2013). Security in cognitive radio networks. In T. Lagkas, P. Sarigiannidis, M. Louta, & P. Chatzimisios (Eds.), *Evolution of cognitive networks and self-adaptive communication systems* (pp. 301–335). Hershey, PA: IGI Global. doi:10.4018/978-1-4666-4189-1.ch013

Dahbur, K., Mohammad, B., & Tarakji, A. B. (2013). Security issues in cloud computing: A survey of risks, threats and vulnerabilities. In S. Aljawarneh (Ed.), *Cloud computing advancements in design, implementation, and technologies* (pp. 154–165). Hershey, PA: IGI Global. doi:10.4018/978-1-4666-1879-4.ch011

Dahl, G. E., Yu, D., Deng, L., & Acero, A. (2012). Context-dependent pre-trained deep neural networks for large-vocabulary speech recognition. *IEEE Trans. Audio, Speech Lang. Process., 20*(1), 30–42. doi:10.1109/TASL.2011.2134090

Dark, M. (2011). Data breach disclosure: A policy analysis. In M. Dark (Ed.), *Information assurance and security ethics in complex systems: Interdisciplinary perspectives* (pp. 226–252). Hershey, PA: IGI Global. doi:10.4018/978-1-61692-245-0.ch011

Dasgupta, D., & Naseem, D. (2014). A framework for compliance and security coverage estimation for cloud services: A cloud insurance model. In S. Srinivasan (Ed.), *Security, trust, and regulatory aspects of cloud computing in business environments* (pp. 91–114). Hershey, PA: IGI Global. doi:10.4018/978-1-4666-5788-5.ch005

Das, S., Mukhopadhyay, A., & Bhasker, B. (2013). Today's action is better than tomorrows cure - Evaluating information security at a premier Indian business school. *Journal of Cases on Information Technology, 15*(3), 1–23. doi:10.4018/jcit.2013070101

De Fuentes, J. M., González-Tablas, A. I., & Ribagorda, A. (2011). Overview of security issues in vehicular ad-hoc networks. In M. Cruz-Cunha & F. Moreira (Eds.), *Handbook of research on mobility and computing: Evolving technologies and ubiquitous impacts* (pp. 894–911). Hershey, PA: IGI Global. doi:10.4018/978-1-60960-042-6.ch056

De Groef, W., Devriese, D., Reynaert, T., & Piessens, F. (2013). Security and privacy of online social network applications. In L. Caviglione, M. Coccoli, & A. Merlo (Eds.), *Social network engineering for secure web data and services* (pp. 206–221). Hershey, PA: IGI Global. doi:10.4018/978-1-4666-3926-3.ch010

Dean, J., & Ghemawat, S. (n. d.). MapReduce: Simplified Data Processing on Large Clusters.

Dean, J., Corrado, G., Monga, R., Chen, K., Devin, M., & Le, Q. et al.. (2012). In P. Bartlett, F. Pereira, C. Burges, L. Bottou, & K. Weinberger (Eds.), *Large scale distributed deep network* (pp. 1232–1240). Retrieved from http://papers.nips.cc/book/advances-in-neural-information-processing-systems-25-2012

Dean, J., & Ghemawat, S. (2004). MapReduce: simplified data processing on large clusters.

Del, B. A., & Park, D. C. (1994). Myoelectric signal recognition using fuzzy clustering and artificial neural networks in real time. In *Proceedings* of *the IEEE World Congress on Computational Intelligence and Neural Networks. IEEE.*

Deng, L., & Togneri, R. (2015). Deep Dynamic Models for Learning Hidden Representations of Speech Features. In Speech Audio Process. Coding, Enhanc. Recognit. (pp. 153–195). Springer. doi:10.1007/978-1-4939-1456-2_6

Denning, D. E. (2011). Cyber conflict as an emergent social phenomenon. In T. Holt & B. Schell (Eds.), *Corporate hacking and technology-driven crime: Social dynamics and implications* (pp. 170–186). Hershey, PA: IGI Global. doi:10.4018/978-1-61692-805-6.ch009

Desai, A. M., & Mock, K. (2013). Security in cloud computing. In A. Bento & A. Aggarwal (Eds.), *Cloud computing service and deployment models: Layers and management* (pp. 208–221). Hershey, PA: IGI Global. doi:10.4018/978-1-4666-2187-9.ch011

Dev, D., & Baishnab, K. L. (2014). A Review and Research Towards Mobile Cloud Computing. *Proceedings of 2nd IEEE International Conference on Mobile Cloud Computing, Services and Engineering (MobileCloud)* (pp. 252-255). doi:10.1109/MobileCloud.2014.41

Ding, S. F., Xu, X. Z., & Nie, R. (2014). Extreme learning machine and its applications. *Neural Computing & Applications*, 25(3-4), 549–556. doi:10.1007/s00521-013-1522-8

Dionysiou, I., & Ktoridou, D. (2012). Enhancing dynamic-content courses with student-oriented learning strategies: The case of computer security course. *International Journal of Cyber Ethics in Education*, 2(2), 24–33. doi:10.4018/ijcee.2012040103

Disterer, G. (2012). Attacks on IT systems: Categories of motives. In T. Chou (Ed.), *Information assurance and security technologies for risk assessment and threat management: Advances* (pp. 1–16). Hershey, PA: IGI Global. doi:10.4018/978-1-61350-507-6.ch001

Dix, A. (2009). Human-computer interaction. In L. Liu & M.T. Özsu (Eds.), Encyclopedia of database systems (pp. 1327–1331). Springer.

Dix, A. (2009). *Human-Computer Interaction. In L. Liu & M.T. Özsu (Eds.), Encyclopedia of Database Systems (pp.* 1327–1331). Springer.

Domingos, P. (2012). A few useful things to know about ML. *Communications of the ACM, 55*(10), 78–87. doi:10.1145/2347736.2347755

Dong, L., Lin, Z., Liang, Y., He, L., Zhang, N., & Chen, Q. et al. (2016). A Hierarchical Distributed Processing Framework for Big Image Data. *J. Latex Cl. Files., 20*, 1–13.

Dong, X., Li, R., He, H., Zhou, W., Xue, Z., & Wu, H. (2015). Secure sensitive data sharing on a big data platform. *Tsinghua Science and Technology, 20*(1), 72–80. doi:10.1109/TST.2015.7040516

Dorigo, M., & Caro, G. D. (1999). Ant Colony Optimization: A New Meta-heuristic. In Proceedings of Evolutionary Computation CEC 99, Washington, DC.

Dougan, T., & Curran, K. (2012). Man in the browser attacks. *International Journal of Ambient Computing and Intelligence, 4*(1), 29–39. doi:10.4018/jaci.2012010103

Dubey, R., Sharma, S., & Chouhan, L. (2013). Security for cognitive radio networks. In M. Ku & J. Lin (Eds.), *Cognitive radio and interference management: Technology and strategy* (pp. 238–256). Hershey, PA: IGI Global. doi:10.4018/978-1-4666-2005-6.ch013

Dunkels, E., Frånberg, G., & Hällgren, C. (2011). Young people and online risk. In E. Dunkels, G. Franberg, & C. Hallgren (Eds.), *Youth culture and net culture: Online social practices* (pp. 1–16). Hershey, PA: IGI Global. doi:10.4018/978-1-60960-209-3.ch001

Dunkerley, K., & Tejay, G. (2012). The development of a model for information systems security success. In Z. Belkhamza & S. Azizi Wafa (Eds.), *Measuring organizational information systems success: New technologies and practices* (pp. 341–366). Hershey, PA: IGI Global. doi:10.4018/978-1-4666-0170-3.ch017

Dunkerley, K., & Tejay, G. (2012). Theorizing information security success: Towards secure e-government. In V. Weerakkody (Ed.), *Technology enabled transformation of the public sector: Advances in e-government* (pp. 224–235). Hershey, PA: IGI Global. doi:10.4018/978-1-4666-1776-6.ch014

Dupuis, A., Ghribi, M., & Kaddouri, A. (2004). Multi-objective genetic estimation of DC motor parameters and load torque. In *Proceedings of Industrial Technology, 2004. IEEE ICIT '04.* IEEE.

Durai, M. S., & Iyengar, N. C. S. N. (2010). Secure medical diagnosis using rule based mining. In *Proceedings of the International Conference on Advances in Information Technology* (pp. 34-42). Springer.

Du, W., & Zhan, Z. (2003, August). Using randomized response techniques for privacy-preserving data mining. In *Proceedings of the ninth ACM SIGKDD international conference on Knowledge discovery and data mining* (pp. 505-510). ACM. doi:10.1145/956750.956810

Du, Y.-C., Lin, C.-H., Shyu, L.-Y., & Chen, T. (2010). Portable hand motion classifier for multi-channel surface electromyography recognition using grey relational analysis. *Journal Expert Systems with Applications*, *37*(6), 4283–4291. doi:10.1016/j.eswa.2009.11.072

Dwork, C. (2008). Differential privacy: A survey of results. In *Theory and Applications of Models of Computation*. Springer Berlin Heidelberg.

Dwork, C. (2011). Differential privacy. In Encyclopedia of Cryptography and Security. Springer US, pp 338-340.

Ebenezer, J. G. A., & Durga, S. (2015). Big Data Analytics In Healthcare: A Survey. *Journal of Engineering and Applied Sciences (Asian Research Publishing Network)*, *10*(8), 3645–3650.

Eisenga, A., Jones, T. L., & Rodriguez, W. (2012). Investing in IT security: How to determine the maximum threshold. *International Journal of Information Security and Privacy*, *6*(3), 75–87. doi:10.4018/jisp.2012070104

Esteves, R. M., Hacker, T., & Rong, C. (2014). A new approach for accurate distributed cluster analysis for Big Data: competitive K-Means. *International Journal of Big Data Intelligence*, *5*(1-2), 50-64.

Eyitemi, M. (2012). Regulation of cybercafés in Nigeria. In *Cyber crime: Concepts, methodologies, tools and applications* (pp. 1305–1313). Hershey, PA: IGI Global. doi:10.4018/978-1-61350-323-2.ch606

Ezumah, B., & Adekunle, S. O. (2012). A review of privacy, internet security threat, and legislation in Africa: A case study of Nigeria, South Africa, Egypt, and Kenya. In J. Abawajy, M. Pathan, M. Rahman, A. Pathan, & M. Deris (Eds.), *Internet and distributed computing advancements: Theoretical frameworks and practical applications* (pp. 115–136). Hershey, PA: IGI Global. doi:10.4018/978-1-4666-0161-1.ch005

Fageeri, S. O., & Ahmad, R. (2014). An efficient log file analysis algorithm using binary-based data structure. *Procedia: Social and Behavioral Sciences*, *129*, 518–526. doi:10.1016/j.sbspro.2014.03.709

Farooq-i-Azam, M., & Ayyaz, M. N. (2014). Embedded systems security. In *Software design and development: Concepts, methodologies, tools, and applications* (pp. 980–998). Hershey, PA: IGI Global. doi:10.4018/978-1-4666-4301-7.ch047

Fauzi, A. H., & Taylor, H. (2013). Secure community trust stores for peer-to-peer e-commerce applications using cloud services. *International Journal of E-Entrepreneurship and Innovation*, *4*(1), 1–15. doi:10.4018/jeei.2013010101

Fayyad, U. M., Piatetsky-Shapiro, G., Smyth, P., & Uthurusamy, R. (1996). Advances in knowledge discovery and data mining.

Fayyad, U., Piatetsky-Shapiro, G., & Smyth, P. (1996). From Data Mining to Knowledge Discovery in Databases. *AI Magazine*, *17*, 37–54. doi:10.1609/aimag.v17i3.1230

Feldman, R. (2013). Techniques and applications for sentiment analysis. *Communications of the ACM, 56*(4), 82–89. doi:10.1145/2436256.2436274

Feng, J., & Darrell, T. (2015). Learning the Structure of Deep Convolutional Networks. In *Proceedings of the 2015 IEEE Int. Conf. Comput. Vis.* (pp. 2749–2757). doi:10.1109/ICCV.2015.315

Fenz, S. (2011). E-business and information security risk management: Challenges and potential solutions. In E. Kajan (Ed.), *Electronic business interoperability: Concepts, opportunities and challenges* (pp. 596–614). Hershey, PA: IGI Global. doi:10.4018/978-1-60960-485-1.ch024

Fernandez, E. B., Yoshioka, N., Washizaki, H., Jurjens, J., VanHilst, M., & Pernu, G. (2011). Using security patterns to develop secure systems. In H. Mouratidis (Ed.), *Software engineering for secure systems: Industrial and research perspectives* (pp. 16–31). Hershey, PA: IGI Global. doi:10.4018/978-1-61520-837-1.ch002

Flores, A. E., Win, K. T., & Susilo, W. (2011). Secure exchange of electronic health records. In A. Chryssanthou, I. Apostolakis, & I. Varlamis (Eds.), *Certification and security in health-related web applications: Concepts and solutions* (pp. 1–22). Hershey, PA: IGI Global. doi:10.4018/978-1-61692-895-7.ch001

Fonseca, J., & Vieira, M. (2014). A survey on secure software development lifecycles. In *Software design and development: Concepts, methodologies, tools, and applications* (pp. 17–33). Hershey, PA: IGI Global. doi:10.4018/978-1-4666-4301-7.ch002

Fournaris, A. P., Kitsos, P., & Sklavos, N. (2013). Security and cryptographic engineering in embedded systems. In M. Khalgui, O. Mosbahi, & A. Valentini (Eds.), *Embedded computing systems: Applications, optimization, and advanced design* (pp. 420–438). Hershey, PA: IGI Global. doi:10.4018/978-1-4666-3922-5.ch021

Franqueira, V. N., van Cleeff, A., van Eck, P., & Wieringa, R. J. (2013). Engineering security agreements against external insider threat. *Information Resources Management Journal, 26*(4), 66–91. doi:10.4018/irmj.2013100104

French, T., Bessis, N., Maple, C., & Asimakopoulou, E. (2012). Trust issues on crowd-sourcing methods for urban environmental monitoring. *International Journal of Distributed Systems and Technologies, 3*(1), 35–47. doi:10.4018/jdst.2012010103

Friedman, A., & Schuster, A. (2010). Data mining with differential privacy. In *Proceedings of the 16th ACM SIGKDD international conference on Knowledge discovery and data mining*. ACM. doi:10.1145/1835804.1835868

Fung, B., Wang, K., Chen, R., & Yu, P. S. (2010). Privacy-preserving data publishing: A survey of recent developments. [CSUR]. *ACM Computing Surveys, 42*(4), 14. doi:10.1145/1749603.1749605

Furnell, S., von Solms, R., & Phippen, A. (2011). Preventative actions for enhancing online protection and privacy. *International Journal of Information Technologies and Systems Approach, 4*(2), 1–11. doi:10.4018/jitsa.2011070101

Fu, Y., Kulick, J., Yan, L. K., & Drager, S. (2013). Formal modeling and verification of security property in Handel C program. *International Journal of Secure Software Engineering*, *3*(3), 50–65. doi:10.4018/jsse.2012070103

Gai, K., Qiu, M., & Zhao, H. (2016, April). Security-aware efficient mass distributed storage approach for cloud systems in big data. In *Proceedings of the 2016 IEEE 2nd International Conference on Big Data Security on Cloud (BigDataSecurity), IEEE International Conference on High Performance and Smart Computing (HPSC), and IEEE International Conference on Intelligent Data and Security (IDS)* (pp. 140-145). IEEE. doi:10.1109/BigDataSecurity-HPSC-IDS.2016.68

Gaivéo, J. (2011). SMEs e-business security issues. In M. Cruz-Cunha & J. Varajão (Eds.), *Innovations in SMEs and conducting e-business: Technologies, trends and solutions* (pp. 317–337). Hershey, PA: IGI Global. doi:10.4018/978-1-60960-765-4.ch018

Gaivéo, J. M. (2013). Security of ICTs supporting healthcare activities. In M. Cruz-Cunha, I. Miranda, & P. Gonçalves (Eds.), *Handbook of research on ICTs for human-centered healthcare and social care services* (pp. 208–228). Hershey, PA: IGI Global. doi:10.4018/978-1-4666-3986-7.ch011

Gandomi, A., & Haider, M. (2015). Beyond the hype: Big data concepts, methods, and analytics. *International Journal of Information Management*, *35*(2), 137–144. doi:10.1016/j.ijinfomgt.2014.10.007

Garg, D., Trivedi, K., & Panchal, B. B. (2013, October). A comparative study of clustering algorithms using mapreduce in hadoop. *International Journal of Engineering Research and Technology*, *2*(10).

Gartner. (n. d.). IT Glossary: Big Data. Retrieved from http://www.gartner.com/it-glossary/big-data

Gelbstein, E. E. (2013). Designing a security audit plan for a critical information infrastructure (CII). In C. Laing, A. Badii, & P. Vickers (Eds.), *Securing critical infrastructures and critical control systems: Approaches for threat protection* (pp. 262–285). Hershey, PA: IGI Global. doi:10.4018/978-1-4666-2659-1.ch011

Gemayel, N. (2016Analyzing Google File System and Hadoop Distributed File System. *Journal of Information Technology*, *8*(3), 66–74. doi:10.3923/rjit.2016.66.74

Getelastic.com. (2014). The Big 9 big data sources [Infographic]. Retrieved 2017 from http://www.getelastic.com/big-data-infographic/

Ghesmoune, M., Lebbah, M., & Azzag, H. (2015). Micro-batching growing neural gas for clustering data streams using spark streaming.

Gkoulalas-Divanis, A., & Loukides, G. (2011, March). PCTA: privacy-constrained clustering-based transaction data anonymization. In *Proceedings of the 4th International Workshop on Privacy and Anonymity in the Information Society* (p. 5). ACM.

Gódor, G., & Imre, S. (2012). Security aspects in radio frequency identification systems. In D. Saha & V. Sridhar (Eds.), *Next generation data communication technologies: Emerging trends* (pp. 187–225). Hershey, PA: IGI Global. doi:10.4018/978-1-61350-477-2.ch009

Gogolin, G. (2011). Security and privacy concerns of virtual worlds. In B. Ciaramitaro (Ed.), *Virtual worlds and e-commerce: Technologies and applications for building customer relationships* (pp. 244–256). Hershey, PA: IGI Global. doi:10.4018/978-1-61692-808-7.ch014

Gogoulos, F. I., Antonakopoulou, A., Lioudakis, G. V., Kaklamani, D. I., & Venieris, I. S. (2014). Trust in an enterprise world: A survey. In M. Cruz-Cunha, F. Moreira, & J. Varajão (Eds.), *Handbook of research on enterprise 2.0: Technological, social, and organizational dimensions* (pp. 199–219). Hershey, PA: IGI Global. doi:10.4018/978-1-4666-4373-4.ch011

Goldman, J. E., & Ahuja, S. (2011). Integration of COBIT, balanced scorecard and SSE-CMM as an organizational & strategic information security management (ISM) framework. In M. Quigley (Ed.), *ICT ethics and security in the 21st century: New developments and applications* (pp. 277–309). Hershey, PA: IGI Global. doi:10.4018/978-1-60960-573-5.ch014

Goldschmidt, C., Dark, M., & Chaudhry, H. (2011). Responsibility for the harm and risk of software security flaws. In M. Dark (Ed.), *Information assurance and security ethics in complex systems: Interdisciplinary perspectives* (pp. 104–131). Hershey, PA: IGI Global. doi:10.4018/978-1-61692-245-0.ch006

Goodfellow, I. J., Erhan, D., Luc Carrier, P., Courville, A., Mirza, M., Hamner, B., & Bengio, Y. et al. (2015). Challenges in representation learning: A report on three ML contests. *Neural Networks*, *64*, 59–63. doi:10.1016/j.neunet.2014.09.005 PMID:25613956

Grahn, K., Karlsson, J., & Pulkkis, G. (2011). Secure routing and mobility in future IP networks. In M. Cruz-Cunha & F. Moreira (Eds.), *Handbook of research on mobility and computing: Evolving technologies and ubiquitous impacts* (pp. 952–972). Hershey, PA: IGI Global. doi:10.4018/978-1-60960-042-6.ch059

Greitzer, F. L., Frincke, D., & Zabriskie, M. (2011). Social/ethical issues in predictive insider threat monitoring. In M. Dark (Ed.), *Information assurance and security ethics in complex systems: Interdisciplinary perspectives* (pp. 132–161). Hershey, PA: IGI Global. doi:10.4018/978-1-61692-245-0.ch007

Grobler, M. (2012). The need for digital evidence standardisation. *International Journal of Digital Crime and Forensics*, *4*(2), 1–12. doi:10.4018/jdcf.2012040101

Guo, J., Marshall, A., & Zhou, B. (2014). A multi-parameter trust framework for mobile ad hoc networks. In D. Rawat, B. Bista, & G. Yan (Eds.), *Security, privacy, trust, and resource management in mobile and wireless communications* (pp. 245–277). Hershey, PA: IGI Global. doi:10.4018/978-1-4666-4691-9.ch011

Guo, X., Yang, P., Chen, L., Wang, X., & Li, L. (2006). Study of the control mechanism of robot-prosthesis based-on the EMG processed. In *Proceedings of 6th World Congress on Intelligent Control and Automation* (pp. 9490-9493), Dalian, China: IEEE.

Guo, X., Yu, H., Zhen, G., Liu, Y., Zhang, Y., & Zhang, Y. (2009). Artificial intelligent based human motion pattern recognition and prediction for the surface electromyographic signals. In *Proceedings of Information Technology and Computer Science ITCS '09*. Ukraine: IEEE. doi:10.1109/ITCS.2009.65

Gururajan, R., & Hafeez-Baig, A. (2011). Wireless handheld device and LAN security issues: A case study. In D. Kerr, J. Gammack, & K. Bryant (Eds.), *Digital business security development: Management technologies* (pp. 129–151). Hershey, PA: IGI Global. doi:10.4018/978-1-60566-806-2.ch006

Hagen, J. M. (2012). The contributions of information security culture and human relations to the improvement of situational awareness. In C. Onwubiko & T. Owens (Eds.), *Situational awareness in computer network defense: Principles, methods and applications* (pp. 10–28). Hershey, PA: IGI Global. doi:10.4018/978-1-4666-0104-8.ch002

Ha, H. (2012). Online security and consumer protection in ecommerce an Australian case. In K. Mohammed Rezaul (Ed.), *Strategic and pragmatic e-business: Implications for future business practices* (pp. 217–243). Hershey, PA: IGI Global. doi:10.4018/978-1-4666-1619-6.ch010

Hai-Jew, S. (2011). The social design of 3D interactive spaces for security in higher education: A preliminary view. In A. Rea (Ed.), *Security in virtual worlds, 3D webs, and immersive environments: Models for development, interaction, and management* (pp. 72–96). Hershey, PA: IGI Global. doi:10.4018/978-1-61520-891-3.ch005

Halder, D., & Jaishankar, K. (2012). Cyber crime against women and regulations in Australia. In *Cyber crime: Concepts, methodologies, tools and applications* (pp. 757–764). Hershey, PA: IGI Global. doi:10.4018/978-1-61350-323-2.ch404

Halder, D., & Jaishankar, K. (2012). Cyber victimization of women and cyber laws in India. In *Cyber crime: Concepts, methodologies, tools and applications* (pp. 742–756). Hershey, PA: IGI Global. doi:10.4018/978-1-61350-323-2.ch403

Halder, D., & Jaishankar, K. (2012). Definition, typology and patterns of victimization. In *Cyber crime: Concepts, methodologies, tools and applications* (pp. 1016–1042). Hershey, PA: IGI Global. doi:10.4018/978-1-61350-323-2.ch502

Hamlen, K., Kantarcioglu, M., Khan, L., & Thuraisingham, B. (2012). Security issues for cloud computing. In H. Nemati (Ed.), *Optimizing information security and advancing privacy assurance: New technologies* (pp. 150–162). Hershey, PA: IGI Global. doi:10.4018/978-1-4666-0026-3.ch008

Han, J., Haihong, E., Le, G., & Du, J. (2011). Survey on nosql database. In *Proceedings of the 2011 6th International Conference on Pervasive Computing and Applications*.

Harnesk, D. (2011). Convergence of information security in B2B networks. In E. Kajan (Ed.), *Electronic business interoperability: Concepts, opportunities and challenges* (pp. 571–595). Hershey, PA: IGI Global. doi:10.4018/978-1-60960-485-1.ch023

Harnesk, D., & Hartikainen, H. (2011). Multi-layers of information security in emergency response. *International Journal of Information Systems for Crisis Response and Management*, *3*(2), 1–17. doi:10.4018/jiscrm.2011040101

Hasan, O., Habegger, B., Brunie, L., Bennani, N., & Damiani, E. (2013, June). A discussion of privacy challenges in user profiling with big data techniques: The excess use case. In *Proceedings of the 2013 IEEE International Congress on Big Data* (pp. 25-30). IEEE. doi:10.1109/BigData. Congress.2013.13

Hawrylak, P. J., Hale, J., & Papa, M. (2013). Security issues for ISO 18000-6 type C RFID: Identification and solutions. In *Supply chain management: Concepts, methodologies, tools, and applications* (pp. 1565–1581). Hershey, PA: IGI Global. doi:10.4018/978-1-4666-2625-6.ch093

Hayes, M. A., & Capretz, M. A. (2014, June). Contextual anomaly detection in big sensor data. In *Proceedings of the 2014 IEEE International Congress on Big Data* (pp. 64-71). IEEE. doi:10.1109/BigData.Congress.2014.19

He, B., Tran, T. T., & Xie, B. (2014). Authentication and identity management for secure cloud businesses and services. In S. Srinivasan (Ed.), *Security, trust, and regulatory aspects of cloud computing in business environments* (pp. 180–201). Hershey, PA: IGI Global. doi:10.4018/978-1-4666-5788-5.ch011

Heger, D. A. (n. d.). An Introduction to Artificial Neural Networks (ANN) - Methods, Abstraction, and Usage. Retrieved from http://www.dhtusa.com/media/NeuralNetworkIntro.pdf

Henrie, M. (2012). Cyber security in liquid petroleum pipelines. In J. Zubairi & A. Mahboob (Eds.), *Cyber security standards, practices and industrial applications: Systems and methodologies* (pp. 200–222). Hershey, PA: IGI Global. doi:10.4018/978-1-60960-851-4.ch011

Herath, T., Rao, H. R., & Upadhyaya, S. (2012). Internet crime: How vulnerable are you? Do gender, social influence and education play a role in vulnerability? In *Cyber crime: Concepts, methodologies, tools and applications* (pp. 1–13). Hershey, PA: IGI Global. doi:10.4018/978-1-61350-323-2.ch101

Hilmi, M. F., Pawanchik, S., Mustapha, Y., & Ali, H. M. (2013). Information security perspective of a learning management system: An exploratory study. *International Journal of Knowledge Society Research*, *4*(2), 9–18. doi:10.4018/jksr.2013040102

Hindman, B., Konwinski, A., Zaharia, M., Ghodsi, A., Joseph, A. D., Katz, R. H., ... & Stoica, I. (2011). Mesos: A Platform for Fine Grained Resource Sharing in the Data Center. In *NSDI* (Vol. 11, pp. 22-22).

Hinton, G. E., Osindero, S., & Teh, Y.-W. Y. (2006). A fast learning algorithm for deep belief nets. *Neural Computation*, *18*(7), 1527–1554. doi:10.1162/neco.2006.18.7.1527 PMID:16764513

Hinton, G., Deng, L., Yu, D., Dahl, G., Mohamed, A. R., Jaitly, N., & Kingsbury, B. et al. (2012). Deep neural networks for acoustic modeling in speech recognition: The shared views of four research groups. *IEEE Signal Processing Magazine*, *29*(6), 82–97. doi:10.1109/MSP.2012.2205597

Hjelmervik, J. M., & Barrowclough, O. J. D. (2016). *Interactive Exploration of Big Scientific Data: New Representations and Techniques*. IEEE.

Holland, J. H. (1973). Genetic algorithms and the optimal allocation of trials. *SIAM Journal on Computing*, *2*(2), 88–105. doi:10.1137/0202009

Hommel, W. (2012). Security and privacy management for learning management systems. In *Virtual learning environments: Concepts, methodologies, tools and applications* (pp. 1151–1170). Hershey, PA: IGI Global. doi:10.4018/978-1-4666-0011-9.ch602

Hoops, D. S. (2012). Lost in cyberspace: Navigating the legal issues of e-commerce. *Journal of Electronic Commerce in Organizations*, *10*(1), 33–51. doi:10.4018/jeco.2012010103

Houmb, S., Georg, G., Petriu, D., Bordbar, B., Ray, I., Anastasakis, K., & France, R. (2011). Balancing security and performance properties during system architectural design. In H. Mouratidis (Ed.), *Software engineering for secure systems: Industrial and research perspectives* (pp. 155–191). Hershey, PA: IGI Global. doi:10.4018/978-1-61520-837-1.ch006

Huang, H.-P., Liu, Y.-H., Liu, L.-W., & Wong, C.-S. (2003). EMG classification for prehensile postures using cascaded architecture of neural networks with self-organizing maps. In *Proceedings of the 2006 6th World Congress on Intelligent Control and Automation*, Taipei, Taiwan: IEEE.

Huang, E., & Cheng, F. (2012). Online security cues and e-payment continuance intention. *International Journal of E-Entrepreneurship and Innovation*, *3*(1), 42–58. doi:10.4018/jeei.2012010104

Huang, G.-B., Zhu, Q., & Siew, C. (2006). Extreme learning machine: Theory and applications. *Neurocomputing*, *70*(1-3), 489–501. doi:10.1016/j.neucom.2005.12.126

Hudgins, B., Parker, P., & Scott, R. N. (1993). A new strategy for multifunction myoelectric control. *IEEE Transactions on Bio-Medical Engineering*, *40*(1), 82–94. doi:10.1109/10.204774 PMID:8468080

Hu, H., Wen, Y., Chua, T.-S., & Li, X. (2014). Toward Scalable Systems for Big Data Analytics: A Technology Tutorial. *IEEE Access*, *2*, 652–687. doi:10.1109/ACCESS.2014.2332453

Hutchinson, L. (2012). Solid-state revolution: in-depth on how ssds really work. ArsTechnica.

Hu, W., Qian, Y., Soong, F. K., & Wang, Y. (2015). Improved mispronunciation detection with deep neural network trained acoustic models and transfer learning based logistic regression classifiers. *Speech Communication*, *67*, 154–166. doi:10.1016/j.specom.2014.12.008

Huynh, D. C., & Dunnigan, M. W. (2010). Parameter estimation of an induction machine using advanced particle swarm optimization algorithms. *IET Electric Power Applications*, *4*(9), 748–760. doi:10.1049/iet-epa.2009.0296

Hwang, Y. H., Seo, J. W., & Kim, I. J. (2014). Encrypted Keyword Search Mechanism Based on Bitmap Index for Personal Storage Services. In *Proceedings of IEEE 13th International Conference on Trust, Security and Privacy in Computing and Communications (TrustCom)* (pp. 140-147). doi:10.1109/TrustCom.2014.22

IBM Big Data Hub. (n. d.). The Four V's of Big Data. Retrieved 2017 from http://www.ibmbigdatahub.com/infographic/four-vs-big-data

Ifinedo, P. (2011). Relationships between information security concerns and national cultural dimensions: Findings in the global financial services industry. In H. Nemati (Ed.), *Security and privacy assurance in advancing technologies: New developments* (pp. 134–153). Hershey, PA: IGI Global. doi:10.4018/978-1-60960-200-0.ch010

Imperva. (2015). Top Ten Database Threats. Retrieved from https://www.imperva.com/docs/gated/WP_TopTen_Database_Threats.pdf

Inden, U., Lioudakis, G., & Rückemann, C. (2013). Awareness-based security management for complex and internet-based operations management systems. In C. Rückemann (Ed.), *Integrated information and computing systems for natural, spatial, and social sciences* (pp. 43–73). Hershey, PA: IGI Global. doi:10.4018/978-1-4666-2190-9.ch003

Isard, M., Budiu, M., Yu, Y., Birrell, A., & Fetterly, D. (2007). Dryad: distributed data-parallel programs from sequential building blocks. In *Proceedings of the 2nd ACM SIGOPS/EuroSys European Conference on Computer Systems EuroSys '07*.

Islam, S., Mouratidis, H., Kalloniatis, C., Hudic, A., & Zechner, L. (2013). Model based process to support security and privacy requirements engineering. *International Journal of Secure Software Engineering*, *3*(3), 1–22. doi:10.4018/jsse.2012070101

Itani, W., Kayssi, A., & Chehab, A. (2012). Security and privacy in body sensor networks: Challenges, solutions, and research directions. In M. Watfa (Ed.), *E-healthcare systems and wireless communications: Current and future challenges* (pp. 100–127). Hershey, PA: IGI Global. doi:10.4018/978-1-61350-123-8.ch005

Ito, K., Tsukamoto, M., & Kondo, T. (2008). Discrimination of intended movements based on nonstationary EMG for a prosthetic hand control. In *Proceedings of Communications, Control and Signal Processing ISCCSP '08*, St. Julian's, Malta. IEEE.

Jacob, A. (2009). The pathologies of big data. *Communications of the ACM*, *52*(8), 36–44. doi:10.1145/1536616.1536632

Jansen van Vuuren, J., Grobler, M., & Zaaiman, J. (2012). Cyber security awareness as critical driver to national security. *International Journal of Cyber Warfare & Terrorism*, *2*(1), 27–38. doi:10.4018/ijcwt.2012010103

Jansen van Vuuren, J., Leenen, L., Phahlamohlaka, J., & Zaaiman, J. (2012). An approach to governance of CyberSecurity in South Africa. *International Journal of Cyber Warfare & Terrorism*, *2*(4), 13–27. doi:10.4018/ijcwt.2012100102

Jasmine, R.M. & Nishibha, G.M. (2015). Public Cloud Secure Group Sharing and Accessing in Cloud Computing. *Indian Journal of Science and Technology,* 8(15). doi:10.17485/ijst/2015/v8i15/75177

Jensen, J., & Groep, D. L. (2012). Security and trust in a global research infrastructure. In J. Leng & W. Sharrock (Eds.), *Handbook of research on computational science and engineering: Theory and practice* (pp. 539–566). Hershey, PA: IGI Global. doi:10.4018/978-1-61350-116-0.ch022

Jeuk, S., Szefer, J., & Zhou, S. (2014). Towards Cloud, Service and Tenant Classification for Cloud Computing. In *Proceedings of 14th IEEE/ACM International Symposium on Cluster, Cloud and Grid Computing (CCGrid)* (pp. 792-801). doi:10.1109/CCGrid.2014.71

Ji, C., Li, Y., Qiu, W., Awada, U., & Li, K. (2012). Big Data Processing in Cloud Computing Environments. In *Proceedings of the 12th International Symposium on Pervasive Systems. Algorithms and Networks (ISPAN)* (pp. 17-23).

Jiang, C., Chen, Y., & Ray Liu, K. J. (2014). *Graphical Evolutionary Game for Information Diffusion Over Social Networks.*

Johnsen, S. O. (2014). Safety and security in SCADA systems must be improved through resilience based risk management. In *Crisis management: Concepts, methodologies, tools and applications* (pp. 1422–1436). Hershey, PA: IGI Global. doi:10.4018/978-1-4666-4707-7.ch071

Johnston, A. C., Wech, B., & Jack, E. (2012). Engaging remote employees: The moderating role of remote status in determining employee information security policy awareness. *Journal of Organizational and End User Computing,* 25(1), 1–23. doi:10.4018/joeuc.2013010101

Jolliffe, I. T. (2002). *Principal Component Analysis.* New York: Springer.

Jones, N. (2014). The learning machines. *Nature,* 505(7482), 146–148. doi:10.1038/505146a PMID:24402264

Jung, C., Rudolph, M., & Schwarz, R. (2013). Security evaluation of service-oriented systems using the SiSOA method. In K. Khan (Ed.), *Developing and evaluating security-aware software systems* (pp. 20–35). Hershey, PA: IGI Global. doi:10.4018/978-1-4666-2482-5.ch002

Jung, K. K., Kim, J. W., Lee, H. K., Chung, S. B., & Eom, K. H. (2007). EMG pattern classification using spectral estimation and neural network. *In Proceedings of the 2007 Annual Conference,* Takamatsu, Japan. IEEE. doi:10.1109/SICE.2007.4421150

Jung, K., Park, S., & Park, S. (2014, November). Hiding a Needle in a Haystack: Privacy Preserving Apriori algorithm inMapReduce Framework. In *Proceedings of the First International Workshop on Privacy and Security of Big Data* (pp. 11-17). ACM. doi:10.1145/2663715.2669611

K.C., A., Forsgren, H., Grahn, K., Karvi, T., & Pulkkis, G. (2013). Security and trust of public key cryptography for HIP and HIP multicast. *International Journal of Dependable and Trustworthy Information Systems,* 2(3), 17–35. doi:10.4018/jdtis.2011070102

Kaiya, H., Sakai, J., Ogata, S., & Kaijiri, K. (2013). Eliciting security requirements for an information system using asset flows and processor deployment. *International Journal of Secure Software Engineering*, *4*(3), 42–63. doi:10.4018/jsse.2013070103

Kalanat, N., & Kangavari, M. R. (2015). Data Mining Methods for Rule Designing and Rule Triggering in Active Database Systems. *Int. J. Database Theory Appl.*, *8*(1), 39–44. doi:10.14257/ijdta.2015.8.1.05

Kalloniatis, C., Kavakli, E., & Gritzalis, S. (2011). Designing privacy aware information systems. In H. Mouratidis (Ed.), *Software engineering for secure systems: Industrial and research perspectives* (pp. 212–231). Hershey, PA: IGI Global. doi:10.4018/978-1-61520-837-1.ch008

Kalpana, V. & Meena, V. (2015). Study on Data Storage Correctness Methods in Mobile Cloud Computing. *Indian Journal of Science and Technology*. doi:10.17485/ijst/2015/v8i6/70094

Kamburugamuve, S., & Fox, G. (2016). *Survey of Distributed Stream Processing*. Bloomington, IN: Indiana University.

Kamoun, F., & Halaweh, M. (2012). User interface design and e-commerce security perception: An empirical study. *International Journal of E-Business Research*, *8*(2), 15–32. doi:10.4018/jebr.2012040102

Kamruzzaman, J., Azad, A. K., Karmakar, N. C., Karmakar, G., & Srinivasan, B. (2013). Security and privacy in RFID systems. In N. Karmakar (Ed.), *Advanced RFID systems, security, and applications* (pp. 16–40). Hershey, PA: IGI Global. doi:10.4018/978-1-4666-2080-3.ch002

Kaosar, M. G., & Yi, X. (2011). Privacy preserving data gathering in wireless sensor network. In D. Kar & M. Syed (Eds.), *Network security, administration and management: Advancing technology and practice* (pp. 237–251). Hershey, PA: IGI Global. doi:10.4018/978-1-60960-777-7.ch012

Kapoor, V., Poncelet, P., Trousset, F., & Teisseire, M. (2006, November). Privacy preserving sequential pattern mining in distributed databases. In *Proceedings of the 15th ACM international conference on Information and knowledge management* (pp. 758-767). ACM. doi:10.1145/1183614.1183722

Karadsheh, L., & Alhawari, S. (2011). Applying security policies in small business utilizing cloud computing technologies. *International Journal of Cloud Applications and Computing*, *1*(2), 29–40. doi:10.4018/ijcac.2011040103

Kar, D. C., Ngo, H. L., Mulkey, C. J., & Sanapala, G. (2011). Advances in security and privacy in wireless sensor networks. In H. Nemati (Ed.), *Security and privacy assurance in advancing technologies: New developments* (pp. 186–213). Hershey, PA: IGI Global. doi:10.4018/978-1-60960-200-0.ch014

Karokola, G., Yngström, L., & Kowalski, S. (2012). Secure e-government services: A comparative analysis of e-government maturity models for the developing regions–The need for security services. *International Journal of Electronic Government Research*, *8*(1), 1–25. doi:10.4018/jegr.2012010101

Karpinets, T. V., Park, B. H., & Uberbacher, E. C. (2012). Analyzing large biological datasets with association networks. *Nucleic Acids Research*, *40*(17), e131. doi:10.1093/nar/gks403 PMID:22638576

Kashyap, H., Ahmed, H. A., Hoque, N., Roy, S., & Bhattacharyya, D. K. (2014). Big Data Analytics in Bioinformatics: A ML Perspective. *J. LATEX Cl. FILES.*, *13*, 1–20.

Kassim, N. M., & Ramayah, T. (2013). Security policy issues in internet banking in Malaysia. In *IT policy and ethics: Concepts, methodologies, tools, and applications* (pp. 1274–1293). Hershey, PA: IGI Global. doi:10.4018/978-1-4666-2919-6.ch057

Kaur, P., & Kaur, P. (2016). A Review on Cloud Computing: Backbone Technologies, Fundaments & Challenges. *Int. J. Eng. Appl. Sci. Technol.*, *1*, 123–129.

Kayem, A. V. (2013). Security in service oriented architectures: Standards and challenges. In *Digital rights management: Concepts, methodologies, tools, and applications* (pp. 50–73). Hershey, PA: IGI Global. doi:10.4018/978-1-4666-2136-7.ch004

Kelarev, A. V., Brown, S., Watters, P., Wu, X., & Dazeley, R. (2011). Establishing reasoning communities of security experts for internet commerce security. In J. Yearwood & A. Stranieri (Eds.), *Technologies for supporting reasoning communities and collaborative decision making: Cooperative approaches* (pp. 380–396). Hershey, PA: IGI Global. doi:10.4018/978-1-60960-091-4.ch020

Kelly, M. F., Parker, P. A., & Scott, R. N. (1990). The application of neural networks to myoelectric signal analysis: A preliminary study. *IEEE Transactions on Bio-Medical Engineering*, *37*(3), 221–230. doi:10.1109/10.52324 PMID:2328997

Kennedy, J., & Eberhart, R. C. (1995).Particle swarm optimization. In *Proceedings of the IEEE International Conference on Neural Networks*. Piscataway, NJ: IEEE. doi:10.1109/ICNN.1995.488968

Kerr, D., Gammack, J. G., & Boddington, R. (2011). Overview of digital business security issues. In D. Kerr, J. Gammack, & K. Bryant (Eds.), *Digital business security development: Management technologies* (pp. 1–36). Hershey, PA: IGI Global. doi:10.4018/978-1-60566-806-2.ch001

Khan, K. M. (2011). A decision support system for selecting secure web services. In *Enterprise information systems: Concepts, methodologies, tools and applications* (pp. 1113–1120). Hershey, PA: IGI Global. doi:10.4018/978-1-61692-852-0.ch415

Khan, K. M. (2012). Software security engineering: Design and applications. *International Journal of Secure Software Engineering*, *3*(1), 62–63. doi:10.4018/jsse.2012010104

Khan, N., Yaqoob, I., Hashem, I. A. T., Inayat, Z., Mahmoud Ali, W. K., Alam, M., & Gani, A. et al. (2014). Big data: Survey, technologies, opportunities, and challenges. *The Scientific World Journal*. PMID:25136682

Khushaba, R. N., Al-Ani, A., & Al-Jumaily, A. (2007). Swarm intelligence based dimensionality reduction for myoelectric control. In *Proceedings of Intelligent Sensors, Sensor Networks and Information ISSNIP '07*, Melbourne, QLD, Australia. IEEE. doi:10.1109/ISSNIP.2007.4496907

Khushaba, R. N., & Al-Jumaily, A. (2007a). Channel and feature selection in multifunction myoelectric control. In *Proceedings of 2007 29th Annual International Conference of the IEEE Engineering in Medicine and Biology Society*, Lyon, France. IEEE. doi:10.1109/IEMBS.2007.4353509

Khushaba, R. N., Al-Jumaily, A., & Al-Ani, A. (2009). Evolutionary fuzzy discriminant analysis feature projection technique in myoelectric control. *Pattern Recognition Letters*, *30*(7), 699–707. doi:10.1016/j.patrec.2009.02.004

Kilger, M. (2011). Social dynamics and the future of technology-driven crime. In T. Holt & B. Schell (Eds.), *Corporate hacking and technology-driven crime: Social dynamics and implications* (pp. 205–227). Hershey, PA: IGI Global. doi:10.4018/978-1-61692-805-6.ch011

Kim, S. H., Kim, N. U., & Chung, T. M. (2013, December). Attribute relationship evaluation methodology for big data security. In *Proceedings of the 2013 International Conference on IT Convergence and Security (ICITCS)* (pp. 1-4). IEEE. doi:10.1109/ICITCS.2013.6717808

Kirubakaramoorthi, R., Arivazhagan, D. & Helen, D. (2015). Analysis of Cloud Computing Technology. *Indian Journal of Science and Technology*, *8*(21). doi:10.17485/ijst/2015/v8i21/79144

Kirwan, G., & Power, A. (2012). Hacking: Legal and ethical aspects of an ambiguous activity. In A. Dudley, J. Braman, & G. Vincenti (Eds.), *Investigating cyber law and cyber ethics: Issues, impacts and practices* (pp. 21–36). Hershey, PA: IGI Global. doi:10.4018/978-1-61350-132-0.ch002

Kline, D. M., He, L., & Yaylacicegi, U. (2011). User perceptions of security technologies. *International Journal of Information Security and Privacy*, *5*(2), 1–12. doi:10.4018/jisp.2011040101

Kohonen, T. (1995). *Self-Organizing Maps*. Berlin/Heidelberg, Germany: Springer. doi:10.1007/978-3-642-97610-0

Kolkowska, E., Hedström, K., & Karlsson, F. (2012). Analyzing information security goals. In M. Gupta, J. Walp, & R. Sharman (Eds.), *Threats, countermeasures, and advances in applied information security* (pp. 91–110). Hershey, PA: IGI Global. doi:10.4018/978-1-4666-0978-5.ch005

Korhonen, J. J., Hiekkanen, K., & Mykkänen, J. (2012). Information security governance. In M. Gupta, J. Walp, & R. Sharman (Eds.), *Strategic and practical approaches for information security governance: Technologies and applied solutions* (pp. 53–66). Hershey, PA: IGI Global. doi:10.4018/978-1-4666-0197-0.ch004

Korovessis, P. (2011). Information security awareness in academia. *International Journal of Knowledge Society Research*, *2*(4), 1–17. doi:10.4018/jksr.2011100101

Koskosas, I., & Sariannidis, N. (2011). Project commitment in the context of information security. *International Journal of Information Technology Project Management*, *2*(3), 17–29. doi:10.4018/jitpm.2011070102

Kotsonis, E., & Eliakis, S. (2013). Information security standards for health information systems: The implementer's approach. In *User-driven healthcare: Concepts, methodologies, tools, and applications* (pp. 225–257). Hershey, PA: IGI Global. doi:10.4018/978-1-4666-2770-3.ch013

Koyuturk, M., Grama, A., & Ramakrishnan, N. (2005). Compression, clustering, and pattern discovery in very high-dimensional discrete-attribute data sets. *IEEE Transactions on Knowledge and Data Engineering, 17*(4), 447–461. doi:10.1109/TKDE.2005.55

Krishna, A. V. (2014). A randomized cloud library security environment. In S. Dhamdhere (Ed.), *Cloud computing and virtualization technologies in libraries* (pp. 278–296). Hershey, PA: IGI Global. doi:10.4018/978-1-4666-4631-5.ch016

Kruck, S. E., & Teer, F. P. (2011). Computer security practices and perceptions of the next generation of corporate computer users. In H. Nemati (Ed.), *Pervasive information security and privacy developments: Trends and advancements* (pp. 255–265). Hershey, PA: IGI Global. doi:10.4018/978-1-61692-000-5.ch017

Kumar, S., & Lopez, D. (2015). Feature Selection used for Wind Speed Forecasting with Data Driven Approaches. *Journal of Engineering Science and Technology Review, 8*(5), 124 - 127.

Kumar, M., Sareen, M., & Chhabra, S. (2011). Technology related trust issues in SME B2B E-Commerce. *International Journal of Information Communication Technologies and Human Development, 3*(4), 31–46. doi:10.4018/jicthd.2011100103

Kumar, P. S., Ashok, M. S., & Subramanian, R. (2012). A publicly verifiable dynamic secret sharing protocol for secure and dependable data storage in cloud computing. *International Journal of Cloud Applications and Computing, 2*(3), 1–25. doi:10.4018/ijcac.2012070101

Kumar, P., & Mittal, S. (2012). The perpetration and prevention of cyber crime: An analysis of cyber terrorism in India. *International Journal of Technoethics, 3*(1), 43–52. doi:10.4018/jte.2012010104

Kumar, S., & Dutta, K. (2014). Security issues in mobile ad hoc networks: A survey. In D. Rawat, B. Bista, & G. Yan (Eds.), *Security, privacy, trust, and resource management in mobile and wireless communications* (pp. 176–221). Hershey, PA: IGI Global. doi:10.4018/978-1-4666-4691-9.ch009

L. 0. Hall, N. Chawla, K.W. Bowyer, Decision Tree Learning on Very Large Data Sets, IEEE, 1998.

Lakshmi, C., & Nagendra Kumar, V.V. (2016, August). Survey Paper on Big Data. *International Journal of Advanced Research in Computer Science and Software Engineering, 6*(8).

Landset, S., Khoshgoftaar, T. M., Richter, A. N., & Hasanin, T. (2015). A survey of open source tools for ML with big data in the Hadoop ecosystem. *J. Big Data., 2*(1), 24. doi:10.1186/s40537-015-0032-1

Laurel, B., & Mountford, S. J. (1990). *The art of human-computer interface design.* Addison-Wesley Longman Publishing Co., Inc.

Lavanya, K., Durai, M. S., & Iyengar, N. C. S. (2015). Site specific soil fertility ranking and seasonal paddy variety selection: An intuitionistic fuzzy rough set and fuzzy Bayesian based decision model. *International Journal of Multimedia and Ubiquitous Engineering, 10*(6), 311-328.

Lawson, S. (2013). Motivating cybersecurity: Assessing the status of critical infrastructure as an object of cyber threats. In C. Laing, A. Badii, & P. Vickers (Eds.), *Securing critical infrastructures and critical control systems: Approaches for threat protection* (pp. 168–189). Hershey, PA: IGI Global. doi:10.4018/978-1-4666-2659-1.ch007

Le Callet, P., Viard-Gaudin, C., & Barba, D. (2006). A convolutional neural network approach for objective video quality assessment. *IEEE Transactions on Neural Networks, 17*(5), 1316–1327. doi:10.1109/TNN.2006.879766 PMID:17001990

Lee, J.-Y. (2015). A Study on the Use of Secure Data in Cloud Storage for Collaboration. *Indian Journal of Science and Technology, 8*(S5), Doi no:.10.17485/ijst/2015/v8iS5/61462

Leitch, S., & Warren, M. (2011). The ethics of security of personal information upon Facebook. In M. Quigley (Ed.), *ICT ethics and security in the 21st century: New developments and applications* (pp. 46–65). Hershey, PA: IGI Global. doi:10.4018/978-1-60960-573-5.ch003

Li, J., Ooi, B. C., & Wang, W. (2008). Anonymizing streaming data for privacy protection. In *Proceedings of the IEEE 24th International Conference on Data Engineering ICDE '08* (pp. 1367–1369). IEEE. doi:10.1109/ICDE.2008.4497558

Li, N., Li, T., & Venkatasubramanian, S. (2007, April). t-closeness: Privacy beyond k-anonymity and l-diversity. In *Proceedings of the 2007 IEEE 23rd International Conference on Data Engineering* (pp. 106-115). IEEE.

Li, S., Dragicevic, S., Anton, F., Sester, M., Winter, S., Coltekin, A., ... (2015). Geospatial Big Data Handling Theory and Methods: A Review and Research Challenges. Retrieved from https://arxiv.org/ftp/arxiv/papers/1511/1511.03010.pdf

Ligaarden, O. S., Refsdal, A., & Stølen, K. (2013). Using indicators to monitor security risk in systems of systems: How to capture and measure the impact of service dependencies on the security of provided services. In D. Mellado, L. Enrique Sánchez, E. Fernández-Medina, & M. Piattini (Eds.), *IT security governance innovations: Theory and research* (pp. 256–292). Hershey, PA: IGI Global. doi:10.4018/978-1-4666-2083-4.ch010

Li, M. (2013). Security terminology. In A. Miri (Ed.), *Advanced security and privacy for RFID technologies* (pp. 1–13). Hershey, PA: IGI Global. doi:10.4018/978-1-4666-3685-9.ch001

Lim, J. S., Chang, S., Ahmad, A., & Maynard, S. (2012). Towards an organizational culture framework for information security practices. In M. Gupta, J. Walp, & R. Sharman (Eds.), *Strategic and practical approaches for information security governance: Technologies and applied solutions* (pp. 296–315). Hershey, PA: IGI Global. doi:10.4018/978-1-4666-0197-0.ch017

Lindell, Y., & Pinkas, B. (2000, January). Privacy preserving data mining. In Advances in Cryptology—CRYPTO 2000 (pp. 36-54). Springer Berlin Heidelberg. doi:10.1007/3-540-44598-6_3

Lindström, J., & Hanken, C. (2012). Security challenges and selected legal aspects for wearable computing. *Journal of Information Technology Research, 5*(1), 68–87. doi:10.4018/jitr.2012010104

Lin, X., & Luppicini, R. (2011). Socio-technical influences of cyber espionage: A case study of the GhostNet system. *International Journal of Technoethics, 2*(2), 65–77. doi:10.4018/jte.2011040105

Liu, R., Li, Q., Li, F., Mei, L., & Lee, J. (2014, October). Big Data architecture for IT incident management. In *Proceedings of the 2014 IEEE International Conference on Service Operations and Logistics, and Informatics (SOLI)* (pp. 424-429). IEEE. doi:10.1109/SOLI.2014.6960762

Looks, M., Levine, A., Covington, G. A., Loui, R. P., Lockwood, J. W., & Cho, Y. H. (2007). *Streaming Hierarchical Clustering for Concept Mining. In Proceedings of the 2007 IEEE Aerosp. Conf.* (pp. 1–12). IEEE. doi:10.1109/AERO.2007.352792

Lopez, D., & Gunasekaran, M. (2015). Assessment of vaccination strategies using fuzzy multi-criteria decision making. In *Proceedings of the Fifth International Conference on Fuzzy and Neuro Computing (FANCCO-2015)* (pp. 195-208). Switzerland: Springer.

Lopez, D., & Manogaran, G. (2016). Big Data Architecture for Climate Change and Disease Dynamics, Eds. Geetam S. Tomar et al. The Human Element of Big Data: Issues, Analytics, and Performance, CRC Press, USA.

Lopez, D., & Manogaran, G. (2016). Big data architecture for climate change and disease dynamics. In G.S. Tomar, N.S. Chaudhari, R.S. Bhadoria et al. (Eds.), *The Human Element of Big Data: Issues, Analytics, and Performance*. FL: CRC Press.

Lopez, D., & Raja, S. K. (2009, January 3-6). Virtual Time Fair Queuing Algorithm for a Computational Grid. In *Proceedings of the 10th International Conference on Distributed Computing and Networking*, Hyderabad, India (Vol. 5408, p. 468-474). Springer.

Lopez, D., & Sekaran, G. (2016). Climate change and disease dynamics-A big data perspective. *International Journal of Infectious Diseases, 45*, 23-24.

Lopez, D., Gunasekaran, M., Murugan, B. S., Kaur, H., & Abbas, K. M. (2014). Spatial Big Data analytics of influenza epidemic in Vellore, India. In Big Data (Big Data), 2014 IEEE International Conference on (pp. 19-24). IEEE.

Lopez, D., Gunasekaran, M., Murugan, B. S., Kaur, H., & Abbas, K. M. (2014). Spatial big data analytics of influenza epidemic in Vellore, India. In *Proceedings of the IEEE International Conference on Big Data (Big Data)* (pp. 19-24). IEEE.

Lopez, D., & Gunasekaran, M. (2015). Assessment of Vaccination Strategies Using Fuzzy Multi-criteria Decision Making. In *Proceedings of the Fifth International Conference on Fuzzy and Neuro Computing (FANCCO-2015)* (pp. 195-208). Springer.

Lopez, D., & Manogaran, G. (2017). Modelling the H1N1 influenza using mathematical and neural network approaches. *Biomedical Research*.

Lopez, D., & Sekaran, G. (2016). Climate change and disease dynamics-A Big Data perspective. *International Journal of Infectious Diseases*, *45*, 23–24.

Lopez-Moreno, I., Gonzalez-Dominguez, J., Martinez, D., Plchot, O., Gonzalez-Rodriguez, J., & Moreno, P. J. (2016). On the use of deep feedforward neural networks for automatic language identification. *Computer Speech & Language*, *40*, 46–59. doi:10.1016/j.csl.2016.03.001

Lu, Y.-L., & Fahn, C.-S. (2007). Hierarchical Artificial Neural Networks for Recognizing High Similar Large Data Sets. In *Proceedings of the 2007 Int. Conf. Mach. Learn. Cybern.* (pp. 1930–1935). doi:10.1109/ICMLC.2007.4370463

Lynch, C. (2008). Big data: How do your data grow? *Nature*, *455*(7209), 28–29. doi:10.1038/455028a PMID:18769419

M. Chen, Z. Xu, K. Weinberger, F. Sha, Marginalized denoising autoencoders for domain

Ma, N., Kumar, D. K., & Pah, N. (2001). Classification of hand direction using multi-channel electromyography by neural network. In *Proceedings of The Seventh Australian and New Zealand Intelligent Information Systems Conference,* Perth, Western Australia. IEEE.

Machanavajjhala, A., Kifer, D., Gehrke, J., & Venkitasubramaniam, M. (2007). l-diversity: Privacy beyond k-anonymity. *ACM Transactions on Knowledge Discovery from Data*, *1*(1), 3. doi:10.1145/1217299.1217302

Mahajan, P., Gaba, G., & Chauhan, N. S. (2016). Big Data Security. *IITM Journal of Management and IT*, *7*(1), 89–94.

Maheshwari, H., Hyman, H., & Agrawal, M. (2012). A comparison of cyber-crime definitions in India and the United States. In *Cyber crime: Concepts, methodologies, tools and applications* (pp. 714–726). Hershey, PA: IGI Global. doi:10.4018/978-1-61350-323-2.ch401

Malcolmson, J. (2014). The role of security culture. In I. Portela & F. Almeida (Eds.), *Organizational, legal, and technological dimensions of information system administration* (pp. 225–242). Hershey, PA: IGI Global. doi:10.4018/978-1-4666-4526-4.ch012

Mani, S., Shankle, W. R., Dick, M. B., & Pazzani, M. J. (1998). Two-Stage ML Model for Guideline Development. Retrieved from http://www.ics.uci.edu/~pazzani/Publications/two_stage_ml.pdf

Manikandan, S. G., & Ravi, S. (2014). Big Data Analysis using Apache Hadoop.

Manogaran, G., & Lopez, D. (2016). A survey of big data architectures and machine learning algorithms in healthcare. *International Journal of Biomedical Engineering and Technology*, *23*(4), 1-27.

Manogaran, G., & Lopez, D. (2016). Disease surveillance system for big climate data processing and dengue transmission. *International Journal of Ambient Computing and Intelligence, 8*(2), 88-105.

Manogaran, G., & Lopez, D. (2016). Health data analytics using scalable logistic regression with stochastic gradient descent. *International Journal of Advanced Intelligence Paradigms, 9*(1), 1-18.

Manogaran, G., & Lopez, D. (in press). Spatial cumulative sum algorithm with big data analytics for climate change detection. *Computers & Electrical Engineering.* doi:10.1016/j.compeleceng.2017.04.006

Manogaran, G., Lopez, D., Thota, C., Abbas, K. M., Pyne, S., & Sundarasekar, R. (2017). Big Data Analytics in Healthcare Internet of Things. In *Innovative Healthcare Systems for the 21st Century* (pp. 263-284). Springer International Publishing.

Manogaran, G., Lopez, D., Thota, C., Abbas, K. M., Pyne, S., & Sundarasekar, R. (2017d). big data analytics in healthcare Internet of Things. In Innovative Healthcare Systems for the 21st Century (pp. 263-284). Springer International Publishing.

Manogaran, G., Thota, C., & Kumar, M. V. (2016). MetaCloudDataStorage architecture for big data security in cloud computing. *Procedia Computer Science, 87,* 128-133.

Manogaran, G., Thota, C., Lopez, D., & Sundarasekar, R. (2017). Big Data Security Intelligence for Healthcare Industry 4.0. In *Cybersecurity for Industry 4.0* (pp. 103-126).

Manogaran, G., Thota, C., Lopez, D., Vijayakumar, V., Abbas, K. M., & Sundarsekar, R. (2017). Big data knowledge system in healthcare. In C. Bhatt, N. Dey & A. Ashour (Eds.), *Internet of Things and Big Data Technologies in Next Generation Healthcare.* Springer International Publishing.

Manogaran, G., & Lopez, D. (2016). Health Data Analytics using Scalable Logistic Regression with Stochastic Gradient Descent. *International Journal of Advanced Intelligence Paradigms, 9,* 1–15.

Manogaran, G., & Lopez, D. (2017a). Spatial cumulative sum algorithm with big data analytics for climate change detection. *Computers & Electrical Engineering.*

Manogaran, G., & Lopez, D. (2017b). Disease surveillance system for big climate data processing and dengue transmission. [IJACI]. *International Journal of Ambient Computing and Intelligence, 8*(2), 88–105.

Manogaran, G., & Lopez, D. (2017e). A Gaussian process based big data processing framework in cluster computing environment. *Cluster Computing,* 1–16.

Manogaran, G., Thota, C., & Kumar, M. V. (2016). MetaCloudDataStorage Architecture for Big Data Security in Cloud Computing. *Procedia Computer Science, 87,* 128–133.

Manogaran, G., Thota, C., Lopez, D., & Sundarasekar, R. (2017c). Big data security intelligence for healthcare industry 4.0. In *Cybersecurity for Industry 4.0* (pp. 103–126). Springer International Publishing.

Manogaran, G., Thota, C., Lopez, D., Vijayakumar, V., Abbas, K. M., & Sundarsekar, R. (2017a). Big data knowledge system in healthcare. In *Internet of Things and Big Data Technologies for Next Generation Healthcare* (pp. 133–157). Springer International Publishing.

Mantas, G., Lymberopoulos, D., & Komninos, N. (2011). Security in smart home environment. In A. Lazakidou, K. Siassiakos, & K. Ioannou (Eds.), *Wireless technologies for ambient assisted living and healthcare: Systems and applications* (pp. 170–191). Hershey, PA: IGI Global. doi:10.4018/978-1-61520-805-0.ch010

Maple, C., Short, E., Brown, A., Bryden, C., & Salter, M. (2012). Cyberstalking in the UK: Analysis and recommendations. *International Journal of Distributed Systems and Technologies*, *3*(4), 34–51. doi:10.4018/jdst.2012100104

Maqousi, A., & Balikhina, T. (2011). Building security awareness culture to serve e-government initiative. In A. Al Ajeeli & Y. Al-Bastaki (Eds.), *Handbook of research on e-services in the public sector: E-government strategies and advancements* (pp. 304–311). Hershey, PA: IGI Global. doi:10.4018/978-1-61520-789-3.ch024

Marchal, S., Jiang, X., State, R., & Engel, T. (2014). A Big Data Architecture for Large Scale Security Monitoring. In *Proceedings of IEEE International Congress on Big Data (Big Data Congress)* (Vol. 2, pp. 56-63). doi:10.1109/BigData.Congress.2014.18

Marinchev, I., & Agre, G. (2015, June). On speeding up the implementation of nearest neighbour search and classification. In *Proceedings of the 16th International Conference on Computer Systems and Technologies* (pp. 207-213). ACM. doi:10.1145/2812428.2812464

Marinescu, D. C., Paya, A., & Morrison, J. P. (2016). A Cloud Reservation System for Big Data Applications.

Markou, M., & Singh, S. (2003). Novelty detection: a review-part 2: neural network based approaches. *Journal of Signal Processing*, *83*(12), 2499–2521. doi:10.1016/j.sigpro.2003.07.019

Martin, N., & Rice, J. (2013). Spearing high net wealth individuals: The case of online fraud and mature age internet users. *International Journal of Information Security and Privacy*, *7*(1), 1–15. doi:10.4018/jisp.2013010101

Martino, L., & Bertino, E. (2012). Security for web services: Standards and research issues. In L. Jie-Zhang (Ed.), *Innovations, standards and practices of web services: Emerging research topics* (pp. 336–362). Hershey, PA: IGI Global. doi:10.4018/978-1-61350-104-7.ch015

Marz, N., & Warren, J. (2015). *Big Data: Principles and best practices of scalable realtime data systems*. Manning Publications Co.

Massonet, P., Michot, A., Naqvi, S., Villari, M., & Latanicki, J. (2013). Securing the external interfaces of a federated infrastructure cloud. In *IT policy and ethics: Concepts, methodologies, tools, and applications* (pp. 1876–1903). Hershey, PA: IGI Global. doi:10.4018/978-1-4666-2919-6.ch082

Matsumura, Y., Mitsukura, Y., Fukumi, M., & Akamatsu, N. (2002). Recognition of EMG signal patterns by neural networks. In *Proceedings of Neural Information Processing ICONIP '02*, Singapore, Singapore. IEEE. doi:10.1109/ICONIP.2002.1198158

Matturdi, B., Xianwei, Z., Shuai, L., & Fuhong, L. (2014). Big Data security and privacy: A review. *China Communications, 11*(14), 135–145. doi:10.1109/CC.2014.7085614

Maumbe, B., & Owei, V. T. (2013). Understanding the information security landscape in South Africa: Implications for strategic collaboration and policy development. In B. Maumbe & C. Patrikakis (Eds.), *E-agriculture and rural development: Global innovations and future prospects* (pp. 90–102). Hershey, PA: IGI Global. doi:10.4018/978-1-4666-2655-3.ch009

Mazumdar, C. (2011). Enterprise information system security: A life-cycle approach. In *Enterprise information systems: Concepts, methodologies, tools and applications* (pp. 154–168). Hershey, PA: IGI Global. doi:10.4018/978-1-61692-852-0.ch111

McCune, J., & Haworth, D. A. (2012). Securing America against cyber war. *International Journal of Cyber Warfare & Terrorism, 2*(1), 39–49. doi:10.4018/ijcwt.2012010104

Melvin, A. O., & Ayotunde, T. (2011). Spirituality in cybercrime (Yahoo Yahoo) activities among youths in south west Nigeria. In E. Dunkels, G. Franberg, & C. Hallgren (Eds.), *Youth culture and net culture: Online social practices* (pp. 357–380). Hershey, PA: IGI Global. doi:10.4018/978-1-60960-209-3.ch020

Microsoft Corporation. (2012). Differential Privacy for Everyone.

Miller, J. M., Higgins, G. E., & Lopez, K. M. (2013). Considering the role of e-government in cybercrime awareness and prevention: Toward a theoretical research program for the 21st century. In *Digital rights management: Concepts, methodologies, tools, and applications* (pp. 789–800). Hershey, PA: IGI Global. doi:10.4018/978-1-4666-2136-7.ch036

Millman, C., Whitty, M., Winder, B., & Griffiths, M. D. (2012). Perceived criminality of cyber-harassing behaviors among undergraduate students in the United Kingdom. *International Journal of Cyber Behavior, Psychology and Learning, 2*(4), 49–59. doi:10.4018/ijcbpl.2012100104

Minami, N. A. (2012). Employing dynamic models to enhance corporate IT security policy. *International Journal of Agent Technologies and Systems, 4*(2), 42–59. doi:10.4018/jats.2012040103

Mirante, D. P., & Ammari, H. M. (2014). Wireless sensor network security attacks: A survey. In *Crisis management: Concepts, methodologies, tools and applications* (pp. 25–59). Hershey, PA: IGI Global. doi:10.4018/978-1-4666-4707-7.ch002

Mishra, A., & Mishra, D. (2013). Cyber stalking: A challenge for web security. In J. Bishop (Ed.), *Examining the concepts, issues, and implications of internet trolling* (pp. 32–42). Hershey, PA: IGI Global. doi:10.4018/978-1-4666-2803-8.ch004

Mishra, S. (2011). Wireless sensor networks: Emerging applications and security solutions. In D. Kar & M. Syed (Eds.), *Network security, administration and management: Advancing technology and practice* (pp. 217–236). Hershey, PA: IGI Global. doi:10.4018/978-1-60960-777-7.ch011

Mitra, S., & Padman, R. (2012). Privacy and security concerns in adopting social media for personal health management: A health plan case study. *Journal of Cases on Information Technology*, *14*(4), 12–26. doi:10.4018/jcit.2012100102

Modares, H., Lloret, J., Moravejosharieh, A., & Salleh, R. (2014). Security in mobile cloud computing. In J. Rodrigues, K. Lin, & J. Lloret (Eds.), *Mobile networks and cloud computing convergence for progressive services and applications* (pp. 79–91). Hershey, PA: IGI Global. doi:10.4018/978-1-4666-4781-7.ch005

Mohammadi, S., Golara, S., & Mousavi, N. (2012). Selecting adequate security mechanisms in e-business processes using fuzzy TOPSIS. *International Journal of Fuzzy System Applications*, *2*(1), 35–53. doi:10.4018/ijfsa.2012010103

Mohammed, L. A. (2012). ICT security policy: Challenges and potential remedies. In *Cyber crime: Concepts, methodologies, tools and applications* (pp. 999–1015). Hershey, PA: IGI Global. doi:10.4018/978-1-61350-323-2.ch501

Molodtsov, D. (1999). Soft set theory—First results. *Computers & Mathematics with Applications (Oxford, England)*, *37*(4-5), 19–31. doi:10.1016/S0898-1221(99)00056-5

Molok, N. N., Ahmad, A., & Chang, S. (2012). Online social networking: A source of intelligence for advanced persistent threats. *International Journal of Cyber Warfare & Terrorism*, *2*(1), 1–13. doi:10.4018/ijcwt.2012010101

Monteleone, S. (2011). Ambient intelligence: Legal challenges and possible directions for privacy protection. In C. Akrivopoulou & A. Psygkas (Eds.), *Personal data privacy and protection in a surveillance era: Technologies and practices* (pp. 201–221). Hershey, PA: IGI Global. doi:10.4018/978-1-60960-083-9.ch012

Moralis, A., Pouli, V., Grammatikou, M., Kalogeras, D., & Maglaris, V. (2012). Security standards and issues for grid computing. In N. Preve (Ed.), *Computational and data grids: Principles, applications and design* (pp. 248–264). Hershey, PA: IGI Global. doi:10.4018/978-1-61350-113-9.ch010

Motwani, R., Nabar, S. U., & Thomas, D. (2008, April). Auditing sql queries. In *Proceedings of the 2008 IEEE 24th International Conference on Data Engineering* (pp. 287-296). IEEE. doi:10.1109/ICDE.2008.4497437

Moujahid, A. (2016). A Practical Introduction to DL with Caffe and Python. Retrieved August 27, 2016 from http://adilmoujahid.com/posts/2016/06/introduction-deep-learning-python-caffe/

Mouratidis, H., & Kang, M. (2011). Secure by design: Developing secure software systems from the ground up. *International Journal of Secure Software Engineering*, *2*(3), 23–41. doi:10.4018/jsse.2011070102

Mulanee, A., Shaikh, A., Dhavale, H., Lambate, S., & Teke, A. R. (2015). Database Security Against Intrusion. *Int. J. Adv. Eng. Glob. Technol.*, *3*, 560–566. http://ijaegt.com/wp-content/uploads/2014/12/409440-pp-560-566-shaik.pdf

Müller, H., Michoux, N., Bandon, D., & Geissbuhler, A. (2004). A review of content-based image retrieval systems in medical applications—clinical benefits and future directions. *International Journal of Medical Informatics, 73*(1), 1–23. doi:10.1016/j.ijmedinf.2003.11.024 PMID:15036075

Murthy, A. S., Nagadevara, V., & De', R. (2012). Predictive models in cybercrime investigation: An application of data mining techniques. In J. Wang (Ed.), *Advancing the service sector with evolving technologies: Techniques and principles* (pp. 166–177). Hershey, PA: IGI Global. doi:10.4018/978-1-4666-0044-7.ch011

Murthy, P. K. (2014). Top ten challenges in Big Data security and privacy. In *Proceedings of IEEE International Test Conference (ITC)*. doi:10.1109/TEST.2014.7035307

Nabeel, M., Shang, N., Zage, J., & Bertino, E. (2010, June). Mask: a system for privacy-preserving policy-based access to published content. In *Proceedings of the 2010 ACM SIGMOD International Conference on Management of data* (pp. 1239-1242). ACM. doi:10.1145/1807167.1807329

Nabi, S. I., Al-Ghmlas, G. S., & Alghathbar, K. (2012). Enterprise information security policies, standards, and procedures: A survey of available standards and guidelines. In M. Gupta, J. Walp, & R. Sharman (Eds.), *Strategic and practical approaches for information security governance: Technologies and applied solutions* (pp. 67–89). Hershey, PA: IGI Global. doi:10.4018/978-1-4666-0197-0.ch005

Nachtigal, S. (2011). E-business and security. In O. Bak & N. Stair (Eds.), *Impact of e-business technologies on public and private organizations: Industry comparisons and perspectives* (pp. 262–277). Hershey, PA: IGI Global. doi:10.4018/978-1-60960-501-8.ch016

Najafabadi, M. M., Villanustre, F., Khoshgoftaar, T. M., Seliya, N., Wald, R., & Muharemagic, E. (2015). DL applications and challenges in big data analytics. *J. Big Data., 2*(1), 1–21. doi:10.1186/s40537-014-0007-7

Namal, S., & Gurtov, A. (2012). Security and mobility aspects of femtocell networks. In R. Saeed, B. Chaudhari, & R. Mokhtar (Eds.), *Femtocell communications and technologies: Business opportunities and deployment challenges* (pp. 124–156). Hershey, PA: IGI Global. doi:10.4018/978-1-4666-0092-8.ch008

Namey, E., Guest, G., Thairu, L., & Johnson, L. (2007). Data Reduction Techniques for Large Qualitative Data Sets. In G. Guest & K. M. MacQueen (Eds.), *Handbook for team-based qualitative research* (pp. 137–163). Rowman Altamira, United kingdom: Team-Based Qual. Res.

Nandakumar, D. R. A. N., & Yambem, N. (2014). A Survey on Data Mining Algorithms on Apache Hadoop Platform. *International Journal of Emerging Technology and Advanced Engineering, 4*(1), 563-565.

Naqvi, D. E. (2011). Designing efficient security services infrastructure for virtualization oriented architectures. In H. Nemati (Ed.), *Pervasive information security and privacy developments: Trends and advancements* (pp. 149–171). Hershey, PA: IGI Global. doi:10.4018/978-1-61692-000-5.ch011

Natarajan, S., Joshi, S., Saha, B., Edwards, A., Khot, T., Moody, E., ... (2012). A ML Pipeline for Three-way Classification of Alzheimer Patients from Structural Magnetic Resonance Images of the Brain. *Int. J. Mach. Learn. Cybern.*, *5*, 659–669. Retrieved from http://pages.cs.wisc.edu/~tushar/papers/icmla12.pdf

Neto, A. A., & Vieira, M. (2011). Security gaps in databases: A comparison of alternative software products for web applications support. *International Journal of Secure Software Engineering*, *2*(3), 42–62. doi:10.4018/jsse.2011070103

Ngugi, B., Mana, J., & Segal, L. (2011). Evaluating the quality and usefulness of data breach information systems. *International Journal of Information Security and Privacy*, *5*(4), 31–46. doi:10.4018/jisp.2011100103

Nhlabatsi, A., Bandara, A., Hayashi, S., Haley, C., Jurjens, J., & Kaiya, H. ... Yu, Y. (2011). Security patterns: Comparing modeling approaches. In H. Mouratidis (Ed.), Software engineering for secure systems: Industrial and research perspectives (pp. 75-111). Hershey, PA: IGI Global. doi:10.4018/978-1-61520-837-1.ch004

Nicho, M. (2013). An information governance model for information security management. In D. Mellado, L. Enrique Sánchez, E. Fernández-Medina, & M. Piattini (Eds.), *IT security governance innovations: Theory and research* (pp. 155–189). Hershey, PA: IGI Global. doi:10.4018/978-1-4666-2083-4.ch007

Nicho, M., Fakhry, H., & Haiber, C. (2011). An integrated security governance framework for effective PCI DSS implementation. *International Journal of Information Security and Privacy*, *5*(3), 50–67. doi:10.4018/jisp.2011070104

Nithya, B. (2016). An Analysis on Applications of ML Tools, Techniques and Practices in Health Care System. *Int. J. Adv. Res. Comput. Sci. Softw. Eng.*, *6*(6), 1–8.

Nobelis, N., Boudaoud, K., Delettre, C., & Riveill, M. (2012). Designing security properties-centric communication protocols using a component-based approach. *International Journal of Distributed Systems and Technologies*, *3*(1), 1–16. doi:10.4018/jdst.2012010101

Ohashi, M., & Hori, M. (2011). Security management services based on authentication roaming between different certificate authorities. In M. Cruz-Cunha & J. Varajao (Eds.), *Enterprise information systems design, implementation and management: Organizational applications* (pp. 72–84). Hershey, PA: IGI Global. doi:10.4018/978-1-61692-020-3.ch005

Okubo, T., Kaiya, H., & Yoshioka, N. (2012). Analyzing impacts on software enhancement caused by security design alternatives with patterns. *International Journal of Secure Software Engineering*, *3*(1), 37–61. doi:10.4018/jsse.2012010103

Oost, D., & Chew, E. K. (2012). Investigating the concept of information security culture. In M. Gupta, J. Walp, & R. Sharman (Eds.), *Strategic and practical approaches for information security governance: Technologies and applied solutions* (pp. 1–12). Hershey, PA: IGI Global. doi:10.4018/978-1-4666-0197-0.ch001

Otero, A. R., Ejnioui, A., Otero, C. E., & Tejay, G. (2013). Evaluation of information security controls in organizations by grey relational analysis. *International Journal of Dependable and Trustworthy Information Systems*, *2*(3), 36–54. doi:10.4018/jdtis.2011070103

Ouedraogo, M., Mouratidis, H., Dubois, E., & Khadraoui, D. (2011). Security assurance evaluation and IT systems context of use security criticality. *International Journal of Handheld Computing Research*, *2*(4), 59–81. doi:10.4018/jhcr.2011100104

Pakize, S. R., & Gandomi, A. (2014). Comparative study of classification algorithms based On MapReduce Model. *International Journal of Innovative Research in Advanced Engineering*, *1*(7).

Pal, A.S. & Pattnaik, B.P. (2013). Classification of Virtualization Environment for Cloud Computing. *Indian Journal of Science and Technology*, *6*(1). doi:10.17485/ijst/2013/v6i1/30572

Palanisamy, R., & Mukerji, B. (2012). Security and privacy issues in e-government. In M. Shareef, N. Archer, & S. Dutta (Eds.), *E-government service maturity and development: Cultural, organizational and technological perspectives* (pp. 236–248). Hershey, PA: IGI Global. doi:10.4018/978-1-60960-848-4.ch013

Pal, S. (2013). Cloud computing: Security concerns and issues. In A. Bento & A. Aggarwal (Eds.), *Cloud computing service and deployment models: Layers and management* (pp. 191–207). Hershey, PA: IGI Global. doi:10.4018/978-1-4666-2187-9.ch010

Panackal, J. J., & Pillai, A. S. (2014, December). An intelligent framework for protecting privacy of individuals empirical evaluations on data mining classification. In *Proceedings of the 2014 14th International Conference on Hybrid Intelligent Systems (HIS)* (pp. 67-72). IEEE. doi:10.1109/HIS.2014.7086174

Panackal, J. J., & Pillai, A. S. (2015). Adaptive Utility-based Anonymization Model: Performance Evaluation on Big Data Sets. *Procedia Computer Science*, *50*, 347–352. doi:10.1016/j.procs.2015.04.037

Pan, Y., Yuan, B., & Mishra, S. (2011). Network security auditing. In D. Kar & M. Syed (Eds.), *Network security, administration and management: Advancing technology and practice* (pp. 131–157). Hershey, PA: IGI Global. doi:10.4018/978-1-60960-777-7.ch008

Parimala, M., & Lopez, D. (2015). K-Neighbourhood Structural Similarity Approach for Spatial Clustering. *Indian Journal of Science and Technology*, *8*(23).

Parimala, M., & Lopez, D. (2016). Spatio-temporal graph clustering algorithm based on attribute and structural similarity. *International Journal of Knowledge-based and Intelligent Engineering Systems*, *20*(3), 149-160.

Parimala, M., Lopez, D., & Senthilkumar, N. C. (2011). A survey on density based clustering algorithms for mining large spatial databases. *International Journal of Advanced Science and Technology*, *31*(1), 59-66.

Parthasarathy, S., Ruan, Y., & Satuluri, V. (2011). Community discovery in socialnetworks: Applications, methods and emerging trends. In C. C. Aggarwal (Ed.), *Social network data analytics* (pp. 79–113). United States: Springer. doi:10.1007/978-1-4419-8462-3_4

Parthiban, P. & Selvakumar, S. (2016). Big Data Architecture for Capturing, Storing, Analyzing and Visualizing of Web Server Logs. *Indian Journal of Science and Technology, 9*(4). Doi:10.17485/ijst/2016/v9i4/84173

Patel, A., Taghavi, M., Júnior, J. C., Latih, R., & Zin, A. M. (2012). Safety measures for social computing in wiki learning environment. *International Journal of Information Security and Privacy, 6*(2), 1–15. doi:10.4018/jisp.2012040101

Pathan, A. K. (2012). Security management in heterogeneous distributed sensor networks. In S. Bagchi (Ed.), *Ubiquitous multimedia and mobile agents: Models and implementations* (pp. 274–294). Hershey, PA: IGI Global. doi:10.4018/978-1-61350-107-8.ch012

Patil, D. V., & Bichkar, R. S. (2006). A Hybrid Evolutionary Approach To Construct Optimal Decision Trees With Large Data Sets. In *Proceedings of the 2006 IEEE Int. Conf. Ind. Technol.* (pp. 429–433). doi:10.1109/ICIT.2006.372250

Patokar, A.A., & Patil, V.M. (2016). Efficient Analysis of Big Data by using Hadoop in Cloud Computing by Map Reducing. *National Conference on Innovative Trends in Science and Engineering, 4*(7), 378 – 381.

Paul, C., & Porche, I. R. (2011). Toward a U.S. army cyber security culture. *International Journal of Cyber Warfare & Terrorism, 1*(3), 70–80. doi:10.4018/ijcwt.2011070105

Pavlidis, M., Mouratidis, H., & Islam, S. (2012). Modelling security using trust based concepts. *International Journal of Secure Software Engineering, 3*(2), 36–53. doi:10.4018/jsse.2012040102

Pawlak, Z. (1982). Rough sets. *Int. J. Comput. Inf. Sci., 11*(5), 341–356. doi:10.1007/BF01001956

Pendegraft, N., Rounds, M., & Stone, R. W. (2012). Factors influencing college students' use of computer security. In H. Nemati (Ed.), *Optimizing information security and advancing privacy assurance: New technologies* (pp. 225–234). Hershey, PA: IGI Global. doi:10.4018/978-1-4666-0026-3.ch013

Peters, J. F. (2007). Near Sets. General Theory About Nearness of Objects. *Appl. Math. Sci., 1*, 2609–2629.

Petkovic, M., & Ibraimi, L. (2011). Privacy and security in e-health applications. In C. Röcker & M. Ziefle (Eds.), *E-health, assistive technologies and applications for assisted living: Challenges and solutions* (pp. 23–48). Hershey, PA: IGI Global. doi:10.4018/978-1-60960-469-1.ch002

Picazo-Sanchez, P., Ortiz-Martin, L., Peris-Lopez, P., & Hernandez-Castro, J. C. (2013). Security of EPC class-1. In P. Lopez, J. Hernandez-Castro, & T. Li (Eds.), *Security and trends in wireless identification and sensing platform tags: Advancements in RFID* (pp. 34–63). Hershey, PA: IGI Global. doi:10.4018/978-1-4666-1990-6.ch002

Pieters, W., Probst, C. W., Lukszo, Z., & Montoya, L. (2014). Cost-effectiveness of security measures: A model-based framework. In T. Tsiakis, T. Kargidis, & P. Katsaros (Eds.), *Approaches and processes for managing the economics of information systems* (pp. 139–156). Hershey, PA: IGI Global. doi:10.4018/978-1-4666-4983-5.ch009

Pirim, T., James, T., Boswell, K., Reithel, B., & Barkhi, R. (2011). Examining an individual's perceived need for privacy and security: Construct and scale development. In H. Nemati (Ed.), *Pervasive information security and privacy developments: Trends and advancements* (pp. 1–13). Hershey, PA: IGI Global. doi:10.4018/978-1-61692-000-5.ch001

Pirovano, A., Lacaita, A. L., Benvenuti, A., Pellizzer, F., Hudgens, S., & Bez, R. (2003). Scaling analysis of phase-change memory technology. In *Proceedings of the IEEE Int. Electron Dev. Meeting* (pp. 29.6.1–29.6.4).

Podhradsky, A., Casey, C., & Ceretti, P. (2012). The bluetooth honeypot project: Measuring and managing bluetooth risks in the workplace. *International Journal of Interdisciplinary Telecommunications and Networking*, 4(3), 1–22. doi:10.4018/jitn.2012070101

Pomponiu, V. (2011). Security in e-health applications. In C. Röcker & M. Ziefle (Eds.), *E-health, assistive technologies and applications for assisted living: Challenges and solutions* (pp. 94–118). Hershey, PA: IGI Global. doi:10.4018/978-1-60960-469-1.ch005

Pomponiu, V. (2014). Securing wireless ad hoc networks: State of the art and challenges. In *Crisis management: Concepts, methodologies, tools and applications* (pp. 81–101). Hershey, PA: IGI Global. doi:10.4018/978-1-4666-4707-7.ch004

Popat, S. K., & Emmanuel, M. (2014). Review and Comparative Study of Clustering Techniques. *International Journal of Computer Science and Information Technologies*, 5(1), 805–812.

Pope, M. B., Warkentin, M., & Luo, X. R. (2012). Evolutionary malware: Mobile malware, botnets, and malware toolkits. *International Journal of Wireless Networks and Broadband Technologies*, 2(3), 52–60. doi:10.4018/ijwnbt.2012070105

Prakash, S., Vaish, A., Coul, N. G. S., Srinidhi, T., & Botsa, J. (2013). Child security in cyberspace through moral cognition. *International Journal of Information Security and Privacy*, 7(1), 16–29. doi:10.4018/jisp.2013010102

Puthal, D., Nepal, S., Ranjan, R., & Chen, J. (2016). DLSeF: A Dynamic Key-Length-Based Efficient Real-Time Security Verification Model for Big Data Stream. *ACM Transactions on Embedded Computing Systems*, 16(2), 51. doi:10.1145/2937755

Pye, G. (2011). Critical infrastructure systems: Security analysis and modelling approach. *International Journal of Cyber Warfare & Terrorism*, 1(3), 37–58. doi:10.4018/ijcwt.2011070103

Qiu, J., Wu, Q., Ding, G., Xu, Y., & Feng, S. (2016). A survey of ML for big data processing. doi:.10.1186/s13634-016-0355-x

Rahman, M. M., & Rezaul, K. M. (2012). Information security management: Awareness of threats in e-commerce. In M. Gupta, J. Walp, & R. Sharman (Eds.), *Threats, countermeasures, and advances in applied information security* (pp. 66–90). Hershey, PA: IGI Global. doi:10.4018/978-1-4666-0978-5.ch004

Raja, C., & Rabbani, M. A. (2014). Big Data Analytics Security Issues in Data Driven Information System. *Int. J. Innov. Res. Comput. Commun. Eng., 2*, 6132–6135.

Rajathi, A. & Saravanan, N. (2013). A Survey on Secure Storage in Cloud Computing. *Indian Journal of Science and Technology, 6*(4). doi:10.17485/ijst/2013/v6i4/31871

Rajeshwari, A., Prathna, T. C., Balajee, J., Chandrasekaran, N., Mandal, A. B., & Mukherjee, A. (2013). Computational approach for particle size measurement of silver nanoparticle from electron microscopic image. *International Journal of Pharmacy and Pharmaceutical Sciences, 5*(2 Suppl.), 619-623.

Rajkumar, D., & Usha, S. (2016). A Survey on Big Data Mining Platforms, Algorithms and Handling Techniques. Int. J. Res. Emerg. Sci. Technol., 3, 50–55. Retrieved from http://ijrest.net/downloads/volume-3/special-issue/ncrtct-16/pid-ijrest-3s1ncrtct2016018.pdf

Rak, M., Ficco, M., Luna, J., Ghani, H., Suri, N., Panica, S., & Petcu, D. (2012). Security issues in cloud federations. In M. Villari, I. Brandic, & F. Tusa (Eds.), *Achieving federated and self-manageable cloud infrastructures: Theory and practice* (pp. 176–194). Hershey, PA: IGI Global. doi:10.4018/978-1-4666-1631-8.ch010

Ramachandran, M., & Mahmood, Z. (2011). A framework for internet security assessment and improvement process. In M. Ramachandran (Ed.), *Knowledge engineering for software development life cycles: Support technologies and applications* (pp. 244–255). Hershey, PA: IGI Global. doi:10.4018/978-1-60960-509-4.ch013

Ramachandran, S., Mundada, R., Bhattacharjee, A., Murthy, C., & Sharma, R. (2011). Classifying host anomalies: Using ontology in information security monitoring. In R. Santanam, M. Sethumadhavan, & M. Virendra (Eds.), *Cyber security, cyber crime and cyber forensics: Applications and perspectives* (pp. 70–86). Hershey, PA: IGI Global. doi:10.4018/978-1-60960-123-2.ch006

Ramamurthy, B. (2014). Securing business IT on the cloud. In S. Srinivasan (Ed.), *Security, trust, and regulatory aspects of cloud computing in business environments* (pp. 115–125). Hershey, PA: IGI Global. doi:10.4018/978-1-4666-5788-5.ch006

Ramaswamy, L., Lawson, V., & Gogineni, S. V. (2013, June). Towards a quality-centric big data architecture for federated sensor services. In *Proceedings of the 2013 IEEE International Congress on Big Data* (pp. 86-93). IEEE. doi:10.1109/BigData.Congress.2013.21

Ranjan, R. (2014). Streaming Big Data Processing in Datacenter Clouds. *IEEE Cloud Computing, 1*(1), 78–83. doi:10.1109/MCC.2014.22

Ranjith, D., Balajee, J., & Kumar, C. (2016). In premises of cloud computing and models. *International Journal of Pharmacy and Technology*, *8*(3), 4685-4695.

Raspotnig, C., & Opdahl, A. L. (2012). Improving security and safety modelling with failure sequence diagrams. *International Journal of Secure Software Engineering*, *3*(1), 20–36. doi:10.4018/jsse.2012010102

Reddy, A., & Prasad, G. V. (2012). Consumer perceptions on security, privacy, and trust on e-portals. *International Journal of Online Marketing*, *2*(2), 10–24. doi:10.4018/ijom.2012040102

Ren, D.-Q., & Wei, Z. (2013). A Failure Recovery Solution for Transplanting High-Performance Data-Intensive Algorithms from the Cluster to the Cloud. In *Proceedings of IEEE International Conference on High Performance Computing and Communications & IEEE 10th International Conference on Embedded and Ubiquitous Computing (HPCC & EUC)* (pp. 1463-1468). doi:10.1109/HPCC.and.EUC.2013.207

Reshef, D. N., Reshef, Y. A., Finucane, H. K., Grossman, S. R., McVean, G., Turnbaugh, P. J., ... & Sabeti, P. C. (2011). Detecting novel associations in large data sets. *science*, *334*(6062), 1518-1524. doi:.10.1126/science.1205438

Reshef, Y. A., Reshef, D. N., Sabeti, P. C., & Mitzenmacher, M. (2015). Theoretical Foundations of Equitability and the Maximal Information Coefficient. Retrieved from https://arxiv.org/pdf/1408.4908.pdf

Richet, J. (2013). From young hackers to crackers. *International Journal of Technology and Human Interaction*, *9*(3), 53–62. doi:10.4018/jthi.2013070104

Rjaibi, N., Rabai, L. B., Ben Aissa, A., & Mili, A. (2013). Mean failure cost as a measurable value and evidence of cybersecurity: E-learning case study. *International Journal of Secure Software Engineering*, *4*(3), 64–81. doi:10.4018/jsse.2013070104

Roberts, L. D. (2012). Cyber identity theft. In *Cyber crime: Concepts, methodologies, tools and applications* (pp. 21–36). Hershey, PA: IGI Global. doi:10.4018/978-1-61350-323-2.ch103

Robertson, I. T. (1985). Human information-processing strategies and style. *Behaviour & Information Technology*, *4*(1), 19–29. doi:10.1080/01449298508901784

Rodríguez, J., Fernández-Medina, E., Piattini, M., & Mellado, D. (2011). A security requirements engineering tool for domain engineering in software product lines. In N. Milanovic (Ed.), *Non-functional properties in service oriented architecture: Requirements, models and methods* (pp. 73–92). Hershey, PA: IGI Global. doi:10.4018/978-1-60566-794-2.ch004

Rogers, Y., Sharp, H., Preece, J., & Tepper, M. (2007). Interaction design: Beyond human-computer interaction. *networker, The Craft of Network Computing*, *11*(4), 34.

Rogers, Y., Sharp, H., Preece, J., & Tepper, M. (2007). Interaction design: Beyond human-computer interaction. *netWorker. The Craft of Network Computing*, *11*(4), 34.

Roldan, M., & Rea, A. (2011). Individual privacy and security in virtual worlds. In A. Rea (Ed.), *Security in virtual worlds, 3D webs, and immersive environments: Models for development, interaction, and management* (pp. 1–19). Hershey, PA: IGI Global. doi:10.4018/978-1-61520-891-3.ch001

Rowe, N. C., Garfinkel, S. L., Beverly, R., & Yannakogeorgos, P. (2011). Challenges in monitoring cyberarms compliance. *International Journal of Cyber Warfare & Terrorism*, *1*(2), 35–48. doi:10.4018/ijcwt.2011040104

Roy, I., Setty, S. T., Kilzer, A., Shmatikov, V., & Witchel, E. (2010) 'Airavat: security and privacy for MapReduce. In *Proceedings of the 7th USENIX Conference on Networked Systems Design and Implementation (NSDI'10)* (Vol. 10, pp. 297–312).

Rwabutaza, A., Yang, M., & Bourbakis, N. (2012). A comparative survey on cryptology-based methodologies. *International Journal of Information Security and Privacy*, *6*(3), 1–37. doi:10.4018/jisp.2012070101

Sabar, N. R., Abawajy, J., & Yearwood, J. (2016). Heterogeneous Cooperative Co-evolution Memetic Differential Evolution Algorithms for Big Data Optimisation Problems.

Sadkhan, S. B., & Abbas, N. A. (2014). Privacy and security of wireless communication networks. In J. Rodrigues, K. Lin, & J. Lloret (Eds.), *Mobile networks and cloud computing convergence for progressive services and applications* (pp. 58–78). Hershey, PA: IGI Global. doi:10.4018/978-1-4666-4781-7.ch004

Saedy, M., & Mojtahed, V. (2011). Machine-to-machine communications and security solution in cellular systems. *International Journal of Interdisciplinary Telecommunications and Networking*, *3*(2), 66–75. doi:10.4018/jitn.2011040105

San Nicolas-Rocca, T., & Olfman, L. (2013). End user security training for identification and access management. *Journal of Organizational and End User Computing*, *25*(4), 75–103. doi:10.4018/joeuc.2013100104

Saravanan, M., Thoufeeq, A. M., Akshaya, S., & Jayasre Manchari, V. L. (2014, October). Exploring new privacy approaches in a scalable classification framework. In *Proceedings of the 2014 International Conference on Data Science and Advanced Analytics (DSAA)* (pp. 209-215). IEEE. doi:10.1109/DSAA.2014.7058075

Satoh, F., Nakamura, Y., Mukhi, N. K., Tatsubori, M., & Ono, K. (2011). Model-driven approach for end-to-end SOA security configurations. In N. Milanovic (Ed.), *Non-functional properties in service oriented architecture: Requirements, models and methods* (pp. 268–298). Hershey, PA: IGI Global. doi:10.4018/978-1-60566-794-2.ch012

Saucez, D., Iannone, L., & Bonaventure, O. (2014). The map-and-encap locator/identifier separation paradigm: A security analysis. In M. Boucadair & D. Binet (Eds.), *Solutions for sustaining scalability in internet growth* (pp. 148–163). Hershey, PA: IGI Global. doi:10.4018/978-1-4666-4305-5.ch008

Schell, B. H., & Holt, T. J. (2012). A profile of the demographics, psychological predispositions, and social/behavioral patterns of computer hacker insiders and outsiders. In *Cyber crime: Concepts, methodologies, tools and applications* (pp. 1461–1484). Hershey, PA: IGI Global. doi:10.4018/978-1-61350-323-2.ch705

Schmidt, H. (2011). Threat and risk-driven security requirements engineering. *International Journal of Mobile Computing and Multimedia Communications, 3*(1), 35–50. doi:10.4018/jmcmc.2011010103

Schmidt, H., Hatebur, D., & Heisel, M. (2011). A pattern-based method to develop secure software. In H. Mouratidis (Ed.), *Software engineering for secure systems: Industrial and research perspectives* (pp. 32–74). Hershey, PA: IGI Global. doi:10.4018/978-1-61520-837-1.ch003

Seale, R. O., & Hargiss, K. M. (2011). A proposed architecture for autonomous mobile agent intrusion prevention and malware defense in heterogeneous networks. *International Journal of Strategic Information Technology and Applications, 2*(4), 44–54. doi:10.4018/jsita.2011100104

Search Cloud Computing. (2013). The state of the enterprise cloud and prepping for AWS re:Invent 2013. Retrieved 2017 from http://searchcloudcomputing.techtarget.com/essentialguide/The-state-of-the-enterprise-cloud-and-prepping-for-AWS-reInvent-2013

Sebelius, F., Eriksson, L., Holmberg, H., Levinsson, A., Lundborg, G., Danielsen, N., & Montelius, L. et al. (2005). Classification of motor commands using a modified self-organising feature map. *Journal of Medical Engineering and Physics, 27*(5), 403–413. doi:10.1016/j.medengphy.2004.09.008 PMID:15863349

Sengupta, A., & Mazumdar, C. (2011). A mark-up language for the specification of information security governance requirements. *International Journal of Information Security and Privacy, 5*(2), 33–53. doi:10.4018/jisp.2011040103

Sen, J. (2013). Security and privacy challenges in cognitive wireless sensor networks. In N. Meghanathan & Y. Reddy (Eds.), *Cognitive radio technology applications for wireless and mobile ad hoc networks* (pp. 194–232). Hershey, PA: IGI Global. doi:10.4018/978-1-4666-4221-8.ch011

Sen, J. (2014). Security and privacy issues in cloud computing. In A. Ruiz-Martinez, R. Marin-Lopez, & F. Pereniguez-Garcia (Eds.), *Architectures and protocols for secure information technology infrastructures* (pp. 1–45). Hershey, PA: IGI Global. doi:10.4018/978-1-4666-4514-1.ch001

Setia, L. (2008). Strategies for Content Based Image Retrieval. Albert-Ludwigs-University. Retrieved from https://www.freidok.uni-freiburg.de/fedora/objects/freidok:6150/datastreams/FILE1/content

Shan, C., Porikli, F., Xiang, T., & Gong, S. (Eds.). (2012). Video Analytics for Business Intelligence. In C. Shan, F. Porikli, T. Xiang et al. (Eds.), Video analytics for business intelligence (Vol. 1, pp. 309–354). Berlin: Springer.

Shaqrah, A. A. (2011). The influence of internet security on e-business competence in Jordan: An empirical analysis. In *Global business: Concepts, methodologies, tools and applications* (pp. 1071–1086). Hershey, PA: IGI Global. doi:10.4018/978-1-60960-587-2.ch413

Shareef, M. A., & Kumar, V. (2012). Prevent/control identity theft: Impact on trust and consumers purchase intention in B2C EC. *Information Resources Management Journal*, 25(3), 30–60. doi:10.4018/irmj.2012070102

Sharma, S., & Sethi, M. (2015). Implementing Collaborative Filtering on Large Scale Data using Hadoop and Mahout, *International Research Journal of Engineering and Technology*, 2(4).

Sharma, K., & Singh, A. (2011). Biometric security in the e-world. In H. Nemati & L. Yang (Eds.), *Applied cryptography for cyber security and defense: Information encryption and cyphering* (pp. 289–337). Hershey, PA: IGI Global. doi:10.4018/978-1-61520-783-1.ch013

Sharma, R. K. (2014). Physical layer security and its applications: A survey. In D. Rawat, B. Bista, & G. Yan (Eds.), *Security, Privacy, Trust, and Resource Management in Mobile and Wireless Communications* (pp. 29–60). Hershey, PA: IGI Global. doi:10.4018/978-1-4666-4691-9.ch003

Shaw, R., Keh, H., & Huang, N. (2011). Information security awareness on-line materials design with knowledge maps. *International Journal of Distance Education Technologies*, 9(4), 41–56. doi:10.4018/jdet.2011100104

Shebanow, A., Perez, R., & Howard, C. (2012). The effect of firewall testing types on cloud security policies. *International Journal of Strategic Information Technology and Applications*, 3(3), 60–68. doi:10.4018/jsita.2012070105

Shen, Y., Li, Y., Wu, L., Liu, S., & Wen, Q. (2014). Data protection in the cloud era. In Y. Shen, Y. Li, L. Wu, S. Liu, & Q. Wen (Eds.), *Enabling the new era of cloud computing: Data security, transfer, and management* (pp. 132–154). Hershey, PA: IGI Global. doi:10.4018/978-1-4666-4801-2.ch007

Shen, Y., Li, Y., Wu, L., Liu, S., & Wen, Q. (2014). Enterprise security monitoring with the fusion center model. In Y. Shen, Y. Li, L. Wu, S. Liu, & Q. Wen (Eds.), *Enabling the new era of cloud computing: Data security, transfer, and management* (pp. 116–131). Hershey, PA: IGI Global. doi:10.4018/978-1-4666-4801-2.ch006

Shirudkar, K., & Motwani, D. (2015). Big-Data Security. *Int. J. Adv. Res. Comput. Sci. Softw. Eng.*, 5, 1100–1109.

Shore, M. (2011). Cyber security and anti-social networking. In *Virtual communities: Concepts, methodologies, tools and applications* (pp. 1286–1297). Hershey, PA: IGI Global. doi:10.4018/978-1-60960-100-3.ch412

Shuman, G. (2009). Using forearm electromyograms to classify hand gestures. In Proceedings of Bioinformatics and Biomedicine BIBM '09. Washington, DC, USA.

Shyamala, K. & Sunitha Rani, T. (2015). An Analysis on Efficient Resource Allocation Mechanisms in Cloud Computing. *Indian Journal of Science and Technology, 8*(9). doi:10.17485/ijst/2015/v8i9/50180

Siddiqi, J., Alqatawna, J., & Btoush, M. H. (2011). Do insecure systems increase global digital divide? In *Global business: Concepts, methodologies, tools and applications* (pp. 2102–2111). Hershey, PA: IGI Global. doi:10.4018/978-1-60960-587-2.ch717

Simpson, J. J., Simpson, M. J., Endicott-Popovsky, B., & Popovsky, V. (2012). Secure software education: A contextual model-based approach. In K. Khan (Ed.), *Security-aware systems applications and software development methods* (pp. 286–312). Hershey, PA: IGI Global. doi:10.4018/978-1-4666-1580-9.ch016

Singh, D., & Reddy, C. K. (2014). A survey on platforms for Big Data analytics. *Journal of Big Data, 2*(1), 8.

Singh, A., Chaudhary, M., Rana, A., & Dubey, G. (2011). Online Mining of data to generate association rule mining in large databases. In *Proceedings of the 2011 Int. Conf. Recent Trends Inf. Syst.* (pp. 126–131). doi:10.1109/ReTIS.2011.6146853

Singh, J. (2014). Real time BIG data analytic: Security concern and challenges with Machine Learning algorithm. In *Proceedings of Conference on IT in Business, Industry and Government (CSIBIG)*. doi:10.1109/CSIBIG.2014.7056985

Singh, P., & Suri, B. (2014). Quality assessment of data using statistical and ML methods. In L. C. Jain, H. S. Behera, J. K. Mandal, & D. P. Mohapatra (Eds.), *Comput* (2nd ed., pp. 89–97). Intell. Data Min.

Singh, S. (2012). Security threats and issues with MANET. In K. Lakhtaria (Ed.), *Technological advancements and applications in mobile ad-hoc networks: Research trends* (pp. 247–263). Hershey, PA: IGI Global. doi:10.4018/978-1-4666-0321-9.ch015

Sivarajah, U., Kamal, M. M., Irani, Z., & Weerakkody, V. (2016). Critical analysis of Big Data challenges and analytical methods. *Journal of Business Research*. doi:10.1016/j.jbusres.2016.08.001

Smith, A., Nanda, P., & Brown, E. E. (2009). Development of a myoelectric control scheme based on a time delayed neural network. In *Proceedings of 2009 Annual International Conference of the IEEE Engineering in Medicine and Biology Society*, Minneapolis, Minnesota. IEEE. doi:10.1109/IEMBS.2009.5332846

Sockel, H., & Falk, L. K. (2012). Online privacy, vulnerabilities, and threats: A manager's perspective. In *Cyber crime: Concepts, methodologies, tools and applications* (pp. 101–123). Hershey, PA: IGI Global. doi:10.4018/978-1-61350-323-2.ch108

Spruit, M., & de Bruijn, W. (2012). CITS: The cost of IT security framework. *International Journal of Information Security and Privacy, 6*(4), 94–116. doi:10.4018/jisp.2012100105

Sqlstream. (2012). Retrieved from http://www.sqlstream.com/products/server/

Srinivasan, C., Lakshmy, K., & Sethumadhavan, M. (2011). Complexity measures of cryptographically secure boolean functions. In R. Santanam, M. Sethumadhavan, & M. Virendra (Eds.), *Cyber security, cyber crime and cyber forensics: Applications and perspectives* (pp. 220–230). Hershey, PA: IGI Global. doi:10.4018/978-1-60960-123-2.ch015

Srivatsa, M., Agrawal, D., & McDonald, A. D. (2012). Security across disparate management domains in coalition MANETs. In *Wireless technologies: Concepts, methodologies, tools and applications* (pp. 1494–1518). Hershey, PA: IGI Global. doi:10.4018/978-1-61350-101-6.ch521

Stallings, W. (2011). *Cryptography and Network Security: Principles and Practice* (5th ed.). Pearson Education.

Stojanovic, M. D., Acimovic-Raspopovic, V. S., & Rakas, S. B. (2013). Security management issues for open source ERP in the NGN environment. In *Enterprise resource planning: Concepts, methodologies, tools, and applications* (pp. 789–804). Hershey, PA: IGI Global. doi:10.4018/978-1-4666-4153-2.ch046

Stoll, M., & Breu, R. (2012). Information security governance and standard based management systems. In M. Gupta, J. Walp, & R. Sharman (Eds.), *Strategic and practical approaches for information security governance: Technologies and applied solutions* (pp. 261–282). Hershey, PA: IGI Global. doi:10.4018/978-1-4666-0197-0.ch015

Storm. (2012). Retrieved from http://storm-project.net/

Sundaresan, M., & Boopathy, D. (2014). Different perspectives of cloud security. In S. Srinivasan (Ed.), *Security, trust, and regulatory aspects of cloud computing in business environments* (pp. 73–90). Hershey, PA: IGI Global. doi:10.4018/978-1-4666-5788-5.ch004

Suryawanshi, S. S., Mulani, T., Zanjurne, S., Inarkar, K., & Jambhulkar, A. (2015). Database Intrusion Detection and Protection System Using Log Mining and Forensic Analysis. *Int. J. Comput. Sci. Inf. Technol., 6*, 5059–5061.

Sweeney, L. (2002). k-anonymity: A model for protecting privacy. *International Journal of Uncertainty, Fuzziness and Knowledge-based Systems, 10*(05), 557–570. doi:10.1142/S0218488502001648

Takabi, H., Joshi, J. B., & Ahn, G. (2013). Security and privacy in cloud computing: Towards a comprehensive framework. In X. Yang & L. Liu (Eds.), *Principles, methodologies, and service-oriented approaches for cloud computing* (pp. 164–184). Hershey, PA: IGI Global. doi:10.4018/978-1-4666-2854-0.ch007

Takabi, H., Zargar, S. T., & Joshi, J. B. (2014). Mobile cloud computing and its security and privacy challenges. In D. Rawat, B. Bista, & G. Yan (Eds.), *Security, privacy, trust, and resource management in mobile and wireless communications* (pp. 384–407). Hershey, PA: IGI Global. doi:10.4018/978-1-4666-4691-9.ch016

Takemura, T. (2014). Unethical information security behavior and organizational commitment. In T. Tsiakis, T. Kargidis, & P. Katsaros (Eds.), *Approaches and processes for managing the economics of information systems* (pp. 181–198). Hershey, PA: IGI Global. doi:10.4018/978-1-4666-4983-5.ch011

Talib, S., Clarke, N. L., & Furnell, S. M. (2011). Establishing a personalized information security culture. *International Journal of Mobile Computing and Multimedia Communications*, 3(1), 63–79. doi:10.4018/jmcmc.2011010105

Talukder, A. K. (2011). Securing next generation internet services. In R. Santanam, M. Sethumadhavan, & M. Virendra (Eds.), *Cyber security, cyber crime and cyber forensics: Applications and perspectives* (pp. 87–105). Hershey, PA: IGI Global. doi:10.4018/978-1-60960-123-2.ch007

Tang, L., & Liu, H. (2010). Community detection and mining in social media. *Synthesis Lectures on Data Mining and Knowledge Discovery*, 2(1), 1–137. doi:10.2200/S00298ED1V01Y201009DMK003

Tan, Z., Nagar, U. T., He, X., Nanda, P., Liu, R. P., Wang, S., & Hu, J. (2014). Enhancing Big Data Security with Collaborative Intrusion Detection. *IEEE Cloud Computing*, 1(3), 27–33. doi:10.1109/MCC.2014.53

Tchepnda, C., Moustafa, H., Labiod, H., & Bourdon, G. (2011). Vehicular networks security: Attacks, requirements, challenges and current contributions. In K. Curran (Ed.), *Ubiquitous developments in ambient computing and intelligence: Human-centered applications* (pp. 43–55). Hershey, PA: IGI Global. doi:10.4018/978-1-60960-549-0.ch004

Tenore, F. V. G., Ramos, A., Fahmy, A., Acharya, S., Etienne-cummings, R., & Thakor, N. T. (2009). Decoding of individuated finger movements using surface electromyography. *IEEE Transactions on Bio-Medical Engineering*, 56(5), 1427–1434. doi:10.1109/TBME.2008.2005485 PMID:19473933

Teo, S. G., Han, S., & Lee, V. (2013, December). Privacy preserving support vector machine using non-linear kernels on Hadoop Mahout. In *Proceedings of the 2013 IEEE 16th International Conference on Computational Science and Engineering (CSE)* (pp. 941-948). IEEE. doi:10.1109/CSE.2013.200

Tereshchenko, N. (2012). US foreign policy challenges of non-state actors cyber terrorism against critical infrastructure. *International Journal of Cyber Warfare & Terrorism*, 2(4), 28–48. doi:10.4018/ijcwt.2012100103

The Guardian. (2013). Tech giants may be huge, but nothing matches big data. Retrieved from https://www.theguardian.com/technology/2013/aug/23/tech-giants-data

Thilagavathi, M., Lopez, D., & Murugan, B. S. (2014). Middleware for Preserving Privacy in Big Data. In *Handbook of Research on Cloud Infrastructures for Big Data Analytics* (pp. 419-443). Hershey, PA: IGI Global.

Thota, C., Manogaran, G., & Sundarsekar, R. (in press). Architecture for Big Data Storage in Different Cloud Deployment Models. In R.S. Segall, J.S. Cook & N. Gupta (Eds.), Big Data Storage and Visualization Techniques. Hershey, PA: IGI Global.

Thota, C., Manogaran, G., Lopez, D., & Vijayakumar, V. (2017). Big Data Security Framework for Distributed Cloud Data Centers. In Cybersecurity Breaches and Issues Surrounding Online Threat Protection (pp. 288-310). Hershey, PA: IGI Global. doi:10.4018/978-1-5225-1941-6.ch012

Thota, C., Manogaran, G., Lopez, D., & Vijayakumar, V. (2017). Big data security framework for distributed cloud data centers. In M. Moore (Eds.), *Cybersecurity Breaches and Issues Surrounding Online Threat Protection*. Hershey, PA: IGI Global.

Thota, C., Sundarsekar, R., Manogaran, G., R., V., & M.K., P. (in press). Centralized Fog Computing Security Platform for IoT and Cloud in Healthcare System. In *Exploring the Convergence of Big Data and the Internet of Things*. Hershey, PA: IGI Global.

Thurimella, R., & Baird, L. C. (2011). Network security. In H. Nemati & L. Yang (Eds.), *Applied cryptography for cyber security and defense: Information encryption and cyphering* (pp. 1–31). Hershey, PA: IGI Global. doi:10.4018/978-1-61520-783-1.ch001

Thurimella, R., & Mitchell, W. (2011). Cloak and dagger: Man-in-the-middle and other insidious attacks. In H. Nemati (Ed.), *Security and privacy assurance in advancing technologies: New developments* (pp. 252–270). Hershey, PA: IGI Global. doi:10.4018/978-1-60960-200-0.ch016

Tiwari, S., Singh, A., Singh, R. S., & Singh, S. K. (2013). Internet security using biometrics. In *IT policy and ethics: Concepts, methodologies, tools, and applications* (pp. 1680–1707). Hershey, PA: IGI Global. doi:10.4018/978-1-4666-2919-6.ch074

Tomaiuolo, M. (2012). Trust enforcing and trust building, different technologies and visions. *International Journal of Cyber Warfare & Terrorism, 2*(4), 49–66. doi:10.4018/ijcwt.2012100104

Tomaiuolo, M. (2014). Trust management and delegation for the administration of web services. In I. Portela & F. Almeida (Eds.), *Organizational, legal, and technological dimensions of information system administration* (pp. 18–37). Hershey, PA: IGI Global. doi:10.4018/978-1-4666-4526-4.ch002

Touhafi, A., Braeken, A., Cornetta, G., Mentens, N., & Steenhaut, K. (2011). Secure techniques for remote reconfiguration of wireless embedded systems. In M. Cruz-Cunha & F. Moreira (Eds.), *Handbook of research on mobility and computing: Evolving technologies and ubiquitous impacts* (pp. 930–951). Hershey, PA: IGI Global. doi:10.4018/978-1-60960-042-6.ch058

Traore, I., & Woungang, I. (2013). Software security engineering – Part I: Security requirements and risk analysis. In K. Buragga & N. Zaman (Eds.), *Software development techniques for constructive information systems design* (pp. 221–255). Hershey, PA: IGI Global. doi:10.4018/978-1-4666-3679-8.ch012

Tripathi, M., Gaur, M., & Laxmi, V. (2014). Security challenges in wireless sensor network. In D. Rawat, B. Bista, & G. Yan (Eds.), *Security, privacy, trust, and resource management in mobile and wireless communications* (pp. 334–359). Hershey, PA: IGI Global. doi:10.4018/978-1-4666-4691-9.ch014

Trösterer, S., Beck, E., Dalpiaz, F., Paja, E., Giorgini, P., & Tscheligi, M. (2012). Formative user-centered evaluation of security modeling: Results from a case study. *International Journal of Secure Software Engineering*, *3*(1), 1–19. doi:10.4018/jsse.2012010101

Tsai, C. W., La, C. F., Chao, H. C., & Vasilakos, A. V. (2015). Big data analytics: A survey. *J. Big Data.*, *2*(1), 1–32. doi:10.1186/s40537-015-0030-3 PMID:26191487

Tsai, C., Lai, C., Chiang, M., & Yang, L. (2014). Data mining for internet of things: A survey. *IEEE Communications Surveys and Tutorials*, *16*(1), 77–97. doi:10.1109/SURV.2013.103013.00206

Tsang, S., Kao, B., Yip, K. Y., Ho, W. S., & Lee, S. D. (2011). Decision trees for uncertain data. *Knowl. Data Eng. IEEE Trans.*, *23*(1), 64–78. doi:10.1109/TKDE.2009.175

Tsenov, G., Zeghbib, A. H., Palis, F., Shoylev, N., & Mladenov, V. (2006). Neural networks for online classification of hand and finger movements using surface EMG signals. In *Proceedings of 2006 8th Seminar on Neural Network Applications in Electrical Engineering*, Belgrade, Serbia. IEEE.

Tsiakis, T. (2013). The role of information security and cryptography in digital democracy: (Human) rights and freedom. In C. Akrivopoulou & N. Garipidis (Eds.), *Digital democracy and the impact of technology on governance and politics: New globalized practices* (pp. 158–174). Hershey, PA: IGI Global. doi:10.4018/978-1-4666-3637-8.ch009

Tsiakis, T., Kargidis, T., & Chatzipoulidis, A. (2013). IT security governance in e-banking. In D. Mellado, L. Enrique Sánchez, E. Fernández-Medina, & M. Piattini (Eds.), *IT security governance innovations: Theory and research* (pp. 13–46). Hershey, PA: IGI Global. doi:10.4018/978-1-4666-2083-4.ch002

Tsuji, T., Fukuda, O., Kaneko, M., & Koji, I. (2000). Pattern classification of time-series EMG signals using neural networks. *International Journal of Adaptive Control and Signal Processing*, *14*(8), 829–848. doi:10.1002/1099-1115(200012)14:8<829::AID-ACS623>3.0.CO;2-L

Tulasi, B., Wagh, R. S., & Balaji, S. (2015). High Performance Computing and Big Data Analytics – Paradigms and Challenges. *International Journal of Computers and Applications*, *116*(2), 28–33. doi:10.5120/20311-2356

Turgeman-Goldschmidt, O. (2011). Between hackers and white-collar offenders. In T. Holt & B. Schell (Eds.), *Corporate hacking and technology-driven crime: Social dynamics and implications* (pp. 18–37). Hershey, PA: IGI Global. doi:10.4018/978-1-61692-805-6.ch002

Tvrdíková, M. (2012). Information system integrated security. In M. Gupta, J. Walp, & R. Sharman (Eds.), *Strategic and practical approaches for information security governance: Technologies and applied solutions* (pp. 158–169). Hershey, PA: IGI Global. doi:10.4018/978-1-4666-0197-0.ch009

Udomsuk, S., Areerak, K.-L., Areerak, K.-N., & Srikaew, A. (2010). Parameters identification of separately excited dc motor using adaptive tabu search technique. In *Proceedings of Advances in Energy Engineering (ICAEE).Beijling*. IEEE. doi:10.1109/ICAEE.2010.5557618

Uffen, J., & Breitner, M. H. (2013). Management of technical security measures: An empirical examination of personality traits and behavioral intentions. *International Journal of Social and Organizational Dynamics in IT*, *3*(1), 14–31. doi:10.4018/ijsodit.2013010102

UK Data Archive. (2011). Managing and Sharing Data. Retrieved from http://www.data-archive. ac.uk/media/2894/managingsharing.pdf

Vadivel, M., & Raghunath, V. (2014). Enhancing Map-Reduce Framework for Bigdata with Hierarchical Clustering. *Int. J. Innov. Res. Comput. Commun. Eng.*, *2*, 490–498.

Vaidya, J., Shafiq, B., Fan, W., Mehmood, D., & Lorenzi, D. (2014). A random decision tree framework for privacy-preserving data mining. *IEEE Transactions on* Dependable and Secure Computing, *11*(5), 399–411.

Vance, A., & Siponen, M. T. (2012). IS security policy violations: A rational choice perspective. *Journal of Organizational and End User Computing*, *24*(1), 21–41. doi:10.4018/joeuc.2012010102

Varatharajan, R., Manogaran, G., Priyan, M. K., Balaş, V. E., & Barna, C. (2017b). Visual analysis of geospatial habitat suitability model based on inverse distance weighting with paired comparison analysis. *Multimedia Tools and Applications*, 1–21.

Varatharajan, R., Manogaran, G., Priyan, M. K., & Sundarasekar, R. (2017a). Wearable sensor devices for early detection of Alzheimer disease using dynamic time warping algorithm. *Cluster Computing*, 1–10.

Vashkevich, A. V., & Zhukov, V. G. (2015) Privacy-Preserving Clustering Using C-Means.

Vavilapalli, V. K., Murthy, A. C., Douglas, C., Agarwal, S., Konar, M., Evans, R., ... & Saha, B. (2013). Apache hadoop yarn: Yet another resource negotiator. In *Proceedings of the 4th annual Symposium on Cloud Computing* (p. 5). doi:10.1145/2523616.2523633

Veltsos, C. (2011). Mitigating the blended threat: Protecting data and educating users. In D. Kar & M. Syed (Eds.), *Network security, administration and management: Advancing technology and practice* (pp. 20–37). Hershey, PA: IGI Global. doi:10.4018/978-1-60960-777-7.ch002

Venkataraman, R., Pushpalatha, M., & Rao, T. R. (2014). Trust management and modeling techniques in wireless communications. In D. Rawat, B. Bista, & G. Yan (Eds.), *Security, privacy, trust, and resource management in mobile and wireless communications* (pp. 278–294). Hershey, PA: IGI Global. doi:10.4018/978-1-4666-4691-9.ch012

Venkataraman, R., & Rao, T. R. (2012). Security issues and models in mobile ad hoc networks. In K. Lakhtaria (Ed.), *Technological advancements and applications in mobile ad-hoc networks: Research trends* (pp. 219–227). Hershey, PA: IGI Global. doi:10.4018/978-1-4666-0321-9.ch013

Victor, N., Lopez, D., & Abawajy, J. H. (2016). Privacy models for big data: a survey. *Int. J. Big Data Intelligence, 3*(1), 61.

Victor, N., Lopez, D., & Abawajy, J. H. (2016). Privacy models for big data: A survey. *International Journal of Big Data Intelligence, 3*(1), 61–75. doi:10.1504/IJBDI.2016.073904

Vijayakumari, R., Kirankumar, R., & Gangadhara Rao, K. (2014). Comparative analysis of Google File System and Hadoop Distributed File System. *International Journal of Advanced Trends in Computer Science and Engineering, 3*(1), 553–558.

Vijayalakshmi, M., & Devi, M. R. (2012). A Survey of Different Issue of Different clustering Algorithms Used in Large Data sets. *Int. J. Adv. Res. Comput. Sci. Softw. Eng., 2*(3), 304–307. Retrieved from http://www.ijarcsse.com/docs/papers/March2012/volume_2_Issue_3/V2I300137.pdf

Vincent, P., Larochelle, H., Bengio, Y., & Manzagol, P.-A. (2008). Extracting and composing robust features with denoising autoencoders. In Proc. of the 25th Int. Conf. Mach. Learn. ICML '08 (pp. 1096–1103). New York, NY: ACM. doi:10.1145/1390156.1390294

Viney, D. (2011). Future trends in digital security. In D. Kerr, J. Gammack, & K. Bryant (Eds.), *Digital business security development: Management technologies* (pp. 173–190). Hershey, PA: IGI Global. doi:10.4018/978-1-60566-806-2.ch009

Vinod, P., Laxmi, V., & Gaur, M. (2011). Metamorphic malware analysis and detection methods. In R. Santanam, M. Sethumadhavan, & M. Virendra (Eds.), *Cyber security, cyber crime and cyber forensics: Applications and perspectives* (pp. 178–202). Hershey, PA: IGI Global. doi:10.4018/978-1-60960-123-2.ch013

von Solms, R., & Warren, M. (2011). Towards the human information security firewall. *International Journal of Cyber Warfare & Terrorism, 1*(2), 10–17. doi:10.4018/ijcwt.2011040102

Wadhwa, A., & Madhow, U. (2014). Bottom-up DL using the Hebbian Principle. Retrieved from http://www.ece.ucsb.edu/wcsl/people/aseem/Aseem_stuff/hebbian_preprint.pdf

Wall, D. S. (2011). Micro-frauds: Virtual robberies, stings and scams in the information age. In T. Holt & B. Schell (Eds.), *Corporate hacking and technology-driven crime: Social dynamics and implications* (pp. 68–86). Hershey, PA: IGI Global. doi:10.4018/978-1-61692-805-6.ch004

Wang, L., Wang, G., & Sng, D. (2015). DL Algorithms with Applications to Video Analytics for A Smart City: A Survey.

Wang, Z., Liao, J., Cao, Q., Qi, H., & Wang, Z. (2015). Friendbook: A Semantic-Based Friend Recommendation System for Social Networks.

Wang, H., Zhao, J. L., & Chen, G. (2012). Managing data security in e-markets through relationship driven access control. *Journal of Database Management, 23*(2), 1–21. doi:10.4018/jdm.2012040101

Wang, J. Z., Wang, R. C., Li, F., Jiang, M. W., & Jin, D. W. (2005). EMG signal classification for myoelectric teleoperating a dexterous robot hand. In *Proceedings of the 2005 IEEE 27th Annual Conference on Engineering in Medicine and Biology*, Shanghai, China. IEEE. doi:10.1109/IEMBS.2005.1615841

Wang, J., Xu, C. F., & Pan, Y. H. (2006, August). An incremental algorithm for mining privacy-preserving frequent itemsets. In *Proceedings of Fifth International Conference on Machine Learning and Cybernetics*, Dalian (Vol. 13, p. 16). doi:10.1109/ICMLC.2006.258592

Wang, L., & Sajeev, A. S. M. (2007, January). Roller interface for mobile device applications. In *Proceedings of the eight Australasian conference on User interface* (Vol. 64, pp. 7-13). Australian Computer Society, Inc.

Wang, L., & Sajeev, A. S. M. (2007, January). Roller interface for mobile device applications. In *Proceedings of the eight Australasian conference on User interface-*(*Vol. 64*, pp. 7-13). Australian Computer Society, Inc.

Wang, S., Gan, W., Li, D., & Li, D. (2011). Data Field for Hierarchical Clustering. *International Journal of Data Warehousing and Mining*, *7*(4), 43–63. doi:10.4018/jdwm.2011100103

Wang, Y., Yu, D., Ju, Y., & Acero, A. (2011). Voice search. In *Lang. Underst. Syst. Extr. Semant. Inf. from Speech*. New York: Wiley. doi:10.1002/9781119992691.ch5

Warren, M., & Leitch, S. (2011). Protection of Australia in the cyber age. *International Journal of Cyber Warfare & Terrorism*, *1*(1), 35–40. doi:10.4018/ijcwt.2011010104

Weber, S. G., & Gustiené, P. (2013). Crafting requirements for mobile and pervasive emergency response based on privacy and security by design principles. *International Journal of Information Systems for Crisis Response and Management*, *5*(2), 1–18. doi:10.4018/jiscrm.2013040101

Wei, S., & Yonggui, W. (2010, February). Association rule mining algorithm based on privacy preserving. In *Proceedings of the 2010 The 2nd International Conference on Computer and Automation Engineering (ICCAE)* (Vol. 4, pp. 140-143). IEEE.

Wei, J., Lin, B., & Loho-Noya, M. (2013). Development of an e-healthcare information security risk assessment method. *Journal of Database Management*, *24*(1), 36–57. doi:10.4018/jdm.2013010103

Weippl, E. R., & Riedl, B. (2012). Security, trust, and privacy on mobile devices and multimedia applications. In *Cyber crime: Concepts, methodologies, tools and applications* (pp. 228–244). Hershey, PA: IGI Global. doi:10.4018/978-1-61350-323-2.ch202

WestinA., F. (1967). *Privacy and Freedom*. New York: Atheneum.

White, G., & Long, J. (2012). Global information security factors. In H. Nemati (Ed.), *Optimizing information security and advancing privacy assurance: New technologies* (pp. 163–174). Hershey, PA: IGI Global. doi:10.4018/978-1-4666-0026-3.ch009

White, S. C., Sedigh, S., & Hurson, A. R. (2013). Security concepts for cloud computing. In X. Yang & L. Liu (Eds.), *Principles, methodologies, and service-oriented approaches for cloud computing* (pp. 116–142). Hershey, PA: IGI Global. doi:10.4018/978-1-4666-2854-0.ch005

Whyte, B., & Harrison, J. (2011). State of practice in secure software: Experts' views on best ways ahead. In H. Mouratidis (Ed.), *Software engineering for secure systems: Industrial and research perspectives* (pp. 1–14). Hershey, PA: IGI Global. doi:10.4018/978-1-61520-837-1.ch001

Wille, R. (2005). Formal concept analysis as mathematical theory of concept and concept hierarchies. In Form. Concept Anal. Springer. doi:10.1007/11528784_1

Wojtczak, P., Amaral, T. G., Dias, O. P., Wolczowski, A., & Kurzynski, M. (2009). Hand movement recognition based on biosignal analysis. *Journal of Engineering Applications of Artificial Intelligence*, *22*(4-5), 608–615. doi:10.1016/j.engappai.2008.12.004

Wu, C., Buyya, R., & Ramamohanarao, K. (2016). Big Data Analytics = ML + Cloud Computing. Retrieved from https://arxiv.org/ftp/arxiv/papers/1601/1601.03115.pdf

Wu, Q., Ding, G., Wang, J., & Yao, Y. D. (2013). Spatial-temporal opportunity detection for spectrum-heterogeneous cognitive radio networks: Two-dimensional sensing. *IEEE Transactions on Wireless Communications*, *12*(2), 516–526. doi:10.1109/TWC.2012.122212.111638

Wu, T. T., Chen, Y. F., Hastie, T., Sobel, E., & Lange, K. (2009). Genome-wide association analysis by lasso penalized logistic regression. *Bioinformatics (Oxford, England)*, *25*(6), 714–721. doi:10.1093/bioinformatics/btp041 PMID:19176549

Wu, X., Kumar, V., Quinlan, J. R., Ghosh, J., Yang, Q., Motoda, H., & Zhou, Z. H. et al. (2008). Top 10 algorithms in data mining. *Knowledge and Information Systems*, *14*(1), 1–37. doi:10.1007/s10115-007-0114-2

Wu, X., Zhu, X., Wu, G. Q., & Ding, W. (2014). Data mining with big data. *IEEE Transactions on Knowledge and Data Engineering*, *26*(1), 97–107. doi:10.1109/TKDE.2013.109

Wu, Y., & Saunders, C. S. (2011). Governing information security: Governance domains and decision rights allocation patterns. *Information Resources Management Journal*, *24*(1), 28–45. doi:10.4018/irmj.2011010103

Xiang, G., Yu, B., & Zhu, P. (2012). A algorithm of fully homomorphic encryption. In *Proceedings of 9th International Conference on Fuzzy Systems and Knowledge Discovery (FSKD)* (pp. 2030-2033).

Xie, Y., Xu, Z., Zhu, X., & Xie, P. (2012, August). A parallel algorithm PMASK based on privacy-preserving data mining. In *Proceedings of the 2012 International Symposium on Instrumentation & Measurement, Sensor Network and Automation (IMSNA)* (Vol. 2, pp. 398-402). IEEE. doi:10.1109/MSNA.2012.6324604

Xu, L., Jiang, C., Wang, J., Yuan, J., & Ren, Y. (2014). Information security in big data: Privacy and data mining. *IEEE Access*, *2*, 1149–1176. doi:10.1109/ACCESS.2014.2362522

Yadav, S. B. (2011). SEACON: An integrated approach to the analysis and design of secure enterprise architecture–based computer networks. In H. Nemati (Ed.), *Pervasive information security and privacy developments: Trends and advancements* (pp. 309–331). Hershey, PA: IGI Global. doi:10.4018/978-1-61692-000-5.ch020

Yadav, S. B. (2012). A six-view perspective framework for system security: Issues, risks, and requirements. In H. Nemati (Ed.), *Optimizing information security and advancing privacy assurance: New technologies* (pp. 58–90). Hershey, PA: IGI Global. doi:10.4018/978-1-4666-0026-3.ch004

Yamany, H. F., Allison, D. S., & Capretz, M. A. (2013). Developing proactive security dimensions for SOA. In *IT policy and ethics: Concepts, methodologies, tools, and applications* (pp. 900–922). Hershey, PA: IGI Global. doi:10.4018/978-1-4666-2919-6.ch041

Yang, K., Han, Q., Li, H., Zheng, K., Su, Z., & Shen, X. (2016). An Efficient and Fine-grained Big Data Access Control Scheme with Privacy-preserving Policy.

Yan, G., Rawat, D. B., Bista, B. B., & Chen, L. (2014). Location security in vehicular wireless networks. In D. Rawat, B. Bista, & G. Yan (Eds.), *Security, privacy, trust, and resource management in mobile and wireless communications* (pp. 108–133). Hershey, PA: IGI Global. doi:10.4018/978-1-4666-4691-9.ch006

Yang, X. S. (2010). *A New Metaheuristic Bat-Inspired Algorithm.Cruz, C.; Gonz'alez, J. R.; Pelta, D. A* (G. Terrazas, Ed.). Springer Berlin.

Yao, Y., Zhang, L., Yi, J., Peng, Y., Hu, W., & Shi, L. (2016, September). A Framework for Big Data Security Analysis and the Semantic Technology. In *Proceedings of the 2016 6th International Conference on IT Convergence and Security (ICITCS)* (pp. 1-4). IEEE. doi:10.1109/ICITCS.2016.7740303

Yaokumah, W. (2013). Evaluating the effectiveness of information security governance practices in developing nations: A case of Ghana. *International Journal of IT/Business Alignment and Governance, 4*(1), 27–43. doi:10.4018/jitbag.2013010103

Yates, D., & Harris, A. (2011). International ethical attitudes and behaviors: Implications for organizational information security policy. In M. Dark (Ed.), *Information assurance and security ethics in complex systems: Interdisciplinary perspectives* (pp. 55–80). Hershey, PA: IGI Global. doi:10.4018/978-1-61692-245-0.ch004

Yau, S. S., Yin, Y., & An, H. (2011). An adaptive approach to optimizing tradeoff between service performance and security in service-based systems. *International Journal of Web Services Research, 8*(2), 74–91. doi:10.4018/jwsr.2011040104

Yazama, Y., Mitsukura, Y., Fukumi, M., & Fukumi, N. (2004). Analysis and recognition of wrist motions by using multidimensional directed information and EMG signal. In *Proceedings of IEEE Annual Meeting of the Fuzzy Information Processing NAFIPS '04*, Banff, Alberta. IEEE.

Yazama, Y., Mistukura, Y., Fukumi, M., & Akamatsu, N. (2003). Feature analysis for the EMG signals based on the class distance. In *Proceedings of Computational Intelligence in Robotics and Automation,* Kobe, Japan. IEEE. doi:10.1109/CIRA.2003.1222292

Yu, D., & Deng, L. (2011). DL and Its Applications to Signal and Information Processing. *IEEE Signal Processing Magazine, 28,* 145–150. doi:10.1109/MSP.2010.939038

Zadig, S. M., & Tejay, G. (2012). Emerging cybercrime trends: Legal, ethical, and practical issues. In A. Dudley, J. Braman, & G. Vincenti (Eds.), *Investigating cyber law and cyber ethics: Issues, impacts and practices* (pp. 37–56). Hershey, PA: IGI Global. doi:10.4018/978-1-61350-132-0.ch003

Zafar, H., Ko, M., & Osei-Bryson, K. (2012). Financial impact of information security breaches on breached firms and their non-breached competitors. *Information Resources Management Journal, 25*(1), 21–37. doi:10.4018/irmj.2012010102

Zakerzadeh, H., & Osborn, S. L. (2011). Faanst: fast anonymizing algorithm for numerical streaming data. In *Data Privacy Management and Autonomous Spontaneous Security* (pp. 36–50). Berlin, Heidelberg: Springer. doi:10.1007/978-3-642-19348-4_4

Zalzala, A. M. S., & Chaiyaratana, N. (2000). Myoelectric signal classification using evolutionary hybridRBF-MLP networks. In *Proceedings of Evolutionary Computation,* La Jolla, California. IEEE.

Zapata, B. C., & Alemán, J. L. (2013). Security risks in cloud computing: An analysis of the main vulnerabilities. In D. Rosado, D. Mellado, E. Fernandez-Medina, & M. Piattini (Eds.), *Security engineering for cloud computing: Approaches and tools* (pp. 55–71). Hershey, PA: IGI Global. doi:10.4018/978-1-4666-2125-1.ch004

Zboril, F., Horacek, J., Drahansky, M., & Hanacek, P. (2012). Security in wireless sensor networks with mobile codes. In M. Gupta, J. Walp, & R. Sharman (Eds.), *Threats, countermeasures, and advances in applied information security* (pp. 411–425). Hershey, PA: IGI Global. doi:10.4018/978-1-4666-0978-5.ch021

ZDnet.com. (2012). Top 10 categories for big data sources and mining technologies. Retrieved 2017 from http://www.zdnet.com/article/top-10-categories-for-big-data-sources-and-mining-technologies/

Zhang, Q., Chen, Z., Lv, A., Zhao, L., Liu, F., & Zou, J. (2013, August). A universal storage architecture for big data in cloud environment. In *Proceedings of the IEEE International Conference on Green Computing and Communications (GreenCom), and Internet of Things (iThings/CPSCom), and IEEE Cyber, Physical and Social Computing* (pp. 476-480). IEEE. doi:10.1109/GreenCom-iThings-CPSCom.2013.96

Zhang, J. (2012). Trust management for VANETs: Challenges, desired properties and future directions. *International Journal of Distributed Systems and Technologies, 3*(1), 48–62. doi:10.4018/jdst.2012010104

Zhang, Y., Chen, M., Mao, S., Hu, L., & Leung, V. C. M. (2014). *CAP: Community Activity Prediction Based on Big Data Analysis.*

Zhang, Y., He, L., Shu, L., Hara, T., & Nishio, S. (2012). Security issues on outlier detection and countermeasure for distributed hierarchical wireless sensor networks. In A. Pathan, M. Pathan, & H. Lee (Eds.), *Advancements in distributed computing and internet technologies: Trends and issues* (pp. 182–210). Hershey, PA: Information Science Publishing. doi:10.4018/978-1-61350-110-8.ch009

Zhao, J. Xie, Z. Jiang, L., Cai, H., Liu, H., & Hirzinger, G. (2005). Levenberg-Marquardt based neural network control for a five-fingered prosthetic hand. In *Proceedings of the 2005 IEEE International Conference on Robotics and Automation*, Barcelona, Spain. IEEE.

Zhao, F., Li, C., & Liu, C. F. (2014). A cloud computing security solution based on fully homomorphic encryption. In *Proceedings of 16th International Conference on Advanced Communication Technology (ICACT)* (pp. 485–488). doi:10.1109/ICACT.2014.6779008

Zhao, J., Wang, L., Tao, J., Chen, J., Sun, W., Ranjan, R., & Georgakopoulos, D. et al. (2014). A security framework in G-Hadoop for big data computing across distributed Cloud data centres. *Journal of Computer and System Sciences*, *80*(5), 994–1007. doi:10.1016/j.jcss.2014.02.006

Zheng, X., & Oleshchuk, V. (2012). Security enhancement of peer-to-peer session initiation. In M. Gupta, J. Walp, & R. Sharman (Eds.), *Threats, countermeasures, and advances in applied information security* (pp. 281–308). Hershey, PA: IGI Global. doi:10.4018/978-1-4666-0978-5.ch015

Zhou, G., Sohn, K., & Lee, H. (2012). Online incremental feature learning with denoising autoencoders. In Proceedings of the Int. Conf. Artif. Intell. Stat. (pp. 1453–1461).

Zhou, P., Lei, J., & Ye, W. (2011). Large-Scale Data Sets Clustering Based on MapReduce and Hadoop. *Journal of Computer Information Systems*, *7*(16), 5956–5963.

Zhu, H., Xu, Z., & Huang, Y. (2015). Research on the security technology of big data information. In *Proceedings of the Int. Conf. Inf. Technol. Manag. Innov.* (pp. 1041–1044).

Zineddine, M. (2012). Is your automated healthcare information secure? In M. Watfa (Ed.), *E-healthcare systems and wireless communications: Current and future challenges* (pp. 128–142). Hershey, PA: IGI Global. doi:10.4018/978-1-61350-123-8.ch006

About the Contributors

Daphne Lopez is a Professor in the School of Information Technology and Engineering, Vellore Institute of Technology University. Her research spans the fields of grid and cloud computing, spatial and temporal data mining and big data. She has a vast experience in teaching and industry. She is the author/co–author of papers in conferences, book chapters and journals. She serves as a reviewer in journals and conference proceedings. Prior to this, she has worked in the software industry as a consultant in data warehouse and business intelligence. She is a member of International Society for Infectious Diseases.

M.A. Saleem Durai received the MCA from Bharathidasan University, Tiruchirapalli, Tamilnadu, India in 1998; M. Phil. from Madurai Kamaraj University, India in 2008 and pursued PhD at VIT University Vellore. He is an Associate Professor in the School of Computing Sciences and Engineering at VIT University, Vellore, Tamilnadu, India. He has authored many International and National journal papers to his credit. His research interests include data mining, fuzzy logic, cloud computing and rough sets. Mr. Saleem Durai is associated with many professional bodies CSI and IEEE.

* * *

Gahana Agarwal is currently pursuing her bachelor's degree in computer science from Vellore Institute of Technology, Vellore. She completed her junior college from FIITJEE, Hyderabad and her schooling from St. Ann's High School. She has completed five grades of Piano from Trinity College of Music, London. Apart from this and more importantly, Gahana is a person who is fair, honest and fearless. She does not stand down from challenges and is open to new ideas. She is most passionate about the idea of simplifying and improving the day to day life of people. Some of the people who have inspired her the most are her parents, who supported her in every way possible. In the end, Gahana Agarwal is her own person, very different from the average crowd. She is a dreamer who converts her dreams into goals to achieve it.

Chitra Dhawale has Master Degree in Computer Science from P.G. Department of Computer Science and Technology (P.G.D.C.S.T), S.G.B.A. University, Amavati and Ph.D. in Computer Science, S.G.B.A. University, Amavati (MS). She having 20 years of rich and quality teaching experience to P.G courses at Shree H.V.P. Mandal, Amravati, Symbiosis International University and P.R. Pote College of Engg. & Mgmt. She is Member of editorial board of various national/international journals, also reviewer for reputed international journals. She is registered supervisor in computer science at S.G.B. Amravati University, R.T.M, Nagpur University, Symbiosis International University and member of Ph.D. panel at R.T.M, Nagpur University, Nanded and Gujrat University. She has published 17 research papers in Journals including SCI-Indexed, Scopus Indexed Journals and other reputed international journals, 41 Research papers presented including various IEEE, Elsevier, ACM and other international and national conferences. She is guiding 09 Ph.D. students. 01 students awarded Ph.D. and 02 has submitted their thesis. She also has also published 01 patent on her name for "Advanced Encryption Standard".

Sreenu G. is working as an assistant professor at Muthoot Institute of Technology and Science. Along with that he is doing his research at VIT, Vellore as an external part-time candidate.

P. Geethanjali received her B.E. degree in Electrical and Electronics Engineering from University of Madras, Tamilnadu, India in 2001. She obtained M. Tech in Electrical Drives and Control from Pondicherry Engineering College, Puducherry, India in 2004. She received her Ph. D degree from VIT University, Vellore, India in 2012. Her Ph.D thesis has been nominated for "Best Thesis" by Indian National Academy of Engineering (INAE). She received grants from the Department of Science and Technology (DST), Government of India. She also received Fulbright-Nehru Academic and Professional Excellence Fellowship for 2014-15. Her research interests include bio-signal and image processing, pattern recognition, development of assistive devices, biomechanics and application of renewable energy in assistive devices.

Jaiti Handa completed his M.Tech in Computer Science and Engineering from VIT University in 2016and B.Tech in Computer Science and Engineering from ITM University Gurgaon in 2014.

Navin Jambherkar is working as an Assistant Professor at Department of Computer Science, S.S.S.K.R. Innani Mahavidyalaya, Karanja Lad(MS). He is an active researcher in security techniques. He has published quality research papers and recently submitted his thesis to S.G.B. Amravati University. He also has published patent for "Method for execution load balancing of Advanced Encryption Standard (AES) asymmetric key dependent dynamic s-boxes."

Balajee Jeyakumar is currently pursuing a PhD in the School of Information Technology and Engineering, Vellore Institute of Technology University. He received his Bachelor of Computer Science degree in University of Madras, Chennai and Master of Computer Application degree from VIT University, Vellore and M.Phil degree Thiruvalluvar University, Vellore, respectively. I have worked as a Project Assistant for a project on Stability and aggregation of silver nanoparticles in natural aqueous matrices funded by the CSIR-Physical Sciences, Chennai, and Government of India. My current research interests include Big Data, Deep learning, Big Data Analytics in Healthcare, and Drug Discovery.

Gunasekaran Manogaran is currently pursuing PhD in the School of Information Technology and Engineering, Vellore Institute of Technology University. He received his B.E. and M.Tech from Anna University and Vellore Institute of Technology University respectively. He has worked as a Research Assistant for a project on Spatial Data Mining funded by Indian Council of Medical Research, Government of India. His current research interests include Data Mining, Big Data Analytics and Health Informatics. He got an award for young investigator from India and Southeast Asia by Bill & Melinda Gates Foundation. He is a life time member of International Society for Infectious Diseases.

Anbarasi Masilamani received the M.Tech(CSE) from VIT University, Vellore, Tamilnadu, India in 2006; she is an Assistant Professor(Senior) in the School of Computer Science and Engineering at VIT University, Vellore, Tamilnadu, India. Her research interests include Data mining, Soft Computing and Bioinformatics.

Chandu Thota is currently working as Technology Analyst in the Infosys Ltd., India. He received his MCA from Jawaharlal Nehru Technological University, Hyderabad. He Qualified UGC-NET (Computer Science and Applications) exam which has been conducted by University Grants Commission (UGC), HRD Ministry, Government of India. Currently he is working on projects with Java, J2EE, Cloud Computing and Infosys Finacle technologies. His current research interests include Cloud Computing, Security, Big Data and IoT.

Nancy Victor is currently working as an Assistant Professor at VIT University, India. She is an active researcher in the field of big data privacy. Her research interests include privacy preserving data publishing, data anonymization, big data privacy, etc.

Index

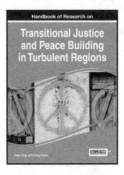
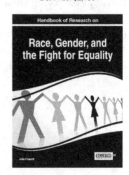

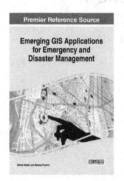   

Printed in the United States
By Bookmasters